Gifted Children

Gifted Children

MYTHS AND REALITIES

Ellen Winner

BasicBooks
A Division of HarperCollinsPublishers

Copyright © 1996 by Ellen Winner.
Published by BasicBooks, A Division of HarperCollins Publishers, Inc.

Designed by Lili Schwartz

Library of Congress Cataloging-in-Publication Data
Winner, Ellen.
    Gifted children : myths and realities / Ellen Winner.
       p.   cm.
    Includes bibliographical references and index.
    ISBN 0-465-01760-6 (cloth)
    ISBN 0-465-01759-2 (paper)
    1. Gifted children.   I. Title.
HQ773.5.W55   1996
155.45'5—dc20   95-49279
                                                       CIP

97 98 99 00 01 ❖/RRD 10 9 8 7 6 5 4 3 2

For Howard

Contents

Preface

No society can afford to ignore its most gifted members, and all must give serious thought to how best to nurture and educate talent. While psychologists have long been interested in the issue of giftedness, the study of giftedness has taken a back seat to the study of the typical and the pathological. In addition, a number of unquestioned assumptions are often made by researchers, educators, and clinicians in this field.

I have organized this book around nine misconceptions about the nature of giftedness. There is nothing magical about the number nine. I might have come up with ten, to make the number even, but the nine that I have identified struck me as the most pervasive and the most problematic. I have tried to synthesize and evaluate the best scientific research on giftedness in the areas of art, music, mathematics, and verbal ability. I begin with nine myths and conclude with what I hope are nine more informed views, which I have bravely called realities.

The children described in this book are real children, but some of their names have been changed. All the children that I studied came to me by word of mouth. I found that all I had to do was mention the topic of my study, and friends and colleagues immediately thought of children who would be good case studies. They were almost always right. The children who people these pages are used to illustrate and make vivid what researchers have learned about giftedness.

Many people helped me in this project. I must begin by thanking the children whom I studied. Except where indicated, the names are real: David (a pseudonym), Michael Kearney, KyLee, Rahela, Peter B., Jacob, Stephen (a pseudonym), Hillary, Peter S., and Alex. I owe a great deal to the parents (and in the case of Hillary, the grandparents) of these children, all of whom provided me with extremely detailed and careful observations about their children's development. Peter S., a seven-year-old described in chapter 9, helped to copyedit the pages devoted to him! Bill Eldridge, Jacob's guitar teacher, and Nina Grimaldi and Judy Ross, Stephen's music teachers, provided me with insights about the musical learning of these children. Robin Schader, from the San Francisco Music Conservatory, put me in touch with students to interview. Anabel Jensen, the director of the Nueva School, and other Nueva staff members Anne Bennet, Alison Barta, and Jo-An Vargo spent much time with me talking about the Nueva School and setting up interviews for me with students. Cynthia Kosut was also very helpful in discussing with me the experience of her sons at Nueva. Al Hastorf and Eleanor Walker opened up the Terman files to me at Stanford University, and they patiently answered many questions for me about the Terman project. They also helped me contact two Terman subjects, Russell Robinson and Beulah Fabris, who graciously agreed to be interviewed.

I wrote most of this book while on leave at Stanford University during 1994 and 1995. John Flavell invited me to join his developmental research group at Stanford and gave me an office, and I am most grateful to him. When I was not at the psychology department at Stanford, I worked at the Center for Advanced Study in the Behavioral Sciences, where my husband was a fellow. I wish to thank Neil Smelser and

Robert Scott for making it possible for me to work at the Center, monopolize the laser printer, and have so many interesting lunch discussions.

I am grateful to my editor, Jo Ann Miller, who provided excellent comments about both substance and style, who urged me to weave case studies of gifted children throughout the chapters, and who pushed me to keep psychological jargon out. I thank Juliana Nocker and Karen Klein at Basic Books for skillfully overseeing the book's editing and production. I owe thanks to colleagues who read all or portions of the manuscript and provided me with important and well-used feedback: Philip Adey, Jere Brophy, Mihaly Csikszentmihalyi, Bill Damon, Elliot Eisner, Lynn Goldsmith, Claire Golomb, Francesca Happé, Helen Haste, Mardi Horowitz, Kay Jamison, Tanya Luhrmann, Constance Milbrath, Robert Ornstein, Dean Keith Simonton, and Robert J. Sternberg. I am also grateful to colleagues with whom I have had profitable discussions about giftedness: Joe Campos, Neil Charness, Anders Ericsson, John Flavell, Howard Gruber, Robert Hogan, Jeanne Lepper, Hank Levin, Ellen Markman, Ruth Richards, Linda Silverman, Annemarie Roeper, John Sloboda, and Joe Tecce. Maria Ortiz and Lorrie Kirchner, my research assistants at Boston College, spent countless hours digging up articles from the library for me and compiling references. I thank Stephen Vedder, Assistant Director of the Audio Visual Department at Boston College, for photographing most of the figures. Finally, I thank my husband, Howard Gardner, who not only read the entire manuscript in several versions and commented on it but also argued with me about the issues over the course of the book's writing.

One

NINE MYTHS ABOUT
GIFTEDNESS

One evening not long ago I took my young son to a concert. A small orchestra was playing a Mozart concerto. As the concert began, I noticed a boy intently reading the orchestral score from a thick book of music. As he read and listened to the performers, he also hummed the music to himself, in perfect pitch. The boy was sitting with his father. At the intermission, I turned to the father and asked whether his child was really reading the music or simply looking at it. Listening to music and following along with a multipart orchestral score was one of Stephen's favorite pastimes, his father told me. Later I noticed Stephen in my son's after-school program. While the other children played basketball or cards, or talked to one another about classmates they did or did not like, Stephen sat in a corner alone and read a music theory book. Sometimes he climbed the stairs to the empty gym to improvise on the piano.

Talented, gifted, creative, prodigious—children with these labels have always intrigued us, inspiring fascination and awe, as well as intimidation and envy. Gifted children have been feared as possessed because they know and understand too much too early. Like retarded children, gifted children have been feared as strange, as oddballs, as freaks. They have been rejected as nerds. Their parents have been derided as overambitious zealots living vicariously through their children's achievements and depriving them of a normal childhood. Our schools often refuse to alter the curriculum for such "extreme" cases and insist that they adapt to the existing programs. When parents get upset about this, they are seen as people who have lost all perspective, people who do not realize how lucky they are to have a child with high, rather than low, abilities.[1]

Deviant people—whether atypical in personality, intellect, or both—have always interested psychologists, especially if the deviance involves negative personality traits or severely limited abilities. We know far more about psychopathological aspects of personality than about ideal traits such as compassion, moral courage, or leadership ability. A similar focus on deficits can be seen in psychological studies of cognition. While standard journals in developmental psychology publish articles on retardation, they rarely publish studies of giftedness. Such articles are relegated to less prestigious journals that specialize in giftedness. This state of affairs reflects the mistaken assumption that giftedness does not have much to tell us about the typical. I believe it is also due to the fact that retardation, like psychopathology, has been seen as a problem in need of solution, while great strengths have been seen as privileges rather than problems.[2]

Despite being split off from mainstream psychology, the study of giftedness has made great progress since its inception in the 1920s at Stanford University. There, the psychologist Lewis Terman, who initiated psychological research on the gifted, conducted a massive longitudinal study of more than fifteen hundred high-IQ children, a study that continues to this day (see chapters 2 and 10). Yet myths and misconceptions about the nature of giftedness abound, perhaps because the study of giftedness is a sensitive, politically charged topic, one often branded as elitist and wrongheaded. I offer here a critical look at some of the myths that have developed about giftedness and that have clouded our understanding.[3]

Let me first make clear that I use the term *gifted* to refer to children with three atypical characteristics:

1. *Precocity.* Gifted children are precocious. They begin to take the first steps in the mastery of some domain at an earlier-than-average age. They also make more rapid progress in this domain than do ordinary children, because learning in the domain comes easily to them. By *domain*, I refer to an organized area of knowledge such as language, mathematics, music, art, chess, bridge, ballet, gymnastics, tennis, or skating.

2. *An insistence on marching to their own drummer.* Gifted children not only learn faster than average or even bright children but also learn in a qualitatively different way. They march to their own drummer: they need minimum help or scaffolding from adults in order to master their domain, and much of the time they teach themselves. The discoveries they make about their domain are exciting and motivating, and each leads the gifted child on to the next step. Often these children independently invent rules of the domain and devise novel, idiosyncratic ways of solving problems.

This means that gifted children are by definition creative. But I distinguish sharply between little *c* and big *C* creativity. Gifted children typically are creative in the former sense: they make discoveries on their own and solve problems in novel ways. But they cannot be creative with a capital *C*, for by this I mean transforming a domain the way Jackson Pollack's renunciation of the paintbrush transformed painting or twelve-tone music transformed music. Only adults who have worked for at least ten years to master a domain can hope to leave it forever altered.[4]

3. *A rage to master.* Gifted children are intrinsically motivated to make sense of the domain in which they show precocity.

They exhibit an intense and obsessive interest, an ability to focus sharply, and what I have come to call a rage to master. They experience states of "flow" when they are engaged in learning in their domain—optimal states in which they focus intently and lose sense of the outside world. The lucky combination of obsessive interest in a domain along with an ability to learn easily in that domain leads to high achievement.[5]

In these three ways, gifted children remain qualitatively different from ordinary children who are motivated to work hard. Children who are alert, bright, and curious may put in many hours while trying to master a domain. Their parents may enroll them in a chess class and play chess with them daily, sign them up for violin lessons at age four, or enroll them in Saturday academic drill classes. Children with such parents, dedicated to helping their offspring develop their full potential, almost invariably impress us with how much they have achieved. And they show us how our expectations of what children can do are embarrassingly minimal and in sharp contrast to the expectations in some other cultures, such as Japan.

Yet these children are not the subjects of this book. These children are not particularly precocious. They do not learn at an especially rapid rate. They require extensive adult scaffolding—instruction, support, and encouragement—in order to make progress. They do not make discoveries about the domain on their own. And they do not show the intrinsic rage to master shown by gifted children. Moreover, they typically do not reach the levels reached so seemingly effortlessly by gifted children. We would not confuse a Suzuki-trained child with a violin prodigy like Midori, or a child socialized to work diligently and efficiently on her math homework with a math prodigy like Norbert Wiener.

Which brings us to the subject of prodigies. A prodigy is simply a more extreme version of a gifted child, a child so gifted that he or she performs in some domain at an adult level. When I use the term *gifted,* I mean all gifted children, including those we call prodigies. When I use the term *prodigy,* I refer only to the most extreme children.[6]

I focus on giftedness in two academic areas, language and mathematics, and two artistic areas, visual arts and music. It is in these four areas that childhood giftedness has most often been noted and studied. One reason for finding gifted children in these domains is that these areas are appealing to children. Another reason is that these areas are rule-governed and highly structured, making it possible to ferret out the underlying regularities. Unlike areas such as law or medicine, they do not require vast accumulations of knowledge and can be mastered when one understands a relatively small set of formal principles.

The more formal and rule-governed the domain, the more likely it is to yield gifted children. Mathematics and classical music, in which it is clear what needs to be mastered and how excellence can be recognized, are prototypical examples. Language is also highly structured, if by this we mean mastery of oral language and of reading; we often find children who are linguistically gifted in these ways. Creative writing, however, is less structured, and we find fewer linguistically gifted children who write at an advanced level than who read at an advanced level. The visual arts are even less well structured. However, drawing systems are highly rule-governed, and it is here that one finds gifted child artists—mastering realistic drawing (in the West) or allusionistic, schematic drawing (in Asia).

Sometimes gifted children are found in the area of biology, a domain that is clearly accessible to children. Charles Darwin, Jean Piaget, and Edward O. Wilson showed an exceptional ability as children to make fine discriminations in the natural world. We rarely notice gifted children in diffuse areas like leadership, interpersonal understanding, or self-awareness. But this does not mean they do not exist; we just do not know how to find them. And we do not classify children who show exceptional empathy, morality, or courage as gifted, but rather as having sterling character.[7]

But this is a cultural decision. The Pueblo residents of New Mexico have no word for "giftedness," but they do have terms for certain valued special abilities—ones that psychologists might call instances of giftedness—such as linguistic ability, the possession of abundant cultural knowledge, and the ability to create with one's hands. But the fourth valued area is one in which we do not normally recognize special abilities—the humanistic area of compassion, self-sacrifice, empathy. Also different from the mainstream Western individualistic view of giftedness is the Pueblo belief that special abilities should not be used as a basis for elevating one person over others. For this group, a special gift is meaningful only if it is used in a way that benefits the community. Even more anti-individualistic is the Confucian view that all can be skilled, and that differences in skill reflect only effort and moral commitment, not any special talents.[8]

Other highly rule-governed areas where Western cultures have identified children as gifted could have been included in this book: chess, bridge, ballet, gymnastics, skating, tennis, or swimming, to name just a few. And of course there are child actors like Shirley Temple, Mickey Rooney, Judy Garland, or today's MacCaulay Culkin, children exceptionally good at mimicry and role play. Instead of trying to cover all areas, I chose what I felt to be representative scholastic and artistic domains. Other domains are mentioned when comparisons to them prove revealing.

Myths and misunderstandings can be identified in any area of study, and the topic of giftedness is no exception. Here are nine strongly held assumptions about giftedness that I believe are wrongheaded.

MYTH 1: GLOBAL GIFTEDNESS

The label gifted *is* most often reserved for children with academic gifts—that is, children gifted in language (oral and written) and mathematics, the two major areas valued in schools. And psychologists and educators have typically measured academic giftedness with an IQ test that yields a global score. Children are admitted into special school programs for the gifted on the basis of their IQ scores, just as they are admitted into psychologists' studies of the gifted on this basis.

The underlying assumption here is that gifted children have a general intellectual power that allows them to be gifted "across the board." I call this the myth of global giftedness. But scholastic giftedness is often not a global capacity that cuts across the two major areas of scholastic performance. The child with a combination of academic strengths and weaknesses turns out to be the rule, not the exception. Children can even be gifted in one academic area and learning-disabled in another. Highly gifted children as young as two or three show clear domain-specific abilities. The specificity of their abilities is a strong indication that these children are predisposed toward particular domains. They are not generally gifted individuals who have by chance chosen to focus on math or language.

MYTH 2: TALENTED BUT NOT GIFTED

While children who are precocious in those kinds of scholastic skills assessed by an IQ test are called gifted, children who show exceptional ability in an art form such as the visual arts, music, or dance or in an athletic area such as skating, tennis, or diving are called talented. Two different labels suggest two different classes of children. But there is no justification for such a distinction. Artistically or athletically gifted children are not so different from academically gifted children. Both classes of children exhibit the three characteristics of gifted-ness mentioned earlier.[9]

MYTH 3: EXCEPTIONAL IQ

Although children with high ability in art or music are called talented, not gifted, we still assume that these children could not do what they do without a high IQ. "Giftedness, however interpreted, nearly always involves high IQ even if this is not to be considered the only ingredient," writes one of today's leading experts on intelligence and giftedness.[10]

But IQ tests measure a narrow range of human abilities, primarily facility with language and number. There is little evidence that giftedness in nonacademic areas such as art or music requires an exceptional IQ. One can even find extraordinary levels of giftedness in so-called *idiots savants*—individuals, often autistic, with IQs in the retarded range and exceptional domain-specific abilities.

MYTHS 4 AND 5: BIOLOGY VERSUS ENVIRONMENT

Where does giftedness come from? The commonsense myth is that giftedness is entirely inborn. This folk myth ignores the environment's powerful influence on the development of gifts.

Diametrically opposed to this view is the myth held by some psychologists that giftedness is simply a matter of inten-sive training by parents and teachers begun at an early age. In the recent words of one psychologist, "With sufficient energy and dedication on the parents' part, it is possible that it may not be all that difficult to produce a child prodigy." This kind of statement suggests that gifted children start out with ordinary brains which are then shaped to become extraordinary. This view ignores the powerful role of biology in determining whether there is any gift for the environment to develop.[11]

MYTH 6: THE DRIVING PARENT

Some people assert that gifted children are "made" by overzealous parents intent on their children's stardom. Parents are cautioned not to push their children, to let them have "normal" childhoods. Otherwise, they are told, their children will resent them and lose all interest in achieving.

It is true that parents of gifted children are highly involved in the nurturance of their children's gifts. But such an unusual degree of investment and involvement is not a destructive force. It is a necessary one if a child's gift is to be developed.

MYTH 7: GLOWING WITH PSYCHOLOGICAL HEALTH

Gifted children often face ridicule, taunts about being nerds or geeks. Most children easily pick out the awkward, unathletic loners, or the show-offs with strange interests out of touch with those of their peers. Psychologists have countered this view with an idealized picture of high-IQ children as popular, well-adjusted, exceptionally moral, and glowing with psychological and physical health. In his 1922 address as the president of the American Psychological Association, Terman defined gifted children not only as academically superior but also as "superior to unselected children in physique, health and social adjustment; [and] marked by superior moral attitudes as measured by character tests of trait ratings."[12]

But children's prejudices may strike close to the truth. We seem to have a need either to deny or to idealize the gifted child. Gifted children are often socially isolated and unhappy, unless they are fortunate enough to find others like themselves. The vision of the well-adjusted gifted child applies only to the moderately gifted child and leaves out the extremes.

MYTH 8: ALL CHILDREN ARE GIFTED

Many principals and teachers assert that all children are gifted. Sometimes this means that all children have some areas in which they have strengths; other times it means that all children have an equal potential for learning. This assumption is not made only about academic abilities. When I tried to study children gifted in drawing, art teachers initially refused to identify individual children for me, telling me that all their students were gifted in art. Sociological consideration of the concept of giftedness has sometimes led to the conclusion that giftedness is just a social construction to buttress elitism.[13]

No one seems to mind the fact that children gifted in music routinely take advanced classes outside of school. But the view that all students are gifted in school skills leads to adamant positions against any form of special education for the gifted. In reaction, parents of the gifted turn to support groups and talk of how misplaced egalitarianism discriminates against their children and makes them stressed as well as bored. When special education for the gifted is offered, it is minimal and is fashioned to fit the moderately gifted.[14]

We need to rethink education for the gifted. First, we should markedly elevate academic standards for all children. The moderately gifted would then no longer find school so unchallenging. We ought then to focus all of our resources for the gifted on the extremely gifted. These children have special needs no less than do retarded or learning-disabled children. Moreover, they are our human capital, the promise of our future.

MYTH 9: GIFTED CHILDREN BECOME EMINENT ADULTS

When I asked an admissions director of a school for the gifted what her office looked for in applicants, she said both high IQ and creativity. Giftedness is usually seen as synonymous not only with high IQ but also with high creativity.[15]

Gifted children are typically seen not only as creative children but also as future creative and eminent adults. But many gifted children, especially prodigies, burn out, while others move on to other areas of interest. Some, while extremely successful, never do anything genuinely creative. Only a very few of the gifted become eminent adult creators. We cannot assume a link between early giftedness, no matter how extreme, and adult eminence. The factors that predict the course of a life are multiple and interacting. Over and above level of ability, important roles are played by personality, motivation, the family environment, opportunity, and chance.

～

THE IMPORTANCE OF STUDYING GIFTEDNESS

These nine myths pervade the intellectually, emotionally, and politically charged concept of giftedness. In confronting these myths, I hope to set them to rest.

But why study giftedness? Some might object that this is an elitist topic, one with little relevance in this time of sharpening economic inequality, violence, and educational crisis. I strongly disagree. An understanding of the most extraordinary levels of the human mind is important both for our society and for the scientific understanding of human potential.

In the United States, despite lip service to the gifted, we

actually pay very little attention to the problem of how to identify and nurture children with exceptional abilities. What public resources we do spend on educating the gifted are primarily reserved for moderately academically gifted children, rather than for those extremely gifted in academics or other areas. Other cultures have done far more to identify and nurture their most gifted. Hungary has produced more than its share of mathematicians and scientists, and much of the creative work in the United States in the twentieth century has been done by refugees from Europe. Today, with our rightful concern for social and economic inequity, we care little about giftedness or about ways to strengthen the tenuous path from childhood gifts to adult achievement and creativity. This outlook is very shortsighted.

In addition, giftedness deserves attention within basic scientific research. Psychological theories of learning and development need to be able to encompass the typical as well as the atypical—the retarded child, the autistic child, the learning-disabled child, *and* the gifted child. As Freud showed, the study of pathology can illuminate the normal, and no sharp dividing line marks where normalcy becomes pathology. The study of the gifted tells us many important things about how the mind in general can operate.

Take just the following few unexpected findings revealed when we look behind the myths shrouding the notion of giftedness:

- Children can be gifted in one area but average or even learning-disabled in another. Thus, abilities can be independent of one another.
- Having a high IQ is irrelevant to giftedness in art or music.
- The brains of the gifted are atypical.
- Families play a far more important role in the development of gifts than do schools.

- As with a disability, giftedness can lead to unhappiness and social isolation.
- Personality attributes predict what will happen to the gifted child in adulthood more reliably than does the child's degree of giftedness.

These findings, interesting in their own right, help us develop a full picture of the human mind. And our understanding of the most gifted has even broader implications. If any individuals are to solve the vast array of problems that threaten human survival, they are surely to be found among this group.

Two

GLOBALLY GIFTED:
THE CHILDREN BEHIND
THE MYTH

There is a reason for the myth of global giftedness. Some children fit the picture perfectly, like David and Michael, described in this chapter. For them, the myth is a reality. These children are gifted across the board in all school-related academic subjects—reading, mathematics, and logical thinking—and score highly on all areas of an intelligence test. Children like this are "notationally" gifted—that is, they seem effortlessly to grasp language and number, the two kinds of notational symbol systems most valued in school. These children have extremely high scholastic ability (as measured by an IQ test or by school performance), they solve problems in divergent and independent ways, and they have a rage to learn. They thus have all three of the components of giftedness.

Children like these do not just strike observers as bright. Rather, they astound those around them. Their exceptional abilities announce themselves at a very early age, before parents could have begun any kind of "training" to "create" a prodigy.

TWO GLOBALLY GIFTED CHILDREN

David's precocity was first noticed in the domain of language. At eight months, he showed excellent language comprehension, about a year ahead of the normal timetable. He could understand simple questions, such as "Where's Daddy?" (he pointed in reply), indirect questions such as "Can you go and get it?" and direct commands such as "Come here" or "Lean forward." At eight months, he also said his first words (most children do this at twelve months), and almost as soon as he began to speak, he was forming two-word utterances (a feat accomplished usually around eighteen months). By fifteen months, when normal children are just beginning to speak, his spoken vocabulary contained about two hundred words.

From eighteen months on, David's language proceeded so rapidly that his mother stopped recording his sentences. She did note what he said the week he turned two, however, when he accurately reported, "I saw a real ditch digger pick up real dirt and put in dump truck, and I saw pretend ditch digger and sat in it and pulled the handles." This is the age at which the typical child has just mastered "Hi, Dada," or "No go." Many parents of children like David say that their children pass almost instantly from just one word at a time to complete sentences.

By five, David began to show an interest in language as a system. Children usually show some ability to reflect on language as an object, rather than to simply *use* language, as young as two. However, the form that such awareness takes is usually rudimentary. For instance, they will correct their own speech errors, starting a sentence over again in midstream, thereby indicating some awareness of grammatical rules. But David's awareness of language took a more adult form when he became eager to learn other languages. When he was five, he asked his mother to check out French, Spanish, and sign-language books from the library. He studied these books avidly and mastered some of the words and signs. He also began to make up his own languages (both spoken and sign) and wrote letters in code for his mother to decode (he provided a key).

From early on, David was fascinated with letters. At twenty-one months, he fashioned the letter *X* from two rectangular blocks and then called it an *X*. At a little over two and a half, he proclaimed that the word *cheers* started with a G. When told that was wrong, he suggested that it started with a J. He also announced that *daddy* and *dive* both started with D. By three, he loved to play an alphabet game in which each player had to come up with words beginning with the consonants, in alphabetical order. To play this, one must be able to reflect on similarities in how words sound and are spelled.

Once he knew all his letters, David began to read. Typically, children begin to read by recognizing the visual pattern of an entire printed word and pairing it with its sound, heard spoken by an adult. Later, usually as a result of explicit instruction, they master the rules of phonics, pairing single letters or clusters with sounds, and can sound out words they have never seen before. David, however, read phonetically from the start. At three, his first read word was *Argo*, which he saw on a box of soap powder. No one had ever read this word to him, so the only way he could have read it was by sounding it out according to phonetic rules. After he sounded it out, he asked what it meant.

David then became driven to master reading. He formulated his own program for how to do it and asked for his mother's help in carrying it out. But he actually needed little help. One day he brought a favorite book to his mother and asked her to read it to him and point her finger at the words as she read aloud. He looked intently at the words as she read and pointed. Then he asked for the book again, and this time he pointed his finger at the words as they were read. He requested this same book to be read in this same way about a dozen times a day, over the course of a week. For a second week, he repeated this procedure with a second book.

After these two weeks, three-year-old David put the two now-memorized books aside and picked up one new book after another, reading each aloud to his mother. He sounded out words when he did not know them, and in those rare cases when he could not sound out a word, he spelled it out loud to his mother. This lasted for another two weeks. After this, David was reading silently on his own, rapidly, and voraciously.

Early and omnivorous reading that begins before kinder-garten is one of the most commonly noted characteristics of globally gifted children. Biographical accounts of prodigies often note that these children apparently taught themselves to read. Some researchers have taken issue with this claim, insist-ing that no child can learn to read without a great deal of help. But the instruction David received lasted only two weeks. Moreover, he received no phonics instruction. His mother simply paired words to sounds, and from this pairing he *induced* the rules of phonics. Most children have reading instruction every day for several years before they can read fluently.[1]

Another telling difference was that David's two weeks of instruction were not imposed by his mother. This was a clear case in which learning was initiated and pursued vigorously by the child, not the teacher. Children like David who ask to learn to read do so because they sense that this is something they can do with ease. Children who do not read until they are made to in school may well sense that the printed squig-gles on a page are going to be very difficult to decode. Glenn Doman, founder of the Institutes for the Achievement of Human Potential, has shown that with the use of flash cards begun in infancy, children can learn to read early. But these children are receiving extensive scaffolding. Children like David need almost none.

As soon as he began to read on his own, David was not content to read one book at a time, in serial fashion. Like adult creators who are involved in many different projects simultaneously, David was immersed in up to a dozen books at a time. By the time he was three and a half, the library waived the limit on how many books David could take out so that his mother would not have to bring him in every day.[2]

Before he entered kindergarten, at age five, David was reading sixth-grade–level books. When he read fiction that was at his level, it was usually about children who were considerably older than he was. Because he found it hard to relate to adventures of children so far beyond his age range, he turned to nonfiction with a passion. From the age of four, he typically pursued a particular subject matter over a period of weeks or sometimes months. His preferred books were biographies and science books. One favorite was a biography of Wilbur and Orville Wright, which he read just as he turned five. But that single biography did not satisfy him, so he read three different biographies of the Wright brothers until he felt he had learned enough about them. Persistence like this is typical of such children. He sought books on how volcanoes work, on how hurricanes and tornadoes differ, and on why the body produces saliva. He pored over his atlas at least once a day, not only reading the words but tracing the paths of territorial boundaries, roads, and rivers. He also began to read the charts in his atlas. At four, after having read several volumes of the *Childcraft Encyclopedia* from cover to cover at the library, what he wanted most for his birthday was an encyclopedia.

Not surprisingly, by seven, he had an enormous store of information, as is typical of children with precocious verbal ability. For instance, by five, he excelled at the game of Geography, in which one must think of places starting with the last letter of the word said by the other player. To play this game, one must know the names of many cities, towns, countries, rivers, and mountains, and one must know how the names are spelled (or at least what letter their names begin and end with). Children who read a great deal soak up much world knowledge from books.

David also started to write early. Just shy of his third birthday, he asked for help in making his first letter, the letter *A*. Within half a year, he wrote his own letter to Santa Claus by sounding out the words himself. He asked for help only with the words *bring* and *thank,* because he realized that he did not yet know how to write nasal sounds. By four, he began to write letters to friends and family members on a regular basis. He also began to do simple crossword puzzles. By five, he was writing stories and nonfiction pieces. Because his thoughts were quicker than his handwriting, and because he had easily taught himself to type on the computer (by using an adult manual), David did most of his writing on the computer. His handwriting has remained a problem throughout elementary school.

David showed as much early interest in numbers as in words. By fifteen months, he could count to ten. By three, he had grasped the concept of zero as meaning nothing; by four, he was fascinated by the concept of infinity. At four, he could easily manipulate numbers in his head, adding and subtracting, and separating numbers into odds and evens. Often he sought stimulation by asking his parents to give him addition and subtraction problems to do in his head. He could mentally add two-digit numbers, provided there was no carrying involved. Because he typically solved math problems in his head, he had difficulty at first in school when his teacher insisted he write out his math problems using conventional symbols like pluses and minuses.

By kindergarten, he could also count to 100 by 2s, 3s, 4s, and 5s, 10s, and 20s. Claiming that 97 consists of nine 10s and seven 1s, he clearly understood place value. He announced that four quarters in a dollar was the same as four 15-minute segments in an hour, and that if four pieces make up a whole, they are called quarters. Similarly, he noted that if ten pieces make up a whole, they are called tenths and that 100 percent must, therefore, mean 100 pieces for a whole.

David seemed to know things about numbers that he had never been taught, like the concept of zero or the meaning of percentages. He simply looked at the numbers and knew the answers. It is not surprising that the parents of some of these children begin to believe that their children have supernatural powers.[3]

All children are curious, and all ask questions that amuse and astound adults. But David's intellectual curiosity had another streak to it: persistence. When he wanted to know something, he would not rest until he had an answer that satisfied him. For instance, at fourteen months, when his mother explained to him that a loud noise heard outside was from a power saw, he insisted on going to see it. For two hours he repeated, "See saw, saw see," until finally his mother gave up, put him in the car, and drove him to see the saw. At two and a half, he asked his mother how a toy worked. He remained dissatisfied with her explanation until she finally made a structure to demonstrate how it worked. When he asked where the wind comes from, David again was not happy with his mother's explanation. He was content only after they went to the library, got out a book on the subject, and read it together over and over. David's rage for knowledge is typical of all gifted children, though what they want to know and do depends on their domain of gift.

David began at a very young age to theorize about how things work. At age four, he posited the existence of sphincter muscles, referred to them as "a gate," and explained how they work and how the mind controls them. By four, he had decided to become a scientist.

If I had to make one generalization about David, I would say that underlying all his behavior was a desire to make his environment stimulating. This explains his persistent questions, his creation of math problems, his scientific theorizing, and his omnivorous reading. His parents did not push him to early mastery. Rather, he was the one who pushed, because of his need for answers to his questions.[4]

David is similar to Michael Kearney, a child who has attracted considerable media attention recently because of his graduation from college at age ten, the youngest American college graduate yet. Michael's development was so extreme as to seem almost freakish; David's, though astounding, may be somewhat more within the realm of human understanding.

According to his parents, Michael scored over 200 in IQ, a level achieved by fewer than one in a million people. Michael began to speak at the age of four months—eight months ahead of schedule. His mother says that at this age he uttered not only single words but also sentences such as "Mom, Dad, what's for dinner?" At eight months, he began to read off the television whenever he saw a commercial with a product name on the screen. He would also read aloud from *TV Guide*, saying "price is right," or "ten o'clock." At ten months, looking like a normal infant, he shocked people by reading words aloud off signs at the supermarket. According to his parents, people first thought the voice must have been the mother's: an infant who could not only talk but read seemed too incredible. Michael figured out the rules of phonics by fifteen months, which allowed him suddenly to be able to read words he had never seen before.

Michael was just as precocious in math as he was in language. At three, his father says, he discovered and proved the commutative, associative, and identity rules in algebra, announcing gleefully, "Dad, what could be more fun than math!" When his father returned home from each workday, Michael would greet his father with, "Dad, let's go do work," then insistently pull his father toward some math books.

Michael showed the same kind of persistence, drive, and rage to master as did David. "Michael has a raging desire to learn," his father said. His parents say they actually tried to slow him down, but nothing could stop him. Michael had so much energy, both mental and physical, that he exhausted his parents. He needed little sleep, and he actually looked hyperactive when he was bored. But when he was interested in something, his concentration was intense. Children like this can easily get misdiagnosed as hyperactive or as having attention deficit disorder (usually called ADD). Such children are stimulus seekers: if they are not sufficiently stimulated, they will produce stimulation for themselves with activity.[5]

At five, Michael entered and completed high school. The next year, his parents moved to Mobile, Alabama, so that he could attend the University of South Alabama. Because of his age, his mother accompanied him to his classes every day. But no one had to help or even urge him to do his work. A professor who knew Michael described him as "one of the most intelligent people on Earth."

When I met Michael, then age ten, he had just graduated from college and was trying to decide what to do next. He was spending his days playing video games and watching TV. But he was also trying to decide between going to graduate school in anthropology to become a primatologist (like Jane Goodall, whose writings had inspired him at age six) or going to Los Angeles to become a game-show host. When I talked to him about why he wanted to be a game-show host, he said, "You have to be smart to really comprehend the questions and get the audience to understand what you are doing." He told me he had wanted to be a game-show host since the age of two. As of this writing, Hollywood has not signed Michael up for any game show, so he is now planning to reenter college. As we will see, high IQ scores in childhood do not necessarily predict great scholarship or creative discovery in adulthood.[6]

TERMAN'S STUDY OF GLOBALLY GIFTED HIGH-IQ CHILDREN

Had David and Michael been born in California in the early 1900s, they would have qualified to be subjects in the first systematic study of academically gifted high-IQ children, which was begun in 1921. In this study, the Stanford psychologist

Lewis Terman tried to pinpoint the traits of high-IQ children and track what became of them as they grew up.[7]

Terman's study involved about fifteen hundred school-aged children born between 1903 and 1917, who were followed over the entire course of their lives. The surviving subjects of this study are now in their eighties, and the sixth volume of the Terman study appeared in 1995. What Terman hoped to show was that these high-IQ children were superior not only in academic areas but also in both social and physical development. He wanted to counter what struck him as a myth: the view that high-IQ children are physically awkward social misfits. He also hoped to show that having a high IQ as a child was a good predictor of achieving eminence in adulthood.

Terman tried to find a representative sample of the upper part of the top 1 percent of the school population of California. First, he asked teachers to nominate their brightest students, as well as their youngest students. He rightly thought that the youngest students in a grade were likely to be among the brightest. Those nominated were then given a group intelligence test, and those who excelled were given an individual but abbreviated Stanford-Binet intelligence test. Finally, those who scored high on this shortened version were given a complete test. Children who scored 135 or higher were invited to participate in the study. Almost all who joined the study in fact scored above 140. These well-studied children came to be known, affectionately, as the "Termites."

The Stanford-Binet IQ test, Terman's revision of Binet's original, is composed of a variety of simple school-like tasks that are artificial and removed from everyday activities. For instance, the test for children asks them to define words, to indicate how two words (for example, *laziness* and *idleness*) are different, to explain how two objects are similar and different, to listen to a paragraph and summarize it, to answer verbal puzzles, to read stories and indicate what the moral lesson is, to repeat seven numbers backward, to solve math problems with known right and wrong answers, and to complete visual patterns. This test, like most intelligence tests, measures language and logic, as well as math and spatial ability to a limited degree.[8]

Average intelligence on this test is defined as a score between 90 and 109. Fifty percent of all people fall into this normal range. A score of 132 is two standard deviations above the mean (a standard deviation is the average distance of scores from the mean score), and it is the score required for entrance into MENSA, a national organization for individuals with high IQs. And a common cutoff for children's admission into gifted programs in schools is 130. About two or three children out of a hundred have IQs of 130 or higher; only about one in a hundred has an IQ of 140 or higher. Only one in ten thousand to thirty thousand will score 160 or higher, and only one in a million will score above 180. Terman's children had IQs ranging from 135 to 196, and the average IQ of the children was about 150. An average Ph.D. holder scores around 130, except in physics, where the average is about 140.[9]

According to retrospective parental reports, Terman's children, just like David and Michael, showed signs of precocious development from infancy. They began to speak about three and a half months ahead of schedule, and about half were reading before starting school. Of those who read early, most began at four, but a few began as young as three or even two. One child, aged twenty-five months, read as well as the typical child at the end of first grade!

Early reading is a reliable sign of a high IQ: not only did the group as a whole read far earlier than average, but IQ differences within the group also predicted age of reading. Those with IQs above 170 were over twice as likely to have read before four than were those with IQs below 170.[10]

Like David and Michael, all the children, regardless of when they had begun to read, went on to read omnivorously.

At seven, they were reading on average almost an hour a day; by thirteen, they were reading on average about two hours a day. And at every age there were children who read around three hours a day or more. These children also read a much wider range of books than do typical children. They did not stick to fiction, but also read nonfiction (science, history, and biography), as well as atlases and encyclopedias.

Other early indications of global giftedness also marked the Terman sample. Parents typically noted that their children seemed to catch on to things effortlessly, were insatiably curious, and had extraordinary memories. Given their early reading ability, and their love of reading, these children quickly acquired a vast store of information and an immense vocabulary. They also were much more likely than ordinary children to make collections, especially scientific collections. In general, Terman's subjects had interests typically held by much older children.

The children in the study were ones a teacher would want to have in class—children sometimes referred to as the "schoolhouse gifted." They excelled in schoolwork, often mastering on their own the curriculum taught to children two or even four grades ahead of them. Some children had skipped grades and thus had had fewer years of schooling than others. However, no relationship existed between number of years in school and degree of mastery of any subject area tested. Terman concluded that these children (like David and Michael) were often teaching themselves. Teachers rated almost all of them as having high willpower and a strong desire to excel.

Terman's subjects were also surprisingly well-rounded. The commonly held generalization that gifted children are unable to relate to other children found no support in the Terman study. His children, in fact, scored somewhat higher than a control group on measures of social adjustment.

These children were even somewhat superior in their physical development. Their motoric development was precocious, and they walked about a month ahead of schedule. They were also superior to a comparison group in health. Anyone drawing conclusions from Terman's study, however, must recognize that almost 33 percent of the subjects came from professional, middle-class families, a socioeconomic group that constituted only about 3 percent of the general population. But Terman clearly did much to change people's conceptions of gifted children as odd, sickly, and unhappy.[11]

Terman had a disproportionate number of boys in his final sample. This probably occurred because of his decision to screen for IQ only after children had been selected by their teachers. Teachers in the 1920s may well have been biased to assume that boys had more academic promise than girls. In a more recent, but much smaller, study of high-IQ children that depended only on IQ scores and no teacher nominations, equal numbers of high-IQ boys and girls were identified.[12]

Terman's dependence on teacher nominations also probably resulted in other biases. When asked to select their brightest children, teachers probably picked their most high achieving, all-round students. Children with much greater strengths in language than mathematics, or the reverse, may have been passed by. Troublemakers, highly creative children, or ones with specific learning disabilities may also have been overlooked. When giving certain children high academic ratings, teachers also may have tended unconsciously to give them positive personality and social adjustment ratings as well (a kind of halo effect). In addition, teachers probably had a social class bias that led them to overlook poor children, resulting in a sample that was disproportionately middle class.[13]

A PROFILE OF THE GLOBALLY GIFTED HIGH-IQ CHILD

The following qualities generally characterize the globally gifted, very high-IQ child. Most parents notice at least some of these signs before their child is five.[14][15]

Earliest Signs
Attention and recognition memory

These children show signs of alertness and long attention spans in infancy, and they recognize their caretakers early. This observation goes beyond potentially biased parents' reports. Studies have shown a positive relation between recognition memory at four to seven months and verbal intelligence scores at age seven.[16]

Preference for novelty

Infants who get bored by a visual array and want to see something new are also those who test higher in IQ at age two.[17]

Precocious physical development

Children of high IQ who show academic giftedness are often precocious in physical development in infancy: they sit, crawl, and walk several months earlier than normal.[18]

Oral language

These children speak early, often progressing directly from one-word utterances to complex sentences. They have a large vocabulary and a large store of verbal knowledge.

Overreactivity

These children have been reported to show unusually intense reactions to noise, pain, and frustration.

Learning Style

Learning with minimal instruction

In general, such children seem to learn with very little help or scaffolding from adults. They need merely access to a domain of knowledge (which they can get from books or adults) and someone to answer their persistent questions.

These children are not just *faster* learners, though. They learn and think *differently* from other children. For example, when high-IQ children were given a spatial logic task called Tower of Hanoi, they asked for minimal help. The task is to transfer a tower of disks stacked from large to small from one vertical peg to another with two constraints: one can move only one disk at a time, and one must not place a larger disk over a smaller one. They eagerly began the activity and tried to challenge themselves by doing the problem faster and with fewer moves. The way they kept pushing themselves to the optimal level of challenge suggests that they were experiencing "flow," a state of intense and pleasurable concentration.[19]

Curiosity

Intellectually curious like scholars, globally gifted high-IQ children ask deep questions. When encountering a problem they want to investigate, they persist until satisfied with the available information.

Persistence and concentration

These children show high persistence and concentration when they are interested in something.

Energy

These children have high energy levels, which not only allow them to concentrate intensely when they are challenged, but also can lead to hyperactivity when they are insufficiently stimulated. Some parents have determined that, as infants, these children needed less sleep than most others their age.

"Metacognitive" awareness

Unusually aware of their own problem-solving strategies, these children can use these strategies to solve new problems that on the surface may seem quite unrelated.[20]

Obsessive interests

They develop almost obsessive interests in specific areas, such as computers, volcanoes, or Greek myths, and become experts in these domains.

School-Related Abilities

Reading

These children almost always read by age four, some even earlier, and they learn with minimal instruction. This was one of the few abilities that differentiated the children in Terman's study with IQs of 170 or above from the rest. It is not unusual for such children to read at sixth-grade level in kindergarten. They also read voraciously, going through books "like potato chips," as one mother told me.

Number

They are fascinated with number and number relations.

Memory

They have prodigious memories for verbal and mathematical information.

Abstract logical reasoning

They excel at logical and abstract reasoning.

Handwriting

While they like to write, they often struggle with handwriting and prefer to type. Sometimes there is a sharp split between their precocious verbal abilities and their handwriting, probably because they can think faster than they can write, and they are bored with the goal of being neat.[21]

Social Aspects
Solitary play

They often play alone and enjoy solitude, not only because they like to but also because they have few people to play with who share their interests. The mother of a six-year-old fascinated with gears told me that her son said of the other children his age, "They don't like the things I play with." Such children feel different from others and are aware of not fitting in.

Preference for company of older children

When they do find friends, they usually find older children who are closer to themselves in mental age.

Affective Aspects
Philosophical and moral concerns

They are interested in philosophical issues, and they worry about moral and political problems such as the existence of evil in the world, the threat of nuclear war, or the destruction of the environment. They may become overwhelmed by such worries, and they may also take unusual moral stands, such as becoming a vegetarian despite having nonvegetarian parents.[22]

Humor

Perhaps as a result of their high verbal abilities, they are often reported to have an excellent sense of humor.

Experiences of awe

All the characteristics described thus far are highly typical of children with very high IQs. A characteristic of the gifted that is probably rarer was described by the psychoanalyst Phyllis Greenacre. She noted that extremely gifted people often experienced sudden intense feelings, images, and memories in childhood. These images were so vivid and the accompanying feelings so intense that the children seemed to experience a kind of wonder, terror, awe, even ecstasy—a spiritual or religious experience. She noted descriptions of such experiences in autobiographical accounts of some eminent people whom she called gifted, though she did not use the term *intelligence* or *IQ.* For example, Albert Schweitzer said that every Sunday morning as he sat in church and listened to the organ, he had a vivid image of the devil that filled him with terror and awe. She was struck by the similarities between these spiritual experiences in people who became eminent and the experiences reported by her patients. This capacity for mystical, hypomanic, intense states is very common in creators.[23]

The abilities of these kinds of extreme globally gifted children must be brain-based, as must the abilities of more singularly gifted children. Such abilities cannot be the product of training alone, for the training is self-imposed and follows from an inner need to learn. These children are not getting intensive training from their parents. Often the parents are not as gifted as the children and can hardly keep up with them. These children manipulate their environments in order to challenge themselves: they ask for books and beg for extra instruction.[24]

These children induce the rules of reading and mathematics just as the ordinary child induces the rules of syntax. Every normal child acquires the complex rules of language before five without explicit instruction of any kind; we take this for granted. But if only a few managed to do this, we would consider those who did to be prodigies like David or Michael or the children studied by Terman.

༻

TERMAN'S LEGACY

Terman launched formal scientific work on giftedness. He moved the field beyond the case study approach and profoundly influenced the research on giftedness that has been carried out ever since. Part of his legacy is that, for the general public as well as for most psychologists and educators, the term *giftedness* continues to refer to a unitary, global ability that is best assessed by an IQ test, or if not that, by school performance, which is known to correlate with IQ. And, in great part as a result of Terman's work, programs for the gifted (that is, academically gifted, high-IQ children) have mushroomed in public schools all over the United States.

How a society conceptualizes giftedness determines how it will test for giftedness. There are many ways in which a society might conceive of giftedness: people who are exceptionally moral, who are charismatic leaders, who can make people laugh, or who can take things apart and fix them might be considered exemplars of the gifted. Although educators, including those in the American Association for Gifted Children, often agree that extraordinary performance in areas such as these ought to be considered gifts, IQ has remained the primary way in which giftedness is thought of and assessed. Giftedness is usually defined by a score of 130 or higher on a paper-and-pencil IQ test, or by school performance in the ninety-fifth percentile or above. These criteria define the top 2 to 5 percent of the population of schoolchildren.[25]

In the United States, IQ tests have been roundly criticized because members of minority groups discriminated against, especially African Americans and Hispanics, tend to score lower than do members of more privileged groups. This scoring pattern shows that some groups in our society are denied the opportunity to develop their gifts. I see this as an indictment of our society, not of IQ tests. However, I agree that educators could more readily identify gifted children from underprivileged backgrounds by using more qualitative observational measures and noting such things as high levels of drive or curiosity. Some also argue that nonverbal tests are more fair than verbal tests, although such tests often identify the spatially, but not the verbally, gifted. The Ravens Progressive Matrices test, for example, is a measure of nonverbal reasoning in which one is shown a matrix with a missing piece. The task is to select from a set of choices the design that completes the pattern.[26]

In the last decade, a small but vocal group of researchers has begun to question the equation of giftedness with general intelligence. Evidence against linking giftedness with general intelligence has come from a study of prodigies by developmental psychologists David Feldman and Lynn Goldsmith. The prodigies they studied were operating at adult levels in chess, music, math, or writing, yet they were not at all advanced on tasks outside their domain of talent. Increasingly, skepticism has been voiced about whether tests of general intelligence and standardized achievement tests are the measures we should be using. And some are beginning to question the use of the IQ test as an overall indicator of intellectual functioning. Researchers are beginning to see that giftedness and IQ are not the same thing, and that a person can be very gifted in one area yet not have a high IQ overall. Thus, we are beginning to develop a broader, more multidimensional view of what it means to be gifted.[27]

In recent years new tests and definitions of academic giftedness have proliferated. Some are argued to be superior to the IQ test because they are better able to predict achievement beyond childhood. Examples include a test developed by the psychologist Robert Sternberg to assess insight and a model developed by Joseph Renzulli, director of the National Research Center on the Gifted and Talented at the University of Connecticut. Renzulli's model emphasizes task commitment and creativity, in addition to high ability. And in a recent study, economically disadvantaged minority children of normal IQ were identified as gifted on the basis of qualities like curiosity, motivation, and imagination. These children fared as well in gifted classes as children selected by traditional measures for "gifted" IQ. Whether these measures actually have greater predictive value for later achievement remains to be seen, but it is likely that they do, since they include factors known to be important in later achievement, such as commitment and creativity.[28]

Three

UNEVENLY GIFTED, EVEN LEARNING DISABLED

Certainly, many academically gifted children are globally gifted, balanced in verbal and mathematical abilities, like David or Michael Kearney, the boys described in chapter 2. But many other academically gifted children look far less balanced. In fact, unevenness between verbal and mathematical abilities may be more the rule than the exception. Many children whom we would clearly call gifted have much higher mathematical than verbal skills, or the reverse. Math prodigies do not also tend to be literary prodigies; nor do writing prodigies tend to excel in math.[1]

CONTRASTING MATHEMATICAL AND VERBAL PROFILES

KyLee and Rahela are two children who present a less global picture of academic giftedness than do David and Michael. KyLee excelled in the numerical domain, and Rahela excelled in language. While both children had high IQs and were academically gifted, they differed markedly, even at an early age.

A "Number Boy"

By one and a half, KyLee was fascinated with both letters and numbers. He would pick up plastic refrigerator letters and say their names over and over. He pointed out a *W* on the frame of someone's glasses. Any objects that he found to play with, such as chopsticks or blocks, were simply materials with which to fashion letters and numbers.

But his initial fascination with letters gave way, at age two, to a more intense fascination with numbers. His favorite toys became plastic numbers and blocks with numbers on them. He loved the actual physical numbers and said their names over and over as he handled the objects.

KyLee never tired of numbers. At two, he was given a calendar, from which he insistently and repeatedly read the numbers aloud. When he stayed in a hotel at age two, he was more interested in the number 304 on the hotel room door than in anything else, and he immediately read it aloud. At two and a half, when his mother brought him into her office for the first time, he was intrigued by the numbers on all the office doors, and he quickly learned that Liz was in 303, Paulina in 323, and Howard in 324. Once KyLee saw a number, it was imprinted in his memory. At three, his parents took him camping. At the park gate, the ranger asked for the license number. Neither parent remembered it. His father turned to KyLee and asked, "What's the license number?" With ease, KyLee answered, "502-VFA."

Even before that he had begun to do mental arithmetic. "Eight plus eight makes sixteen," he had announced at two after seeing a license plate with two 8s on it. When his startled parents asked him how he knew this, he couldn't explain. When he was two and a half, his grandmother lined up three blocks to form the equation $1 + 1 = 2$. KyLee realized instantly that one could play with numbers, and he asked for this game again and again. At this age, his favorite book was one about addition, with objects pictured with numbers written under each, forming equations (for example, 2 apples plus 2 apples equals 4 apples).

His father had begun to hold KyLee at five months on his lap while playing computer games. KyLee had been allowed to fiddle with the keyboard, and he had become immersed in using the computer. By three, he had mastered the Macintosh and played math computer games every day.

KyLee refused to let anyone teach him how to play these games, insisting on figuring them out himself. "Go away, I do it myself," he would insist. His understanding of math leaped ahead, and he mastered addition and multiplication.

Through a computer game, KyLee discovered prime numbers. In this game, the player sees a grid partially filled in with numbers and must fill in the grid with other numbers of the same kind. On one occasion, KyLee faced a grid partially filled in with prime numbers. Thus, the implicit rule was to find other numbers that were prime. By chance, he picked a prime number for one of the empty cells. When the computer told him that this choice was correct, he picked out all the other prime numbers by trial and error. He then memorized all the prime numbers and said that he knew how they were all alike. For every ten numbers, he could identify the prime numbers. No one taught him a rule for this, and his amazed parents did not know what rule he was using that was allowing him to identify prime numbers so effortlessly.

By three, he had mastered all of the easy levels of his math computer games. At this age he could add, in his head, any pair of numbers that equaled fifteen or less. By five, he was able to subtract, multiply, divide, estimate, and do word problems. When he added and multiplied, he knew how to carry. He could solve problems in his head using these operations. For instance, when asked how many 10s in 1,030, he immediately said 103. Even more astounding was his reply to his mother's exceedingly difficult question, "Five 100ths are how many thousandths?" (that is, $5/100 = ?/1000$). "Fifty," he replied casually. I asked him if he ever got tired of numbers. "No," he replied, "never."

His ability to add in his head was astonishing. When KyLee was four, one of his favorite, and most difficult, computer games involved adding mentally and estimating. Players are given a number to which they must each add numbers. The player whose final sum is closest to a target number wins. So, for example, one might be given 57 and a choice of 5, 8, or 1 to add to 57, with the target sum being 63. Players add one number to 57 at a time. KyLee played against the computer and always beat it. He would survey his choice of three numbers and pick one that would leave the computer with only two bad choices. So, in this case, he chose 5, giving him a sum of 62, and giving the computer the choice of ending up with 65 or 58. What he was thus able to do was add all three numbers to the original number, compare the sums, and recognize which one was closer to the goal of 63.

Like David, who had trouble solving arithmetic problems linearly on paper, KyLee could not explain how he calculated. "I just figured it out," he would say, or, "I just think in my head." This is typical of children precocious in math. Perhaps they have a visual image of numerical relations that they cannot translate in a linear way in school.[2]

KyLee's parents never drilled him in math. They simply supplied him with materials because they recognized his single-minded love of numbers. All that KyLee needed were the materials; the rest he did on his own. When his father showed him the multiplication tables, three-year-old KyLee soaked them up effortlessly, on his own. By age five, KyLee had all of the arithmetic and math skills expected of a child at the end of elementary school: he could add, subtract, multiply, carry, divide, estimate, and solve complicated word problems.

Here is an example of how another mathematically gifted child like KyLee solved an algebra problem. The problem was to solve for X, given the following equation:

$9 + X + X = 29 + 29 + 29$. The child just looked at the problem and then wrote down 39. He explained that because 29 is 20 more than 9, he split the 20 in half and added 10 to the other 29s. Like KyLee, he seemed to grasp the relations among the numbers and solved the problems by an intuitive leap rather than with an algorithm. Both this child and KyLee obviously learn math in a different way than do most other children.[3]

When I observed KyLee, at age five, he could easily spend up to three hours doing solitary math activities—arranging cards or sticks, counting, playing math games on the computer, and so on. He loved being alone and often played by himself, writing numbers on a blackboard, for instance, rather than interacting with other children in the same room.

Five-year-old KyLee called himself a "number boy." He was in the grip of numbers and had been since age two. He imposed numbers on his world. Where other children saw people or stories or events, KyLee saw numbers and their patterns. He reminded me vividly of another mathematically precocious child I observed who used the occasion of meeting someone new to create a math problem: he would immediately ask for the person's birthday and would then compute in his head the age difference in years and months between him and his new acquaintance. Case studies of mathematically gifted children always mention this kind of self-imposed, obsessive fascination with numbers. These children read numbers in the phone book for pleasure; they pay more attention to the page numbers in a book than the words. The physicist Edward Teller, who would clearly have qualified as a mathematically gifted child, apparently put himself to sleep by reciting math tables and by figuring out the number of seconds in a minute, hour, day, week, and year. While KyLee was an excellent mental calculator, the ability to calculate is far less predictive of later mathematical achievement than is such mathematizing of everyday experience.[4]

Eavesdropping on the kinds of conversations that extremely gifted math students have shows that what these children are interested in is not calculating but reasoning mathematically. For example, a teenager at an international math competition described the topic of conversation one night: "The next night, we started talking about a system in which all universal constants are 1, discovering that (a) this couldn't be done, and (b) even if it could, it would make things so darn weird that no one would seriously want to use such a system."[5]

KyLee's intense interest in numbers and, to a lesser extent, letters did not extend to other areas. His parents tried to interest him in music and in drawing, but he paid little attention. KyLee was an early reader. He was spelling simple words with his letters at two and a half, and he taught himself to read much like David did (chapter 2), sometime between the ages of two and three. However, it is clearly numbers that delight and seduce him. After playing number games with him for a while, I asked him if he liked to read. "Give me another number problem," he replied.

A Five-Year-Old Who Could Read *Chrysanthemum*

When I first met Rahela, she was five and a half—the same age as KyLee—and in preschool. Rahela was also extremely precocious, but her precocity and interests were far more verbal than mathematical.

Rahela began to speak early, like David. She said her first Bengali word at nine months, and by two, she spoke in long, complex Bengali sentences. For example, her parents translated one of her two-year-old sentences as, "Daddy is putting shaving cream on his face." (At this age, most children would describe such an event by saying, "Daddy shave.")

At three months, she sat patiently and looked at books with her mother. As soon as she was shown books, she developed several favorites. Her parents knew her favorites by how her eyes and face lit up.

By two, she could recognize and name all the letters of the alphabet. At two and a half, she surprised her mother by recognizing and naming simple English words like *milk*. At that point, but not before, her mother started to point to words as she read aloud to her daughter from books. Rahela looked with fascination at the words as her mother pointed to them and read them. By three, she could read many words, and she surprised her preschool teacher when she showed that she could read the names of all her classmates. By four, she was reading books for pleasure. By five, she read chapter books omnivorously. Her parents had long since given up reading to her.

Rahela was at first probably reading words by recognizing the whole word. However, she quickly began reading phonetically, with no formal instruction from her parents. At five, she could read difficult words that she had never encountered before and could not understand, such as *chrysanthemum, asymptotic,* and *business.*

I watched Rahela read aloud at age five and a half. She read like an adult—totally fluently, with expression, even reading the italicized words with extra emphasis. When she read silently, she read rapidly. For example, it took her twenty minutes to read *One Morning in Maine*, a sixty-four–page picture book with about 280 lines of print. This clocks to fourteen lines (or about a half a page of print) per minute. Although Rahela could read anything, she resisted reading books whose content was too sad. Thus, her reading choices were limited, but not by her ability.

Rahela's writing was equally advanced. At five, she could easily and neatly write lowercase letters, and she could even read cursive writing. Unlike most children of this age, who use invented spelling, Rahela's words were almost always spelled correctly, including English words that are known to cause problems such as *walk, almost, first, prayed,* and *you.* She must have soaked up these words from her extensive reading and then recalled exactly how they had looked on the page.

Rahela was advanced in math, but not like KyLee. For example, whereas KyLee could multiply, carry, divide, estimate, and solve word problems at five, Rahela at this same age could count by 2s, 3s, 5s, and 10s, and add up to three digits together, but she could not yet perform the other operations that came so effortlessly to KyLee. Nor did she, like KyLee, think of the world in terms of its numbers. Obsessed with words and with the printed page, Rahela stood out most sharply in the linguistic domain.

In other domains, she was proficient, but not unusually so. Her drawings were careful but age appropriate. As for physical development, she had crawled and walked a few months later than average.

IS UNEVENNESS THE RULE?

An unevenness between mathematical and verbal abilities should have been evident even to Terman. Many of his subjects had greater strengths and interests in reading than in math, or vice versa. However, because Terman was interested in overall, general intelligence, he dismissed this fact by claiming that the unevenness in ability found in gifted children was no different from the amount of unevenness found in children of ordinary IQ. When he compared a group of his children to a nongifted group, he found that the gifted were slightly more uneven in their profile of verbal and numerical skills. But he chose to emphasize the fact that the differences between the gifted and nongifted groups were small. "Gifted children may be more successful specialists and thus attract more attention, but it should be observed that they are superior in all abilities," wrote James DeVoss, the author of a chapter, in Terman's first volume, on specialization of abilities in the Terman sample. "The 'one-sidedness' of precocious children is mythical," wrote Terman in the conclusion to his first volume. He also found that his subjects expressed no more than average interest in drawing, painting, and music.[6]

More recent work has shown, however, that unevenness is the rule among academically gifted children, while global giftedness like that of David or Michael is the exception. Adults with high IQs show *less* correlation among subabilities measured by an IQ test than do those with ordinary IQs, an effect noted even by British educational psychologist Charles Spearman, the proponent of general intelligence, or "g" as it is called. Thus, we are more likely to find a high-IQ individual with mathematical ability far exceeding verbal ability than we are to find a low-IQ person with such a striking disparity. In one recent study, sharp discrepancies were found between verbal and performance IQ scores in children with IQs of 120 or higher. One reason that lower IQs are associated with more even performance might be that a deficit in some critical cognitive process places a limit on all subabilities.[7]

Despite the greater variability in profiles of academically gifted versus ordinary children, mathematical and verbal precocity are correlated to some extent among the gifted. Evidence of this relationship has come largely from the work of psychologists Julian Stanley and Camilla Benbow in their efforts to identify mathematically precocious children for the Study of Mathematically Precocious Youth (SMPY), a program started at Johns Hopkins University that offers intensive accelerated summer mathematics courses. Children identified as mathematically precocious by this program are those who, at age twelve or thirteen, score at least 500 on the math portion of the Scholastic Aptitude Test (SAT). The average score for college-bound seniors is 500 for boys, 453 for girls. Stanley and Benbow have argued that a high score on the math SAT at an early age is a reflection of advanced mathematical reasoning. These children cannot be spitting back math strategies they have been taught, since the test assesses skills they have not yet covered in school. While these children are far more precocious in math than in the verbal domain (as measured by SAT test scores), they still often perform far above the average for college-bound high school seniors on the verbal SAT as well.

Nonetheless, in a study of over a thousand highly academically gifted adolescents, over 95 percent of them showed a strong disparity between mathematical and verbal ability. And many mathematically gifted children identified for SMPY show an enormous discrepancy between their math and verbal skills. For instance, one of the program's best math students scored 760 on the math portion of the SAT but only 310 on the verbal SAT portion at age twelve. And one eight-year-old from Australia scored 760 on the math SAT portion and 290 on the verbal SAT portion. However, one year later, his verbal score had risen to 380. If his verbal score continued to increase, he may have had little discrepancy between his verbal and math scores by age fourteen. Thus, the SAT scores of older children may mask a discrepancy between verbal and mathematical ability that is picked up by the SAT scores of younger children. Perhaps it is relevant that in a retrospective study of the development of mathematicians conducted by the educational psychologist Benjamin Bloom, none of the mathematicians reported that they had learned to read before attending school, and six of the twenty had had difficulty learning to read.[8]

While mathematically gifted children who are weak in verbal ability exist, it is far rarer to find verbally precocious children who do poorly in math, probably because they use verbal strategies to solve math problems. For instance, twenty-two children who scored 700 or higher on the math SAT portion scored under 430 on the verbal portion. In contrast, only one verbally precocious child tested in another study had a math SAT score under 500.

Thus, at least according to paper-and-pencil test measures, children who are mathematically precocious are less balanced in their skills and are more likely to achieve lower overall IQ scores than are those who are verbally precocious. Programs for the gifted that use overall IQ scores as an entrance criterion are likely to miss those children precocious in math but average in verbal ability. In addition, overall IQ scores will not tell the school anything about the area in which the child is gifted and, thus, about the area in which greater challenge is needed.[9]

LEARNING DISABLED, YET GIFTED

The Nueva School, just outside San Francisco, is a school for academically gifted children. On a visit there, I learned that applicants are given the widely used Wechsler Intelligence Scale for Children (WISC). Children of average intelligence score somewhere between 90 and 109, but the average score at Nueva is in the 140s. Children must score at least 125 to be eligible for admission.

The WISC yields a verbal subscore and a performance one. The verbal score is based on responses to tasks such as verbal problem solving and vocabulary definition. The performance score is based on visual-spatial tasks such as assembling puzzles and building block designs. I learned there that about a third of the children admitted achieve only average scores on one subscale, but score one or two standard deviations above average on the other. These are academically gifted children with very uneven profiles. Academically gifted children are sometimes so uneven in their scholastic profiles that they are learning disabled in some domain. The Nueva School also has plenty of these children, and they receive a great deal of individual attention. Typically, these children excel at abstract verbal reasoning and seem very bright and motivated outside of school, but they encounter serious problems with school tasks. They may have dyslexia and have difficulty learning to read, they may have serious problems with math, or they may have perceptual-motor problems leading to number reversals (e.g., writing 12 instead of 21) or difficulties in handwriting. Disabilities in reading and math tend to be more disruptive than problems in perceptual and motor skills. Sometimes these children also have an inability to focus and attend, and they are classified as having an attention disorder. These children often develop negative self-images in school and become unmotivated underachievers. They are in as much need of special intervention as are the nongifted learning disabled. Because of the pervasive myth of global giftedness, it was not until fairly recently that educators and psychologists began to recognize cases of gifted children with learning disabilities.

Of course, children—gifted and not gifted alike—are often incorrectly labeled as learning disabled, given the difficulty of distinguishing between a bored child, a disturbed child, and a learning-disabled one. It is possible that gifted children are misdiagnosed more often than nongifted children because it is so common for gifted children to be bored and restless in an unchallenging classroom and to end up classified as having an attention disorder or as being hyperactive. However, though some gifted children diagnosed with an attention disorder are merely bored, others do have a problem. The academic tutor of learning disabled children at the Nueva School described these children to me as trying desperately to attend, but being unable to screen out irrelevant background information. She spoke of the emotional damage that such a problem can cause if undiagnosed, and the relief felt by the child and the family when the problem has been diagnosed and treated medically.

We do not know the overall incidence of high-IQ children with learning disabilities. By one estimate, there are between 120,000 and 180,000 gifted and learning-disabled students in American schools today. Many of these children have language-based disabilities. About 10 percent of high-IQ children read two or more years below grade level, and 30 percent show a discrepancy between their mental age and reading achievement. This finding is consistent with a recent study by three educational researchers at the National Research Center on the Gifted and Talented: Sally Reis, Terry Neu, and Joan McGuire. These researchers found that all of the academically gifted students in the University of Connecticut program for students with learning disabilities had a language-based disability, from spelling problems to severe dyslexia. In addition, all these students with a language problem had gifts in spatial areas. We will return in chapter 6 to the combination of language problems with visual-spatial strengths.

One reason for the lack of information about the incidence of learning disabilities in gifted populations is the lack of clarity with which various categories of learning disability are often defined. However, the notion that academic giftedness can coexist with academic learning disabilities is no longer in dispute.

Students with a combination of gifts and learning disabilities suffer in school because they are kept out of gifted programs but are considered too smart for remedial work. Also, because they excel in certain abilities, teachers sometimes consider them unmotivated. Students like this are also clever enough often to hide their disability.[10]

PROBING BENEATH THE SURFACE

Children who are gifted mathematically differ in many ways from those who are gifted verbally. These two groups of children differ in their spatial abilities, in the kinds of information they can most readily manipulate and recall, and in the proportion of males to females in the group.

Mathematical Gifts and Spatial Ability

Mathematics has long been argued to involve visual and spatial thinking. The mathematicians studied by Bloom had spatial interests in childhood: they were curious about how things like gears worked and took pleasure in taking toys apart. And mathematically gifted children score higher on spatial tests such as those in which one must mentally rotate an image, and on nonverbal reasoning tests such as the Ravens Progressive Matrices, while verbally gifted children score higher on tests of general information and verbal ability. One piece of evidence for a link between mathematics and spatial thinking is that children who score well on the math portion of the SAT also score very well on tests of spatial ability. And college students majoring in math or in science fields that require many math courses excel over those majoring in verbal fields such as history or English when asked to manipulate and rotate images mentally.[11]

As suggested earlier, one explanation for the wide range in verbal ability among the mathematically gifted is that high scores on a test such as the math portion of the SAT can be obtained through either verbal or nonverbal reasoning. Mathematically precocious children who score poorly on the verbal SAT portion tend to have high scores on the Ravens Progressive Matrices test. (The Australian child mentioned earlier, who scored so much higher on his math SAT portion than the verbal one, also scored extremely high on the Ravens at age nine.) It is rare to find a mathematically precocious child who scores poorly on both the verbal SAT portion and the Ravens. Thus, high performance on the math SAT portion must reflect either verbal intelligence (use of verbal strategies) or nonverbal reasoning.[12]

Three kinds of children with mathematical talent have been identified: those who use visual–spatial reasoning to solve math problems, those who use verbal strategies, and those who use both. This would account for why verbally gifted children can do well on math tests, since they can use verbal strategies. However, these kinds of children may excel only at moving symbols around on paper-and-pencil tests. Perhaps they would reveal weaknesses in mathematics if the tests were not multiple-choice and required them to discover rules never taught to them.[13]

Kinds of Memories

The kind of gift one has tells a lot about the kinds of information one can best hold in memory. Underneath the surface of mathematical giftedness is the ability to remember numerical and spatial information; underneath verbal giftedness is the ability to remember linguistic information. There is no general, across-the-board enhancement of memory just because one is verbally or mathematically gifted.

Psychologists who search for the kinds of information best stored in the memories of gifted minds are adopting what is called an information-processing approach to the study of giftedness. Information-processing psychologists seek to understand how bits of information are processed, or operated on, by the brain, much like bits of information, or data, are processed by a computer. Researchers who adopt an information-processing approach to giftedness search for the basic, underlying components, or bits, of complex ability as measured by very simple tasks. Thus, they might search for the components of mathematical talent by measuring the number of digits that can be remembered and manipulated in working memory, or the speed with which one can rotate an image mentally. Similarly, they might search for the components of verbal talent by measuring the speed with which a string of letters can be classified as a word or not. A distinction is made between *working memory,* the system in which information is stored temporarily while it is manipulated, and *long-term memory,* the system in which information is stored permanently as one's knowledge base.[14]

Camilla Benbow showed that the basic information-processing capacities of working memory in the gifted differ depending on whether the gift is primarily mathematical or verbal. She compared two groups of undeniably precocious adolescents: thirteen- and fourteen-year-olds who scored on both the math and verbal SAT portions at or above the level of the average college-bound male senior. This means that they achieved scores of at least 500 and 430 on the math and verbal portions of the test, respectively. These adolescents were recruited as part of a talent search run by the Johns Hopkins University's Center for Talented Youth (CTY), an organization similar to SMPY. Like SMPY, CTY runs intensive academic summer programs for youths who have college-level skills.

The students were subdivided into three groups: the "globally" gifted, who scored high on both portions of the SAT (averaging 664 on the math portion and 546 on the verbal portion); the mathematically gifted (averaging 649 on the math portion and 408 on the verbal portion); and the verbally gifted (averaging 453 on the math portion and 526 on the verbal portion). They were then given a set of information-processing tasks predicted to underlie one or the other kind of talent.

The tasks were designed to assess very simple abilities that were thought to be at the core of mathematical and verbal talent. The first kind of task assessed how accurately subjects could maintain information in their short-term, working memory. Subjects were shown various kinds of lists for brief periods of time, after which they were asked to recall the lists, in the correct temporal order. The lists were composed of either letters, words, numbers, or locations. The location task consisted of a grid and an asterisk that moved around to different cells in the grid; the task was to mark each cell that had contained an asterisk, in the order in which the asterisk had moved there. The letter and word lists were considered to be linguistic stimuli; the number and location lists were considered to be mathematical stimuli. The location task was considered to be related to mathematical ability because of the heavy spatial component underlying mathematical reasoning.

The prediction was that linguistic stimuli should be better recalled by the verbally gifted, while numerical and spatial stimuli should be better recalled by the mathematically gifted. With one exception, this was what was found. Those with math talent (the math and global group) outperformed the verbal group on both digits and locations. Their facility with these kinds of stimuli was not due to global ability, since the math group did just as well as the global group. Similarly, those with verbal talent (the verbal and global group) outperformed the math group on words, but not letters. Again, this was not due to global ability, since the verbal group did just as well as the global group.[15]

Mathematically talented children not only excel in recalling numbers and locations. They also excel over those with verbal ability in recalling visual information that cannot be coded verbally. Scientists, who are commonly mathematically precocious as children, often report using visual imagery in their thinking. For instance, suppose you wanted to remember the shape of a Chinese character. You could not readily attach a verbal label to it, because it would not look like anything you could name. What you would have to do is store it in your visual memory as a pattern. When children with mathematical talent were asked to remember such nonverbalizable patterns (in this case, Persian letters), they excelled over a comparison group matched in verbal IQ. These children's facility thus had nothing to do with verbal ability and everything to do with mathematical talent, a subcomponent of IQ. Now suppose you were shown a meaningless visual pattern but were not asked to remember it. In this case, superior memory for the pattern would show that even when you did not make the effort, patterns would be effortlessly "photographed" by you and stored in your visual memory. Individuals with talent in math also excel in such a "noninstructed" visual memory task. When asked to copy a complex, nonrepresentational image, and later, after the image was removed, asked to reproduce it from memory, those college students who excelled were those who had chosen to major in fields requiring extensive math.[16]

Benbow also showed that children with verbal talent are faster at accessing words in their long-term memory, and that this is not due to global giftedness. She showed her subjects a list of words and of pronounceable nonwords, such as *floor* and *flome*. They had to decide, as quickly as possible, whether each was a word. This task shows how long it takes for a word to activate its representation and move the representation from long-term memory into working memory. Here, the verbally talented group excelled.[17]

When a relevant context makes it easier for us to access information in our memory, we say that the context has "primed," or jogged, our memory. Thus, if I hear the word *baby* just before I hear *infant,* I will be quicker to access *infant* from my long-term store of English words, and to decide that it is indeed a word, than if I had just heard the word *infant* following an unrelated word such as *book.* Semantic priming helps people recognize words. However, such priming effects are much smaller for good readers than for poor ones, probably because the former rely on more automatic processes than do the latter. Similarly, verbally gifted children need such help less than do the mathematically gifted.[18]

What these kinds of findings show is that types of gifted children differ in the kind of information they can most easily hold in working memory. Those with mathematical talent most readily retain numerical, spatial, and visual information; those with verbal talent most readily retain words. Thus, contrary to what many assume, there is no *general* enhancement of memory capacity in the gifted. Rather, enhanced memory is a function of a match between the kind of information to be recalled and the kind of talent possessed. Only those globally gifted with talent in both the verbal and mathematical areas recall both types of information equally well. Experts have superior memories not for any kind of information, but specifically and only for information within their field of expertise. Ten-year-old chess experts, for instance, have superior memory for chess positions, but not for numbers. High ability in one area does not mean high ability in general.[19][20]

Sex Differences

Yet another way in which mathematical talent diverges from verbal talent is in the striking sex difference found at the high end of math, but not verbal, ability. Among the thirteen- to fourteen-year-olds who take the verbal and math portions of the SAT as part of the SMPY talent search, a large sex difference is found on the math, but not the verbal, portion. (Only those who score in the top few percentiles on school-administered standard math and verbal tests qualify to take the SATs as part of the talent search. Roughly the same number of girls as boys qualify at this level.) Boys in the talent search score about half a standard deviation above the girls on the math SAT portion, and their advantage is especially great at the upper range. The ratio of high-scoring boys to girls is 2 to 1 for those scoring at or above 500; it is 4 to 1 for those scoring at or above 600; and it is 13 to 1 for those scoring 700 or above. These sex differences persist after the early adolescent years and relate to later math and science achievement in high school and college. These differences at ages twelve to thirteen cannot be due to boys having taken more math courses, since at this age all students have taken the same courses. But the differences may be due at least in part to sex differences in spatial ability.[21]

Despite the fact that in all of the many countries tested a sex difference favoring males has been found, the size of this sex difference is substantially lower for one particular group: Asians. Whether those tested were Chinese students in Shanghai or

Asian-American students, the ratio of males to females at the 700 to 800 range was only 4 to 1. Thus, culture may play a role in mathematical aptitude. It is possible that attitudes about girls in math are more positive among Asians, and that students of both sexes are expected to do well in math. Asians may place more stress on visual-spatial thinking for both sexes. However, we also cannot rule out at this point the possibility of a biological, brain-based explanation favoring Asian females over other females.[22]

It appears clear that unevenness is more the rule than the exception. To be sure, globally gifted children exist. But uneven profiles are more common. And underlying differences in ability are differences in how information is processed and remembered. In extreme cases, children are gifted in some academic areas, but actually learning disabled in others. The smooth and even image of the globally gifted child thus gives way to the more complex, irregular picture of the singularly gifted individual.

How should schools and special programs try to identify gifted children? Given the uneven picture of the academically gifted child, it would seem to make far more sense to use domain-specific achievement tests to identify kinds of gifted children than to rely on full-scale IQ scores that pool scores on various subtests. Domain-specific achievement tests are also far more useful than the subtest scores of an IQ test, both because the subtest scores are not highly reliable and because the relationship between a performance score (based on tasks such as block designs and puzzles) and school performance is not particularly evident. Our new understanding of the nature of academic giftedness ought to be having more of an effect on how schools and programs are identifying such children.[23]

Four

ARTISTIC AND MUSICAL CHILDREN

We are more likely to call children with exceptional ability in art or music "talented" than "gifted." The term *gifted* is usually reserved for the scholastically able. But children with high ability in art and music actually resemble the scholastically gifted in important ways. They have all three components of giftedness: they are precocious, they march to their own drummer, and they have a rage to master. And, like the scholastically gifted, they often have a singular, domain-specific gift existing alongside more ordinary abilities in other areas.[1]

A CHILD WITH A RAGE TO DRAW

The case of Peter B. shows how visually artistic children resemble scholastically gifted ones. When I discovered Peter, he was a six-year-old obsessed with drawing. The intensity of his obsession rivaled David's and Michael's obsession with language, books, and mathematical concepts. The singularity of his obsession rivaled that of KyLee's with number and Rahela's with the printed word. As with all four of these other children, Peter's unusual ability made itself clear in infancy.

Peter first tried to draw at ten and a half months. One day his mother was paying bills at the kitchen table. Peter kept trying to grab her pen. To distract him, she gave him a piece of paper and two markers and sat him in his high chair across from her. It was love at first sight. He was enthralled. While children do not ordinarily begin making marks on paper until about two, drawing on paper became Peter's favorite pastime from that day forward. His first drawings were, of course, mostly scribbles, but he was able to hold pens, pencils, and crayons easily.

At age five and a half, he was given the Goodenough Draw-a-Person Test, which is sometimes used as an IQ test. On this test, one must draw a person, and the more details included, the higher one's score. Although the test correlates only weakly with IQ, it does give some indication of how advanced a child is in drawing. Peter was given this test at the suggestion of his preschool teacher so that his gift would be clearly documented with a "score," thus making it more likely that he would be placed in a kindergarten with a teacher who had empathy for his kind of ability.

Peter's drawing was scored at a level higher than that of a typical fourteen-year-old. His drawings were reported by the tester to "reflect an exceptional degree of perspective, dimension, and detail." The report read: "[Peter] draws with incredible fluidity. . . . What makes it even more remarkable is the fact that he is self-taught and seems to work so effortlessly." Figure 4.1 shows one of the drawings he made for this test. What stands out here are the details (eyelashes, pupils, neck, sleeves, cuff) and the accurate, fluid shapes of things (lips, eyes, head shaped as an oval rather than a sphere, nose). Compare Peter's drawing of a human figure with the one shown in figure 4.2. This is by a five-year-old with no special drawing ability. Shapes are drawn as formulaic schemas (for example, head and eyes are round, mouth is a U), and few details are provided (for example, no neck, no waist, no eyelashes or pupils).

4.1. Drawing by Peter B. at five and a half when given the Goodenough Draw-a-Person Test. Drawing shows unusual detail and accurate, fluid contours.

Reprinted by permission of Lois Borelli.

4.2. Drawing by a typical five-year-old showing schematic shapes and minimal details.

From the collection of the author.

Until he was six, Peter drew with either his left or his right hand—it made no difference. Sometimes he would draw with one hand, while coloring in another part of the same drawing simultaneously with the other hand. It was as if he could not get his images down on paper fast enough, and he realized he could work faster by using both hands at once. At six, he began to draw with his right hand only.

Almost an Obsession

Peter wanted to draw more than do any other activity. Soon he was waking up in the mornings and calling out for paper and markers before getting out of bed. As he waited at the breakfast table for his food to be served, he drew. He continued to draw as he ate his breakfast. When breakfast was something messy, like oatmeal, he alternated between drawing and eating (with more drawing than eating). When he was served something that he could hold in his hand, like a waffle, he drew with one hand while feeding himself with the other. When he had finished eating, he pushed his dish aside and continued with his drawings, despite his mother's pleas that he stop and get dressed for school. Usually he had made several drawings by the time breakfast was over. On his return home from school, where he was not able to draw much, his first question was routinely, "Mom, can I draw?" He was like Michael, whose daily request of his father as he returned from work was that they do math together.

Peter would have drawn all day if allowed to do so. He was willing to participate in other activities, but he almost always tried to incorporate drawing into whatever he was doing. When friends came over to play, he would reluctantly disengage himself from drawing for a while, but he soon would begin to cajole his friends into sitting and drawing with him or posing for him. And he would use the television as an opportunity to get ideas for drawings. While watching a video or playing Nintendo, he often saw something that he wanted to draw. He would then insist on pausing the tape (over the protests of his younger brother) as he dashed around the house to find paper and pencil. When the image he wanted to draw was on TV and could not be paused, Peter became disgruntled.

Peter's Drawings

By two, Peter was drawing perfect balloons in motion, all blown up with a triangle for a knot and a long string (figure 4.3). At an age when most children draw "tadpole" human figures (figure 4.4a), Peter drew strikingly accurate figures with all their parts, as shown in figure 4.4b.

By four, he had developed a favorite and quite unusual theme: he drew flying, falling, walking, and dancing female figures in flowing, glittery robes (figures 4.5 and 4.6). The contours of these figures were far more realistic and less schematic than drawings typical of this age. By seven, in reaction to being teased at school for drawing "ladies," he added muscular or flabby wrestlers to his repertoire, as well as wildlife and portraits (figures 4.7a and b, 4.8, and 4.9), though he continued to develop his female-figure theme (figures 4.10a and b).

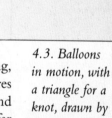

4.3. Balloons in motion, with a triangle for a knot, drawn by Peter B. at age two.

Reprinted by permission of Lois Borelli.

(a)

4.4. (a) Typical tadpole drawing by a three-year-old. (b) Human figure with all its parts, by Peter B. at age three years, seven months. Note the striking contrast between the age-typical and the gifted child's drawing.

Figure a from the collection of the author.

Figure b reprinted by permission of Lois Borelli.

(b)

4.5. *Peter B.'s favorite theme, emerging at age four: moving female figures in flowing robes. This drawing was made just as Peter turned four.*

Reprinted by permission of Lois Borelli.

4.6. Drawing of a girl by Peter B. at age four and a half, showing a fluid contour line that fairly accurately captures the shape of the body and facial features.

Reprinted by permission of Lois Borelli.

(a)

4.7. (a) *Drawing of the back view of a flabby wrestler, by Peter B. at age six years, eleven months. (b) Drawing of a muscular wrestler at age seven years, four months. Peter added males to his repertoire after being teased at school for drawing "ladies."*

Reprinted by permission of Lois Borelli.

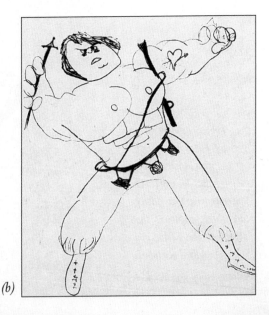

(b)

4.8. Drawing of an owl by Peter B. at age seven years, two months as he expanded his repertoire.

Reprinted by permission of Lois Borelli.

4.9. Portrait by Peter B. at age seven years, two months.

Reprinted by permission of Lois Borelli.

(a)

4.10. *Peter B. continued to draw female figures even after being teased. (a) Drawing of seated girl, from observation, age six years, eleven months. (b) Cheerleader leaning over, showing foreshortening, drawn just as Peter turned seven.*

Reprinted by permission of Lois Borelli.

(b)

Young children rarely draw observationally, even when asked to. When I taught an art class in my son's kindergarten, I tried to get my five- and six-year-old students to draw profiles and still lifes from models. Some realized that this meant looking closely and trying to draw what they actually saw. But others looked at the model, felt defeated, and proceeded to keep their eyes on their paper and draw schematically, from their visual concepts. Peter not only often drew from observation, but he got the idea to do so on his own. No one ever suggested that this was a way in which one might draw. And when he did draw from observation, he never just copied slavishly, but rather drew a whimsical interpretation of what he observed.

One morning, at age six, he caught sight of a photograph of Bill and Hillary Clinton about eleven feet away from him. Without moving closer to study it, he made a quick sketch of the picture (figure 4.11). This sketch of the Clintons reminds me of a sketch by Paul Klee drawn somewhere between four to six years of age (figure 4.12). A few months later, while eating waffles, Peter caught a brief glimpse of a woman singing on the country music TV channel. While he ate, he dashed off a picture of a woman singing with her arms outstretched and a microphone on a stand nearby (figure 4.13).

Creating Challenge

Like the academically gifted children described in the previous chapters, Peter manipulated his environment to make it more stimulating. Academically gifted children do this by reading increasingly difficult books or accelerating themselves in math. Recall the way in which they solved the Tower of Hanoi problem, trying to do it faster and in fewer moves. Peter created visual-spatial challenges for himself. He chose complex things to draw—human figures moving (figures 4.14a, b, and c) and figures in noncanonical positions, shown from the back (figure 4.15) or in three-quarters view (figure 4.16). At six, he

(right) 4.11. *Drawing of Bill and Hillary Clinton by Peter B. at age six, after a quick glimpse of a photo.*

Reprinted by permission of Lois Borelli.

(below) 4.12. *Drawing by Paul Klee (made between ages four and six), called* Lady with Parasol (Kindheit 15; Dame mit Schirm).

Both figures 4.11 and 4.12 show contour, detail, and subtle motion. Notice the swinging handbag in Klee's drawing, and the way Hillary leans to her right in Peter's drawing.

Kunstmuseum Bern, Paul-Klee-Stiftung, Bern. Copyright by Artists' Rights Society, New York, N.Y.

drew a foreshortened image of a person lying down, a most unusual and challenging picture even for an adult to draw (figure 4.17). And he started his drawings from odd points—the hem of a dress, a shoulder, or a shoe—and a picture emerged.

Just shy of his sixth birthday, Peter discovered that he could create movies. He took a long sheet of computer paper and drew different scenes from *The Little Mermaid*. He then asked his mother to get out the video camera and record each picture, from left to right. He had created an animated film. Peter was pushing at the boundaries of the drawing domain and discovering animation on his own. Peter's discovery of film animation compares with Michael Kearney's discovery of some of the rules of algebra. This capacity to make discoveries in a domain with little or no adult support is why gifted children look so different from others, and it is what makes gifted children march to their own drummer.

4.13. Singer with arms outstretched, by Peter B. at age six years, five months.

Reprinted by permission of Lois Borelli.

Other Visual-Spatial Abilities

Peter's fascination with drawing extended to other kinds of visual-spatial activities such as jigsaw puzzles and Lego blocks. When his puzzles became too easy for him,

(a)

(b)

(c)

4.14. *Drawings of figures in motion by Peter B.*
(a) Ballerina drawn at age four and a half.
(b) Woman with hand on hips throwing a book,
drawn at age six and a half. (c) Girl dancing on
stone over a waterfall (a rather imaginative choice
of subject), drawn at age seven years, four months.

Reprinted by permission of Lois Borelli.

4.15. Figure drawn from the back, by Peter B. at age five.

Reprinted by permission of Lois Borelli.

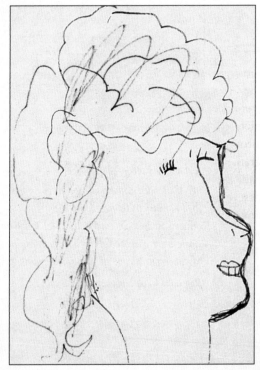

4.16. Self-portrait in three-quarters view, by Peter B. at age six years, one month.

Reprinted by permission of Lois Borelli.

he sought greater challenge by mixing up the pieces of four different ones and then putting them back together as separate puzzles.

Peter also had an exceptional visual memory. At eighteen months, he visited his grandparents in Florida and noticed a set of seashells lined up at the back window of his grandparents' car. Fourteen months later, he

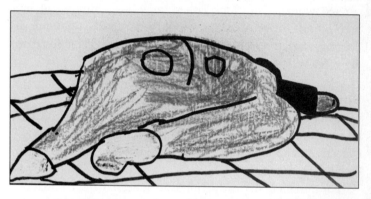

returned to Florida, got into his grandfather's car, and noticed that the seashells were gone. His grandfather, having completely forgotten about the shells, was astounded that his two-and-a-half-year-old grandson remembered and wanted them so badly. Peter looked at the world intently. He described pictures that he discerned in the grain of wood, and angels and harps in the shapes of clouds—further examples of a need to create visual stimulation for himself.

At about eighteen months, Peter was looking through a colorfully illustrated book of the Beatles' lyrics as his mother was packing up household items for a move to

4.17. Fore-shortened view of person lying down, by Peter B. at age six years, nine months.

Reprinted by permission of Lois Borelli.

Florida. Soon after, the book went into a packing box and remained there for the next several years. Finally, over two and a half years later, when he was four, the box was unpacked. As his mother took the Beatles book out of the crate, Peter spotted it and insisted that his mother stop unpacking and help him find a particular illustration in the book. He had talked about this illustration before, but his parents had not known what he was talking about and so had ignored him. They found the page he was looking for: a picture of a very exaggerated woman with long lashes, huge lips, a tiny waist, and high, almost caricatured cheekbones—not unlike the kinds of flowing, curvilinear human-figure forms that Peter liked to draw. He was thrilled.

Scholastic Abilities

Peter showed little interest in school-related subjects. But he sometimes managed to manipulate verbal and mathematical activities so that they fit with his drawing interests. Then he became engaged.

For instance, his early language reflected his fascination with the visual. At only twelve months, he could correctly label objects as blue, red, green, or orange. By the time he was a year and a half, he could even describe off-colors. For instance, at this age he examined a maroon crayon, thought for a while, and then declared that it was "dark red." By the time he was two years old, he could describe (and he loved to describe) virtually any color: lavender was "light purple," the sky was "light blue," his shirt was "dark blue," teal was "a little bit of blue and a little bit of green," and so on. For ordinary children, color terms are typically acquired considerably later and are very difficult to learn. Peter's language clearly reflected his fascination with the visual world.[2]

Peter's drawing also leaked into his writing. He could "draw" all his uppercase letters by the time he was two. Again, this interest was not initiated by his parents. Peter simply decided that he wanted to write his letters. By the time he was three years, three months, he began to write actual words. But he did this solely to create a dialogue between the characters in his pictures. His words were in the service of his pictures.

He did not like to write his letters and numbers in the standard way, but insisted on decorating them with fancy, curly arches and designs (figure 4.18). His kindergarten

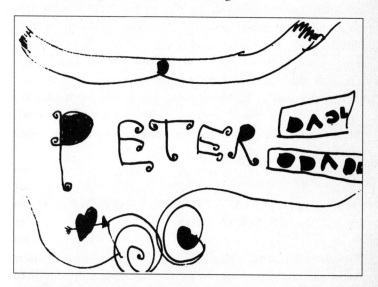

teacher continually reprimanded him for making his letters and numbers differently from the standard style she insisted on. But he engaged in a battle of wills, refusing to conform. The desire to do things in their own way is a recurrent theme in descriptions of gifted children, no matter what the domain. They are inveterate noncon-formists.

4.18. Peter B.'s decorated letters. He refused to write his letters in the standard way.

Reprinted by permission of Lois Borelli.

Peter's reading progressed slowly. While he was able to recognize the letters of the alphabet by age two, at the age of six and a half and in first grade, he could not yet read. Peter's performance in math, which he found boring, was ordinary, and he hated addition. While he could work out a simple, age-appropriate math problem, doing so did not come easily like drawing, and he showed no interest in making the required effort. And while he could make most of his numbers by age six, he still had some trouble recognizing written numbers. For instance, when his mother wrote down the number 20 and asked him what it was, he said "twelve." He liked to do math only if this meant drawing and decorating numbers. Like Picasso, who drew pigeons all over his schoolbooks, Peter drew pictures all over his math worksheets. In first grade, while all the other children were working on some assignment, Peter was in his own world. He would often get up, walk over to the paper supplies, and begin to draw. Fortunately, his teacher understood his need to draw and did not interfere.

SOME GENERALIZATIONS ABOUT GIFTED CHILDREN'S DRAWINGS

The core ability of the visually artistic child is a visual-spatial-motor precocity that makes it possible to capture the contour of three-dimensional objects on a two-dimensional surface. This ability enables children to make drawings that resemble the work of adult artists in a number of ways.

Recognizable Shapes

While children typically scribble until about three, gifted drawers make clearly recognizable shapes by the age of two. Recall Peter's balloons at age two. Figures 4.19a and b contrast a typical two-year-old's drawing of apples and a precocious two-year-old's drawing. The age-typical child drew a slash for each apple. A slash could stand for anything. The precocious

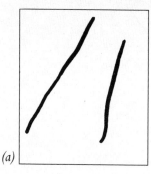

(a)

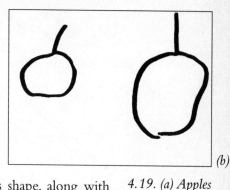

(b)

child drew each apple's shape, along with the stem. For him, the representation had to capture the apple's contour in order to depict an apple. A similar ability is seen in the drawing of a fish by a two-year-old, Eitan, a child whose work was studied in detail by the child psychologist Claire Golomb (figure 4.20). This drawing also reflects an ability to render the contour of the object drawn. Ordinary children draw from schemas (for example, a circle for a head, a line for an arm), but gifted drawers seem to notice the actual shapes of things.[3]

4.19. (a) Apples drawn as slashes by a typical two-year-old, and (b) apples drawn by Ryan Sullivan, a gifted two-year-old artist.

Figure a from the collection of the author.

Figure b reprinted by permission of Ryan Sullivan.

Fluid, Confident Contour Lines

Preschoolers typically draw additively, juxtaposing geometric shapes. A horse consists of an oval for the head, another oval for the body, rectangles joined to the oval for legs, and triangles for ears (figure 4.21). These drawings are called schematic because they do not capture the contour of

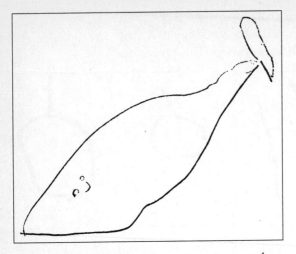

4.20. Fish by Eitan at age two years, two months showing fluid contour line.

From Golomb (1992a) and reprinted by permission
of Claire Golomb.

*4.21. Horse by a
typical five-year-old.*

Reprinted by permission of
Betsy Goldman.

the object, but represent it through simplified geometric shapes or "schemas." In contrast, precocious children draw the whole object with one fluid contour line (recall figure 4.4b, Peter's drawing of a girl in a bathing suit).

Gifted drawers do not depict a generic object, but include a rich amount of detail. Peter dressed his figures in robes. Eitan added gas tanks, axles, grills, bumpers, headlights, and brake boxes to his vehicles (see figures 4.23–4.25). Another child drew dinosaurs with scientific accuracy, using paleontology books to acquire the needed information. Including details is one way precocious children achieve realism in their drawings.[4]

Gifted drawers draw recognizable, complex images quickly and with ease. Like Peter, they do not labor over and erase their lines. And like Peter, they can start a drawing from just about any part of the object drawn. Picasso used to do this. He could draw a dog by starting with the ear (not the usual starting point), with no decrement in speed or confidence.[5]

Showing Volume and Depth

Gifted drawers achieve the illusion of realism not only by drawing differentiated shapes and details but also by depicting the third dimension. They use all of the known Western techniques to show depth—foreshortening, occlusion, size diminution, modeling to show volume, and even the most difficult technique of all, linear perspective—and they do so years earlier than normal children.[6] Linear perspective is used by precocious drawers sometimes almost as soon as they begin to draw (figures 4.22, 4.23, 4.24, and 4.25). These children may well be using a figural, perceptual strategy, rather than a conceptual one. That is, they just *see* the shapes of things, including the distortions of shapes as they recede into depth and diminish in size or become foreshortened. They do not need to rely on a learned system of perspective drawing. Typically, children do not begin to draw in perspective until late childhood or even early adolescence, and when they begin to do

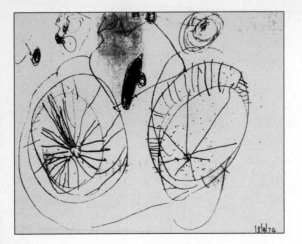

4.22. Tractor or bicycle by Eitan at age two years, two months, showing a juxtaposed side and top view of the wheels, making them look three-dimensional.

From Golomb (1992a) and reprinted by permission of
Claire Golomb.

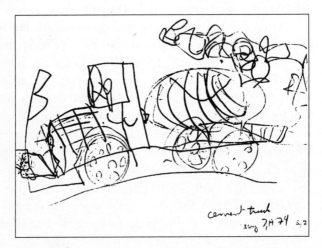

4.23. Cement truck by Eitan, age two years, seven months, showing the side view of the truck, the top view of the hood, and a frontal view of the grill and bumper.

From Golomb (1992a) and reprinted by permission of Claire Golomb.

4.24. Truck by Eitan, age three years, seven months, showing isometric perspective, in which the third dimension is represented by parallel oblique lines.

From Golomb (1992a) and reprinted by permission of Claire Golomb.

4.25. Near Accident, *by Eitan at age six years, six months, showing the systematic use of isometric perspective.*

From Golomb (1992a) and reprinted by permission of Claire Golomb.

so, they are probably using a conceptual strategy, applying rules that they have learned. Here again is an example of how gifted children are not just faster, but do things in a qualitatively different way from ordinary children. If you naturally see the shapes of things—the distorted shapes, the shapes formed by objects being partially occluded, the negative spaces between objects—then you do not draw formulas for the way you think things look (for example, a circle for a head), and you do not need to use the various strategies (meant to help you see) found in books on how to draw. For instance, in the popular book *Drawing on the Right Side of the Brain*, Betty Edwards suggests copying pictures upside down so that one's knowledge of what one is drawing does not interfere with seeing. Visually gifted children do not need to rely on such strategies, just as verbally gifted children do not need to rely on priming to jog their verbal memories.

The perspective systems used by visually gifted children are at first primitive ones, and they are applied locally to separate objects on the page, rather than in a unified fashion to the entire scene. Nonetheless, the invention of perspectival drawing systems by very young children is astounding to see.[7]

Drawing Objects in Challenging Orientations

Gifted drawers vary the orientation of figures, in contrast to the front or side view shown by ordinary children. One study found that ordinary children ages eleven through fourteen drew human figures in three-quarters view only 15 percent of the time. In contrast, precocious drawers as young as six used this orientation in half of their figure drawings (as in Peter's drawing shown in figure 4.16). These three-quarter views appeared abruptly between six and seven years. Note that a three-quarters view is a distortion, just as are foreshortening, size diminution, and occlusion. These children are will-

ing to distort the size and shape of objects in order to show them as they appear to the eye.[8]

Composition

How children compose their drawings has not been studied much, but we do know that there is a difference between ordinary and gifted children in this arena as well. At first, children typically compose pictures randomly. Within a few years they are composing pictures fairly symmetrically, aligning objects along a ground line. Gifted drawers are more likely to use what Rudolf Arnheim calls "dynamic balance." Here, a large form on the right might be balanced by a small form on the left, which acquires extra weight by being intensely colored. Thus, the drawing is not symmetrical, yet it is still balanced. This is a far more sophisticated and subtle strategy than strict mirror symmetry.[9]

Realism

All the characteristics just described make precocious drawings look exceptionally realistic. The ability to draw realistically at an early age also marks the childhoods of those who have gone on to become recognized artists.[10]

Picasso claimed that he bypassed the typical stage of early fanciful, nonrealistic drawing. "I have never done children's drawings. Never." When he went to see a show of children's drawings, he said, "As a child, I would never have been able to participate in a show of this kind: at age twelve I drew like Raphael." Picasso recalled one of his early drawings (figure 4.26) in this way: "I was perhaps six. . . . In my father's house there was a statue of Hercules with his club in the corridor, and I drew Hercules. But it wasn't a child's drawing. It was a real drawing, representing Hercules with his club." In fact, this drawing was done at nine, so we do not really know whether Picasso ever produced childlike drawings. One of Picasso's biographers, John Richardson, points out how important it

was for Picasso to see himself as a child prodigy.[11]

Although almost all Western children identified as gifted in drawing have drawn realistically, there have been some exceptions. Golomb studied two visually gifted children whose drawings were distinguished by their advanced sense of composition and color. Their works were filled with decorative properties; colors were used in a highly expressive manner; and colors and shapes were endlessly and inventively varied. Thus, although an ability to draw realistically may be the most typical and striking characteristic of Western children who draw precociously, exceptional nonrepresentational skill with design, form, and color also occurs in children who draw precociously.[12]

4.26. Hercules, *a realistic drawing by Picasso at age nine. Museu Picasso, Barcelona, Spain.*

Copyright by Artists' Rights Society, New York, N.Y.

Realism as an early indicator of precocity in drawing may well be culturally determined. In the West, at least from the Renaissance until the twentieth century, artists have striven to capture the illusion of space, volume, and depth. While precocious drawers probably begin to draw realistically long before they have looked closely at examples of Western realistic art, they have certainly been exposed to illusionist images on billboards, magazines, picture books, TV,

and so on. What of children not exposed to such examples?[13]

We have one well-known case, Wang Yani, a Chinese child who, because she grew up in China, probably saw fewer examples of Western, illusionist images than do Western children. In addition, she was exposed to the impressionistic style of Chinese painting. Yani was spared traditional Chinese drawing instruction, which involves the copying of schemas, because her artist father felt such instruction killed the artistic imagination. However, Yani spent many hours a day in her father's art studio painting alongside her father. Although her father insists that he did not teach her, we really do not know whether Yani received any kind of instruction from her father. But we do know that she painted all the time (she made four thousand paintings in three years), and she painted far in advance of her years.[14]

Yani's paintings look very different from those by Western gifted children. She painted in the allusionistic, impressionistic style of traditional Chinese brush painting (figures 4.27, 4.28, and 4.29). What I think she shares with Western children who draw precociously is the ability to master the pictorial conventions of her culture. In the West, this means mastering the conventions of perspective and realism. In China, this means mastering the convention of capturing the spirit of objects, not their exact likeness. Thus, like Peter and Eitan, Yani was able to make pictures that looked remarkably like the adult art of her culture. Visually gifted children also often draw in cartoon style, another indication that at the heart of their talent is the ability to master a cultural convention, since cartoons are not realistic but are highly conventionalized. While some visually artistic children draw in cartoon style because doing so is easier than drawing realistically, others can do both equally well.[15]

The near-adult-level skill displayed in Yani's paintings contrasts surprisingly with her childlike calligraphy. In Western children, too, there is no relation between skill in drawing and in handwriting. Recall how Peter refused to master handwriting in the canonical style, preferring instead to turn his letters into fanciful drawings.[16]

Visual Narratives

Particularly in middle childhood and adolescence, artistically gifted children create ate imaginary settings and fantasy characters in their drawings, and their drawings depict episodes in the lives of these invented characters. This is the age when gifted children begin to create superheroes and science fiction characters modeled after the images they see in comic books. One child studied by psychologists Brent and Marjorie Wilson said, "Most people . . . just look at them and say 'that's a pretty picture' without understanding what the people are really like and the story behind them." The Wilsons found that some gifted children were more interested in inventing imaginary worlds in their drawings than in experimenting with form and design. But in the process, they produced countless drawings, and thus gained fluency and technical skill. Recall Peter, who, at around six,

4.27. Kitty, *painting by Yani at age three.*

Reprinted by permission of Wang Shiqiang.

4.28. Pull Harder, *painting by Yani at age five.*

Reprinted by permission of Wang Shiqiang.

4.29. A Happy
Troop, *painting by
Yani at age six.*

Reprinted by permission of
Wang Shiqiang.

discovered that he could create animated narratives out of drawings. His mother told me that he related long and involved stories, using his drawings as illustrations: the drawings functioned as shorthand for points in a complex plot.[17]

A JIMI HENDRIX REINCARNATION?

Many parallels can be drawn between artistically and musically gifted children. The case of a child named Jacob, once called a Jimi Hendrix reincarnation, is not unlike the story of Peter B.

The electric guitar is not a typical instrument for a musically gifted child to play. Most are given classical lessons, generally on the piano or violin. But Jacob's choice of instruments was his own. From the age of three, he had wanted to play his mother's acoustic guitar. When Jacob, at age six and a half, happened to hear a heavy metal rock band, it was a "crystallizing" experience. From that point on, he wanted to play heavy metal music more than anything else. He proceeded to plead for an electric guitar for a year and a half. When he was eight, his parents relented.[18]

The teacher Jacob's parents found set up a standard half-hour lesson. But from the first, Jacob would not leave at the end of his appointed time. Although the lesson time was officially switched to sixty minutes, it often expanded to ninety minutes. Still, his teacher often had to push Jacob out the door at the end of his session.

"Jacob played intense, avant-garde pseudo-music that was genuinely interesting," his teacher said. When the teacher began to show Jacob how to play "for real," Jacob "took off like a rocket." By the second lesson, the teacher realized that Jacob was not just gifted—he was a likely prodigy. He had never encountered a student like this in his eighteen years of teaching.[19]

Like Peter's Rage to Draw

In his single-mindedness, Jacob was similar to Peter, who would not stop drawing. Jacob wore his guitar around his neck while at home and played constantly as he walked around the house. On weekends or school holidays, he would typically play his guitar three or four hours a day. Like Peter, who cajoled his friends to draw with him, Jacob kept this up even when a friend had been invited over, oblivious to the friend's boredom. For recreation, Jacob read guitar magazines and interviews with rock stars. Most of all, he liked to go to music stores and try out all the guitars.

Jacob had to convince his parents to let him play the guitar. In most cases, the situation works the other way around—parents have to convince their children to play an instrument. Parents also often have to convince their children to practice, even when their children are musically gifted. Most of the world-class pianists studied by Benjamin Bloom did not at first go to the piano to practice voluntarily. But when children are doing rock improvisation, like Jacob, or starting a band, parents do not need to tell their young musicians to get to work. Jacob's parents never used the word *practice*. They never had to ask him to play. Instead, they had to ask him to stop, just as Michael's parents tried (unsuccessfully) to slow their son down so they would not run out of teaching materials, and just as Peter's mother had to plead with him to stop drawing and get ready for school. In their ability to focus on activities in their domain of gift, and in their single-minded rage to master, gifted children look a lot alike, no matter what their domain of gift.

An Astounding Musical Memory

Jacob played entirely by ear, in the tradition of rock improvisation. His teacher tried to teach him to read musical notation, but Jacob resisted and found it difficult. When he wanted to learn a new piece, he simply listened to a backup or lead guitar part from a recording and played it back from memory. His memory for long guitar solos was as extraordinary as Peter's memory for visual information. After concentrated listening, Jacob could master and play back any piece by Eric Clapton or Jimi Hendrix.

Jacob began to invent music as soon as he began to play. Since he did not read music, he could not notate formally what he composed. He simply remembered it. One day he was taken by his teacher to a studio to record a composition he had been preparing for a school talent show. Jacob remembered every note of a piece that he had composed in his head, a long, five-part, complex piece with difficult fingering. He spent three hours in the studio, recording multiple sound tracks. At the end of the session, his teacher was exhausted. But when Jacob listened to what he had recorded, he was not happy. At one point he could hear two beats that should not have been there. And so he insisted on returning again with his teacher to record it all over again. This kind of perseverance and perfectionism is typical of children gifted in any domain.

Improvising

When his teacher first showed Jacob how to play the blues scale in E, Jacob immediately started to improvise on this scale. In fact, he improvised and varied everything he was taught. His mother bought him a background tape so he could improvise along with it, "on-line." Because he could hear the musical structure, his improvisation fit perfectly with the background.

After fewer than six months of lessons, Jacob came upon a rock band performing on the sidewalk. Jacob asked to join in. The lead guitarist amusedly handed Jacob his guitar, expecting a childlike performance. All were astounded to hear a seven-year-old improvising with the competence of an adult player. "He must be the reincarnation of Hendrix," murmured people in the crowd.

Creating Challenges

Like Peter, Jacob created challenges for himself and thrived on doing this. He happily worked on the scales and exercises his teacher gave him, challenging himself to improve his speed and accuracy. He worked hard on what was difficult, playing something over and over until he got it right. He was able to hear in his mind's ear how a piece should sound, and he worked at a piece until it sounded like he knew it should.

Jacob was very aware of his playing. When I asked him to show me all the things that he could do that were out of the ordinary, he showed me, along with a running commentary, how he could do slides, octave changes, and harmonics.

Like Peter, who refused to write in a way he found boring, Jacob wanted to do things his own way. He had regular struggles with his guitar teacher over control of the lesson agenda. This independence and stubbornness extended to school, where he was continually engaged in a battle of wills with his teachers. He wanted to do things his way, and he challenged everything his teacher requested of him if it did not make sense to him. Yet, he had no difficulty whatsoever with academic skills. He was an excellent student when he wanted to be.

A CHILD WHO READS ORCHESTRAL SCORES

Stephen, the child described in chapter 1 who read orchestral scores, shows us a different side of musical giftedness. Stephen was much more interested in music theory and in composition than in performance. His preferred activity was to listen to classical music or attend a classical concert and read the orchestral score to himself as he listened to the music. He said that he heard the music in his head as he read.

At five, he began to take very simple piano lessons at his after-school program with someone who was not a professional music teacher. He immediately figured out how to read musical notation. Within a few months of lessons, his teacher contacted Stephen's parents and told them that their son had exceptional musical aptitude, that he just "soaked it up," and that his parents should find him a "real" music teacher.

So Stephen began weekly hour-long lessons at age five with a professional teacher. But he refused to practice systematically. Instead, what he loved to do was sight-read piano or orchestral scores (he could play the part of any instrument). He also loved to improvise and harmonize (beginning at age six) and to compose (beginning at age seven). Often what he composed was more advanced than what he could play.[20]

A Music Notator and Theorist

At nine, Stephen read advanced adult music theory books and began to take theory lessons at the Longy School of Music in Cambridge, Massachusetts. One of the things he did in these lessons was to take musical dictation—that is, to write down in musical notation whatever his teacher played for him. He was unfailingly accurate. The fact that he had perfect pitch helped in this task, but he also could do this flawlessly when the task was simply to notate rhythm. At nine, he was awarded the music theory prize at the Longy School, a prize that had always before gone to an adult student.

His piano teacher thought she understood why Stephen was not more advanced in performance ability. When he had the desire to play something, he could play well beyond his years, she told me. But he got little physical pleasure from the act of playing. If he goes on in music, Stephen is more likely to become a composer or a conductor than a performer. Jacob would probably be more likely to become a performer who improvises as he plays.

A Fascination with All Kinds of Notations

Stephen had a number of other advanced abilities, all of which involved manipulating abstract notations. He began to read without instruction at age three, while studying lists of songs on cassette tapes. He also began to write at three and by four was able to read cursive. He drew complex maps, charts, and diagrams, but he had no interest in drawing observationally or in color. He mastered highly technical computer-programming books at age eight, and he began to write programs in a variety of computer languages. He was fascinated with foreign languages and different alphabets. One of his amusements for years was to invent new alphabets. When he played chess, he seemed more interested in recording his moves in chess notation than in actually moving the pieces, much as he seemed to prefer playing with music notation to playing music.

Stephen did not interact socially with others unless they were interested in talking about music or computer programming or in listening to a piece of music together while following along with a score. Needless to say, this choice of activities limited his partners to a select few adults, typically his parents. Here again he resembles Jacob, who bored his friends by making them listen to him play his guitar, or Peter, who made his friends pose for a drawing.

GENERALIZATIONS ABOUT MUSICALLY GIFTED CHILDREN

Jacob and Stephen show us how many ways one can be gifted in music. This is because there are so many roles in music: one can perform (as does Jacob), compose and read music (as does Stephen), or conduct (as Stephen might). Musically gifted children most typically emerge in performance. There are far more Jacobs than Stephens.

It is more common to find a musically gifted child engaged in classical music training, playing from the score and not by ear, than it is to find a child like Jacob playing rock by ear. But this is no doubt a cultural and a class phenomenon. Rock bands and heavy metal electric guitars are seen by middle-class parents as countercultural and not as serious or as good for the mind as classical piano or violin. We know little about children like Jacob who are gifted in nonclassical forms of music. We also know little about the emergence of musical giftedness in cultures with non-Western music.

The core ability of the musically gifted child involves a sensitivity to the structure of music—tonality, key, harmony, and rhythm. This sensitivity allows the child to remember music and to play it back with ease, either by voice or instrument. This sensitivity to structure also allows the child to transpose a theme to a new key, to improvise on a given theme, and to invent melodies, all of which musically gifted children do easily. Musically gifted children show great sensitivity to musical structure, and this astounds us because it is rare. In contrast, all children show great sensitivity to linguistic structure, and this we take for granted because it is universal.

Musical giftedness reveals itself very early. In fact, giftedness in music may appear earlier than giftedness in any other domain of skill. Many great performers and composers have demonstrated musical giftedness as young as one or two, and almost always before six. Mozart started picking out tunes on the piano at three, and he was composing by six. The pianist Lorin Hollander said that after hearing a rehearsal of a Haydn quartet at age three and a half, and then being shown the score, he "fell into music; that's the only way to describe it. Within four minutes I knew the notes, the clefs, everything." The violinist Yehudi Menuhin performed with symphony orchestras at the age of seven. A survey of forty-seven musicians revealed that their ability had been detected on average at four years, nine months. Most of the world's great violinists were prodigies as children. It may be because music is such a highly rule-governed, formally structured domain that musical giftedness manifests itself so early in life.[21]

Earliest Signs

Sheer auditory discrimination ability is not the skill that reveals musical giftedness. Rather, the earliest clue that a child is gifted in music is a strong interest and delight in musical sounds.[22]

Another early sign of musical giftedness is the ability to sing back accurately songs one has heard. This ability is made possible by exceptional musical memory, which is seen by many as the ability most central to musical talent. Both Jacob and Stephen excelled in musical memory. Jacob could play back anything after one or two hearings. And Stephen at age two learned many Hungarian folk songs and could sing them back perfectly.[23]

While children typically begin to sing at about eighteen months, musically gifted children begin to sing at a younger age, and often before they can speak. Erwin Nyiregyhazi, a seven-year-old Hungarian musical prodigy, had not spoken until three; but before the age of one, he had begun to sing back songs he had heard. Handel also sang before he could speak.[24]

Normally, children do not even attempt to imitate heard songs until about two or two-and-a-half years of age. They can sing portions of these songs accurately at around three, and they can sing whole songs by three or four. However, the intervals in their songs are only approximate, and children are not yet able to maintain the same tonality through a single song. It is not until about five that children typically can reproduce with accuracy the familiar tunes of their culture. Musically gifted children present a striking contrast: these children sing with great accuracy, demonstrating the ability to match pitches with precision by their second year.[25]

Musically gifted children can imitate a song after only one exposure, and they learn familiar themes from TV rapidly and effortlessly. A prodigy named Pepito Areola could play twenty pieces from memory by the age of three and a half. At three, the pianist Arthur Rubinstein listened to his older sister playing the piano and surprised his family by faultlessly playing the pieces she had been practicing. At the beginning of his fourth year, Erwin Nyiregyhazi could accurately reproduce on the piano any tune that he overheard. By seven, he could play complex Beethoven sonatas from memory. And Mozart, at fourteen, was able to write down Allegri's *Miserere*, a complex piece of music with nine parts, after listening to it only a few times. Music psychologist Jeanne Bamberger observed young adolescent performers amusing themselves while waiting for their lessons at the Longy School of Music by playing pieces in the styles of well-known performers.[26]

At seven, Nyiregyhazi had a musical memory equal, and in some ways superior, to that of an adult musician to whom he was compared. He performed as well as the musician when asked to listen to pieces of music, commit them to memory, and play them back. And only Nyiregyhazi, but not the adult musician, could flawlessly reproduce music heard twenty-four hours earlier.[27]

Nyiregyhazi's memory was "structure-dependent." That is, he was better able to recall familiar structure, harmony, and rhythm than random harmonies, and he had better recall for the music in the diatonic scale than for dissonant music built on the twelve-tone chromatic scale. The fact that his musical memory was somewhat dependent on familiar structure showed that it was not eidetic, mindless, or literal but was based on musical understanding.

Superior recall for familiar form indicates some representation of familiar form, at least at an unconscious level. Jacob's ability to improvise at will would not have been possible if he had not internalized the structure of Western rock music. But the extraordinary ability of musically gifted children to play back what they hear is nonreflective and tacit. Such children often say that they cannot imitate a piece if they think about it.[28]

Perfect Pitch

Perfect pitch is a very rare ability, estimated to be found in about 1 in 10,000 people in the general population. However, perfect pitch is far more common among musicians and typically makes its appearance before age five. Stephen had perfect pitch, as did Nyiregyhazi, who, at three, could locate on the piano any note sung to him. Nyiregyhazi also had other, related acoustic skills: he could recognize intervals and the notes in a chord and analyze chords in a manner that has hardly ever been equaled. At three and a half, Lorin Hollander identified a car horn as an F-sharp and a glass clinking as a B-flat. And by age four, Mozart could tell when violins were a quarter out of tune.[29]

However, perfect pitch is not consistently associated with musical giftedness. Wagner did not have perfect pitch, and neither did Tschaikovsky, and many lesser composers did have it. Perfect pitch is thus not a necessary component of musical talent.[30]

Some have suggested that perfect pitch is a function of training. One study showed that the possession of perfect pitch was related to the age at which musical instruction was initiated. Of those who had begun instruction before age four, 95 percent had perfect pitch; of those who had begun instruction at age twelve, 55 percent had perfect pitch. However, this evidence does not prove that perfect pitch is a function of training. Perhaps children who begin instruction at a very early age already have perfect pitch and are more gifted than those who begin later.[31]

One serious adolescent pianist told me that while perfect pitch allows her to notate or play back any music that she hears, it has made it difficult for her to transpose. She told me of her difficulty in choir when the director wanted her to sing a piece one quarter pitch higher than the written notation. She had to struggle not to sing exactly what was notated. She wished that instead of perfect pitch she had been blessed with relative pitch, the ability to recognize a G, for example, only after one has heard another note that has been appropriately labeled. Relative pitch does not tie the individual to the literal notations.[32]

Sight-Reading

As with the skill of perfect pitch, the ability to sight-read is also not consistently associated with giftedness in music. Mozart, like Stephen, possessed this skill. At the age of eight, Mozart could play without hesitation a piece he had never seen before, like an adult reading text. Nyiregyhazi also possessed this ability, noted by the age of seven. The pianist Glenn Gould said that he could read notes before words. But Jacob, like many rock performers, did not know how to sight-read.[33]

Musical Generativity

A clear distinction exists between performing existing music and creating new music. A further distinction exists between composing new music and two more constrained forms of creation: transposing a given piece to a new key while retaining the melody, and improvising, in which one starts from and builds on a musical theme.

As mentioned before, all children begin to produce their own spontaneous songs at around eighteen months. During this time, they are experimenting with intervals. Their spontaneous songs grow in length and internal organization between the ages of two and three. However, by five, spontaneous singing declines in frequency, as the child becomes concerned with making mistakes and shows an interest in accurately imitating heard songs. Thus, the ordinary child, at least in Western culture, stops generating music by the end of the preschool years. This decline in playful experimentation with song has its parallel in the decline of flavorful, preconventional drawings of the preschooler and a growing concern for literalness in drawing.[34]

Musically gifted children like Jacob and Stephen tell a different story. Most musically gifted children learn to play an instrument, and soon after they begin, they show "musical generativity." This generativity first takes the form of the ability to transpose tunes to new keys and to improvise on themes. Jacob and Stephen both had this ability. Nyiregyhazi could transpose pieces to new keys at age seven. By ten, he could accurately and easily transpose complex pieces at first sight into any key.

Jacob and Stephen both improvised as soon as they started to play. Nyiregyhazi could improvise at the beginning of his fourth year, and until seven, he improvised more than he composed. He was able to improvise on his own themes as well as on those of others. When he had just turned six, for example, he was given a pastoral theme and asked to improvise a funeral march on it, which he did with great skill. He was then asked to improvise a children's song on the same theme, which he again did effortlessly. These improvisations showed remarkable spontaneity and musical imagination. Areola could, given a few bars, continue a melody in the same style. And Mozart improvised at four. A musically gifted adult recalled being an improviser in childhood and described himself as "one of those kids who would play the piano, play it wrong and keep playing it wrong, fooling around with the themes." He continued, "At a young age, I would pick things off the radio by ear, and then change them and rearrange them."[35]

A gift for composing entire pieces from scratch (and notating them), as distinct from improvising on a given theme, is rarely seen before late childhood. J. S. Bach, Handel, Beethoven, and Brahms are examples of great musicians who were performing virtuosi in early childhood, but who did not begin to compose until at least early adolescence, if not early adulthood.[36]

Nyiregyhazi was, like Stephen, one of the rare cases of children who began to compose music at an early age. Haydn, Mozart, Chopin, Mahler, Meyerbeer, Saint-Saëns, and Strauss also produced their first compositions before the age of ten. Mozart started composing at four, and by the age of eight, he had already written six sonatas for piano and violin, and three symphonies for small orchestras.[37]

Representing Music Mentally: Further Divergence

Bamberger, who has studied musical ability in both ordinary and gifted children, has found that musically gifted children have a capacity to represent musical relations in multiple ways. These children move freely among four ways of attending to a piece of music, shifting their focus of attention among the instrument and the actions performed on it, the score, the sound, and the music's structure.[38]

When one focuses on the instrument, the music is represented as a felt path, a sequence of actions performed on the instrument. For instance, one might think of a pitch on a violin as the third finger on the E string. The musical score is a very different kind of representation, and students must connect the kinesthetic representation to the notational one. The imagined sound toward which the performer is striving is yet another representation. When thinking of the music in terms of sound, one listens to one's own playing to keep it in tune, or one matches one's sound to remembered models of others' playing. And finally, there is the level of musical structure, in which one attends to the organization of a piece and the relations among its parts.

Bamberger noted that teachers shift continually among comments that highlight music as a felt path, as a set of notations, as sound, and as structure. The gifted children she observed shifted their attention readily with the teacher.

Bamberger has argued that such easy shifting from one mode of representation to another is a significant aspect of musical giftedness.

She devised a task to reveal how gifted children entertain multiple representations of music. The task involved using a set of bells, all of which looked alike, but each of which had a different pitch when struck with a mallet. The set of bells included all the pitches of the C major scale, plus three matched pairs: two Cs, two Gs, and two Es. The bells were laid out in arbitrary order, and children were instructed to try three things. First, they were to construct the tune of "Twinkle Twinkle Little Star" using the bells. Next, they were to notate this tune in any way they wanted. And finally, they were shown a notation of the song different from their own and asked to arrange the bells to make the same tune.

She gave these tasks to four different groups: gifted children, musically untrained children, musically untrained adults, and musically trained adults who had not, however, been particularly gifted in music as children. Thus, musically gifted children could be compared to nongifted children, and to nongifted adults with and without training.

The construction task was meant to disturb the familiar structure of the instrument field, because the bells were arbitrarily arranged. Thus, the felt path of pitch relations (low to high) was violated. In addition, some pitches in "Twinkle" are identical but have a different function. For instance, when performed in the key of C, the note G occurs on *twinkle* and again on *star,* but the second time it occurs at the end of a phrase and thus has a different structural function from the first G. Some people hear these Gs as the same, and some hear them as different. If one responds to the context, the two notes sound different; but if one can focus on the single dimension of pitch, the two notes sound the same.

The musically gifted children shifted strategy during the construction task, and with each shift, they attended to different dimensions of the music. In contrast, the other subjects maintained a single, consistent strategy during the entire task, including the trained adults who were students at a prestigious American university and had had at least five years of music instruction.

The children and adults with no musical training always added new bells to the bell path in their order of occurrence in the tune, never moving backward to hit the same note a second time. The result was a row of bells, one for each pitch. Thus, they needed to use two different bells for the two Gs. Each was heard as a different event. These nongifted and non-trained subjects were using what Bamberger calls a "figural" strategy, because they were focusing on the shape, or figure, of the tune and hearing individual notes within the context of the tune's shape. Thus, these subjects heard the two Gs as dif-ferent events because of the different functions within the tune.

The nongifted but trained adults used a "formal" strategy. They built a C major scale out of the bells and played the tune on the scale, moving back and forth as needed. Unlike the untrained individuals, these people focused on the tune as it relates to the formal structure of the C major scale.

The gifted children did something different. They switched strategies as they went about the task. At first, they looked like the untrained subjects. They began with a figural strategy by searching for each pitch, lining them up from left to right. The first part of the piece ("Twinkle twinkle little star") was played on bells lined up as C-G-A. But when they got to *star*, they switched to a formal strategy: they moved backward to hit the G already used for *twinkle*. Thus, they rec-ognized the two Gs as the same. They then faced a dilemma when they got to the F for the first note of "How I wonder what you are." If they followed their initial figural strategy of lining up bells in order of occurrence, they would have to put F to the right of A. But this move would not represent the downward pitch from G to F; and such a move would not have yielded a purely figural strategy, since it would have required skipping from G over the A to F. If, on the other hand, they had followed their new formal strategy, the F would have had to go to the left of the previous G, since it is lower. But the C bell was already to the left of G, because of the initial figural strategy of placing the bells in order of occurrence.

The gifted children felt this conflict between figural and formal strategies, and they made different choices at this point. For instance, one child responded to the fact that F is lower than G, and he moved left. But the bells were not ordered from low to high, so he realized that he had to search for the F bell. He then recognized that the F had a double meaning: it was next in the tune but also was lower than G and higher than C. So, he pushed the C to the left and inserted F between C and G. The added notes beginning with *star* were placed in order of occurrence (backward) but also classified according to a low-high series (D-E-F). Thus, for the gifted children, multiple dimensions came into conflict.

When asked to notate the song so someone else could play it, none of the gifted children used standard notation, though they all knew such notation well. Instead, they invented their own ways of notating the task. When asked to make sense of another form of notation different from what they had constructed, no one in the nongifted group, whether trained or not, could make sense of notations other than their own. It was as if the internal representation and the notation were locked into one another. In contrast, all but one of the gifted children could easily grasp the alternative notation and were able to rearrange their bells so that the new notation would yield the same tune. For instance, those who had used numbers as names for scale positions were able to make sense of notations in which numbers referred to order of occurrence in the tune.

Thus, musically gifted children have multiple internal representations for the same piece of music. They can move freely from one kind to another and can easily see one *as* the other. In contrast, nongifted individuals, irrespective of age and musical training, use a single strategy and focus consistently on a limited set of musical dimensions.

Bamberger noted that musically gifted children face a crisis at adolescence when they must learn to integrate a formal mode of representation with their initial and intuitive figural mode of representation. They have to learn to rely more on fixed referent structures of scales, yet they must not lose their figural understanding, in which music representation is tied to motor patterns executed on an instrument. When the primacy of figural knowledge is questioned at adolescence, musically gifted children often experience a "midlife" crisis. Some turn away from music at this time.[39]

Gifted children—whether gifted in math, language, art, or music—learn faster and represent information in their domain in an atypical way. Children gifted in math solve problems in idiosyncratic (apparently intuitive) ways, and they may thus have difficulty when forced to shift to formally established methods. Recall David's difficulties when he was asked in school to write down in linear fashion the steps he used in solving a math problem. Children gifted in language simply see the way words should sound, and they do not have to sound them out bit by bit, using a deliberate phonetic strategy. Children who draw realistically use a figural strategy, drawing what they *see* without thinking about it much. When forced to think about the rules of unified perspective, say in a high school art class, they may have difficulty shifting to this more conscious, conceptual, and rule-governed system.[40]

Children gifted in academic and aesthetic domains should be labeled either all talented or all gifted. There is not enough of a distinction between academically and aesthetically gifted children to warrant two different labels.

If those gifted musically and artistically bear a strong resemblance to the scholastically gifted, does this mean that, like the scholastically gifted, they have high IQs? Does a high IQ lurk behind all high achievements? It is to this question that we now turn.

Five

THE IQ MYTH

We have seen that academically gifted children often have uneven profiles, with much higher abilities in verbal than mathematical areas, or the reverse. Such unevenness can bring down an overall IQ score. Thus, a strong, singular gift may go undetected if all one looks for is overall IQ.

Strong gifts in art or music would also go unnoticed if one sought them by obtaining IQ scores. While many of us assume that the artistically gifted need not have high IQs (perhaps because we think of artists as nonverbal and countercultural), we tend to assume that the musically gifted do have high IQs (perhaps because some mathematicians are musical). Yet children gifted in art or music have abilities that are unrelated to most of those measured by an IQ test. Even those most outstandingly gifted in their domain can be but average in *intelligence,* if what we mean by that term is verbal and mathematical ability, those skills assessed by an IQ test. We even find strange cases of severely retarded individuals who show astonishing abilities in art and music. These "savants," as they are called, show us that giftedness in art and music can operate even in the absence of "normal" intelligence.

ARTISTIC GIFTEDNESS AND IQ

In the many studies of high-IQ children, Terman's included, none reports an association of IQ and drawing ability. And visually artistic children do not show a tendency to be scholastically gifted. Peter was bored in school, and so was Varda, one of the children studied by Claire Golomb. The "class artist" in my son's third-grade class read slowly and laboriously at a first-grade level. A very small group of Terman's subjects were called "special ability" cases. These were children nominated by their teachers not for high IQ but for a special talent such as ability in art or music, or mechanical aptitude. Fifteen of these were nominated for artistic ability. Only one would have passed the standard IQ cutoff of 130 for a gifted program. Their IQs ranged from 79 to 133 and averaged 107. These children were not included in the final sample selected for study.[1]

The most systematic study to date of academic achievement in the artistically gifted was conducted by Mihaly Csikszentmihalyi. Teenagers gifted in art, music, math, science, and athletics were followed over four years. The artistically gifted adolescents did not do as well in school as the musically gifted teenagers, and the artistically gifted teens actually had a lower commitment to academic achievement than all of the other groups, including the athletes. These artistic teenagers performed in the sixtieth percentile of their high school class. Fewer than half elected to take the kinds of tests required for selective U.S. colleges—the PSAT and the SAT. Yet in art class they were highly committed, took the most advanced and challenging courses, and often won art scholarships after graduation. A lack of interest in academic achievement and an early focus on art as a primary career path are typical of adolescents gifted in art. This singleness of purpose was also demonstrated when Csikszentmihalyi found that art students rated aesthetic values above all others, rating them, in fact, more highly even than theology students rated religion.[2]

Children gifted in drawing have a higher incidence of reading problems such as dyslexia in comparison to the normal population. Peter had difficulty learning to read. Joel, a gifted drawer studied by the psychologist Constance Milbrath, was dyslexic and did not read until age ten. Even in college he said that he could understand concepts only if he could image them. The reading difficulty so often associated with artistic giftedness (explored in the next chapter) is probably one of the factors that prevents artistically gifted children from excelling in or loving school.[3]

A disjunction between artistic and IQ giftedness is actually not surprising. Drawing giftedness relies on visual-spatial skills, while IQ tests primarily measure verbal and numerical ability and abstract reasoning. Where gifted drawers excel is not in reading, reasoning, or math, but in the ability to see, remember, visualize, and transform images. While mathematics involves spatial skill, it may well call on a more abstract kind than the ability to draw.[4]

Visually artistic children excel in their ability to recognize geometric shapes camouflaged in complex designs. As a child, the surrealist painter Max Ernst saw human forms in the patterning of his bed's mahogany footboard. And Paul Klee, as a child, saw human forms in polished marble tabletops. Recall that Peter said that he saw figures in the undefined shapes of visual patterns.[5]

This ability of the artistically gifted to see hidden shapes is a skill that is independent of verbal IQ (though it may well be tapped by the Embedded Figures subtest of the IQ). We know that imagery ability is unrelated to verbal IQ from a study in which children gifted in drawing were compared on imagery tasks to children with only average drawing ability but who were matched to the gifted group in verbal IQ. If IQ were related to imagery, children in both groups would show the same imagery skills. But the group gifted in drawing far outperformed their verbal IQ-matched control group. Similarly, children gifted in drawing excel in visual imagination, as measured by the ability to recognize incomplete pictures (for example, readily seeing a portion of a sailboat as a sailboat where others just see it as meaningless lines). Visually artistic children may excel in such a task because they can readily store and access an internal visual lexicon of images. Again, using the comparative method just described, this ability was shown to be independent of verbal IQ.[6]

Like mathematically gifted children, visually artistic children also excel in their visual memory. Michelangelo was reputed to have had an astonishing visual memory for paintings, even those only seen once. Wang Yani (see chapter 4) was able to learn a Chinese character after seeing her father "write it" in the air just one time. And Picasso was excellent at remembering visual details as a child.[7]

Experimental evidence has also demonstrated that artistically gifted children excel in both long- and short-term visual memory. In one study researchers found that children gifted in drawing excel in recalling aspects of pictures such as color, composition, form, line quality, and content. And other researchers showed that this kind of ability is not correlated with verbal IQ. Like the mathematical children discussed earlier, children gifted in drawing were given the memory test for nonverbalizable Persian letters. Despite the fact that the gifted drawers had significantly lower verbal IQs than the gifted math students, the drawers remembered the letters better. And like the math gifted, the art gifted performed significantly better than a control group matched in verbal IQ but without any artistic inclination. This suggests that there is no relationship between verbal IQ and the ability to store nonverbalizable shapes in short-term memory or to access such shapes from memory. Yet these are exactly the kinds of skills that seem to underlie drawing giftedness, and they may well form a component of math giftedness as well.[8]

MUSICAL GIFTEDNESS AND IQ

On first glance, it would appear that musical giftedness bears more relationship to IQ than does artistic giftedness. There are many reports of musical children with a high IQ. Erwin Nyiregyhazi was extremely advanced academically. Mendelssohn was translating Caesar and Ovid at age ten. And the eleven children in Terman's special ability group who had been nominated for musical ability had IQs ranging from 95 to 139, but averaging 121. While this is not particularly high, four were above 130, and the average was fourteen points higher than for the art special ability cases. But closer scrutiny shows that musical ability does not depend on IQ. Attempts to correlate musical aptitude with IQ have yielded positive but low correlations. Once an IQ of about 90 is attained, intelligence is not very predictive of musical ability. Nor does high musical ability necessarily predict high intelligence.[9]

Csikszentmihalyi's study of talented teenagers provides us with some interesting comparative information. The musical teenagers performed very well in school. Their PSAT scores placed them in the eighty-seventh percentile nationally for the verbal portion of the test and in the eighty-third percentile for the math portion. On the American College Test (ACT), they placed in the ninetieth percentile of high school juniors nationally. A third of them even had strong enough abilities in math or science to be nominated for study in these domains as well as music. They contrasted sharply with the visual artists.[10]

Another piece of evidence showing that musical students have academic strengths is found in the IQ scores of students at the Yehudi Menuhin School of Music. These highly musical students' IQs ranged from 93 to 166 and averaged about 130, the usual cutoff for a school gifted program. However, evidence that a high IQ is not a *necessary* component of musical giftedness comes from the fact that the student with the lowest IQ, who was deficient in both reading and math, won an award for musicianship.[11]

We do not know whether the academic performance and IQs of musically gifted children improve once music lessons are undertaken, or whether these children start out with academic strengths. If academic strengths were gained as music lessons were undertaken, we might conclude that the dedication learned from music lessons transfers to schoolwork. But if these children were to show high levels of academic performance irrespective of time spent in music lessons, we would have to conclude that musical and academic abilities often co-occur.

We also do not know much about the academic performance of children like Jacob (the electric guitar player described in chapter 4), who are not trained in classical music, and who are not taught to read music. Jacob was an excellent student, but we do not know how typical he was of children engaged in his kind of improvisational music. Nor do we know anything about the academic skills of children who form rock bands or rap groups or engage in other rebellious, antiauthority musical activities.

Why is it that musical children do better in school than children gifted in art? I can only speculate here, since no systematic study of this question has been carried out. One reason may be that this finding is based entirely on children taking classical lessons. Such children are likely to have educated parents who provide a stimulating, intellectual atmosphere at home. Perhaps also, visually artistic children fare less well in school because, as discussed in the next chapter, they often have reading-related difficulties, suggestive of some kind of deficit in the left hemisphere of the brain, the seat of language.

Yet another possibility for the superior school performance of the musical over the artistic child is that the musically gifted child (taking classical lessons) is engaged in regular reading of musical texts, a linear activity that requires the student to sit still. This is precisely what schools require, and thus we might predict that any child, gifted or not, who reads musical texts regularly would do well in school. Then too, musically gifted children might do well simply as a result of the sheer hard work and perseverance required by formal music lessons. Artistic children rarely take formal lessons, and they draw when they feel like it. Musical children typically begin lessons early and practice on a rigorous daily schedule imposed by their parents.

But hard work and perseverance are probably insufficient for superior schoolwork, as the example of athletes shows us. Athletes certainly have to work hard on a regular, often grueling basis. But in Csikszentmihalyi's study, adolescents gifted in athletics were less scholastic than those in music (though not as weak as those in the visual arts). Their mean PSAT scores placed them in the seventy-ninth percentile nationally on the verbal portion of the test and in the eighty-second percentile on the math portion. Although they exceeded the national average in academic achievement, their group included a very wide range of students, from some of the strongest to some of the poorest students in the school. Thus, regular and disciplined drill probably is not sufficient to account for musical children's good school performance. More likely, a set of factors are at play: highly educated parents, the regular habit of reading musical notation, and disciplined practice.[12]

Where the musically gifted excel is not in IQ but in visual-spatial-perceptual skills, much like children gifted in drawing. Musicians (as well as painters and writers) have been noted to have prodigious visual and auditory memories. This has been shown experimentally, in tasks such as finding hidden patterns or combining apparently disconnected visual stimuli into a single image. Sometimes musicians even excel over visual artists. For instance, on a spatial reasoning task, musicians (both composers and instrumentalists) surpassed both painters and a control group gifted in neither music nor the visual arts. Asked to recognize patterns hidden in larger patterns, musicians surpassed painters, who in turn surpassed the control group.

Music training might even help spatial skills develop. A recent study showed that spatial reasoning in preschoolers was enhanced by eight months of music lessons. Similarly, listening to Mozart was shown to increase children's spatial reasoning ability when tested a few minutes later.[13]

GIFTEDNESS AND RETARDATION

The strongest evidence that there is no necessary link between overall IQ and ability in either art or music comes from savants. At Gateway Crafts, an unusual art studio in Brookline, Massachusetts, I watched a group of odd adults working with intense concentration. They were hunched over, drawing, painting, or working with clay. Loud, incomprehensible grunts filled the eerie silence. No one made eye contact with me. One young woman, whose name I later learned was Cathy, was using colored markers to draw a large landscape of buildings and trees (figure 5.1). The scene was a highly realistic depiction of Boston buildings along the Charles River. It was in full linear perspective. She drew without looking up, with no model except one remembered in her mind, and with great motor confidence. She could not erase, given her medium, and she did not start over, as she had made no "mistakes." She drew rapidly. Next to the one she was working on was a large pile of other drawings. Many were scenes of Boston, most of which she had seen at some time in pictures. Some were expressionistically painted faces (figure 5.2).

When I tried to talk to her about what she was doing, she did not look up, and she made no attempt to respond to me.

5.1. Realistic cityscape of Boston painted by Cathy Andersen, an artist with moderate retardation and autistic tendencies.

Cathy Andersen, © 1994, Gateway Crafts, Brookline, Massachusetts. Reprinted by permission of the artist.

5.2. Expressive portrait by Cathy Andersen.

Cathy Andersen, © 1994, Gateway Crafts, Brookline, Massachusetts. Reprinted by permission of the artist.

She made noncommunicative vocalizations as she drew. Cathy had autistic tendencies, as did most of the people in this exceptional studio set up for mentally handicapped artists. Figure 5.3 shows a painting by an adult with Down's syndrome. This non-realistic painting is brilliantly colored and the shapes are varied. It reminds me of work by twentieth-century expressionists such as Kandinsky.

WHO ARE THE SAVANTS?

Individuals like the ones I observed have been studied for at least a hundred years. They were originally called "idiots savants," but because of the cruel and also non-scientific nature of the term *idiot*, these individuals are now referred to as *savants,* or as possessing the "savant syndrome." Savants are usually either retarded, autistic (a severe social and communicative disorder), or both. The term *idiot* is also misleading, for savants are never found at the most severe and devastating levels of retardation. The IQ range of reported savants is almost always between about 40 and 70. Typically, savant skills do not run in families.

Ordinary savants (as opposed to prodigious ones) usually possess just one kind of

5.3. Painting by Sahar Pick, a young Israeli adult with Down's syndrome.

From the collection of Reuven Feuerstein. Reprinted by permission of Sahar Pick.

ability at a normal level, but are retarded in all other abilities. In contrast, prodigious savants have an island of skill at the prodigy level. Fewer than 100 cases of true prodigious savants have ever been reported. The incidence is thus certainly far rarer than that of normally gifted children (though we have no precise numbers for the incidence of normal giftedness outside of that assessed by IQ tests).[14]

The savant syndrome occurs six times more often in males than in females. About two-thirds of all savants are retarded, while the remaining third are also autistic, though even savants classified as retarded almost always show some autistic characteristics. We do not know whether within a particular domain of gift there are differences between autistic and retarded savants.[15]

Some of the characteristics of autistic individuals were depicted accurately in the Academy Award–winning movie *Rain Man*. Dustin Hoffman played an autistic man with flattened and sometimes inappropriate affect; he was aloof and socially odd, and he was impaired in language and communication. He had an obsessive desire for sameness: he always wanted to eat the same number of fish sticks and the same flavor of Jell-O, and his bed always had to be near a window. He engaged in obsessional, ritualistic, repetitive behavior: whenever he was anxious, he repeated lines from a movie he had seen as a child.

People with autism differ sharply from those who are retarded because autism is not accompanied by deficiencies in all areas. People with autism have excellent visual-spatial abilities, as shown by their skill in recognizing hidden figures in pictures and by their high scores on two parts of the IQ test— block design and object assembly. They also often excel at assembling jigsaw puzzles, which they can solve just by fitting local shapes together, without using the overall picture as a guide. Some autistic individuals have low IQs, while others are high functioning and have high IQs and good language skills, despite profound social problems. Like savants, autistic children tend to be male, with a ratio of four to one.[16]

Savants most often exhibit their extraordinary abilities in one of four domains: the visual arts (usually realistic drawing), music (reported cases so far have almost always been pianists), rapid "lightning" mental calculation, and calendrical calculation. There have been a few cases reported of other kinds of savants, ones with mechanical ability, sensory discrimination skill, and foreign-language–learning proficiency.[17]

Savants have often been dismissed as slavish imitators incapable of any innovation, expression, or understanding of rules. But savants could not do what they do without relying on rules, even if unconsciously. Indeed, the four domains in which savants are usually found are highly formal and rule-governed, and savants may need such domains. (While the visual arts are far less formally structured than is calculation or classical piano performance, realistic drawing is the primary style in which savants work, and realism is certainly more rule-governed than styles such as expressionism, impressionism, cubism, or abstraction.) As discussed later, savants do not merely imitate mindlessly but show an understanding of the rules of their domain. And they can be innovative and expressive.

Despite the differences that do certainly exist between savants and prodigies in art and music, savant gifts in these domains are close enough to those of prodigies to provide strong evidence against the IQ myth even for music. And savants in calculation show us that this splinter skill of mathematical ability can be performed in the absence of other forms of more conceptual intelligence.

SAVANT ARTISTS

The woman I observed at Gateway had artistic skills, which not only were impressive in contrast to her deficiencies but also were far in advance of what the typical adult can produce. Her work would surely have earned her entrance to an art school.

All of the realistic-drawing savants who have been discovered are autistic. The work of some savants in the visual arts is even more impressive than Cathy's and rivals work by adult masters. And autistic savant drawings are wholly unlike drawings by other atypical populations, such as children who are psychotic, deaf, or retarded. But most autistic children are not savants, and they draw at a level consistent with their mental age.

5.4. Horse by Nadia at age five and a half, resembling a sketch by a Renaissance master.

From Selfe (1977). Reproduced courtesy of the publisher, Academic Press London Limited.

Perhaps the savant with the most astonishing gift in the visual arts is Nadia. At six, Nadia had a mental age of three years and three months (and thus was a retarded, "low-functioning" autistic child) and had poor fine motor control, except in the area of drawing. But when she was given a fine pencil or a ballpoint pen, she gripped it in an adult fashion and drew pictures of horses and riders that resembled sketches by Renaissance masters in their proportion, foreshortening, motion, and surety of line, as exemplified in figure 5.4. Her lines were drawn rapidly and confidently. It looked as if she were tracing an image: instead of first sketching an overall outline and then adding the details, she could place lines at disconnected points all over the page and later make them join up perfectly in a completed figure.[18]

Nadia sometimes drew from direct observation, as seen in figure 5.5. More often, however, she drew from pictures. She looked intently at pictures in her children's books, and then sometimes weeks or even months later she would draw these pictures from memory. This delayed rendition ability was like that of autistic children who accurately sing back music long after having heard it, or repeat sentences or entire dialogues heard on TV or in real life.[19]

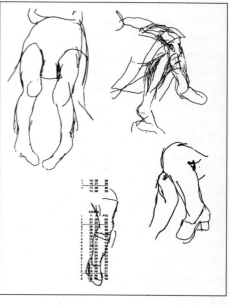

The fact that her original model was typically itself a picture meant that she did not have to translate a three-dimensional scene into two-dimensional form, but simply had to recall what was already a two-dimensional translation. But this feat should not be lightly dismissed. Any normal child, shown a perspectival drawing, copies it, omitting the perspective. Moreover, she was able to draw from observation. Drawing

5.5. Observational drawings of crossed legs by Nadia at age six.

From Selfe (1977). Reproduced courtesy of the publisher, Academic Press London Limited.

from the three-dimensional world is more difficult than draw-ing from pictures, because one must translate the three-dimensional world onto a two-dimensional page.

Despite the realism of her drawing style, the skill shown by Nadia cannot be dismissed as literal, mindless mimicry. She altered the orientations of the objects that she drew and often added or omitted details. For instance, after having seen a sim-ple drawing of a rooster in a coloring book, she drew a wide variety of roosters from this initial stimulus. She drew them in different sizes. She tried beaks in various orientations, and on one she added a tongue. She also sometimes altered propor-tions, drawing the heads of her horseback riders as pinheads, and sometimes omitting heads and drawing headless riders. She seemed to be experimenting and challenging herself, just as do normally gifted children.

We have no drawings by other savants produced at as young an age as Nadia did hers. And Nadia is usually consid-ered the most extraordinary of all known savant artists. How-ever, she is similar in many ways to other autistic artists. For instance, Lorna Selfe, the psychologist who worked closely with Nadia, compared Nadia to four other autistic artists. All had prototypical autistic symptoms: delayed language, impaired social relationships, ritualistic behaviors, and severe learning difficulties (they were in the lowest 2 percent of the IQ range). All also had poor gross motor coordination: they walked late, and they had trouble learning to tie their shoes and catch balls. Yet all were able to draw highly realistic draw-ings. Like Nadia, they showed little interest in color or deco-ration and focused exclusively on naturalistic rendering. They could readily capture accurate contour and proportion, and they used occlusion, foreshortening, and linear perspective to show depth. A drawing of a foreshortened body lying down, by one fifteen-year-old autistic child, is strikingly similar to Peter's drawing at age six. Compare figure 5.6 by the autistic child with figure 4.17 by Peter.[20]

Nadia was first diagnosed as autistic at age six, when her mother brought her to the Child Development Research Unit at the University of Nottingham in England. She was then placed in a special school for

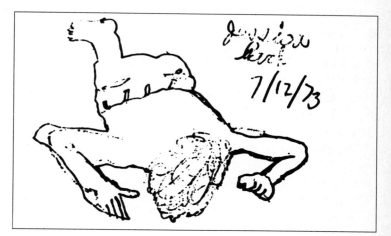

autistic children, where she began to acquire a limited amount of language. There, she sometimes tried to draw like the other children, and her interest in drawing realistically declined dramatically. She also drew less and less and after the age of about eight, for reasons not well understood, her drawings stopped developing. Today, as a young adult living in a residential home, she draws simple, childlike drawings that accurately reflect her low mental age of five to six years.

It is not uncommon for savant skills to disappear, and we do not know why they do. Some have attributed Nadia's lost skill to the fact that she had begun to acquire

5.6. Foreshortened drawing by a fifteen-year-old autistic girl. Note the striking resemblance to six-year-old Peter's foreshortened human in figure 4.17.

Reprinted by permission of Clara Claiborne Park.

some language and therefore no longer needed to communicate through drawing. This assumes, however, that drawing served as a form of communication for her. Moreover, other autistic artists have continued to draw even as they have acquired some language.[21]

Stephen Wiltshire is an example of an autistic artist whose gift continued to flourish even as he acquired language. While Nadia specialized in horses, Stephen specializes in detailed architectural drawings (his drawings of people are far more schematic), and several books of his drawings have been published. Like Nadia, he draws from observation, but more often from memory. Also like Nadia, his drawings are not photographic copies. Although his buildings are curiously the mirror image of the model he is reproducing, just as a photograph would be, his pictures also depart somewhat from the model, and he produces variations on what he has seen (see figures 5.7a and b).[22]

Like normally gifted artistic children, artistic savants draw almost every day and produce many more drawings than do average children. Also like the normally gifted, savants typically prefer using implements that make fine lines, rather than thick crayons or wide brushes. Nadia's drawings disintegrated when she was forced to use a thick crayon. Pencils and pens are far better for making the kind of detailed, realistic renderings that both normally gifted children and savants usually make.[23]

One Japanese savant, Yamamura, shows us that savant realism is a phenomenon found even in a culture whose artistic tradition does not feature realism. Yamamura painted insects and other animals, such as frogs, using the traditional Japanese ink brush, rather than the fine pencil or pen typically used by Western savants. And his paintings were done in the flat style of Asian art. Nonetheless, as shown in figure 5.8, his drawings show the same kind of highly accurate and confident grasp of contour that Nadia's drawings had.[24]

(a)

(b)

5.7. Drawings by artistic savant Stephen Wiltshire. (a) The Rialto, *a realistic drawing of Venice.*

Copyright Stephen Wiltshire, from Floating Cities, *Michael Joseph, 1991.*

(b) An Xciting Day, *a drawing of people. Note that the people are drawn simply and schematically, in contrast to the wealth of realistic detail in his drawing of the Rialto.*

Copyright Stephen Wiltshire, from Drawings, *Dent, 1987.*

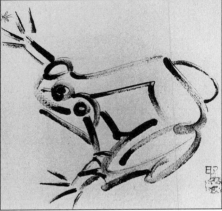

5.8. Finger drawing of frog by Japanese artistic savant showing realism despite its allusionistic, Asian style.

From Morishima and Brown (1977). Reprinted by permission of American Association of Mental Retardation. Copyright by American Association of Mental Retardation.

Savants have been said to be interested only in the *process* of drawing, not the final product. But this does not seem to have always been true of Nadia, since she sometimes tried to make corrections on her drawings either as she drew, or later on an old drawing. She also used to sit back and look at her work from different angles. She took great pleasure in viewing her drawings when she was satisfied with them. Yet, while normally gifted artistic children talk about their drawings to others and show them to their parents with pride, savants do not talk about or show their drawings. They seem to draw for themselves only and to display little interest in others' reactions to what they have made. Cathy did not look up or react in any way when I showed interest in her drawing, though the more high-functioning Stephen does clearly take pride in the acclaim that his drawings have received.[25]

People have debated whether savant realism is a *result* of the autistic condition or whether the realism is not pathological but simply a very high level, prodigylike skill operating independently of other intelligences. The debate has continued, probably because there is truth on both sides. Savant drawing skill is a high-level skill, just like that of normal artistic child prodigies. Yet savant drawing skill is far more limited and constricted than the drawing ability of prodigies. This constriction of options is probably a result of the pathological condition of autism.

AN IMPAIRMENT IN HIERARCHICAL ORGANIZATION?

One account of how savant artists differ from normal artists is that they do not grasp the hierarchical organization by which parts are subsumed into a larger whole. Savants, it is argued, focus on the particulars of a visual scene instead of the overall whole, because the global has no special status for them. This abnormal attentional focus, along with a vivid visual memory, could account for Nadia's and other savants' ability to begin a drawing by starting with disconnected details rather than by first sketching the overall outline. It could also account for the local precision of their drawings.[26]

This hypothesis was examined in one adult savant, called E. C., who had such heightened visual memory that he seemed to be simply reading off his mental images and translating these into a graphic image on a page (figure 5.9). Most artists, asked to draw from a model, begin by sketching an overall outline of the major shapes, and then fill in the parts. As they add details, they often go back and revise the global outline. But E. C. did not draw like this. Instead of beginning with an overall outline, he began with a detail and then added contiguous details. But instead of finishing each detail as an integral part before moving on to the next, he often went from parts of one detail to parts of another, if the two parts were contiguous. It was as if he did not care whether the lines he moved on to described the same form he had begun or another one next to it. Moreover, unlike normal artists (and

5.9. *Two drawings by E. C., a drawing savant, showing extreme realism and precision. The top drawing was done spontaneously. The bottom drawing was done after he was shown the two depicted objects, and then asked to rotate them mentally and draw them from different angles.*

From Mottron and Belleville (1993). Reprinted by permission of Laurent Mottron and by Academic Press. Copyright by Academic Press.

also unlike Nadia), he never altered any part as he worked. No one part affected another. E. C. was not using any kind of conceptual strategy when he drew. That is, he did not seem to be classifying a part as a part and then working on that part. Thus, for example, instead of conceptualizing a part as a leg of a table and then drawing the leg, he just drew lines in a kind of contiguous strategy, so that eventually they would show the whole.[27]

Because E. C. was not attending to the whole, he found it difficult to copy "impossible" figures such as Penrose's triangle or the devil's fork, figures whose impossibility becomes clear only if one relates all of the parts to one another. Local focusing on one part at a time, without relating the parts, will not reveal the amusing impossibility of these figures. Figure 5.10 shows Penrose's triangle and E. C.'s drawings from memory. E. C. showed the same local focus when shown the letter *C* formed out of small *O*s. He found it difficult to say that he was looking at a large *C* made out of small *O*s, and he often said he was looking at an *O*. The local parts, the *O*s, interfered with the larger global shape, the *C*.

E. C.'s focus on the local rather than the whole, his lack of hierarchical organization, could be why he drew human-made, inanimate objects like chairs and tables (which are distinguished by their parts) rather than organic ones like human bodies (which are distinguished by their proportions). The fact that the global outline of things had no special status for E. C. is consistent with the visual-spatial skills associated with autism. The facility of autistic people in recognizing hidden figures probably rests on their ability to overlook the more obvious outlines that hide these figures. And the two IQ subtests on which autistic people excel—block design and object assembly—can both be solved by a local matching strategy. E. C.'s drawing strategy is also consistent with how some autistic individuals solve jigsaw puzzles, not by using the overall picture that is being built up but, as mentioned earlier, by fitting local shapes to one another.

However, Nadia drew primarily organic forms, as did Yamamura. Savants also have been shown to excel in the depiction of

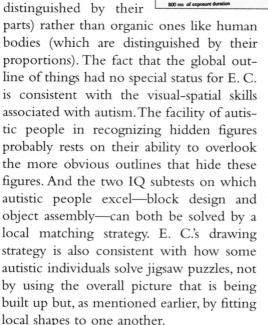

5.10. An "impossible" figure, called Penrose's triangle (top), and E. C.'s four drawings of the triangle done from memory after increasingly longer looking times. Note that none are correct.

From Mottron and Belleville (1993). Reprinted by permission of Laurent Mottron and by Academic Press. Copyright by Academic Press.

proportions on the Draw-a-Person Test, clearly a case of drawing organic forms. Thus, we do not know how general an explanation is offered by E. C.'s exclusive focus on parts instead of the whole.[28]

PHOTOGRAPHIC MEMORIES WITHOUT UNDERSTANDING?

According to another account, savant realism is made possible by visual memories that are not only rich and precise but also entirely nonconceptual. This hypothesis again explains savant realism in terms of savant deficiencies.

All known savant artists (as well as all savants in other domains as well) have unusually good visual memory skills. We know that savant artists have exceptional visual memories from the fact that their drawings are highly accurate and typically drawn from memory. Moreover, as just discussed, while normal children complete a drawing part by part, showing no sense of advance planning, savants like E. C. or Nadia can draw details in various places on the page and later connect these details with perfectly fitting larger lines. This suggests that they can hold the imagined finished product in mind as they draw. Other evidence showing their extraordinary visual memory skills comes from tests of their ability to recognize incomplete pictures. The fact that they can identify images from mere fragments of the images shows that, like normally gifted artistic children, they have richly detailed stored images.[29]

Savant memory has been characterized as automatic and nonconscious, and described as "verbal adhesion" or "memory without reckoning." Savants have been described as paying more attention to the physical characteristics of stimuli than to their meaning. For example, the British psychiatrist J. Langdon Down described a child savant who could remember entire books verbatim. When he read *The Rise and Fall of the*

Roman Empire, he skipped a line on page three. When he realized his error, he went back and read it correctly. Afterward, he was able to recite the book from memory, but he always included this initial mistake and its correction. Nadia provides us with a similar example. After having seen a picture of pelicans scattered on a page, with some above others, she later drew a pelican and showed the feet of another pelican above the head of the one she had drawn in full, because that was how it was in the model.[30]

These descriptions suggest a kind of memory in which conceptualization and understanding do not intervene, a kind of tape-recorder memory that requires no effort and admits no thought. It could be argued that this kind of noncomprehending memory would lead to excessively realistic rendering. Savants may, in fact, draw complex objects with precision because, when looking at the object, they see it merely as a cluster of lines and shapes, not as a three-dimensional object.

Evidence that knowledge and conceptualization interfere with realistic rendering comes from studies showing that people pay greater attention to form when they are not thinking about what the form represents. For instance, children draw more realistically when copying nonrepresentational designs than when drawing recognizable objects. And people can copy pictures more faithfully when the models are upside down and thus unrecognizable.[31]

There is some evidence that Nadia did not conceptualize what she drew. She was apparently unable to match two pictures of the same object unless both were in the same orientation, and she could not match pictures of different types of chairs. Assuming that she understood the instructions and what was expected of her, this performance suggests an impaired ability to generalize and classify.[32]

Such an impairment in classification ability could be causally related to the ability to draw naturalistically. Normal children show their conceptual understanding of an object in their drawings, and their simple schemas are evidence of generalization and abstraction. A circle used as a head, for instance, is an abstraction, albeit a crude one: a circle is somewhat like all heads and overlooks the individual variations in head shape.[33]

In contrast, the realistic drawings produced by savants are not generalizations but, like those of Eitan and other gifted child artists, are snapshotlike depictions of individual objects from particular, fixed vantage points—for example, not a generic house but a specific church seen from a particular angle. Thus, the high realism of autistic drawings could result from an inability to form visual concepts. Perhaps savants have no choice but to render every detail of a figure; they may be unable to grasp the general form of objects. They may draw realistically because they do not know or recognize or classify in any way what they are drawing. Perhaps they are just translating formal, nonrepresentational patterns from their vivid visual memories.

EVIDENCE THAT SAVANT MEMORY IS CONCEPTUAL

A problem exists, however, in explaining savants' realism by pointing to a conceptual impairment. Normally gifted children like Eitan draw very realistically, yet they clearly have no such conceptual impairment. Moreover, the British researchers Beate Hermelin and Neil O'Connor have shown that artistic savants do in fact classify and label what they see. This finding conflicts with the finding that Nadia could not classify together pictures of chairs.

Hermelin and O'Connor demonstrated the normal classification abilities of savant artists in several ways. First, they compared savant artists' ability to remember abstract (scrambled) versus representational pictures. When asked to repro-

duce pictures from memory, the savants were able to reproduce the representational pictures better than the scrambled
pictures. If they had been unable to classify the representational pictures (for example, as a house, as a tree), they should
have remembered them as sheer form, like the abstract pictures, and both kinds should have been recalled at an equal
level. The fact that the representational pictures had priority in
their memories shows us that their memory cannot be dismissed as entirely unthinking and automatic.[34]

In another study, savants, along with artistically gifted normal children, were shown sets containing four pictures, all of
which were related either by shape or by category. In the
shape sets, the "target picture" belonged to a different category
from the other pictures. For example, one shape set consisted
of a pear, an apple, a strawberry, and a light bulb. All four are
round, but a light bulb is not a member of the class of fruits.
In the category sets, the target picture was different because it
did not share the same shape as the other three, even though
all four belonged to the same category. For instance, a harp lay
next to a banjo, a guitar, and a violin. The harp, while still a
string instrument, clashed in shape with the others. After
being allowed to look at the pictures for fifteen seconds, the
subjects were asked to draw as many of the pictures as they
could recall. The measure was how many of the targets of each
type were reproduced.[35]

If savants recall what they see like a camera, they should
remember both kinds of targets equally well. But if they classify and label and interpret what they see, then they should
remember the targets that clash in terms of category better
than those that clash in terms of shape. And this is what happened. Both the normal gifted subjects and the savants
recalled the category-clashing targets the best.

Even when asked directly to classify pictures, and when
given a choice of shape versus category classification, the
savants, like the normal comparison group, used the category

framework. Hence, they placed a picture of a butterfly next to that of a caterpillar, but not next to a bow, even though the bow was shaped just like the butterfly. Thus, savant artists' memory cannot be described as memory without understanding. Nor can we explain savant realism in terms of a putative lack of ability to conceptualize.

A LACK OF INTEREST IN THE GENERAL?

Of course, conceptualization is not an all-or-nothing thing, and the question may be not whether savant artists conceptualize at all but whether they do so naturally and automatically, like normal people. While capable of classifying, savants may not be *interested* in the classification of the thing they are drawing. Instead, they may be attracted to all its local details and particulars. This lack of interest in the thing as categorized may help them to focus only on the form, not on what kind of a thing it is. In the words of the neurologist Oliver Sacks, who has written extensively about the savant syndrome, "The abstract, the categorical, has no interest for the autistic person—the concrete, the particular, the singular, is all."[36]

It is the focus on detail that may also explain why there is often so little emotional expression in the drawings of savants. To be sure, they do sometimes draw and paint expressive pictures, as Cathy's picture in figure 5.2 attests. But more typically, savant art mirrors the external world with astonishing faithfulness and shows us little emotional expression.

SAVANT ARTISTS AND
ARTISTICALLY GIFTED CHILDREN

We have seen how in many ways savant artists are like normally gifted children. They draw constantly, they are years ahead of their mental age in their ability to draw realistically, and at least sometimes they seem interested in the final product.

Yet they are not quite like gifted children. The savant's gift is more constricted. For one thing, savants almost always focus on the external world in all its particularity. They rarely show people relating to one another, and they rarely draw or paint expressively. In fact, they rarely draw people at all. Nadia drew animals primarily; Stephen Wiltshire draws buildings. Autistic people in general have constricted abilities and interests. For instance, they may memorize train schedules yet show no interest in actually riding on a train.

Savant drawings do not reflect the savant's inner world, probably because his or her inner world is impoverished. Artistically gifted children create visual narratives that seem to have powerful emotional meaning for them—scenes from *Star Wars* or *Batman,* for example—and they create fictional worlds that they return to in each drawing. Recall Peter's invention of animation, when he drew scenes from *The Little Mermaid.* They also sometimes inject humor into their drawings. One artistic child described by Milbrath drew a woman reading while absentmindedly stroking a pineapple instead of the cat on her other side. But savants do not make jokes in their drawings (autistic individuals have difficulty understanding many types of humor). And, despite the fact that they can classify pictures and thus understand *what things are*, their drawings have less personal and narrative meaning imbued in them than those of the normally gifted child or prodigy in art.[37]

Nonetheless, savant art is not totally unrelated to the art of the normally gifted. I take this as suggestive evidence that the art of the normally gifted is carried out by visual-spatial intelligence at least somewhat independently of the kinds of verbal and numerical abilities measured by an IQ test.

SAVANTS AT THE PIANO

As is the case with child prodigies, the domain in which savants
have most frequently been noted is music. Musical savants are
typically blind and retarded, though as noted earlier, there is
no sharp distinction between retarded and autistic savants, and
all show autistic characteristics. We know nothing about the
role of culture in musical savantism. For example, we do not
know whether musical savants emerge in cultures with non-
Western scale structures, and if so, whether their pattern of
abilities resembles that in Western savants. At least in the case
of drawing savants, we have one Japanese example, and he
showed the same kind of abilities as do Western savants.[38]

As with drawing savants, music savants resemble the normally gifted in many important respects. Like the normal
musically gifted child, music savants display signs of their gift
in early childhood. In fact, there is only one known music
savant whose talent emerged after early childhood. This is
Stephen Wiltshire, discussed earlier, who was found to have
extraordinary musical ability after he was already known as a
drawing savant. Wiltshire also is one of several exceptions to
the general rule that savants show gifts in only one domain. To
the extent that savants have skills in more than one domain,
the same underlying explanation is likely to account for all
savant skills.[39]

The early signs of talent displayed by musical savants are
identical to the signs shown by musical prodigies. Parents of
such savants have noted that at the age of one or two, their
children could sing in perfect pitch and rhythm, and could
sing many long and complex songs. These children show an
intense interest in and emotional reaction to music at an early
age. One three-year-old sat raptly through a three-hour opera
on TV, yet was unable to sit through one program of *Sesame
Street*, showing extraordinary attentional abilities limited to
the domain of music. Another child was unresponsive to his

environment but was drawn to music and, like Mozart, was easily disturbed by loud noises.[40]

These children have been reported to play many songs on the piano in any key by three, and to pick out melodies on the piano from sonatas they have heard by the age of four. Like musical prodigies, musical savants all have a phenomenal memory, and are able to play back faithfully most anything they hear. Like artistic savants, musical savants produce works that are highly faithful to the physical stimulus. The artist savant makes drawings that capture all of the details of the object represented; the music savant reproduces music from memory without missing a note.[41]

Just as artistic savants are constrained to a focus on external reality and visual realism, music savants are usually constrained to the piano. Perhaps this is because the piano is the most common instrument that allows a one-to-one mapping of key to sound, since the keys are arranged in a coherent, linear, spatial organization. Contrast this to the violin, for example, which requires bowing and fingering techniques to produce accurate pitches.[42]

While, as we saw, many great (nonsavant) performers and composers do not have perfect absolute pitch, almost all reported music savants do. They can recognize any note no matter where in the scale and no matter what instrument it is played on. The near universal incidence of perfect pitch in music savants may be related to the high incidence of perfect pitch in autistic populations in general (one in twenty). Another special population with a high incidence of perfect pitch consists of people with Williams syndrome, individuals who have high auditory, musical, and linguistic skills, along with retardation in the areas of drawing and reasoning. Thus, perfect pitch may be a marker of musical ability, particularly in special populations.[43]

Like Hungarian gypsy violinists or jazz improvisers, savant musicians play by ear and rarely read music. Here again they are unlike normally gifted musicians. Also unlike normally gifted musicians, savant musicians are often born prematurely and are blind. Their blindness is usually the result of a disease called retrolental fibroplasia, a condition caused by the administration of high doses of oxygen to premature infants. The recurring triad of blindness, retardation, and musicality, to be discussed in the next chapter, may be a clue to the biological basis of savantism.[44]

One famous example of a blind, retarded piano savant was Blind Tom, a slave child who at four could play any piece of music performed on the piano, with all the accents and rhythm correct, after having heard it only once. His gift was first discovered by Colonel Bethune, the slaveowner to whom he had been sold. Bethune heard piano playing late at night and went down to investigate, where he found the four-year-old Tom playing without mistake a Mozart sonata that he had heard the Bethune daughters practicing.[45]

Tom never received any formal instruction in music, but he soon could replay perfectly any piece he had heard but once. At age eleven, he was tested and shown to be able to play back even twenty-page compositions that he had only heard once. By adulthood, Tom had a repertoire of hundreds of pieces in his memory.[46]

Tom's memory extended to other auditory information besides music: he could repeat without error conversations of up to fifteen minutes that he had overheard. He could also sing back songs in French or German (which, of course, he could not understand) after only one hearing.[47]

ATTEMPTS TO EXPLAIN MUSIC SAVANTS

It is tempting to try to dismiss the gifts of music savants as unrelated to musical giftedness by describing their memories as mindless tape recorders, just as it is tempting to explain away the gifts of artistic savants by describing their memories as mindless cameras. But just as we saw that drawing savants are capable of conceptualizing and classifying pictures, so also musical savants show a grasp of the underlying structure of music. Tom's skill was not sheer imitation, for he could improvise on any tune by the age of six. And he could play an accompaniment to music that he had never heard before. So, like Nadia, Tom could go well beyond the information given.

Research by Hermelin, O'Connor, and their colleagues provides experimental evidence that musical savants are like normal musicians in their understanding of music. Their research suggests that musical savants are not dependent on rote auditory memory. Rather, musical savants have absorbed the structure and rules of music, and this structure influences the way they remember music. Just as the musical prodigy Nyiregyhazi remembered notes linked by familiar harmonies and rhythms better than random notes, so also did the musical savant N. P., whose memory was compared to that of a professional musician of the same age who had the same number of years of piano experience. Both were given two pieces to remember, one a traditional classical piece based on the diatonic scale, and one a semi-atonal composition by Bartók. N. P. recalled the traditional piece better than did the musician, and he recalled the atonal as well as did the musician. Most importantly, he recalled the tonal piece better than the atonal piece.[48]

If N. P.'s memory had been purely imitative, he should have recalled both pieces equally well, like a tape recorder (just as the artistic savants should have recalled abstract pictures as well as representational ones). The fact that N. P. showed superior memory for the piece based on familiar Western rules of music means that his memory was "structure-based," just like that of Nyiregyhazi. Thus, just as artistic savants show conceptually based memory (remembering pictures more readily by their category than by their shape), musical savants show structure-based memory (remembering music more readily if it conforms to familiar rules). In neither case can we conclude that the memory system operating here is totally automatic and unhampered by conceptualization.[49]

Indeed, their skills at improvisation and even composition show that they have internalized musical rules. When musical savants and musically gifted children were asked to compose, the savants outperformed the children. They were better able to continue an unfinished tune and to invent new tunes, including ones with both melody and accompaniment lines. Moreover, their inventions were also judged to be more complex, more well-balanced, and better timed.[50]

Of course, this was composition on request. Only one savant, L. L., has been noted to compose on his own. The typical musical savant is one who can play back pieces from memory and improvise. No savant has become known whose major activity is composing. Just as artistic savants typically make drawings that "play back" the external world, rather than ones that construct an imaginary one, the musical savant plays back (and improvises on) heard pieces rather than constructing new ones.[51]

Some musical savants have been described as playing in a wooden, mechanical style, with no feeling. Such a position would be consistent with an early view of savants as incapable of abstraction and as pathologically concrete. Their music has been called colorless, stereotyped, and mechanical. And in this respect, musical savants have been likened to artistic savants, whose drawings depict lines and edges rather than feelings. But just as savant artists do sometimes make expressive pictures, musical savants also sometimes play with feeling and expression. Savants often have strong emotional reactions to the music they play, they take delight in playing, and they have strong preferences for certain types of music over others. Savants, like autistic people in general, may experience emotion but have difficulty expressing and communicating their feelings.[52]

Like artistic savants, musical savants resemble their non-pathological counterparts. Their musical abilities are essentially indistinguishable from those of musical prodigies, especially from those with absolute pitch. But again, they are more constricted in their options than are child prodigies in music. Savants are limited to the piano, they cannot read music notation, and they rarely compose. As mentioned, such constriction of abilities is characteristic of all autistic people, not just savants.

SAVANTS WHO CALCULATE

The existence of calculating savants provides evidence that one aspect of mathematical ability, the ability to calculate, can be performed independently of other forms of intelligence. But this seems to be the only part of math that can operate without more conceptual thought.

Calculating savants are thus also highly constricted in their numerical abilities. Calendrical calculators, who can instantly figure out on what day of the week any given date will fall, can calculate, but only in the context of the calendar. Lightning calculators, who can mentally calculate huge sums at great speed, can calculate but do no other form of math. Thus, these calculators possess just one "splinter" of mathematical ability. (Some mathematicians are not even particularly good at calculating, and calculation is not considered a skill central to mathematics.) For this reason, calculating savants are like "normal" calculators, but they are not like mathematicians.[53]

Calculating savants are obsessed with numbers. Like mathematically gifted children, they mathematize the world, turning everything into numbers. But while math prodigies are fascinated by patterns and relationships among numbers, calculators seem more fascinated by the mechanical, dull activity of counting. One lightning calculator, taken to the theater, occupied himself by counting the number of words that each actor uttered, and the number of times that each exited and entered.[54]

Lightning calculators, those who can calculate complex numerical problems with "lightning" speed, never use a paper and pencil, and are sometimes faster even than a computer. Fuller, a slave boy like Blind Tom, was obsessed with counting. He counted the hairs on the tail of a cow, and whether his answer of 2,872 was correct or not is less interesting than is the fact that he not only could bear to do this boring task but felt driven to do it. He performed nine-digit multiplication problems easily and rapidly in his head. It took him two minutes to figure out the number of seconds in one and a half years.[55]

These calculators seem to have a photographic memory for numbers. For example, Fuller could begin a long calculation, stop, and then months later resume just where he had stopped, as if he were going back to old notes. In this he shows the excellence of delayed memory reported in artistic savants who can draw things they saw years earlier, or musical savants who can play back pieces they heard years earlier.

The photographic memory of savant calculators for numbers allows them to look at a string of twelve digits for a split second and then recite the numbers backward, forward, or starting from anywhere within the string. This ability is like that of the artistic savants who can start drawing from any part of the picture and end up with a completely proportioned rendition. Both seem to be based on a very strong and vivid internalized representation.[56]

A GRASP OF RULES

Savant calculators do not simply rely on rote memory. Multiplying any two 3-digit numbers instantly and retrieving the answer from memory, which any savant calculator can do, would require one million bits of information. Studies have shown that savants make the same kinds of errors on calculating tasks as do normal mathematicians, and this indicates that they are calculating using algorithms like normal mathematicians, and not pulling answers out of a vast memory vat. There is no evidence that they are conscious of these rules, however. Here again they differ from nonsavant mathematicians, who are certainly operating with explicit understanding of mathematical rules.[57]

Thus, what calculating savants do is not totally mindless and rote. These savants make use of numerical regularities just as musical savants make use of the structure of music and as artistic savants make use of the structure of graphic representation.

Calendrical savants are perhaps even more bizarre than calculating savants because they engage in an activity that scarcely any normal adult or child prodigy would ever think about. These savants can tell the day of the week on which any given date, in the past or the future, will fall—March 10, 1795; December 1, 1400; July 8, 2201; and so on. They can also do the reverse—quickly identify the year in which March 15 will fall on a Monday.

The most famous calendrical savants are a pair of identical, retarded twins, George and Charles, born three months prematurely. Their IQs were assessed twice and ranged between 40 and 70. Both were fascinated by calendars and spent hours as young children playing with perpetual calendars. George began to do calendar calculations at age six; Charles showed an interest in calendars a few years later and could perform the same feats as his twin brother.[58]

Like lightning calculators, calendrical calculators are not relying on rote memory but are using rules and regularities of the calendar. Clear evidence for this exists. For instance, calendrical calculators can calculate into the future, and this shows that they are not reading off from memory, since they would not have seen calendars of future dates. In addition, they are particularly rapid in calculating dates twenty-eight years apart, showing that at some level they know the rule that calendrical patterns repeat themselves every twenty-eight years.[59]

Thus, calendrical calculators seem to be using some kind of knowledge (probably unconscious) of calendrical regularities, just as musical savants use some kind of knowledge of musical regularities. They cannot explain what they do, though. "It's in my head and I do it," said one of the twins.[60]

⌣

THE LIMITATIONS OF SAVANTS' GIFTS

Savants often surpass prodigies in the accuracy of their memories. Nadia drew with a higher degree of realism than do prodigies at the same age. Blind Tom's memory for music was surely greater than that of most music prodigies. And math prodigies do not show the ability (or the inclination) to memorize vast sets of numbers and dates. Savant memory seems to be more automatic and literal than that of a prodigy of any sort.

However, the findings that calendrical and lightning calculators use rules and rely on calculation rather than sheer memory, that musical savants use musical structures, and that artistic savants use object classifications, all force us to reject any generalization savants rely totally on "dumb" rote memories. The very fact that savantism occurs only in domains that have clear, well-defined rules (visual realism, tonal piano playing, calculation, calendar calculation) must be important. If savants were not dependent on the use of rules, then one would find savants in domains without such clear regularities—atonal music, abstract painting, fiction.

In other ways, too, savants resemble the most highly gifted children. Savants are obsessed with their domain of gift. They have an unstoppable drive to exercise their special skill. And like gifted children, they need little encouragement, support, and instruction to discover the structure of their domain.

Thus, despite the fact that savants are so severely impaired in all domains besides their domain of gift, they are in important respects similar to the "normal" gifted child or child prodigy. This conclusion suggests that gifts—at least those in the domains in which we find savants—can operate almost entirely independently of IQ. To the extent that savant artists' abilities are no different from those of normally gifted artists, we can conclude that the abilities found in the normally gifted can operate independently of other intellectual, social, and emotional capacities.

However, because savants can call on no other forms of intelligence besides their one area of gift (for example, they lack interpersonal intelligence and self-awareness), they are far more constricted in what they can do, and they seem to have fewer options than do gifted children. Drawing savants mostly draw realistically; music savants stick to the piano; and mathematical savants can only calculate. If they had normal IQs, artistic savants might be able to draw and paint in a wide range of styles and imbue more meaning and feeling in their works. Musical savants might be able to play the violin, where there is no one-to-one mapping of sound to physical position of the note. And calculating savants might also be able to explain and prove how they arrived at a certain answer.

While some prodigies become creative adults who make innovations in their domains of expertise, to date savants have never altered their domains in any way. This lack of domain-altering creativity may also be a function of their low IQs. To the extent that the abilities of gifted children diverge from those of savants, we must conclude that the abilities we find in the gifted are not entirely domain-specific and must involve some other forms of intelligence as well, forms that are lacking in the savant.

The abilities of gifted children and savants are so exceptional that we are often at a loss to explain them. Where do these abilities come from? Are they attributable to motivation and practice, or are they due to innate "talent," built into the brain?

Six

THE BIOLOGY
OF GIFTEDNESS

When it comes to the origins of giftedness, there are really two myths, diametrically opposed. The commonsense "folk" psychology is that giftedness is entirely inborn: you either have it or you don't. The abilities of Mozart, Picasso, Newton, or Einstein are so unfathomable to us that we explain them by saying that these individuals were just born geniuses. The environment has no interesting role to play if talents are inborn and largely fixed.

Of course, this explanation offers almost nothing unless we can determine how and why gifted people are different from birth. Psychologists like to attack folk psychologies in general, and the folk psychology of giftedness is no exception. But psychologists have their own myth: that giftedness is entirely a product of the environment. They argue that the right kind of intensive training, begun at an early age, is sufficient to account for even the very highest levels of giftedness—the levels attained by child prodigies, savants, or adult creators.

A similar view was proposed by Shinichi Suzuki, the founder of the Suzuki method of music teaching. "Every child is born with the capacity for becoming richly musical so long as he or she is brought up properly. . . . There is no inborn talent for music ability," he wrote. The high levels of music performance attained by ordinary children trained in the Suzuki method show us that all children have considerable musical ability, much as the high levels of scholastic performance attained by ordinary Japanese children show us that all children have more academic ability than we might think. But Suzuki's results do not lead to the conclusion that there are no innate differences in musical ability. Nor do they allow us to conclude that all children with proper training could attain the heights of a Mozart. To argue that all achievements are entirely a product of the right regimen of training is to return to the now discredited behaviorism that dominated psychology in the first half of the twentieth century. Nonetheless, an environmental explanation of giftedness is gaining hold today among some experimental psychologists interested in learning.[1]

Consider some evidence on which a strong environmental view might rest. Benjamin Bloom, who studied world-class achievers in a variety of fields, including math, art, music, and athletics, found that not one of his cases had achieved expertise without a supportive and encouraging environment, including a long and intensive period of training, first from loving and warm teachers, and then from demanding and rigorous master teachers. This study is often taken as strong evidence that eminent adults started out as perfectly ordinary children who had dedicated parents and teachers who motivated them to work long and hard.

However, a reading between the lines of the descriptions of these eminent individuals in childhood shows that at a very young age, before much if any training, signs of unusual ability were clearly evident. The musicians recalled being quick to learn at the piano, and both their parents and teachers recognized them as special. The sculptors recalled drawing constantly as children, usually realistically, and also enjoying working with their hands, building, and nailing. The mathematicians recalled a fascination with gears, valves, gauges, and dials, and they were considered "brilliant" as children. Most of the interviewees said that they had learned easily in their chosen domain but had not learned so quickly in other areas in school. A similar story is portrayed in the book and subsequent movie *Searching for Bobby Fischer, the True Story of a Chess Prodigy.* Here the prodigy, Josh Waitzkin, invented a sophisticated strategy the very first time he played chess, after having watched the game only a few times: he launched an attack using a combination of several pieces. No one had taught him to do this. To be sure, Josh went on to acquire countless hours of practice and training. But he was unusual from the start. Examples such as these allow us to conclude that hard work is necessary for the acquisition of expertise, but *not* that it is sufficient.[2]

Further evidence that has been used to support an environmental view of giftedness comes from the work of psychologist Anders Ericsson. Ericsson has shown that levels of achievement reached in piano, violin, chess, bridge, and athletics correlate highly with the sheer amount of "deliberate practice" in which individuals have engaged. Those who spend more time working on difficult problems over and over in order to perfect them (deliberate practice) are the ones who reach the highest levels. In addition, in music, ballet, and chess, Ericsson found that the higher the level of attained performance, the earlier the age of first exposure to the domain, and hence the earlier the onset of deliberate practice. An earlier onset leads to greater accumulation of hours of deliberate practice.[3]

But again, such evidence points to the necessity of deliberate practice, not to its sufficiency. Those children who have the most ability are probably those who are most interested in a particular activity, who begin to work at that activity at an early age, who work the hardest at it, and who can most profit from practice. One is likely to want to work hard at something when one is able to advance quickly with relatively little effort, but not when every step is a painful struggle. One cannot get a more typical child to sit at a piano for hours or to draw or work on math puzzles all day. The kinds of children I have described in this book are like Josh Waitzkin: they cannot be stopped. Their fortunate combination of obsessional perseverance *and* high ability is what leads to their remarkable achievements.

Of course, the daily work on a skill leads to improvement and is necessary for the development of talent. In the words of psychologist Howard Gruber, who has studied creative adults such as Charles Darwin and Jean Piaget, "Practice is not everything but it may be everywhere." But the desire to work so hard at something, to practice and explore for long hours, comes from within, not without. Such intrinsic motivation typically occurs when there is a high innate ability, as long as there is sufficient parental encouragement and support. The rage to master is an ineluctable part of talent.[4]

Thus, while researchers such as Bloom and Ericsson have demonstrated the clear importance of hard work, their findings fail to rule out the role of innate ability. Occasionally one finds examples of hard work without innate talent. In the domain of art, a published record exists of drawings produced by Charles, a child who was obsessed with drawing, who drew constantly, but who never made much progress. Charles produced over two thousand drawings of trains from the time he was two until he was eleven, most of them drawn between the ages of seven and nine. Charles clearly drew two to three years ahead of his age. But as figures 6.1, 6.2, and 6.3 show, while he made some progress, his drawings never reached a skill level anywhere near that of Eitan's or Peter's. True, his drawings became more complex, more realistic, and more controlled. But after age four, his drawings showed little development, and even at age eleven, his drawings were fairly schematic and showed neither Eitan's mastery of perspective nor Peter's ability to capture contours in motion.[5]

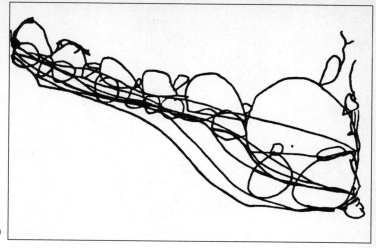

(a)

6.1. Series of train drawings by Charles showing the fruits of drawing practice without much innate talent. (a) Drawing at age two,
showing tracks and differentiation between engine and passenger cars.
(b) Drawing at age three, showing non-canonical front view, and
showing tracks smaller behind the train, but with no converging lines.

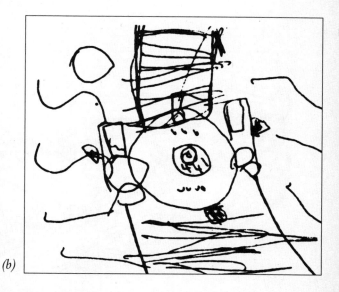

(b)

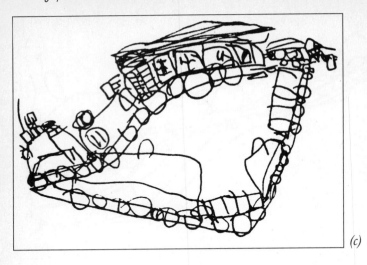

(c)

(c) Drawing at age four, showing three-dimensional space by vertical positioning (the farther trains are placed higher up). (d) Drawing at age five, showing differentiated passenger and freight trains.

All Charles's drawings are from Hildreth (1941). Copyright 1941 by Kings Crown Press. Reprinted with permission of Columbia University Press.

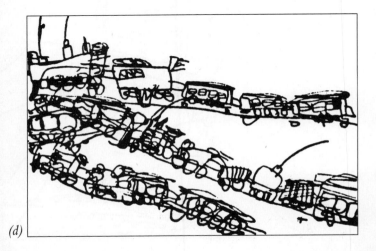

(d)

6.2. *More trains by Charles, ages six to nine. (a) Drawing at age six, showing trains receding in distance and diminishing in size. (b) Drawing at age seven, which seems no more advanced than drawing at age six. (c) Drawing at age eight, in canonical side view.*

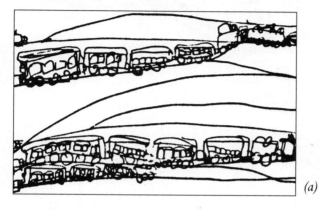

(a)

(b)

(c)

(d) Drawing at age nine, showing technique of diminishing size to suggest depth.

(d)

(below) 6.3. Charles's trains at ages ten and eleven. (a) Drawing at age ten, in canonical side view. (b) Drawing at age eleven, showing increase in detail, still drawn in canonical side view.

(a)

(b)

Other examples of the effects of hard work without talent can be found in any urban preschool or elementary school in contemporary China. Chinese children are given explicit practice in drawing from the age of three, when they enter kindergarten; and from the age of six, they have daily practice in mastering calligraphy through copying. These children are taught in a meticulous, step-by-step manner how to produce the wide variety of graphic schemas found in traditional Chinese painting. They learn how to draw or paint monkeys, bamboo, goldfish, shrimp, chickens, roosters, and so on. They are taught precisely which lines to make, and the direction and order in which to make them. They learn by copying, but eventually they are able to go beyond copying and draw from life. While ordinary Western children are given virtually no instruction in drawing and are simply given materials with which to explore and experiment, ordinary Chinese children are given very detailed instruction in drawing as a skill. Thus, the drawings and paintings of ordinary Chinese children appear controlled, neat, skilled, and adultlike, while those of ordinary Western children appear free, messy, unskilled, and childlike. Compare figures 6.4 and 6.5 by typical Chinese children to figures 4.2 and 4.21 by typical American children. The instructional regimen imposed on the Chinese child undoubtedly accounts for this difference.[6]

One can see the same phenomenon in the domain of music. Ordinary Japanese children trained in the Suzuki method of violin begin to play the violin at a very young age and practice every day. These children play in a disciplined, controlled, musical manner, and on the surface they all appear to be musical prodigies.[7]

While Chinese drawers and Suzuki violinists perform at a level that makes them look highly skilled, they are very different from the other kinds of children I have described thus far—those who not only choose to draw, play music, or solve math problems, but who *insist* on doing so, and who master their domain with very little explicit instruction. Ordinary Chinese children become very proficient at drawing but would never be confused with Wang Yani, nor would Suzuki violinists ever be confused with a young Yehudi Menuhin or the

6.4. *Typical nongifted Chinese child's painting, age six.*

From the collection of the author.

Japanese violin prodigy Midori. Yani far surpasses the average Chinese child in skill and inventiveness, as does Midori the average Suzuki-trained violinist.

In short, the psychologist's myth of adult-made prodigies does not hold up. Hard work is not sufficient, and precocious children are not mere drudges. They are not ordinary children who know how to work hard. Not only can one not make ordinary children spend hours a day at drawing or chess or math, but even if one could, as in

China or Japan, these children would not achieve with instruction what precocious children achieve on their own.

What about the commonsense view that giftedness is inborn? In its extreme form, this view must also be wrong. Giftedness cannot be entirely a product of birth: as discussed in later chapters, family support, education, and hard work can determine whether a gift develops or dies on the vine. Nonetheless, there is considerable evidence for a strong inborn, brain-based component to giftedness.

6.5. Typical nongifted Chinese child's painting, age five.

From the collection of the author.

THE SEARCH FOR THE BRAIN BASIS OF GIFTEDNESS

In 1995, a striking finding was reported in the journal *Science*. The planum temporale, an area of the brain that processes auditory information, was shown to be considerably larger on the left than on the right in musicians who have perfect pitch. This finding was based on a magnetic resonance imaging (MRI) study of the brains of thirty professional musicians and thirty nonmusicians matched in age and sex to each professional musician. Although the planum temporale was larger on the left than on the right in both groups, the difference was two times as large in those with perfect pitch as it was for the other subjects, whether or not they were musicians. It would be interesting to determine whether special populations with a high incidence of perfect pitch (for example, people with autism, musical savants, and those with Williams syndrome) also have this enlargement.[8]

The study reported in *Science* represents an effort to discover how gifts may be reflected in the physical structure of the brain. In recent years, less systematic efforts along these lines have also been made. On a segment of the television show *60 Minutes,* a reporter noted that Soviet scientists had studied slides of brain tissue taken from Stalin, Lenin, and other Soviet leaders to try to determine whether there was anything exceptional about their brains that could be seen under the microscope. But because this research was never reported in a scientific journal, and Western scientists were never permitted access to the slides, we have no idea what, if anything, was discovered. Moreover, unless brain cells are preserved in very specific ways, and unless those examining the neurons have the right hypotheses about what to look for, this kind of research is not likely to be fruitful.[9]

Brain tissue from Albert Einstein has also been scrutinized by psychologist Marian Diamond and her colleagues. One atypical feature was discovered: the left inferior parietal lobe of his brain had a relatively greater number of glial cells than are found in normal brains, yielding a lower than average ratio of neuronal to glial cells. But we do not know whether the elevated glial count had anything to do with Einstein's exceptional powers, as the parietal lobe is involved in so many different kinds of skills—integration of visual, auditory, and tactile modalities; self-awareness; imagery; memory; and attention. In addition, we do not fully understand the functions of glial cells.[10]

Another problem is that studies showing something special about the brains of gifted adults tell us nothing about the *origin* of the gifts. We do not know whether Einstein was born with more glial cells or whether these cells developed in response to greater metabolic need as a result of all the mental work in which he engaged. While neurons never increase in number in the adult brain, glial cells can increase. Similarly, the larger left planum temporale in the brains of those with perfect pitch could be either an inborn characteristic that made perfect pitch possible or the result of training. Just as animals raised in rich, stimulating environments have better connected and larger cortical areas of the brain than those raised in impoverished environments, differences found in the brains of exceptional people could be the *result* of stimulation, training, or hard work.

However, both biology and training may be important and undoubtedly interact. A recent study in the journal *Science* reported a dramatic difference in the brains of violinists who started training early versus late. Those who began training before age twelve had larger and more complex neural circuits than those who started training after thirteen. This finding was demonstrated by stimulating the fingers of the left hand (violinists must develop greatest dexterity in their left hands) and recording the response of the cerebral cortex through magnetic imaging. Assuming the two groups were similar except for the age of beginning training, we can conclude that training affects the brain, but that training can exert this effect only if it is begun at an early age, while the brain is at its most malleable. Training begun too late cannot restructure the brain.

Although our knowledge of the potential neurological and genetic bases of giftedness is in its infancy, new techniques are pushing the search forward. Positron emission tomography (PET) measures blood flow and metabolism to areas of the living brain while the brain is at work. And MRI shows where in the brain glucose is being metabolized, a process necessary for neural activation. These techniques allow us to pinpoint areas of the brain involved in different tasks—listening to music, composing music, creating a visual image, conversing, and so on.[11]

New techniques have also been developed to reveal information at the microscopic, cellular level of the brain. Brain banks are now storing brains for the study of psychiatric disorders, but there is no reason why these brains could not be used for the study of giftedness. And the field of genetics is developing ways of analyzing the molecular basis of genes so that we may ultimately be able to relate specific traits to specific genes or clusters of genes. All these techniques may make it possible eventually to determine the neurological embodiment of gifts, and the extent to which the potential for giftedness may be genetically transmitted. But this research is highly controversial and open to multiple interpretations.

Brain Size

Perhaps the crudest notion of how high-ability brains might differ from average ones is that they might just be bigger. But there is no consistent evidence for this hypothesis. When we compare across species, there is an almost perfect correlation between the brain size of the animal and the amount of cortical surface area. But when we look only at human brains, there is no relation between brain weight and amount of cortical surface area. Brain size is critical to intelligence, but only up to a minimal point, estimated to be 800 or 900 grams. The average human brain weighs three pounds, which is far more. While two studies have shown a relationship between human brain size and IQ, the relationship was found only in males, thus leaving the issue unresolved.[12]

When researchers have examined more specific abilities in relation to very local brain areas, some suggestive findings have emerged. For instance, the study of brains of musicians with perfect pitch has shown how a specific ability may be reflected in differential brain structure. And the preserved brain of one artist with eidetic imagery was found to have a visual area that was also thicker than usual.[13]

Perhaps brain size or brain weight is too crude a measure. A potentially finer measure of the size hypothesis might be length and complexity of the connections between neurons, called dendrites. Dendrites are longer and have more complex branching in brain areas that are involved in more complex tasks. For instance, one study showed the dendrites in the language area of the left hemisphere to be longer than those in the corresponding area in the right hemisphere. And reduced dendritic branching is found in brains of those with senile dementia.[14]

But the fact that dendrites are longer and more complex in areas subserving higher-level abilities in the normal individual does not allow the inference that the gifted have longer or more complex dendrites in the areas of their brains that control these gifts. In addition, as with the musicians' brains or Einstein's brain, such a finding would not allow us to conclude that the dendritic length was the *cause* of the giftedness. In fact, there is some reason to believe the opposite—that dendrites grow as a function of the use of a particular brain area. In the study just described of dendrites involved in complex tasks, the dendrites in the brain region controlling finger movement were especially long in a typist and a machinist.

Brain Speed

If having high ability does not mean having a larger-than-average brain, could it mean having a brain that works more quickly than the average one? This is an old idea, put forth by the polymath Sir Francis Galton over a hundred years ago, when he tried to assess intelligence by measuring speed of reaction time to simple sensory stimuli. Galton's idea was revived by Hans Eysenck, Arthur Jensen, and other psychologists, who believe that neurons in high-IQ brains fire more rapidly and more efficiently than those in normal brains.

These psychologists believe that synaptic speed and efficiency are the biological underpinnings of intelligence, and are inborn and entirely unmodifiable by the environment.[15]

Jensen developed a simple reaction-time task with no "knowledge content" to measure mental speed. A person is seated at a table in front of a circle of buttons that light up intermittently, one at a time. The person rests a finger on the "home button" and tries to push the lit button as quickly as possible. People with lower IQs have more variable reaction times, especially when many buttons are used in the test. Jensen believes that this reaction-time measure is a direct measure of the speed of neuronal processing, a pure measure of intelligence uninfluenced by the environment. But critics such as psychologists Stephen Ceci and Michael Anderson point out that we can never assume that reaction time is not influenced by a person's knowledge, experience, attention, and motivation. Experience in taking laboratory tests, experience in working quickly with one's hands, and motivation to try hard on tests—these are all factors that could speed up one's reaction time.[16]

Brain Efficiency

Brain efficiency may be a better indication of high ability than brain size or brain speed. Studies of brains at work on various tasks, using PET scans to measure the glucose metabolism in the brain, have shown that the brains of high-ability people use less glucose and therefore function more efficiently.[17]

But again we must ask whether brain efficiency is the *result* or the *cause* of having a high IQ. There is reason to believe that when people learn to become experts at a task, their brains function more efficiently. Take, for example, a study of glucose use by people as they played Tetris, a spatial computer game in which one must rotate downward-moving shapes as quickly as possible to make them fit into odd spaces at the bottom of the screen. After practice at this game, scores increased sharply, and glucose use decreased in most of the brain regions examined. But it was only those people with high spatial intelligence (as measured by scores on a spatial reasoning test) who showed a statistically significant reduction in glucose use after mastering Tetris.[18]

In two brain areas, however, there was actually greater glucose use after training. A reasonable interpretation is that when people first attempt a difficult task, they try out a variety of strategies, most of which will not work. As they gain expertise, they become more selective in strategy use. Brain areas not related to the task are then no longer activated. Greater selectivity could mean greater efficiency.[19]

Efficiency, thus, is a function of learning rather than an inborn property of the brain, since efficiency increased after training. Rat brains also show decreased glucose use when rats are raised in enriched environments. However, the Tetris findings do not allow us to rule out *any* inborn differences in brains, since those who showed the greatest increase in efficiency after training were those who had the highest spatial reasoning scores to begin with. Moreover, in theory the ability to develop efficiency could be inborn.[20]

Atypical Brain Organization

Norman Geschwind was a brilliant neurologist who noticed a strange cluster of abilities and disabilities in certain kinds of gifted individuals. Geschwind was intrigued by his observation that individuals with high right-hemisphere abilities (this would include the spatial domains of math, music, and art) tended to be non–right-handed. Geschwind rejected the notion of a dichotomy between right- and left-handers, and argued instead that handedness was a continuum. Non-right-handers are all those who are not strongly right-handed: strong left-handers, weak left-handers, and those who are ambidextrous. Geschwind noted that these individuals also had a higher-than-average frequency of linguistic deficits—

dyslexia, stuttering, delayed language acquisition, even autism, which is associated with impaired language. And they had a higher-than-average frequency of immune system disorders such as asthma and allergies. Geschwind noted that these traits sometimes clustered within individuals, or, if not in individuals, in families.[21]

Geschwind referred to these peculiar clusters of gifts and deficits as "pathologies of superiority." With his colleague Albert Galaburda, Geschwind theorized that the association between right-hemisphere (spatial) gifts, left-hemisphere (linguistic) deficits, non-right-handedness, and immune disorders was due to the effect of the hormone testosterone, which altered the organization of the developing fetal brain.

Geschwind and Galaburda noted that elevated testosterone *in utero* after the twentieth week of gestation inhibits growth in certain posterior areas of the left hemisphere, because the left hemisphere is slower to develop than the right and is thus more vulnerable to insult. When growth in a brain site is inhibited, there is compensatory growth in parallel areas in the other hemisphere, as well as in adjacent areas in the same hemisphere. Thus, a delay in the posterior left hemisphere (relevant for language) could lead to growth in areas nearby (related to calculation ability) and to parallel right-hemisphere areas (related to spatial and musical abilities). This should result in gifts in right-hemisphere skills such as art, music, and math, and in calculation ability, as well as in pathologies of language such as dyslexia, delayed speech, and stuttering.[22]

Such compensatory stimulation of the right hemisphere could also lead to an atypical brain organization called "anomalous dominance." Geschwind estimated that about 70 percent of all people have "standard dominance"—a strong left-hemisphere dominance for language and hand (yielding right-handedness), and a strong right-hemisphere dominance for other functions (for example, visual-spatial and musical processing). Anomalous dominance, defined as any pattern deviating from the standard one, is associated with more anatomically and functionally symmetrical brains, with language less lateralized to the left hemisphere, and visual-spatial functions less lateralized to the right side. In addition, about a third of those with anomalous dominance were estimated to be non-right-handed.[23]

In addition, testosterone can interfere with the development of the thymus gland, known to play an important role in the development of the immune system. Hence, Geschwind and Galaburda argued that excess testosterone exposure leads to immune disorders such as allergies, asthma, colitis, and myasthenia gravis.[24]

Excess testosterone exposure may occur for a variety of reasons. Male fetuses are exposed to more testosterone because they are exposed not only to testosterone provided by the mother but also to that which they themselves produce. (Fetuses of either sex with a male twin fetus are exposed to more for the same reason.) Thus, the syndrome should be more frequent in males. The sex difference favoring males in math would be consistent with Geschwind's hypothesis, as would the fact that more males than females are non-right-handed and have learning disorders. Smoking and stress in pregnancy can also increase testosterone. In addition, some fetuses have more sensitive testosterone receptors, perhaps for genetic reasons.[25]

At its extreme, this syndrome sounds like the savant syndrome: excellence in calculation, music, or art, along with impaired linguistic skills. If the theory is correct, individuals gifted in spatial, "right-hemisphere" skills—mathematics, visual arts, and music—should show the following five tendencies, and males should show more of all of these than females:

1. Superior spatial skills (a measure of enhanced right-hemisphere development)

2. Non-right-handedness (a measure of anomalous dominance)
3. Bilateral representation of language (a measure of anomalous dominance)
4. Language-related problems
5. Immune system disorders

Some intriguing evidence, discussed in the following sections, supports each one of these predictions. Many aspects of the theory, though, are heatedly contested, and many of its specific predictions either have been refuted or have not been clearly supported. Yet some general aspects of the theory may well turn out to be correct, and if so will advance our understanding of giftedness and the brain. Brain researchers can no longer ignore associations between the seemingly unrelated phenomena that Geschwind and Galaburda attempted to explain by one unified theory. At the very least, then, the theory will have stimulated us to think about brain organization and giftedness in a new way. And so far, no new theory has been proposed that can explain these associations.[26]

Superior Spatial Skills?

We have already seen that people gifted in math, music, and art have superior visual-spatial skills. One study provides more direct evidence of enhanced right-hemisphere development. Academically gifted adolescents were asked to look at pictures of faces, a visual task known to involve the right hemisphere. The mathematically gifted subjects showed enhanced electrical brain activity in their right hemispheres, an indication that their right hemispheres were more activated during this task than were those of a control group. This is just one study, but it is consistent with the prediction that people with right-hemisphere gifts have enhanced right-hemispheric functioning during tasks known to involve the right hemisphere.[27]

Non-Right-Handedness?

Individuals gifted in math, art, and music are disproportionately non-right-handed, in comparison to the population at large.

Math

Mathematicians have a tendency to be non-right-handed, as do those who simply rate themselves as having mathematical ability. For instance, researchers in one study found that 20 percent of those who rated themselves as having special ability in math were non-right-handed, in contrast to only 10 percent of those without any self-reported math gift. And among young adolescents who score at the highest levels on either the math or verbal portions of the SAT, or both, the frequency of left-handedness was found to be more than twice that of the general population. Although these youths had family members who were left-handed (showing a genetic influence), the frequency of left-handedness was higher in the gifted youths than in their immediate relatives (consistent with the possibility that intrauterine hormones played a role). Of those who were not left-handed, many were ambidextrous or had relatives who were left-handed.[28]

One might well expect this finding among the mathematically gifted. While doing mathematical computations and reading and writing mathematical signs are activities carried out by the left hemisphere, conceptualizing mathematical relations and concepts is a right-hemisphere ability. But why should verbal ability (a left-hemisphere function) be associated with non-right-handedness? For one thing, verbal ability was assessed by the verbal portion of the SAT, which is more a measure of verbal reasoning than a measure of pure linguistic ability, such as sensitivity to syntax. For another, perhaps the adolescents with high verbal ability also had fairly high mathematical ability. Thus, their increased incidence of non-right-handedness could have been associated with their mathematical giftedness.[29]

Art

Artists show the same disproportionate incidence of non-right-handedness. One survey of art students found 21 percent to be left-handed (in contrast to 7 percent of other students at the same institution), and 48 percent to be non-right-handed (in contrast to 22 percent of other students). In another study, 20 percent of the children identified by their teachers as gifted in art drew with their left hands. A disproportionate number of non-right-handers also go into architecture, and a disproportionate number of male (though not female) non-right-handers go into chess.[30]

Music

Musicians too are disproportionately non-right-handed. For instance, in one study, 11 percent of people who considered themselves musically gifted were non-right-handed, in contrast to 4 percent of those who did not feel they had musical ability. However, the evidence for a relationship between handedness and musical ability is more mixed than it is for art or math.[31]

There is thus a fair amount of evidence for an association between non-right-handedness and giftedness in math, art, and music. However, two qualifications must be made. First, while left-handers turn up in disproportionate numbers in areas requiring right-hemisphere abilities, most people in all fields are of course right-handed. This leads one to wonder whether, among those who go into such "right-hemisphere areas," left-handers are any more gifted than right-handers. The answer is probably no. Non-right-handers in music, art, or math have not been found superior to right-handers in these fields.[32]

The second qualification is related. When we compare non-right-handers and right-handers taken from the normal population, we do not find higher spatial abilities in the former group. Some studies show no difference, some show higher spatial abilities in non-right-handers; some show just the opposite. Such conflicting findings may arise from non-right-handers being a mixed group. Recall that only about a third of non-right-handers actually have anomalous dominance. Of this group, some may have language in both hemispheres, while others may have spatial skills in both hemispheres. To complicate matters, some right-handers from non-right-handed families also have anomalous dominance.[33]

Those with bilateral representation of language may have poor spatial skills, due to spatial abilities being "crowded out" by language skills, and/or have heightened verbal skills, since their language is more widely represented in the brain. These would certainly not be the non-right-handers who go into art or music or math, but they might be those who go into law or other verbal areas. Those with bilateral representation of spatial ability may have poor language skills due to crowding, and perhaps also increased spatial skills, since these are more widely represented in the brain. These could be the non-right-handers who eschew verbal areas and go into the visual arts.

Bilateral Representation of Language?

Since non-right-handedness identifies only about a third of those with anomalous dominance, it would be useful to have a more direct measure of dominance. And there is now some evidence that various forms of giftedness are associated with a more bilateral, symmetrical kind of brain organization, with the right hemisphere participating in tasks ordinarily reserved for the left hemisphere.

Processing words is normally a strongly left-hemisphere task. But academically gifted youth have brains less lateralized for language: they use their right hemisphere as much as their left to process words, in contrast to ordinary people who make more use of their left hemisphere in verbal processing. This can be shown by using what is called an interference task. For instance, mathematically gifted and average students were asked to tap a key as quickly as possible while reading a paragraph aloud at the same time. When one is tapping with the right hand, the left hemisphere is in control; when one is tapping with the left hand, the right hemisphere is in control. Reading a paragraph is a verbal task, and if verbal tasks are processed in the left hemisphere, this should interfere with the tapping rate in the right hand. For the average students, the verbal task slowed the tapping rate in the right hand, but not the left, showing that only their left hemisphere was involved in the verbal task. In contrast, for the mathematical subjects, the verbal task slowed down the tapping rate of both hands, showing that both hemispheres were being used to process the paragraph. Thus, mathematical giftedness was shown to be associated with decreased language lateralization.[34]

Language-Related Problems?

The hypothesis that left-hemisphere–related disorders are associated with right-hemisphere talents can be tested either by looking for heightened right-hemisphere abilities in learning-disabled children, or by looking for an elevated frequency of learning disorders in children with right-hemisphere talents. Both ways of testing the hypothesis yield a clear and consistent answer: there is indeed a relationship between visual-spatial abilities and language-related learning disorders.

To begin with, children with language-related learning disabilities display high right-hemisphere abilities. Dyslexic children do very well on tests that assess right-hemisphere spatial skills (for example, making patterns, putting together puzzles), but poorly on tests assessing left-hemisphere, sequential skills (for example, remembering a string of numbers). These findings fit with more anecdotal observations of visual-spatial talent in dyslexic individuals. They also fit with the fact that autistic individuals (who have language and communication impairments) have high visual-spatial skills.[35]

The same association shows up when adults or children with visual–spatial talent are examined for verbal problems. Children with mechanical ability who become inventors as adults often do poorly in verbal areas in school but excel in math. Artists (but not musicians) score poorly on verbal fluency. Art students report more reading problems than do other college students and also make more spelling errors, including more of the kind associated with poor reading skills —non–phonetically based errors that do not preserve letter-sound relationships. Dyslexic children with high spatial abilities may be just a more extreme case of those many children who are much more gifted in math than in verbal areas.[36]

Musical giftedness may also be associated with language-related problems. In one study, 20 percent of musically gifted individuals reported a history of learning disabilities such as dyslexia, delayed speech, stuttering, math difficulties, or hyperactivity. In contrast, only 10 percent of the non–musically gifted subjects in this study reported any of these disabilities. And those reporting a history of dyslexia were more likely to report music talent than those without a history of reading problems.[37]

Despite the fact that high mathematical ability is sometimes associated with lower verbal ability, mathematically gifted children do not appear to have reading problems. One reason may be that math involves a strong left-hemisphere as well as right-hemisphere component, as mentioned previously.

From an evolutionary perspective, one might wonder why dyslexia has survived. But of course there would have been no survival disadvantage for dyslexia in a preliterate society. We cannot have evolved for phonologically based written languages, since these were invented far too recently.[38]

The tendency of artists and possibly musicians to have language problems of some sort may shed light on why children gifted in these areas do or do not go on to become artists or musicians. Reading problems may lead these children to avoid fields that require extensive reading. By default, then, they may drift into music or art. Given that modern cultures place a higher value on language than on art or music, it would not be surprising to find individuals who possess verbal as well as visual or musical gifts being drawn to verbal fields rather than to art or music.

Immune System Disorders?

High-IQ individuals have a higher-than-average frequency of immune disorders of childhood onset, as do non-right-handers. About 60 percent of Camilla Benbow's academically gifted adolescents had allergies, a rate over twice that in the population at large. (This effect may have been a function of the high mathematical—rather than verbal—ability of these adolescents, as would be predicted by the theory.) In the 1960s, it was noted that high-IQ children attending a school for the gifted run by Teachers College in New York City had more allergies and asthma than normal. However, because there was no biological theory by which to explain this, the high rate of immune problems was attributed to the strains of urban living. There has been far less research investigating a potential link between immune disorders and either artistic or musical giftedness, and so far only a glimmering of evidence that such a link exists.[39]

In Summary

Although the research picture is mixed, and studies do not all show the same thing, the overall findings can still be summarized. Giftedness in abilities subserved by the right hemisphere is associated with enhanced right-hemisphere development. Consequently, individuals with such gifts are likely to have anomalous brain dominance. They are more likely to be non-right-handed, and possibly also to have language bilaterally represented in the brain, than are individuals in the population at large.

Individuals with such brains are likely to have not only gifts but also disorders of two general kinds: first, language-related learning disorders such as dyslexia and, second, at least among the math gifted, immune system disorders of childhood onset such as asthma and allergies. All these findings are consistent with the Geschwind-Galaburda theory that testosterone inhibits some areas of the brain while simultaneously enhancing others.

The model may well end up modified and even rejected as we learn more about the brain, especially from brain-imaging studies of high-ability people at work. But no future theory will replace the Geschwind-Galaburda theory unless it can either account for the clustering of gifts in math, art, and music with non-right-handedness, immune problems, and language-related learning deficits, or show that these traits do not in fact cluster.[40]

SAVANTS: EXTREME CASES OF THE PATHOLOGY OF SUPERIORITY?

Many investigators have tried to explain the biological basis of the savant syndrome, but most of the efforts have been speculative ones based on scant evidence. One suggestion has been that the savant has simply by chance inherited a gift in one domain and retardation in all others. According to this view, both the ability and the deficit are genetically transmitted, and they are transmitted independently of each other. But if this explanation were valid, we ought to find savants who have family members with the same kind of talent, or with retardation. This has not been found.

Explanations in terms of learning, rather than innate gifts, have also been put forth, as they have for normally gifted children and adults. For instance, one hardworking, normal graduate student given intensive training was able to perform as well as a savant in calendar calculation. Evidence like this has been used to argue that savants achieve their high skill levels because they spend countless hours obsessively practicing.

However, both the genetic and the learning explanations leave unanswered the questions of why it is only in certain domains of ability that one finds savants, why their abilities are more rigid and constricted than those of nonsavant gifted individuals, and why musical savants are so often blind.[41]

A more promising explanation of savants draws on the Geschwind-Galaburda hypothesis of the pathology of superiority. Savants are like extreme versions of nonpathologically gifted children with certain patterns of abilities and disabilities. Savants tend to have highly developed right-hemisphere, visual-spatial abilities and severe deficits in the left-hemisphere function of language.

The Geschwind-Galaburda model might even account for calculating savants whose gift is a left-hemisphere one. Geschwind noted that delays in some portions of the left hemisphere (as a result of testosterone) could result not only in stimulation of the right hemisphere but also in stimulation of unaffected regions of the left (and these could thus include left-hemisphere calculation areas). It is also possible that calculators use right-hemisphere, visual-spatial strategies, as there are some reports that they actually *see* numbers when they calculate. Savants who are hyperlexic also fit the model. Although reading is a left-hemisphere, linguistic skill, hyperlexics see letters more as spatial patterns than as meaningful linguistic symbols.[42]

Since there is a higher-than-average incidence of non-right-handedness in autism, savants too probably have a tendency toward non-right-handedness. This would be consistent with the predictions of the Geschwind-Galaburda model. If researchers were to find that savants had a tendency not only toward non-right-handedness but also toward immune disorders, we would gain further support for an explanation of the syndrome in terms of this model.[43]

To date, only scant direct brain evidence exists to confirm this theory. Of the four autopsies that we know of which have been performed on savants' brains, only one presented clear evidence for some form of left-sided damage. However, autopsies are crude measures when one does not know exactly what to look for. X rays of savants' brains point more clearly to left-sided damage. For instance, the musical savant Leslie Lemke apparently had some kind of left-sided brain damage, as did J. L., another musical savant. And there is some evidence that autistic individuals have left-sided damage. For instance, in one study of seventeen autistics, including a few savants, fifteen showed left-sided abnormalities. But what is really needed are studies revealing differences between those few autistic and retarded individuals who are savants, and the rest who are not.[44]

According to Darold Treffert, an expert on savants, the fact that so many savants were premature babies fits with the notion of left-sided brain damage and resultant compensation by the right hemisphere. Toward the end of a normal pregnancy, massive cell death in the fetal brain, called pruning, occurs. If the fetal brain suffers some form of injury to the left hemisphere before pruning, a vast number of uncommitted neurons on the right side still can take over the functions of the lost cells. But if brain damage occurs after birth, fewer excess neurons are available on the right to take over. This would explain why there are more cases of congenital than acquired savants: left-hemisphere brain damage after birth would not lead to as much right-hemisphere compensatory growth. However, if a baby is born prematurely, pruning may not yet have taken place. Hence, if postnatal injury occurs (for example, due to excess oxygen administration, which causes brain damage), there are still massive numbers of right-hemisphere neurons uncommitted and ready to take over. Oxygen given to premature infants is now known to lead to blindness. By this line of reasoning, we could account for the triad of prematurity, savantism, and blindness in music savants.[45]

Treffert also speculates that brain damage can account for the savant's extraordinary memory, emotional detachment, and highly focused, narrow attention. Treffert argues that the kind of high-fidelity memory of the savant could result from injury to the cortex, which is involved in conscious, meaningful memory. We remember best that which we can form associations to and which has meaning for us, especially emotional meaning. When the cortical basis of memory is damaged, Treffert speculates, memory may shift to a more primitive level, mediated by the cortico-striatal system. Memory at this level is nonconscious, noncognitive, and automatic. While this extreme caricature of the savant memory may not be warranted, there is truth to it, in modified form. Savant memory *is* more automatic and meaning-free than is the memory of prodigies.[46]

Thus, the best explanation we yet have for the savant syndrome is that it is caused by injury to selective areas of the brain. This injury leads to an overcompensation by certain other areas of the brain, including a shift to a noncortical form of automatic, narrow, rote memory. Undoubtedly, many causes of this kind of initial brain injury exist, ranging from excess testosterone at a certain point in pregnancy to anoxia at birth to excess oxygen administered to premature infants. This explanation helps to explain why there are so many more male savants, since the male fetal brain is slower to develop and is hence more susceptible to injury (and is exposed to more testosterone). This explanation also helps account for the fact that savants are restricted to certain domains. These are domains mediated either by the right hemisphere (drawing, music) or by the left-hemisphere areas adjacent to the posterior language area (calculation).

IS GIFTEDNESS INHERITED?

It used to be thought that if a trait could simply be shown to run in families, we could assume that this trait was inherited. For example, in one of the first books on giftedness, *Hereditary*

Genius: An Inquiry into Its Laws and Consequences, Francis Galton examined 100 eminent male historical figures, such as Darwin, Bach, and Newton, as well as their male siblings and male offspring. He found that 23 percent of the brothers and 36 percent of the sons of these eminent men also had achieved eminence, rates much higher than Galton's estimate of 1 in 400 in the normal population. Galton concluded that genius ran in families and therefore was genetically transmitted. Terman too noted that the close relatives of his high-IQ children were also intellectually superior, and he concluded that giftedness was inborn.[47]

But Galton's and Terman's conclusions were unwarranted, since family members share both environments and genes. More recently, behavioral geneticists have tried to disentangle the effects of genes and environment. Researchers have compared identical and nonidentical twins in terms of the concordance of some ability, that is, the degree to which a characteristic is shown by *both* members of a twin pair. A higher rate of concordance in identical pairs is taken to indicate a genetic contribution to the ability under study, since identical twins share all of their genes, while nonidentical twins, like ordinary siblings, share only half. A number, referred to as a "heritability coefficient," is used to estimate the extent to which genetic differences in a group are correlated with differences in some ability among members of that group.

But greater similarity between identical twins than between nonidentical twins could also be due to some environmental factor, since identical twins may create a more similar environment for themselves simply because they perceive themselves as identical. A better method is to compare the concordance of an ability in identical twins reared apart to such a concordance in adopted siblings reared together. Here we can compare genetically identical siblings in different environments to genetically unrelated siblings in the same environment. Using the same logic, we can also look at the concordance rates between adopted children and their adopted versus biological families.

Twin studies have told us a lot about the heritability of IQ, but little about the heritability of specific abilities such as music, art, math, or linguistic skill. There is, however, evidence from identical versus nonidentical twins on the heritability of musical ability showing a genetic component to musical giftedness. Nonetheless, we know far more about the heritability of IQ. Most IQ studies have involved only populations selected at large, not high-IQ populations. Thus, much of what we can say about the heritability of high IQ must be extrapolated from the findings about the heritability of ordinary IQ.[48]

Most studies have shown IQ to be highly (though never 100 percent) heritable. For instance, the average correlation between identical twins' IQs is .86, while that for nonidentical twins is .60. If identical twins are reared apart, the correlation remains as high as .75 or .78. Specific abilities such as verbal reasoning, spatial reasoning, and visual memory also yield a high heritability coefficient. Since statistical correlations can range only from -1.0 (a perfect inverse correlation) to +1.0 (a perfect positive correlation), these correlations are strikingly high.[49]

Surprisingly, heritability coefficients for IQ do not decrease with age and experience—just the opposite is true. The effects of the environment on IQ decrease with age, while the effects of genes grow stronger. Thus, the environment imposed on a child seems to affect a child's IQ while that child is young and living at home, but then seems to decline in importance after the child grows up, moves away from home, and chooses an environment compatible with her innate abilities.[50]

Evidence also exists for a genetic influence on *high* IQ. The behavioral geneticists Robert Plomin and Lee Ann Thompson compared identical and nonidentical twins chosen on one criterion from a larger sample of twins: at least one member of each twin pair had to have a high IQ, at least 1.25

standard deviations above the average for all of the twins' mean. The identical twins were far more likely both to have high IQs (62 percent) than were the nonidentical twins (25 percent), which points to a genetic influence on high IQ.[51]

These researchers also compared the IQ distributions of three groups: individuals with an identical twin of high IQ, individuals with a nonidentical twin of high IQ, and all of the twins from the original, unselected sample. The IQs of those who had a high-IQ *identical* twin were higher than the IQs of individuals with a high-IQ *nonidentical* twin.

Some traits that do not run in families may still be genetically transmitted according to a principle called "emergenesis," by which traits are passed on by a package of genes, but only if the *entire* package is transmitted. Part of the package does not result in part of the trait. This claim runs counter to standard models of behavioral genetics, according to which genetic traits must, by definition, run in families. According to the standard model, the concordance rate in nonidentical pairs should be half that of identical pairs. However, some traits simply do not fit this model. Examples include voice timbre (identical twins have identical voices; nonidentical twins rarely have even similar voices), schizophrenia and bipolar affective psychosis (both have concordance rates in identical twins far more than twice that in fraternal twins), and idiosyncrasies of personal style (identical, but not fraternal, twins reared apart are highly concordant in traits such as humor, fearfulness, and cautiousness).[52]

Most traits are determined by the combined action of many genes. Each gene contributes a little bit to the end product. Genes that work in this additive fashion either are on different chromosomes or are far apart on the same chromosome, so that they do not stick together when the chromosome divides into two and gets passed on to the offspring. Height is an example of such a trait. Identical twins are almost identical in height (correcting for placental nutrition); nonidentical twins are about half as similar in height as are identical twins.

But some traits can be described as "all-or-nothing," or as "emergent." These traits do not vary with the combined action of many genes but depend for their emergence on a specific configuration (or package) of genes. Nonidentical twins, or siblings, are unlikely to all receive the entire package, since each gets only half of the parental chromosome that contains this package. However, identical twins share 100 percent of their genes. Thus, if one gets the package, the other one does too.

Extremely rare traits that are qualitatively different from the norm may fit this emergenesis model. Genius, including the genius of savants, may be one such "trait." A child who inherits only half of the right genetic cocktail for being a genius will not end up half a genius. Some of Galton's geniuses—Newton, Beethoven, and Michelangelo—had no other eminent family members and seemed to emerge out of nowhere. Perhaps child prodigies and savants also fit this model. If they do, then the Geschwind-Galaburda model, which is based on prenatal nongenetic influences, would have to be revised.[53]

If traits for genius or prodigiousness do not run in families, they will not be picked up as genetically based through the adoption method, in which one compares concordance rates of children with their adoptive versus their biological families. These traits will be discovered to be genetically mediated *only* through the much more difficult method of comparing identical and nonidentical twins. I say more difficult because identical twins are much rarer than are adopted children. Given the rarity also of prodigies, the number of prodigies who have twins is going to be vanishingly low.

If prodigies fit this model, then one would not expect to find extremely high familial resemblance in cognitive abilities in an extremely high ability group. And this is exactly what Benbow and her colleagues reported when they noted that the scores of their extremely precocious youth were considerably higher than those of their parents. Perhaps we can use the emergenesis notion to account for both Benbow's findings of low familial resemblance and Plomin and Thompson's findings of high familial resemblance. If the precocious youth in Benbow's study were child prodigies, and if being a prodigy is an emergent genetic trait, then one would predict low familial resemblance among them. If the high-IQ subjects in Plomin and Thompson's study were simply moderately high IQ individuals, then one would predict high familial resemblance, because a high IQ is not an emergent genetic trait.

The field of behavioral genetics is moving in yet a new direction today. Geneticists like Plomin are now trying to pinpoint the DNA markers (extracted from blood or saliva) for particular traits. This method has been used so far in the study of disorders, but it is now being used in the study of high ability. Plomin predicts that we will eventually be able to identify the DNA markers of individuals at the high end of the IQ spectrum.[54]

Problems with Genetic Arguments

Claims that IQ is in part genetic have met with strong resistance. Some have criticized the IQ measure as an unfair, culturally biased measure. Some have criticized the twin methodology, noting that identical twins reared apart are often adopted into families similar to one another. For example, Stephen Ceci reanalyzed some of the identical-twin data, separating the pairs of twins reared in similar environments (both members were adopted into urban or rural families) from those reared in dissimilar ones (one member was adopted into a rural family and the other into an urban one). When twins were reared apart in dissimilar environments, the IQ concordance rates were only .27. Thus, the twins-reared-apart method may not disentangle genetics from environment as cleanly as has been touted.[55]

Ceci also makes another important point: what is inherited may not be IQ but some other factor, such as temperament, which may then interact with the environment to affect IQ. For instance, suppose a child is born with an excessive activity or anxiety level that makes it impossible to pay attention in school. This child could end up with a low IQ score because of failing to attend to, and thus take in, information. But what was inherited was temperament, not IQ. The path from what is actually inherited to one's ultimate IQ score is not necessarily a direct one.[56]

We also too easily slip into causal and mechanistic language when drawing conclusions from research findings in behavioral genetics. Heritability tells us only the extent to which genetic *differences* within a group are correlated with differences in a particular trait as measured at one point in time. If heritability for IQ is .50, this simply means that 50 percent of the IQ differences within a group of people are correlated with their genetic differences. The figure tells us nothing about any particular individual, because it is a group measure. It also does not mean that 50 percent of people's IQ is due to genes and 50 percent to the environment. We cannot separate genes and environment in this additive way, since the cause of development always results from the *joint* action of genes and environment. Genes are part of the developing system and are thus susceptible to influence from all levels during development. But note that this same kind of critique can be made of the way in which we so often talk about any result involving an interaction of factors. For instance, if we find that education and race interact to predict income, we easily slip into additive language and talk about how much of income is predicted by each variable. We should watch our language but not throw out the findings.[57]

High heritability of a trait does not mean that this trait cannot be modified. No one has ever shown a genetic effect for ability so strong that it is invulnerable to environmental enrichment or deprivation. Height, for example, though genetically transmitted, is affected by nutrition. Still, innate differences in ability must place a limit on how much and what kind of modifiability by the environment is possible. Recall Charles, who drew so many trains. Because he had little innate gift to begin with, training did not lead to quantum leaps in improvement.[58]

The critiques of behavioral genetics amount to a critique of how we talk about the findings. We should not conclude that some percentage of our abilities are caused by genes and the rest by our environment. We should not think of genes and environment operating separately and additively. And we must remember that heritability tells us only the extent to which differences among people are associated with differences in their genes. Nonetheless, there have been so many very carefully designed twin studies that demonstrate fairly high heritability for intelligence and even personality that it would be foolish to disregard these studies and conclude that genes have nothing to do with our intelligence or personality. One of the most striking findings is that heritability of intelligence increases with age, a finding not easily explainable in environmental terms.

If there is a genetic component to intelligence, then it is likely (but certainly not yet demonstrated) that there is a genetic component to other forms of giftedness. And if so, then it is likely that gifted children do not have ordinary brains.

Psychologists would never assert that retardation is due to too little training or not enough drill. No one disputes the biological basis of retardation (with the exception of that due to extremely impoverished environments). But if biological retardation exists, why not biological acceleration?

Most of the evidence discussed in this chapter suggests that there are neurological and genetic differences between the gifted and the ordinary, and among different kinds of gifted people. A skeptic might argue that these differences are not inborn but arise as a result of how these individuals choose to use their brains. But the suggestive evidence for the brain basis of giftedness, as well as the evidence for a genetic component to IQ, makes it increasingly likely that all forms of giftedness have some biological basis. It is highly improbable that any amount of deliberate practice by ordinary people could bring them up to the level reached so quickly by a child prodigy or a savant. And so, with respect to the origins of giftedness, the commonsense view turns out to be less of a myth than the psychologists' view.

Seven

GIFTEDNESS AND
THE FAMILY

Some people say that gifted children are driven and pushed by overly ambitious parents. Children whose parents drive them to achieve too early, it is believed, can only end up as resentful, disengaged, depressed adolescents who have lost all interest in achieving. Parents are told to leave their children alone and let them play like normal children.

But this view merely reflects our culture's low expectations for our children, and our contentment with modest levels of achievement. In some nontechnological cultures today, children are expected to engage in adult activities from an early age. In Japan, academic expectations for children are higher than in the U.S.[1]

Gifted children do sometimes lose interest in their domain of talent, but this is rarely because they were simply pushed very hard. Rather, such disaffection results from extreme pushing *in combination* with several other factors: parents whose own needs lead them to exploit their gifted child, parents who dominate and deny their child autonomy, and parents who deprive their child of emotional contact.

SIX GENERALIZATIONS

Six generalizations characterize the family environments of highly gifted children.

1. Gifted children occupy "special positions" in the family: they are often either first-born or only children.[2]
2. These children grow up in "enriched" environments.
3. Their families are child-centered: parents focus almost all their energies on making sure that their children receive early training in the domain in which they have shown a gift.
4. Their parents are driven: they both model and set very high standards and hold high expectations for achievement. But when parents are overinvolved, push to excess, and love their children's achievements more than their children, gifted children are at risk for dropping out.
5. At the same time, their parents grant them considerable independence.
6. Family environments most conducive to the development of talent combine high expectations and stimulation, on the one hand, with nurturance and support, on the other.

With the exception of the birth-order effect, none of these generalizations demonstrates definitively that particular family characteristics *cause* or even necessarily *contribute to* giftedness and high achievement. It remains possible either that inborn characteristics in the child create certain family characteristics (such as enriched or child-centered environments) or that certain parental characteristics (such as high drive) are passed on genetically rather than environmentally.

Special Positions in the Family

Gifted children and adults who become eminent occupy special positions in their families. As noted, they are typically either first-born or only children. This has so often been found that the finding is widely accepted.[3]

The association of childhood giftedness, as well as adult eminence, with particular positions within the family must be explained in terms of an environmental, rather than a genetic, advantage. There can be no plausible genetic reason why first-born children have a systematic advantage over later-born children. One explanation for the advantage of being a first-born is a motivational one. First-borns spend their early years in a position of prominence, which they lose when a sibling is born. They may thus be driven to achieve in order to regain their lost position of centrality.

But what about only children, who never lose their special position? The motivational account does not help us here. A genetic account is conceivable: parents who choose to have only one child could be people of high ability who want less time spent child rearing and more time for work. However, an environmental explanation could account for the advantage of being *both* an only and a first-born child. First and only children receive more adult stimulation in their early years in comparison to children born into families where siblings already exist. Later-born children spend more of their time in the company of other children. Greater adult stimulation might lead to a cognitive advantage.[4]

Enriched Environments

Gifted children typically grow up in "enriched" environments—interesting, varied, stimulating ones. They have houses filled with books and are read to at an early age. They get taken to museums and concerts. Their parents do not talk down to them, but from an early age engage them in sophisticated discussions.[5]

David Feldman and Lynn Goldsmith have described in detail the conscious efforts of one prodigy's parents, who tried to surround their child with constant and varied stimulation. As an infant, Adam was exposed to bright colors, interesting shapes, visually active displays, musical and nonmusical sounds, and a great deal of interpersonal interaction. This stimulation was always under the supervision of one of the parents so that it could be varied in response to Adam's reactions. Stimulation took other forms after infancy. The parents discussed abstract concepts with their son, and they posed interesting questions and thought experiments. A walk in the woods with his parents, Fiona and Nathaniel, became a science class for Adam:

> On our first walk with Adam, Fiona, and Nathaniel into the forest preserve near our home, we spent the better part of an hour barely penetrating 100 yards into the woods: Fiona would see a cluster of particularly interesting ferns which we all stopped to inspect, and the three Konantoviches launched into an extended discussion of reproduction of different plant types. Two steps later, Nathaniel would find some decomposing something-or-other, and he and Adam would speculate about how long it had been decaying, what kinds of chemical reactions you would find going on, and how long the entire process would take. Then Adam would spy an interesting species of bird and describe its nesting habits. Nearly every experience provided the potential for lively and interesting discussion.[6]

The level of education attained by the parents plays a strong role in the development of a child's gift, probably because educated parents have the means and the desire to provide enriched environments. But families of gifted children need not be well educated. For one thing, while families of children gifted in music tend to be well educated, most of the children identified as musically gifted have been those who take formal lessons and study Western classical music. It is certainly possible that musically gifted children who have no formal instruction, and who participate in "alternative" music activities such as rock bands, come from less well educated families. These children and their families have not been studied. And parents of children gifted in the visual arts are not necessarily highly educated. For instance, in Bloom's study, the families of the sculptors ranged widely in level of parents' formal education as well as socioeconomic level. Nonetheless, these parents almost always provided their artistically inclined children with the kind of enrichment necessary for the development of their talent: they bought them art materials, gave them space to work, and took them to museums.[7]

Giftedness can certainly develop in families without much money, as long as the families value education. Poor parents of children identified as gifted have been found to be responsive and stimulating, and to provide opportunities for reading, playing, and talking. Recent refugees to this country from Vietnam and Cambodia are clear examples of children who achieve highly but come from poor families. The black psychiatrist James Comer tells how he and his siblings grew up in a poor family with parents of little education. Yet Maggie Comer, their mother, valued education so highly that she made sure that her children read and studied and achieved in school. All of them were success stories.

Thus, what is critical are those cultural values that make education a priority. These values are linked to upper levels of social class and education, but only imperfectly. There are poor and uneducated families who value education and achievement, just as there are many upper-income families who do not invest much in their children's education, do not provide enriching environments, and allow their children to spend the bulk of their time in front of the television or at the mall.

Of course, poorer parents are less likely to be able to provide varied stimulation than are richer ones. This is probably why gifted programs always have a disproportionate number of children from middle- and upper-middle classes. And there are undoubtedly many children never identified as gifted because of their disadvantaged environments. Some psychologists are trying to develop non-IQ methods of assessing academic giftedness so that gifted children from disadvantaged backgrounds will be identified.[8]

Thus, a strong association exists between giftedness and enriched family environments. Enriched environments also play a role in fostering normal levels of development, while impoverished ones stunt normal development. Children who grow up with little social and verbal interaction in orphanages are slow to develop. But when they are taken out of such environments and are placed in stimulating ones, they catch up.[9]

Still, *high* ability could be genetically transmitted and have nothing whatsoever to do with the enriched environments that educated parents create. High-ability parents may pass on high abilities genetically and create enriched environments simply because they themselves have high ability. Or perhaps high-ability children need more stimulation and thus seek out enriched environments. Gifted children make more demands on their parents for such extracurricular activities as lessons, clubs, and hobbies. Adam was described as making "omnivorous intellectual demands" on his parents. Psychologists Sandra Scarr and Kathleen McCartney have pointed out that the environment is not necessarily what acts on the child; rather, the child's genetic traits may lead the child to select certain kinds of environments.[10]

Even if high-ability children did not demand enriched environments, parents of such children might create enriched environments *in response to* the high ability they perceive in their children. Parents can identify giftedness in their children even when they are infants. Parents may simply interact socially and verbally with their children on a higher level when they recognize that their children can understand such interaction.[11]

In all likelihood, children who get identified as gifted are usually born into families with already enriched environments. But because of their inborn high ability, these children go on to seek out even higher levels of enrichment. And once the parents recognize that they have a gifted child, they react by increasing the enrichment level of the already enriched environment. Thus, the environments of children recognized as gifted become increasingly enriched over time, in comparison to those of nongifted children (or of children whose gifts go unnurtured). And this enrichment probably stimulates the development of the child's initial gift.[12]

Child-Centered Families

Families of gifted children in our culture are extraordinarily child centered. The child perceived as gifted is typically selected as special, and all the family's energy becomes focused on this child. The Menuhin family reportedly selected as gifted one child in each generation and then focused all their resources on developing the talents of this child. In the twentieth century, this child was the violinist Yehudi. At last report, Menuhin's mother was still alive, actively supporting him into her late nineties. Before Yehudi, those selected had become religious scholars.[13]

Families focus in two ways on the gifted child's development: either one or both parents spend a great deal of time stimulating and teaching the child themselves, or parents make sacrifices so that the child gets high-level training from the best available teachers. In both cases, family life is totally arranged around the child's needs. Parents channel their interests into their child's talent area and become enormously invested in their child's progress.[14]

Yehudi Menuhin's father gave up his job as a teacher to help his children's careers. The fathers of Mozart and of Picasso devoted themselves to nurturing their extraordinary sons' talents. Yani's artist father eventually gave up painting so his style would not influence his daughter. The father of three female chess prodigies in the Polgar family worked with his daughters on chess, and they cited the Talmud as dictating that Jewish parents should be the child's first teachers. Sometimes the demands on family resources are so great that even when more than one child shows potential, only one is helped to develop. When one is a boy and the other a girl, all too often only the boy is nurtured.[15]

The most extreme cases of child-centered families occur when the child's gift is in a performance domain such as athletics, or even music and chess. In these families, the child is being groomed for a public performance: an athletic event, a recital, a chess competition. Bloom's future pianists, swimmers, and tennis players came from more child-centered families than did the sculptors, neurologists, and mathematicians. The music and athletic parents (usually the mother) drove their children often considerable distances to lessons and athletic events. Parents sat with their children when they practiced the piano. Sometimes families even moved to be near the best teachers. Families made these sacrifices even when they did not have much money.

The story of Tara Lipinski vividly portrays a child-centered family of a skating prodigy. At twelve, Tara was the youngest winner at the Olympic Sports Festival. Her life was wholly organized to support her goal of competing in the 1988 Winter Olympics at age fifteen. Tara may well have been born with unusual athletic talent. But she would probably never have become a prodigy had her family not made extreme sacrifices so that she could get suitable training.

The sacrifices were financial, social, and educational ones. Tara had five 45-minute skating sessions a day, and she frequently traveled to competitions. She had a private tutor two hours each morning, since her demanding schedule precluded attending school. She and her mother lived in Maryland so that Tara could train at an elite training center at the University of Delaware, while her father remained behind in Houston, where he worked. And to cover the staggering costs of skating (coaches' fees, ice time, travel, and skating costumes, plus living expenses—in total about fifty thousand dollars a year), Tara's father transferred to a new job, and the family refinanced their mortgage.

Although Tara's parents disliked living apart, they adamantly believed that their sacrifice was for a higher good. "I'd give my daughter anything," her mother said. "She loves it. And we're seeing results. I can't just demand that she stop. For the rest of my life, I'd have to sit around and think, 'What if, what if?' " Her father sounded an equally sacrificing note: "You have a child and you want to do everything for that child that you can possibly do."[16]

Academically and artistically gifted children also typically come from child-centered homes. Parents of academically talented children sometimes make their children's precocity a performance by parading them on talk shows and allowing them to be written up in the press as wunderkinds. Like music and athletic families, such families may move so that their children can attend the best schools or can attend college at an early age. For instance, the family of Michael Kearney (chapter 2) moved to Alabama so the six-year-old, accompanied by his mother, could attend college. Even those academically gifted children whose parents do not make their children into showpieces usually have highly child-centered homes. In Wales, a mother of four prodigies spent every waking hour with her children, with the conscious intention of stimulating their development.[17]

As a young child, Adam, mentioned above as he walked in the woods, was almost always in the care of one or both parents. Adam's need to acquire information was his parents' highest priority. When he went to school, his parents tried to shape that environment as well, as can be seen from the following excerpts from a letter written by his mother to the director of Adam's first school. Speaking of her four-and-a-half-year-old, she wrote:

> Adam will absorb content and fact effortlessly when that content is interesting and relevant to a wider learning experience. . . . His requirements in teaching personnel are for persons of the greatest degree of professional competence so that the theoretical as well as the specifics, the developmental, historical, the possible as well as the known and the scope as well as the praxis of any field can be a part of this work with these skilled mentors. . . . Adam does not, I think, need to pursue a unit on the Eskimo, land and people. Rather I believe that it makes sense for him to have access to anthropologists, cross-cultural psychologists, economists, political historians, geographers, folklorists, [and] psychiatrists . . . so that he may inquire, explore, question, and perhaps, finally, begin to comprehend the nature of the society of humans. . . . To enclose him in the preconceived limits of a customary educational experience is to deprive him of what he needs.[18]

Not surprisingly, no teacher or mentor was ever able to give Adam the intensity of focus his parents demanded. Only his parents could provide this. Like the fathers of John Stuart Mill and Thomas Edison, many parents of academically gifted children in our culture believe that they can do a better job of educating their children than can the schools. And so they turn their backs on conventional education in favor of home schooling.

A few reports exist of similar kinds of family-centeredness in the families of children gifted in the visual arts. As mentioned, Picasso's father devoted himself to his son's artistic development; and the father of Wang Yani has devoted himself to his daughter's artistry. But in both of these cases, the father was already an artist. In most families of artistically gifted children, the parents are not themselves artists. These families do not reorganize their time and energies around their child's artistic endeavors. Instead, they simply give their artistically inclined children the space and the time to pursue their artistic endeavors on their own. In so doing, they convey to their children that such endeavors are worthwhile.[19]

The fact that parents spend an enormous amount of time with their gifted child, and thereby foster the development of talent, does not mean that parents *create* their child's giftedness. The gift makes itself known first. Parents notice signs of exceptionality in their child, and then respond by devoting themselves to the development of this exceptionality.

Modeling and Setting High Standards

High achievement seems almost never to occur without at least one parent (or parent surrogate) who both models hard work and pushes the child to work hard. More often it is the mother who pushes, at least in our culture. (According to one informal source, both parents in China play an equally strong role.) For instance, a study of the lives of eminent adults revealed that one-fourth of those studied had mothers who pushed, but only one-twentieth had fathers who did so. These ambitious mothers also firmly believed that their children would succeed, and they conveyed this belief to their off-spring. The strong role of the mother is also evident in the stories told by gifted black science students admitted to the Meyerhoff Scholarship program at the University of Maryland in Baltimore County. These students are just as likely to come from noneducated homes as educated ones. Nonetheless, they all come from close families who value achievement, and most report that they owe much of their success to their mothers' high expectations and unflagging belief in their potential.[20]

Parents of children who get identified as gifted believe in work before play. They disapprove of wasting time, doing sloppy work, and shirking responsibility. They model these values themselves by working hard and by engaging in active kinds of leisure. When the parents in Bloom's study relaxed, they carpentered, gardened, sewed, engaged in sports, read, played music, or developed photographs; they did not channel surf on television. Children in these families were not allowed to be bored, idle, and passive. They learned the value of daily work. Tara's father revealed what he valued when he said that the most important thing his daughter was learning was that hard work pays off. Tara's mother made it clear to Tara that she must work to her utmost every day at practice, and that she must earn all A's on the exams she took long distance in connection with a Houston school. Josh Waitzkin's father said that Josh probably would not have worked so hard at chess if he had not been there to urge him on, and noted that all of the top chess players have had at least one parent behind them, encouraging, worrying, and pushing them to win. Parents of "underachieving" gifted children tend to have parents who do not set high standards.[21]

Parents must practice what they preach. Parents who push their children to achieve, but who are not themselves hard workers, have considerably less influence on their children's achievement than do parents who both expect a great deal and accomplish much themselves. But note that this could be genetically mediated: hardworking parents may have high abilities to pass on.

Parents must not only achieve but also have time for their children. Nobel Prize winners are likely to have little time for their children, while parents who achieve less—who are successful but do not reach the peaks—may in fact prove the most effective parents. Similarly, parents who value achievement but who were themselves deprived of the opportunity to achieve, as in some immigrant groups, often pour all their energies into their children's accomplishments and end up with high-achieving offspring.[22]

Although gifted children grow up in families who set high

standards, just how directive the families are seems related to the kind of gift the child has. Families of children in performance domains like music and athletics are the most directive, families of children in visual arts are the least directive, and families of academically gifted children are in between.

This difference can be seen in the families studied by Bloom. Take the families of the future pianists. These parents were almost always involved with music themselves, either actively (they played instruments themselves) or passively (they attended concerts, listened to music at home). In all but two of the cases studied, it was the parents, not the children, who decided to initiate piano lessons. And the parents were very involved in the day-to-day piano playing of their children. A third of them sat in on the lessons, taking notes to be sure that the child would follow instructions in later practice sessions. And half sat next to their young children and supervised them as they practiced. The value placed on practicing and the parents' active role in ensuring that it happened are revealed in these words of one mother: "We always had our vacations, but never any break time from [lessons and practice]." They did not let their children get away with sloppy playing, and they gave them strong approval for hard work at the piano.[23]

The families of the sculptors Bloom studied were far more free-spirited. First, with one exception, they were not themselves artists. About half were interested enough in art to go to museums. A fourth knew little about art but saw it as worthwhile, and another fourth had no particular appreciation of art. These parents did not steer their children into art the way the music parents steered their children into piano lessons. The message that they conveyed to their children was that it is important to work at whatever one likes and to work to the best of one's ability. Self-fulfillment was the message, not academic achievement (these parents cared little about their children's schoolwork). When these children began making it clear that what fulfilled them was working with their hands, drawing, and making things, their parents supported them. Half helped their children find special museum classes, and the half who did not at least did not discourage their children's artistic inclinations. But none set aside special time when their children *had* to work at art: there were no art practices. The children were not groomed to win prizes at art shows. Instead, they were just allowed and encouraged to make art whenever they wanted to.

The families of Bloom's academically gifted children fell in between the directive music families and the self-actualizing sculptor families. The parents of those who became mathematicians valued working hard at school and achieving academic success. While the parents of the future sculptors stressed self-fulfillment, the parents of the future mathematicians stressed academic achievement. However, like the parents of the sculptors, the parents of the mathematicians did not try to steer their children into math. When their children excelled in math, the parents were pleased and made it known that math was a valued intellectual pursuit. Other studies of the families of academically gifted children converge: parents in these families do not steer their children into a particular domain, but do clearly convey a love of learning and of intellectual inquiry and achievement.

These differences in family directiveness make sense. To achieve in a performance domain, one must submit to rigorous and early training. On their own, even highly gifted children might be unlikely to stick to such a grueling regimen, despite their rage to master. As mentioned earlier, very few of the twenty pianists studied by Bloom went to the piano to practice voluntarily as children. Families of visually artistic children are probably the least directive because of the low value our culture places on becoming an artist. Or perhaps they share personality characteristics with their relatively nondisciplined artistic children. Families who are very involved when their children are young, like the families of musicians and athletes, face the challenge of letting go and granting independence later on. Parents who have been so directive often find letting go very difficult.[24]

The powerful influence of parental expectations cuts across socioeconomic levels. In studies of disadvantaged adolescents who were academically gifted, as measured by high scores on both the math and verbal portions of the SAT, it was found that in every case, the families played a pivotal role. The families, whether the parents or grandparents, all monitored their children's academic performance and not only encouraged but also pushed: they made it clear that the children were to work hard and achieve what their parents had not. Among academically gifted black science students selected for the Meyerhoff Scholarship program, almost all of these teenagers have a parent who believed in their ability to achieve. As mentioned earlier, in most cases, this parent is the mother.[25]

It might be argued that parents' high expectations play no causal role at all. People who are talented and driven in some area may have children who are also talented and driven, not because of high parental expectations or hardworking parental role models, but rather because they have inherited their parents' ability and drive. None of the studies of giftedness and the family have proper control groups. So we do not know the influence of high expectations and parental pushing on children selected at random. However, findings from adoption studies discussed earlier showing a genetic component to IQ would support the hypothesis that pushing alone is not enough; a purely genetic explanation remains logically possible.

But cultural comparisons provide a kind of control group and support the environmental position that high expectations of parents play some causal role in their children's high achievement. One telling comparison is that between academic performance levels of American and Japanese children. In first grade little difference exists between these two groups in math. But by fifth grade, there is virtually no overlap. Japanese students have soared ahead. There is no reason to attribute the superior performance of the Japanese to higher ability, since in first grade there is considerable overlap in the math scores of American and Japanese children. Hungary provides another cultural comparison, for there all children are reading by the middle of first grade, and the math accomplishments of Hungarian children are far higher than those of American children. The explanation must be cultural. Japanese and Hungarian parents (and teachers) have much higher expectations for their children than do American parents. Whenever a culture values high achievement in a domain and sets high expectations, children achieve higher-than-average levels. This phenomenon can also be seen in the performance levels of Asian immigrants to the United States, in the drawing levels attained by average Chinese schoolchildren, and in the violin performance levels attained by Japanese children trained in the Suzuki method. The exceedingly low achievement expectations that contemporary American parents have for their children are associated with disturbingly low achievement levels in comparison with those in many other cultures.[26]

Granting Independence

Parents of gifted, high-achieving children expect a high level of performance and monitor their children to make sure they are making continual progress. But these parents are rarely rigid, domineering, and authoritarian. Valuing and nurturing independence in their children, these parents expect their children to make decisions for themselves and even to take some risks.

The desire to achieve seems to come not from being driven but from being given the chance to master challenges on one's own. Children who are given no autonomy to pursue their own interests often stop achieving as soon as they can escape the parental pressure.[27]

The value placed on independent development can be seen at its most extreme in the parents of children gifted in the visual arts in our culture. As mentioned, in Bloom's study, these parents provided supplies, space, and encouragement but left their children alone to do art if and when they pleased.

Parents who grant their children autonomy while at the same time setting clear standards have been described as authoritative, in contrast to authoritarian. Authoritarian parents are rigid and dictatorial; authoritative ones convey a clear set of moral standards but respect their children's independence and tolerate early errors. Studies with nongifted children have shown that the most effective families in terms of child outcomes are those that are authoritative rather than either authoritarian or permissive.[28]

Again, the causality question can be raised. Do the parents of gifted children encourage independence because they recognize high ability in their children, or does the encouragement of independence lead to high achievement, just as the discouragement of independence may lead to low achievement? An experiment in which children of equally high ability were randomly assigned to different kinds of upbringing could answer this question, as could studies of achievement in cultures that discourage independence in children.

While it is certainly likely that a parent's recognition of high ability in a child may lead the parent to grant the child independence, it seems just as likely that encouragement of independence in a high-ability child, along with high standards, leads to an intrinsic motivation to achieve. Domination can lead to rebellion, resentment, and disaffection.

Stimulation and High Standards, Harmony and Nurturance

Families of gifted children are usually described in glowing terms as harmonious, loving, and warm. These families are more cohesive and less conflictual than those of nongifted children. (As noted in chapter 10, this generalization does not hold for the subset of gifted children who go on to become highly creative in their domains as adults.) Most of Bloom's high achievers came from families that had remained intact at least throughout the achievers' childhoods. Other researchers too have shown that families of gifted children have lower-than-average divorce rates. However, in a recent study of high-IQ children, no difference in divorce rates between gifted and nongifted children's families was found. This finding is likely due to the overall rise in divorce rates, a trend that may bode ill for the development of talent if family cohesion plays a causal role.[29]

Perhaps because their families are more harmonious, gifted children have more positive relationships with their parents than do children in control groups. And in at least one study, extremely high IQ children were found to have far more positive feelings about their families than they did about school. These children do not typically rebel against their parents, but rather tend to incorporate their parents' values. Other studies have shown that high-achieving children tend to have affectionate parents, while low achievers tend to have rejecting, hostile parents.[30]

When familial warmth and nurturance are combined with stimulation and high expectations, the optimal setting for the development of talent is created. This critical combination was demonstrated in Mihaly Csikszentmihalyi's longitudinal study of teenagers talented in math, science, visual art, music, and athletics.[31]

Csikszentmihalyi's families fell into four separate groups. "Differentiated" families provided a great deal of stimulation but little support. "Integrated" families provided emotional support with little stimulation. "Complex" families provided both stimulation and support, while "simple" ones provided neither. These four types of families were not distinguished in terms of other factors such as socioeconomic level, family size, marital status, ethnicity, or religious background; nor were they distinguished in terms of characteristics of their children such as sex, talent area (art, music, math, science, athletics), or intelligence as measured by the PSAT.

Compared to the three other groups of teenagers, those from complex families were the most fortunate. They were the happiest, as measured by the moods they experienced and reported eight times a day for a week. They reported higher levels of alertness and greater levels of goal directedness. They more often experienced states of flow when involved in productive work, and they reported being engaged in challenging activities involving high skill levels. They spent more time in study and homework, and with one telling exception, they achieved higher levels in their area of talent.

The exception was in the domain of athletics. Here the teenagers from the differentiated families achieved the highest levels. Apparently, teenagers with athletic talent achieve more when they are challenged but not strongly nurtured than when they are both challenged and nurtured. Perhaps this is because energy fueled by anger helps in athletic competitions.

When subjective experience at home was measured, the teenagers from complex families again reported more states of flow and more states of high energy. They preferred interacting with their families to watching TV, even though they spent the same amount of time watching TV as did the other kinds of teenagers. They reported being the most satisfied and feeling that they were living up to their expectations and pursuing important goals. When teacher ratings were considered, teenagers from complex families were reported to have higher levels of concentration than those from simple families. In addition, those from complex families were reported by their teachers to be working up to their potential more often than those from simple families, and to be more independent and original. Teenagers who lost interest in their domain of talent saw their parents as either too intrusive (that is, too differentiated) or too disinterested (that is, too simple). These teenagers had lost their intrinsic motivation to work.

These findings are correlational ones. But assuming that the complexity of the family leads to the outcomes in the teenagers, how can we explain these findings? Csikszentmihalyi argues that family integration leads to positive affect and high energy, while family differentiation leads to willingness to meet great challenges. Children from complex families described their parents as having high expectations but as giving them great freedom. They described exactly the kind of authoritative families studied by Bloom who challenged but provided support.

WHEN PARENTS PUSH TOO HARD

In an oft-cited book called *The Hurried Child*, the psychologist David Elkind makes a strong case against too much parental pushing at an early age. Taking the opposite tack, another psychologist, William Damon, has argued that American parents' expectations are far too low, and that we push our children too little.[32]

While I side with Damon in the view that we need to hold all of our children to much higher standards, it is also true that parents who push too hard, who do not nurture the "whole child" but care only about their child's gifts and are overly critical and demanding, can end up with disengaged, depressed, resentful children. Gifted children who stop achieving in response to excess parental pressure will, of course, never be included in a retrospective study such as Bloom's. Although retrospective studies like Bloom's show us that parental pushing and high expectations are typically associated with high achievement, such studies cannot show us whether too much pushing results in stunted, underachieving children. Only prospective studies can tell us this.

Many famous adults have indeed reported that they were pushed to extremes by their parents and as a result were scarred for life. John Ruskin had a domineering mother and suffered breakdowns as an adult, though mood disorders also ran in his family. John Stuart Mill's father pushed him mercilessly and allowed him no holidays, lest he break the habit of daily hard work. Mill experienced a serious depression at twenty (though mood disorders also ran in his family). The mathematician and inventor of cybernetics, Norbert Wiener, had a father who disciplined him in everything, granted him no independence, and never allowed him to have a "casual" interest. Wiener entered college at eleven, graduated at fourteen, and earned a doctorate from Harvard at eighteen. But he was often depressed in young adulthood, and he felt handicapped throughout his life. Wiener wrote poignantly in his autobiography about how he felt oppressed by his father:

> Every mistake had to be corrected as it was made. He would begin the discussion in an easy, conversational tone. This lasted exactly until I made the first mathematical mistake. Then the gentle and loving father was replaced by the avenger of the blood.

Pushing too much often occurs in the families of musical prodigies, when parents derive vicarious pleasure from their children's public fame and push them on to more and more performances. Some music schools believe that even prodigies should not be pushed too young to perform publicly. Pushing a prodigy to work all the time can also be damaging. Yeou-Cheng Ma, the older sister of Yo-Yo Ma, studied the violin and was made to practice eight hours a day. "I traded my childhood for my good left hand," she said.[33]

Adragon De Mello is a contemporary example of an extremely academically gifted child who dropped out as a result of a father who pushed him ceaselessly and lived entirely through his son's precocious achievements. Adragon's father told Adragon that he was smarter than his teachers and got him admitted to MENSA, the society for people with high IQs. He taught his son advanced math, forced him to study every waking minute, and enrolled him in college-level math courses at age eight. Adragon was doing calculus by age nine, as well as writing screenplays. He skipped grades and graduated from college in three years with a math major at age eleven.

Adragon's mother eventually left his father and gained custody of her then twelve-year-old son. She tried to reverse everything the father had done. Her goal was to give her son the childhood he had never had. So she enrolled him in Little League, and although he already had a college degree, she put him in the local public junior high school. Probably in reaction to his father's excessive pushing, Adragon had lost all interest in scholarly activity. His schoolwork became unexceptional. He replaced his Einstein posters in his bedroom with baseball cards and posters of comic book characters. He hid his unusual past and tried to blend in with the crowd. "If I could go back in time, I would," he said. "I'd like to go back and live normally."[34]

Adragon's relation with his father calls to mind a famous and sad case, that of William James Sidis. William James was born to a psychologist father, Boris Sidis, who believed fervently that the brain is most capable of learning in the first few years of life. When his son was born in 1898, Boris tried out his theories on the child, whom he named after the pioneering psychologist William James (who almost surely would not have approved of Boris's methods). Boris Sidis was a colleague of Norbert Wiener's father, and both knew of each other's educational experiments.[35]

Boris Sidis drove his son mercilessly. He disapproved of all nonacademic interests. Sports, games, and exploration of nature were all considered trivial. He taught his son to read and spell at the age of two. By three, William could type coherently in both English and French. At five, he wrote an essay on anatomy and had also become a calendrical calculator. Like an autistic savant, he could calculate the date on which any day of the week had fallen within the past ten thousand years. When he entered school at the normal age of six, he sped through seven years of curriculum in half a year. At eight, this math prodigy invented a new table of logarithms. At ten, he could speak six languages. The father continually allowed his son to be pursued by the media, probably to satisfy his own craving for publicity.

At eleven, as a nervous boy in velvet knickers, William James Sidis delivered a lecture on "Four-Dimensional Bodies" to professors and graduate students in math at Harvard, where he was enrolled as a student. This lecture prompted a professor of mathematics at the Massachusetts Institute of Technology, Daniel Comstock, to predict that Sidis would become a world-class mathematician. Seemingly on his way to fulfilling Comstock's prediction, William James Sidis, a mathematics major, graduated *summa cum laude* from Harvard at age fifteen.

However, after this brilliant beginning, everything went downhill. Sidis lost all interest in math after a year in graduate school, entered law school but lost interest in that, and ended up thereafter taking clerical jobs that required neither thought nor responsibility. He amused himself with obsessive hobbies suggestive of autistic behavior. At age twenty-eight, he wrote a book on the classification of the transfer slips that streetcar conductors give to passengers. He could state precisely which transfer slips were needed to reach any street in the United States on a single streetcar fare.

This obsessive and autisticlike interest was surely a strange and sad outcome for such mathematical precocity. Sidis could no longer bear to do any real math. "The very sight of a mathematical formula makes me physically ill. All I want to do is run an adding machine but they [the press] won't let me alone," he was quoted as saying in a 1937 article about him in the *New Yorker*.[36]

Sidis bitterly resented his father, who had driven him, lived through him, and starved him emotionally. He lived in a rooming house, and his landlord described him in the article as having "a kind of chronic bitterness, like a lot of people you see living in furnished rooms." The article went on to describe him as getting "a great and ironic enjoyment out of leading a life of wandering irresponsibility after a childhood of scrupulous regimentation." When he was asked about Comstock's prediction, he smiled and pointed out that he was born on April Fools' Day. He died alone of a brain hemorrhage at age forty-six.[37]

The fathers of Adragon and Sidis are examples of "creator parents," driving parents who live through their children's high achievements. Such parents believe that they have created their child's gift, and they exhibit the child in the media to gain attention themselves. The fathers of Wiener and Mill took credit for their sons' precocity. Adragon's father described his son tellingly as "my greatest accomplishment."[38]

Children of creator parents typically submerge their own personality and become what the parents want them to become. At some level these children probably feel that their parents' love is conditional on their success. The father of Josh Waitzkin had an insatiable desire for his son to win at chess championships, and Josh knew full well that winning was the way to his father's heart. Parents of artistically gifted children may support artistic talent only when it meets the parents' needs, and not when it means that their children may not be able to make a decent living. The psychoanalyst Alice Miller has vividly described such high-achievement–oriented parents in *Prisoners of Childhood*. The children of creator parents have to become the nurturers of their needy parents.[39]

Gifted children of such demanding parents certainly report feeling oppressed and depressed. It is possible, however, that the depression they report is not always the result of a difficult environment, but forms part of the individual's personality and is related to the person's creativity. The relationship between creativity and depression is one to which I return in chapter 10.

While some parents are destructive by overpushing, I have also seen another kind of subtler destructiveness—parents who are never satisfied with their gifted children's schooling, even when they are getting the best, most challenging kind of gifted education our country offers. I have seen such parents repeatedly pull their children out of one school after another, often ending up with home schooling. Such parents strike me as invested in having nothing work for their children. This way they can see their children as brilliant victims, and themselves as saviors.

When pondering how families affect giftedness, we often assume that the relationship is one-way and that the family determines the outcome of the gifted child. But the relationship is two-way, for a gifted child dramatically affects the organization of the family. The presence of a gifted child serves to focus a family's attention and mobilize its resources, just as does the presence of a retarded or handicapped child. One or both parents typically select that child as special, often causing resentment in the other siblings. Parents develop extraordinarily high expectations for the child not only because they themselves have high standards but also because they recognize their child to be gifted. They invest a great deal of energy in seeing that these expectations are fulfilled. Thus, family characteristics that may well profoundly shape the gifted child's development are at least in part initially set in motion by the presence of the gifted child. It is not only the family that creates the child: the child also plays a role in creating the family.[40]

Because children who are pushed too hard sometimes drop out, the myth has developed that all parents of gifted children drive their children destructively. "Early ripe, early rot" is a proverb that suggests that pushing a child too hard to bloom early will inevitably lead to dropout later on. However, high achievement in any domain is always associated with high standards set by an adult who also models high achievement. What leads some gifted children to disengage from talent is never high expectations, but rather extreme pushing, domination, exploitation, and emotional deprivation.

While we can describe the characteristics of families of gifted children, we should not conclude that these characteristics actually *create* the gifts in the children. We do not know how many children there are with responsive, stimulating, child-centered families who never made it, because most studies have started with children who succeeded and then have looked back retrospectively at their families. We certainly all know of such cases. The family characteristics described here are ones that can keep a gift alive, nourish it, or kill it. But families cannot themselves create the gift.

Eight

SO DIFFERENT FROM OTHERS: THE EMOTIONAL LIFE OF THE GIFTED CHILD

Hillary, a twelve-year-old living in a small rural community in Maine, is an academically gifted child. She has no siblings. The social and emotional aspects of her life are characteristic of children gifted not only in academics but also in the arts.

A straight-A student, she was selected for the gifted and talented program in her local public school in the third grade. Students who qualified were pulled out of their normal classroom each week for several hours of enrichment, in which they were engaged in various kinds of projects such as writing and acting. At age eleven, she took a test to determine whether she qualified for the Center for Talented Youth (CTY), a summer program like SMPY, but one not limited to math. Only those who have already scored at or above the ninety-seventh percentile on an academic achievement test are even qualified to take the test for CTY. Of the ten thousand already top students who qualified to take the test, Hillary scored in the top 10 percent, and her verbal score was the highest in the state of Maine. That summer she attended a six-week program of courses at CTY. A year later, on school-administered standardized tests, she scored in the ninety-ninth percentile nationally in all subjects: reading, language, mathematics, social studies, and science.

Like all other academically gifted children, Hillary reads omnivorously, and it is adult books that she reads. When she became interested in Freud's views about women, she checked out library books not about but *by* Freud. When she discovered her partly Jewish roots, she devoured books on Jewish history. She is hooked on the TV show *Night Court* and reads every article she can find about the prosecutor in this show. When I met her, she was in the midst of reading six books (both fiction and nonfiction), including the biographies of various actors. Hillary thrives on doing several things at once. Not only can she keep many books in her head at the same time, but she also typically has the TV on while reading or doing homework. Neither reading nor homework appears to suffer.

Hillary is probably most gifted in the verbal arena, and her interests reflect this. She wants to be a director and an actress. She studies musicals on videotape, attends plays whenever she can, critiques the directing and the acting in whatever she watches, and is a connoisseur of the style and approach of many directors. The desire to be a director is an unusual one for a person so young. But the clear sense of where she is going (even if she ultimately ends up going in a different direction) is, as discussed later in this chapter, typical of adolescents with any kind of exceptional ability, whether in an academic or an artistic domain. These youth have a strong sense of their abilities and interests, and they are highly goal directed.

Hillary is a nonconformist. This fact first emerged in her play interests as a young child, when she resisted playing with dolls. As an adolescent today, she has no interest in boys or clothes, and she has a certain amount of disdain for the mainstream culture. She looks down on materialism and does not like to spend money. She became a vegetarian at twelve, and she proudly considers herself to be a tomboy and a feminist. A moral critic of the society around her, she is particularly concerned about any unfair, discriminatory treatment of girls. While acting in a play, she counted the number of lines for boys versus girls and then told her director that the boys had more lines.

Consistent with her strongly independent views and values, Hillary is often critical of her teachers. When she attended Sunday school at age six, she was taught that Jesus watches over everyone, but that those who do not obey the Bible go to hell. She came home ready to "tell off" her teacher for spouting what she called "fairy tales." In the third grade, during a lesson on the distinction between facts and opinions, she challenged her teacher's statement that it was a matter of *opinion* that George Washington planted a cherry tree. Hillary argued reasonably that this should count as a fact, since there is some evidence in support of it. After all, she insisted, saying that Washington planted a cherry tree is the kind of thing that *could* be proven; it is not like stating that red is nicer than blue, which would certainly be just an opinion. Hillary was grappling with the distinction between the truth or falsity of a factual statement, on the one hand, and a subjective opinion, on the other. This distinction was lost on her teacher, who said that the book said it was an opinion, and therefore it was an opinion. Far from cowed, Hillary lost her respect for this teacher, who gave her a B. Hillary told me that this teacher hated her simply because she refused to comply.

Even in the CTY summer program, she questioned her teachers. Hillary felt that her drama teacher was unwilling to entertain alternative interpretations of Shakespeare. "How do critics *know* what Shakespeare meant?" she challenged in class. "Maybe he meant just what he said." But echoing her third-grade teacher, the drama teacher said that the interpretation she, the teacher, was pushing came from scholars who knew what they were talking about. Hillary's independent thinking exasperated the teacher even in a program in which one would expect students to be encouraged to challenge authority. "They say everything we do is great," she said of her teachers at CTY, "so that we will all come back next summer." The standards she set for herself were higher even than those set at a highly competitive summer program.

Hillary's nonconformism and dominant personality made her a natural leader. She had a big influence on her local school, and in the CTY program she was picked as the lead speaker in debates and the director of plays. Hillary clearly thrives on being in control.

But being looked up to is not the same as having intimate friends. Since Hillary is so different from most of her peers, she does not have close friends. She has no classmates in her small rural school who are even remotely like her. She is acutely aware of how different she is from her peers. She perceives the other girls in her school as interested only in boys and clothes, while she prides herself on liking "research projects" such as studying the Aztecs, the Ukraine, ants, or astronomy. The gifted and talented program in her school was no help to her on the social end: she called the other, more moderately gifted students in this program boring "goodie-goodies." They did not share Hillary's passion for learning.

Hillary likes being different, and she does not mind being alone much of the time. This is a typical story. Gifted youth spend more time alone than average youth. While they feel happier when with others (as most people do), they do not mind solitude as much as most. Hillary would like to find a soul mate in her school, but the only time she ever made friends with people like herself was when she attended the CTY summer program. The most important and influential aspect of that summer experience was finding other "odd kids," to use Hillary's words.

Hillary is driven; she has a strong sense of her identity; she is independent, strong-willed, and nonconforming; and she spends a great deal of time alone, without a close friend to confide in. This social and personality profile is typical of children gifted in all domains—academic areas, art, music, athletics, chess, and so on.

A NEW MYTH REPLACES THE OLD

As noted in earlier chapters, Terman prided himself on having dispelled the myth of the high-IQ child as a clumsy and nearsighted "nerd," friendless, bullied, and teased. Terman believed strongly that his high-IQ subjects were advanced not only cognitively but also socially and emotionally. Parents and teachers in Terman's study rated children on traits such as leadership, popularity, freedom from vanity and egotism, sympathy and tenderness, fondness for large groups, social adaptability, emotional stability and common sense, and honesty and dependability.

But Terman went too far in his claims for the glowing psychological health and adjustment of the gifted child. One of the pioneers in the field of gifted education, Leta Hollingworth, pointed out the special social and emotional problems faced by the profoundly gifted high-IQ child. While most gifted children are socially and emotionally well adjusted, a rather substantial minority of the gifted do have social and emotional problems that stem from the consequences of being gifted. The ones who face the most problems are those with the most extreme gifts. It is estimated that about 20 to 25 percent of gifted children have social and emotional difficulties, a rate about twice as high as one finds in populations of schoolchildren at large.[1]

This percentage is not to be taken lightly. And yet the myth of the gifted child as glowing with psychological health persists today. The typical article or textbook on giftedness is still likely to echo Terman and assert that gifted children are popular, well adjusted, and self-confident. While Terman found his subjects to be well adjusted, note that he studied a select group—those nominated by their teachers as potential subjects. Troubled, dreamy, or rebellious students may not have been seen by their teachers as gifted. Note also that educators who hold this view tend to be people who work with children selected for gifted programs rather than gifted children who underachieve, drop out, or become behavior problems in the classroom.[2]

Children with exceptionally high ability in any area face certain kinds of social and emotional problems just by virtue of being out of step with their peers. These children have a different personality profile from the average child, and the quality of their emotional and social lives is in many ways distinct. While these children and adolescents are by no means all "troubled," those with the highest levels of giftedness do face social problems that lead to emotional pain.

THE RIGHT PERSONALITY STRUCTURE FOR MASTERY

There are three particularly notable ways in which the personality structure and social and emotional experience of the gifted differ from the norm. The first has to do with work: gifted children are highly motivated to work to achieve mastery, they derive pleasure from challenge, and, at least by adolescence, they have an unusually strong sense of who they are and what they want to do as adults. The second has to do with value structures: they are fiercely independent and nonconforming. And the third has to do with relationships with peers: they tend to be more introverted and lonelier than the average child, both because they have so little in common with others and because they need and want to be alone to develop their talent. These qualities of thought and feeling add up to a kind of subjective experience that is both more pleasurable and fulfilling, and more painful, isolating, and stressful than that of the average child.

Work

Motivation and Enjoyment of Challenge

Josh Waitzkin, the chess prodigy who is the subject of the book and movie *Searching for Bobby Fischer*, studied chess at age six as intensively as a college student studies for a comprehensive exam. Michael Kearney's father described Michael as having an unquenchable "rage" to learn. Recall that upon his father's return from work in the late afternoon, Michael used to greet his father with his math books and beg to work with his father on his math. The prodigies described by David Feldman and Lynn Goldsmith all were distinguished by their passion to achieve excellence in their area of talent.[3]

We have already seen how gifted children are highly motivated to achieve and how they can persevere in hard work. They are also more likely than average children to be motivated for intrinsic, rather than extrinsic, reasons: they work because they love doing so, not because they have to. "There was never a time in my life when I did not want to do math," said Aleksandr Khazanov, a fifteen-year-old Westinghouse Science Talent Search finalist in 1995.[4]

High ability may well lead to the belief, shared by most gifted children, that effort pays off. Although they might attribute their achievement to talent, they do not, probably because they all work so hard. Gifted children are far more likely than average ones to believe that what they have achieved came from hard work and effort, not luck or genes. Underachieving gifted children, in contrast, attribute their difficulties to external causes like fate. This is not surprising, since we are all far more likely to attribute our successes to our intentional efforts and our failures to rotten luck.[5]

Gifted children also work hard simply because they enjoy doing so. Mihaly Csikszentmihalyi pioneered a systematic way of sampling the subjective experience of gifted individuals at work. Adolescents who had shown high levels of ability and achievement in five domains—math, science, art, music, and sports—were studied through use of an ingenious method. Each student wore an electronic pager for one week, which beeped at random intervals. Whenever the pager beeped, students filled out a self-report booklet, recording in minute detail what they were doing, thinking, and feeling. This method, the Experience Sampling Method (ESM), is likely to be much more accurate than retrospective interviews, since the ESM catches people in the midst of experience and asks for an immediate self-evaluation.

The reports that the gifted youth gave in this study showed that they enjoyed working in their talent domain. Indeed, many reported higher enjoyment when involved in work in their domain than when involved in any other activity. Challenges difficult enough to cause most people anxiety, and to cause most people to quit, were ones that these youth found most enjoyable. These adolescents achieved "flow" states from the activities that lead to talent development: when working in their domain of talent, they reported high concentration, ease of concentration, and loss of self-awareness—just those qualities that characterize states of flow.

Flow states are critical to the development of talent. When in a flow state, one is mastering challenges that are neither too easy nor too difficult. Mastery of each challenge leads to mastery of a higher level of challenge. According to Csikszentmihalyi, the kind of person who is able to achieve flow is characterized by high curiosity, achievement and endurance, openness to experience, and strong attunement to sensory information. The gifted youth in his study fit this profile exactly.

Not only did Csikszentmihalyi's talented youth derive pleasure from work, but they spent a great deal of time at it.

On average, they spent 13 percent of their waking hours at work in their area of talent, which means about thirteen hours a week. This translates to over two hours a day. Two hours a day, seven days a week, spent in activities that lead to the development of skill is in fact a considerable amount of time and leads to high performance levels. (Such a rate adds up to 728 hours a year, which comes to 91 eight-hour workdays.) In addition, these teens spent more time than average teens on *structured* leisure activities. While their nontalented peers amused themselves by "hanging out," talented teens spent their leisure time often with others but engaged in activities related to their domain of talent—for instance, studying, programming computers, collecting stamps, or just "thinking." Time spent in structured leisure activities is more likely to lead to skill development than is time spent in passive, unstructured activity.

Setting High Standards

As a very young child, Hillary loved to take her grandmother's jar of miscellaneous buttons and sort the buttons into precise piles distinguished by size, material, and color. She showed a strong need for order and precision. She wanted to get those piles just right, and she did not stop until she did. In her grandfather's words, "She doesn't direct an eye on something that interests her; she directs a laser beam." Gifted children are well known to be perfectionists. The term *perfectionism* has a negative ring to it, suggesting someone never satisfied with his or her work or even paralyzed by the fear of not achieving perfection. But being a perfectionist could well be a good thing if it means having high standards, for high standards ultimately lead to high achievement.[6]

Self-Esteem About Work

The one area in which the gifted consistently show high self-esteem is in the area of work and school. Most studies find that the academic self-concept of the high-IQ child is positive and is higher than that of ordinary children, though in Csikszentmihalyi's study, the talented adolescents showed only normal positive scores on academic self-concept. Csikszentmihalyi's subjects, however, no matter what their domain of talent, all had a clear sense of identity and a much stronger sense of what they wanted to become as adults than did the comparison group of average teens. Such confidence in one's abilities probably derives both from having supportive parents and from the experience of seeing that one is often right when others, including teachers, are wrong.[7]

High academic self-esteem is more common among gifted boys than girls, perhaps because girls in our society are more conflicted about achieving. Males gifted in science in Csikszentmihalyi's study had higher-than-average confidence in their academic and intellectual abilities, while females in science scored at the low end of the normal range. And another study found that while academically gifted boys had higher academic self-esteem than did average boys, gifted girls did not differ from their nongifted counterparts.[8]

Csikszentmihalyi also uncovered some differences among the various kinds of talent. The most striking contrast was between the male science students and all the others. As mentioned, the male science students had very high self-confidence about their abilities, and all other groups were close to average, with the exception of males in music, art, and math, who expressed somewhat lower-than-average confidence about their abilities. Perhaps males in the arts are insecure because they are perceived as working in "nonmale" domains; perhaps males in math are insecure because they are perceived as "nerds," though I would expect males gifted in science also to be perceived as nerds.

Feeling positive and confident about one's abilities is clearly associated with high performance, just as feeling poorly about one's abilities is linked to low levels of achievement. As one might expect, gifted children who "underachieve" have low academic self-concepts, as do gifted children diagnosed with learning disabilities.[9]

It is tempting to assume that high levels of confidence about one's abilities lead one to work hard and hence achieve. Then we could foster high levels of achievement simply by helping children believe that their work is excellent. All too often, this is what our schools do. Teachers feel that the most important thing they can give their young pupils is self-esteem, and just about any work that is done is praised as excellent. But children know that when everything is equally praised, praise means nothing. When all work is equally valued, what motivation is there for the child to strive for excellence? The excessive focus on self-esteem in our schools can be a destructive force.[10]

It is more likely the other way round—that high achievement leads to confidence in one's abilities. And thus, the best thing we can do to foster high ability is to set high standards of excellence. Students who gain skill will then develop confidence, which in turn will keep them motivated to keep working. When six-year-old Peter B. (chapter 4) was invited to submit a drawing for a contest, he refused because the drawings were not going to be returned. He told his teacher that he did not need anyone to tell him whether his drawing was good, because in his heart his drawing had already won, and that was good enough for him.

Independence of Thought and Values

No matter what the domain of gift, children with high ability typically are independent, self-directed, willful, dominant nonconformists (as measured by both parent and teacher evaluations). These children are not passive goody-goodies. They are often difficult to be around because they want to "run the show." Yet this same quality also makes them most interesting and stimulating to be around.

Autonomy, Will, and Nonconformity

Self-confidence in one's abilities leads to independence of thought. Hillary prides herself on being different, in particular, in having a different set of values from those of the mass culture. Gifted children in all areas seem to march to their own drummer. They are argumentative, they do not "suffer fools gladly," and they often correct others' errors, even if the other is their teacher. These children are able to reject criticism if they perceive the criticism as silly, just as they are able to criticize their teachers if they perceive themselves to be more able than their teachers.[11]

Recall how Hillary argued with her teacher about the nature of facts versus opinions, and how she came home from Sunday school disdainful of the fairy tales her teacher had tried to put over on her. Josh Waitzkin at first rejected formal chess instruction because he wanted to invent his own strategies. Jacob (chapter 4) battled constantly with his music teacher to play the guitar "his way." At the time of this writing, Jacob had quit taking lessons. Whenever a school rule seemed silly to Jacob, he insisted on asking for its justification. And Peter B. refused to submit to the school curriculum, insisting on making decorative, rather than standard, letters, and engaging in a nonstop power struggle with his teacher. "Peter wants to call the shots," said the psychologist who administered the Draw-a-Person Test to Peter. Children like this are often difficult to manage in the classroom. They refuse to submit to any task that does not engage them and, as a result, often end up labeled as hyperactive or with an attention deficit disorder.

Perhaps because gifted children reject mainstream values, they reject gender-stereotyped traits as well. Recall how Hillary refused to play with dolls as a young child. She went on to reject an interest in boys and in clothes as an adolescent. Csikszentmihalyi's talented females scored highly on achievement motivation and dominance, two traits typically associated with males, and rejected traditional feminine values such as neatness. The gifted boys in his study scored highly on measures of sensitivity and aesthetic values, two traits typically associated with females, and rejected the stereotypical male trait of physical bravado. The fact that gifted children and adolescents have taken on traits typically associated with the opposite sex, and that they are hence less stereotyped by gender, is a function of the fact that these children follow their own promptings.[12]

It takes strong resistance to our cultural norms to work hard as a child and as a teenager. The independent thinking of gifted children allows them to go against the culture and work to develop their talent. While others hang out, they stay in the studio or sit at the piano or the computer screen. It takes someone who does not particularly care what others think, like Peter B., or who prides herself on being different, as does Hillary, to do this.

Advanced Moral Reasoning

Hillary became a vegetarian at age twelve because of a strong sense that it is not morally right to kill animals. She does not even permit herself to kill a bug. Hillary's intense concern with moral issues is common among children with a high IQ, probably because these children reason about issues and think things through to their logical conclusion. Children with extremely high IQs often have passionate concerns about all kinds of ethical and political issues—injustice, violence, abortion, gun control, nuclear war, pollution, animal rights, and so on. They also reason about moral issues at a level far in advance of their peers.[13]

The advanced levels of moral reasoning in the IQ gifted is part and parcel of their independence of thought and nonconformity. Formal measures of moral reasoning show clearly how advanced these children are. The study of moral reasoning as an aspect of cognitive development was initiated by Jean

Piaget, the Swiss developmental psychologist, and developed considerably further by the psychologist Lawrence Kohlberg in the United States. Kohlberg presented children with ethical dilemmas and asked them to evaluate what ought to be done and why. The most famous of these dilemmas told of a man whose dying wife could be saved only by a drug that was too expensive for the man to buy. The druggist would not give him the drug without full payment. Should he steal the drug?[14]

How people justify their answer reveals a lot about their level of moral thinking. Kohlberg found that young children reason at a "preconventional" level: they are self-centered, think of no higher abstract principles, and obey only to avoid punishment. Later, they reason at a "conventional" level. Here they justify actions on the basis of what the community thinks is the right thing to do. A few make it past the conventional stage and reason at the "postconventional" level, in which answers are justified in terms of universal ethical principles, such as the supreme value of human life. People at this stage talk about how society *ought* to be structured, rather than how it *is* structured.

Children with above-average IQs reason morally at a more advanced level than do children of normal IQs. Fewer than 10 percent of ordinary adults ever reason beyond the conventional level. But some high-IQ elementary school-age children have been shown to reason at the postconventional level. Thus, these children are often able to reason morally at a level that few adults ever attain.[15]

We know nothing about the moral reasoning levels of children gifted in art or music. However, since we know that these children tend to be nonconformists, they may well be like high-IQ children, able to reason at the postconventional level. On the other hand, scoring high on a moral reasoning test may have more to do with being good at verbal and abstract thinking. If so, we would expect to find high-IQ children scoring well (since IQ tests pick out those who are skilled in abstract and verbal thought), but not artistic or musical children.

Advanced moral reasoning is not the same thing as having compassion or taking moral action. The psychologists Anne Colby and William Damon studied people who selflessly devoted themselves to some moral cause. Many of these individuals did not score at a particularly high level on Kohlberg's moral reasoning test. Nor does advanced moral reasoning necessarily translate into a particular moral code. Textbooks about the gifted commonly talk about the moral sensitivity of the gifted child as if this were synonymous with kindness, pacifism, and concern for the environment. But there is no reason to assume that an interest in ethical and moral issues would translate into such "liberal" moral values. Recently I read a news report about a local chapter of MENSA that got itself into trouble by advocating coldhearted killing of the old and the sick. A concern with moral questions can lead to a position either for or against any given issue. While the fascination with ethical issues may come with the territory of a high IQ, the *content* of one's moral code seems far more likely to be determined by the values of one's family.[16]

The very high IQ twelve-year-old son of an acquaintance of mine was a good example of the distinction among the concern for moral questions, the content of one's moral views, and one's level of compassion. This child had for several years been interested in politics and had been intensely concerned with social and ethical issues. His views were best described as libertarian. And according to his father, he had never been particularly compassionate. The shape his political views took seemed in part determined by the desire to be different. He attended a very liberal, progressive school for gifted children, most of whom had the predictable liberal values of families who send their children to progressive schools. Being a self-pronounced libertarian in such an environment was one way to demonstrate independence and nonconformity. But of course, libertarianism is just as much a stance about moral and political issues as is liberalism or socialism.

A concern with social and moral issues, along with the ability to reason things through to their logical conclusion, can lead to anxiety and pessimism. In one study children were asked about whether they thought a nuclear war was possible. The pessimistic children had IQs that averaged 142, while the optimistic ones had IQs averaging 129. In another study, 80 percent of high-IQ children and adolescents said they were more worried than their peers about world problems like war and hunger. And of course, high-IQ children are far more likely to know about world problems, since they read the newspaper more than do their peers. One child (Peter S., described in the next chapter) got so upset about the environment that his parents had to censor all news about pollution.[17]

The Pain and Pleasure of Solitude

Although they may reason about moral dilemmas at a high level, academically gifted children do not stand out on interpersonal sensitivity tests. Nor are they children particularly advanced in social skills. In fact, a high level of moral reasoning could well lead to poor social skills. Children who reason at the postconventional level are likely to be judgmental of those who reason at lower levels, and to feel alienated from peers who think so differently from themselves. And it is in the social arena that gifted children, including those in art or music, suffer the most. Gifted children are often alone and lonely. Yet these children suffer less from solitude than do average children. This is fortunate, for solitude is necessary for the development of talent.[18]

Introversion

Hillary spends a great deal of time alone, and though she wishes she had a soul mate, she also does not mind being alone. This ambivalent attitude about solitude is very typical of the gifted. These children like to be in the company of peers with whom they can relate, but they also do not feel a desperate need to be with just anyone. Although they wish for companionship, they also know how to be alone and how to like being alone, since they enjoy the solitary activity of work.

The formal psychological term for this ability to tolerate solitude is *introversion*, in contrast to *extroversion*. Introverts derive their energy from themselves, they prefer low levels of stimulation from the outside, and hence they often avoid social occasions. They do not make friends easily, they spend a great deal of time alone, and they are less in tune with the values of the dominant culture. Extroverts are the mirror image. Since they derive their energy from other people, they seek out others and make friends easily.[19]

It is not only the high-IQ gifted who are introverted. Csikszentmihalyi found that students talented in math, science, music, art, and athletics all spent more time alone than did his nontalented comparison group. Using the electronic pager method, Csikszentmihalyi discovered that these teens spent about five more hours per week by themselves than did average adolescents.

Some gifted children certainly turn inward because they are ostracized for being so different. But gifted children of all types are also introverted because they know how to be alone, they are able to derive pleasure from solitude, and, most importantly, they need to be alone in order to develop their talent.[20]

Heightened Sensitivity

Gifted children are typically described as acutely sensitive and highly alert, even as infants. One thing this means is that they are extremely observant. Elvis Presley had a perpetually watchful air about him, an acute sensitivity once described as a sensibility as heightened as that of a novelist. Recall that

Hillary's grandfather described her as directing a laser beam on whatever she looked at. Gifted children are also said to be extremely sensitive to stimulation, whether sensory or emotional. Albert Schweitzer almost fainted when he heard the sound of brass instruments for the first time. Rahela (chapter 3) could not stand to see or read anything scary or sad. Even *Charlotte's Web*, a favorite of countless children her age, was too sad for her at age five, and she put down *Winnie the Pooh* because she could not tolerate the sadness when Pooh gets stuck in a tree. Because she feared displays of emotion, there were only a few television shows for children that she would watch. She also overreacted to auditory stimulation. Her mother remembered once uttering with excitement, "Oh look, it's snowing," and was surprised to see her daughter startle sharply from her mother's excited tone of voice.[21]

These descriptions echo the observations of the psychoanalyst Phyllis Greenacre, who described intense visual hallucinatory experiences recalled from childhood by extremely gifted adults. It may be that an exceptionally intense sensory response to the environment characterizes many people with heightened abilities of some kind. This would be consistent with the fact that such people are introverted: introversion and shyness often accompany intense sensory responses. For example, the developmental psychologist Jerome Kagan has found that inhibited children are more excitable and physiologically reactive to threat than are noninhibited children.[22]

Loneliness

The majority of gifted children, especially those who are of moderately high IQ, have only the normal social problems of childhood. But for the most extremely gifted, including those in art and music, being so different from others makes it difficult to relate to the children in whose company they find themselves, usually in a classroom. The artistically gifted Peter B. (chapter 4) had great difficulty fitting in with his classmates, and his teacher kept describing him to his parents as "different" and "unique," though she could not quite pin down his distinctiveness. Musically gifted Jacob and Stephen (chapter 4) both had difficulties relating to other children because their interests were so focused and so different from those of their peers. Musical children studied in England felt that they had to hide their musical interests so as not to be teased. One reported that he was called a "brain-box" because he played the piano: while his peers socialized, he stayed home and practiced and felt acutely embarrassed. Only those in special schools for music felt that their peers understood them. In his autobiography, Norbert Wiener wrote poignantly about the suffering he experienced from having to straddle the adult world and the world of the children about him. Many eminent individuals recall extreme loneliness as children.[23]

The mother of one of Terman's subjects wrote this about her son:

> I have tried very hard to push him out with boys but have not succeeded very well. He has his friends but does not seek the large gatherings. He is fond of his books, his radio which he assembled, a quiet home life.

Even Terman admitted that children with very high IQs faced acute social problems. Terman's subjects who scored 170 or higher on IQ tests were said to have "one of the most difficult problems of social adjustment that any human being is ever called upon to meet." At age fourteen, 60 percent of the boys with such high IQs and 73 percent of the girls were described by their teachers as solitary and as poor mixers. Note that the adolescent girls had more social problems than the boys, probably because being a smart girl was less socially acceptable in adolescent culture at that time than being a smart boy. The teachers felt that these children were alone not because of social ostracism but from preference. However, if a child finds no one like herself to relate to, she may choose solitude while still longing for a soul mate. Interestingly, the adult ratings of these subjects no longer showed any social problems.[24]

Terman's most successful subjects (*success* meant going into the professions) had more positive social relationships than the less successful subjects, as adults. However, as young adolescents, those who were going to go on to become the most successful rated themselves as feeling more different from their classmates, as feeling at more of a social and physical disadvantage, and as having more difficulties entering into social activities and making friends, all in comparison to the group destined to be less successful.[25]

Thus, the social problems of the profoundly high-IQ subjects in Terman's study, or of those who were destined for some reason to be the most successful, seemed to occur primarily at adolescence. Presumably, as adults, these individuals chose their own environments and were able to find others like themselves.

Hollingworth also noted the acute social problems of children with IQs over 160. Moderately gifted children, those whose IQs measure between 125 and 155, were ones she found to be emotionally well balanced. These children had what she called a "socially optimal" IQ level and had no problem making friends. But those with IQs over 160 typically suffered from social isolation. These children were isolated, Hollingworth wrote, because they had the intellect of an adult, along with the body and emotions of a child.[26]

Many other recent studies have confirmed the picture of the socially alienated, highly gifted child. Such children are described as introverted, not liking to mix with others, bossy, unpopular, often teased, anxious, depressed, and insecure. The problems that the gifted have with their peers stand out in sharp contrast to their family relations: as we saw, most have unusually supportive family relations.[27]

Highly gifted children have trouble relating to their peers in part because they have so little in common with them. For one thing, their sensitivity and intensity make them different from others. And they also have very different interests, hobbies, and even play preferences as young children. Recall how Hillary disliked playing with dolls. The children in Terman's study liked chess and puzzles, while their peers preferred playing guessing games and house. One of Terman's seven-year-olds reported reading Gibbon's *Decline and Fall of the Roman Empire.* How could this child, who undoubtedly talked about things far in advance of his peers, using the vocabulary and syntax of an adult, possibly connect to other seven-year-olds?[28]

Not surprisingly, the high-IQ gifted usually have older friends. They are searching for mental, rather than chronological, age equivalents. This solution is not optimal, however, because often older children find such children odd. After all, they are far less mature physically, socially, and emotionally. Moreover, older children are not always the mental equivalents of young gifted children, since gifted children are not just children who develop more quickly than normal, but also ones who develop and think differently from others. Older children may not share the gifted child's intensity of interests and love of challenge.[29]

Gifted children are well aware of being different: they report feeling different, and they report that others see them as different. Most, however, like Hillary, say they are proud of being different. After all, since they reject the dominant values of their culture, why would they want to be like everyone else? The psychoanalyst Anthony Storr, in a book called *Solitude*, described the need of creative individuals to be alone. While solitude is painful, it also has its rewards.[30]

Lowered Social Self-Confidence

Despite taking some pride in being different (which could serve as a good defense mechanism), those who feel the most different also have the fewest friends and the lowest self-esteem about their social relationships. Psychologist Miraca Gross examined the self-esteem of a small group of extremely high IQ children. When she administered the Coopersmith Self-Esteem Scale to twelve of her subjects, seven scored below average on the subscale measuring confidence about relationships with peers. These children reported that they were not popular with children their own age, felt that other children did not follow their ideas, and felt that they were picked on. A number of her subjects were assessed as showing moderate to severe levels of depression. And depression can lead to loss of motivation. Some studies have even shown elevated rates of suicide among the gifted. The reason given is that they cannot cope with failure.[31]

When one looks at peer ratings of popularity, rather than self or teacher ratings, a somewhat different picture emerges. Here the high-IQ gifted receive positive ratings. Perhaps the positive peer ratings are mostly ratings of moderately gifted children rather than the ones who are most extremely gifted and thus most extremely different from others. At any rate, it is noteworthy that gifted children report feeling less popular than would be predicted by their peer ratings. One reason could be that they are more critical or have a higher standard of what counts as a friend and what counts as intimacy, or that they know they do not really have much in common with their friends. Also, perhaps self-report is the best measure of one's social relationships. If a child plays with others, he may appear to be popular, but he may in fact not be terribly well liked. Wiener remarked, "I played a great deal with other boys but I was not greatly welcomed by them."[32]

Whether gifted in art, music, or academics, talented adolescents also lack confidence about their social skills and their potential sexual attractiveness. High-IQ children have a less positive body image than their more average peers. And talented adolescents are more conservative than the average teen in their sexual attitudes, with the exception of female visual artists. Csikszentmihalyi found that girls talented in the visual arts have an open attitude toward sexuality, along with a negative attitude toward their family. They were the most rebellious group of those Csikszentmihalyi studied, rejecting family ties and asserting sexual liberation. Nonconventionality is generally seen as typifying visual artists more than musicians, but why female adolescent artists are more rebellious than male ones is not clear.[33]

Talented adolescents may be more conservative in their sexual attitudes because they feel different and hence feel less confident of their attractiveness. But their conservatism could also be related to their need for solitude in order to develop their talent: perhaps they need to guard against intimate entanglements so that they will have sufficient energy for work. If so, sexual conservatism serves as a form of sublimation, in which sexual energy is channeled into work. This would be consistent with the Freudian view that creative work is made possible by a rechanneling of forbidden sexual energy into productive, socially valued work.[34]

Note that these talented children and adolescents seem to have problems not because of any inherent social and emotional difficulties but rather because they are so different from others. They are "out of synch." If they could find others like themselves, their social problems might well disappear.

Does the Label "Gifted" Itself Cause Problems?

Children labeled as gifted have more social problems than ones not so labeled. For instance, Joan Freeman, a psychologist in England, compared children of high IQ whose parents had joined the National Association for Gifted Children in Britain to children of equally high IQ whose parents had not joined. Presumably parents who join such an association talk freely of their child as gifted. These parents were more likely than the others to describe their children as friendless. Other studies have also found that children labeled as gifted are less well adjusted than equally high-ability children not so labeled. One plausible explanation is that labeling a child as gifted pressures the child to perform as a gifted child and compounds the child's feeling of being different. However, we have no proof that the labeling itself is the cause. Perhaps children who get labeled as gifted are "odder" to begin with. Or perhaps parents who label their children as gifted tend to be parents who pressure their children too much. It could be that it is the pressure from the parents to excel, rather than the label itself, that leads to the problems.[35]

UNDERACHIEVEMENT TO BE "NORMAL"

Academically gifted children often underperform, not only because they are underchallenged but also because they work below their level to win social acceptance. While almost all American children perform at levels lower than they can achieve, given our lax and unchallenging educational system, the gap between ability and achievement may be the greatest for the most gifted, who not only are more unchallenged than the rest but who also must confront the conflict between excellence and intimacy.[36]

Alarmingly, it is girls far more than boys who "dumb themselves down," pretending to know less than they do and underachieving more, as early as the fourth grade. This seems to be because gifted girls have much more trouble socially than do gifted boys. For example, in one study, academically gifted boys were shown to be *more* popular than average ones, while gifted girls were *less* popular than average girls. In fact, the most popular of all four groups were the gifted boys, and the least popular of all were the gifted girls. The gifted boys were perceived as funny, smart, and creative, while the gifted girls were classified as moody, melancholy, self-absorbed, aloof, and bossy. What is seen as leadership in a boy is seen as bossiness in a girl. Perhaps this is because the traits of independence and achievement displayed by the gifted violate the stereotype of the girl so much more than that of the boy. These sex differences in popularity recall Csikszentmihalyi's findings that adolescent boys talented in science showed above average self-confidence in their abilities, while adolescent girls gifted in science came out on the low-normal end.[37]

Girls then are particularly at risk, especially at adolescence, for feeling that they must hide their ability. Miraca Gross notes that all gifted children face a conflict between achieving excellence and finding intimacy and acceptance among peers. If they pursue the route of excellence, they lose intimacy with peers. But if they pursue intimacy, then they must "dumb down" to conform, and hence they lose excellence. Apparently, girls are more likely to choose intimacy over excellence than are boys. Girls with high grade-point averages report more depression, lower self-esteem, and more psychosomatic symptoms than do boys with such grades.

The conflict between intimacy and excellence is also felt acutely by children from minority groups in which it is not "cool" to excel at school. "I'd let the other kids answer . . . and I'd hold back. So I never really got into any arguments, you know, about school and my grades or anything," said one high-achieving black student in a study published in the *Harvard Educational Review*. The anthropologist John Ogbu has argued that this tendency to hide being smart characterizes minorities who came to the United States involuntarily (for example, blacks) in contrast to voluntary immigrants (for example, Cubans or Jews who fled Hitler). Voluntary immigrants come to the United States because they believe they and their children will achieve greater well-being; hence they strive to adopt the culture's values. Involuntary minorities resent the dominant culture and define themselves in opposition to it. [38]

Thus, it is clear that the myth of the popular, well-adjusted gifted child is just that—a myth. Despite having unusually strong and positive family relationships, many of the most gifted children continue to feel different and see their gifted-ness as a social barrier. Three children studied by Gross whose IQs were above 200 agreed, saying poignantly, "It's pretty tough to be me."

THE TRADEOFF BETWEEN SOCIALIZATION AND TALENT DEVELOPMENT

The gifted are socially isolated because they have no one like themselves to relate to. But there is another, more positive reason, too. Gifted children, like those studied by Csikszentmi-halyi, spend less time with friends because they need to spend more time developing skill in their area of talent. They spend so much time practicing the piano, working on science experiments, or drawing that they have less time available for the company of others and less desire for company. Whether spending time alone at work is a defense against intimacy or whether it simply makes it more difficult to achieve intimacy is not clear.[39]

One thing that is clear, however, is that gifted children in all domains do not suffer from being alone as much as do ordinary children. True, many children of extremely high IQ report severe loneliness, and Csikszentmihalyi's teenagers reported a less positive quality of experience overall: they were alone a great deal, and solitude can be painful. Nonetheless, these teens also found solitude less difficult to endure than did their more average peers. The father of Josh Waitzkin noted Josh's conflict between wanting to play with other children and wanting to master chess. "Some days he'd look mourn-fully at the kids on their bikes and lose his concentration, but mostly he didn't seem to notice them." If Josh had found soli-tude and perseverance as difficult as the average child, he would have solved this conflict by spending less time at the chessboard.[40]

⌒

The social and emotional problems faced by the gifted are caused not by their being gifted but by the consequences of their being so different from others. These children see things differently, and they have different interests and values. They face a sharp conflict between intimacy and excellence, due to the dyssynchrony they experience between their high ability and their average emotional development and age-appropriate size. Choosing intimacy, they risk losing their motivation to excel and may disengage from their domain of talent. Choosing excellence, they must face loneliness and isolation. It is only those who are willing and able to choose excellence who have a chance at successfully traversing the route from gifted child to eminent adult.

Although gifted children suffer from isolation, solitude also has its rewards. The hours spent alone, either by choice or not, lead to the development of skills and the acquisition of knowledge that could never be gained by time spent socializing with friends.

Nine

SCHOOLS: HOW THEY FAIL, HOW THEY COULD HELP

The mayor of a city in the process of disbanding its gifted programs was recently quoted as saying: "I don't agree with the concept of more and less gifted. I think that all students can and will learn. We don't want to run a separate system for those *who are perceived to be* brighter" (italics mine).[1]

Gifted programs are on their way out in many cities and states, in the name of egalitarianism. Often the argument against special education for the gifted is that *all* children are gifted. This view has developed as definitions of intelligence have broadened beyond IQ and children's gifts in areas not measured by IQ tests have been recognized. Teachers and administrators argue that all children have strengths and that schools should nurture the strengths in each child. This broad nurturing is a worthy goal, one that all teachers certainly should strive for. But the fact that all children have relative strengths does not mean that all are equally gifted. An egalitarian, anti-elitist ideology has become dominant in our culture, even though our culture is in reality far from truly egalitarian.[2]

This egalitarian ideology buttresses our profound ambivalence about intellectual excellence. We do not mind if someone is a star in music, art, athletics, or chess, because it is not considered shameful to lack skills in these domains. But when some children are classified as academic stars, we *do* mind, because such a classification implies the existence of children who are not as strong academically.[3]

Not only are gifted programs on their way out but what limited resources we do have for education for the gifted we spend on the moderately gifted. The extreme kinds of children described in this book are not well served by the existing programs set up for gifted children.

The parents and children that I studied all faced a crisis of sorts when the children were ready for school. Each child had abilities and desires that ordinary schools could not readily accommodate. Different solutions were adopted by different families. The parents of globally gifted Michael Kearney (chapter 2) accelerated him radically through school so that he graduated from college at age ten. The mother of globally gifted David (chapter 2) worked out an individualized education program for him with his teachers and kept him in a regular classroom with children his own age. The parents of verbally gifted Rahela (chapter 3) sent her to a private school that they felt would be more challenging and more able to meet her needs than the available public school. The parents of mathematically gifted KyLee (chapter 3) had no choice but to enroll him in a traditional public school. However, they urged his teachers to give him extra math challenges. Fortunately, the teachers agreed. In addition, his parents supplemented his education at home with extensive reading and math computer games.

The parents of musically gifted Jacob and visually gifted Peter B. (chapter 4) faced different issues. They did not expect the schools to address their children's artistic and musical gifts. Peter's parents were actually given a report, after Peter scored so highly on the Goodenough Draw-a-Person Test, that said: "Unfortunately, while he is gifted in the artistic domain, this will not be a sufficient qualification for a gifted program. Parents are advised to seek art instruction for this youngster either through Jacksonville University or the services of an art teacher who can facilitate this youngster's extraordinary talent." (The Goodenough test was originally designed as an IQ test, but the tester apparently realized that this test is not in fact a particularly good indicator of IQ.) Despite the recommendation, Peter, like most artistically gifted children, did not take private art lessons and simply drew on his own at home with a great deal of parental encouragement (although at the time of this writing, he was about to enroll in a studio art class taught by an artist). Jacob's parents chose the route typically taken for children with musical gifts and sought out private instrumental instruction.

Here are two other more extreme, but not atypical, school stories, both of which ended up with the children being taken out of the system. First story: At nine, Alex was not faring well in school. According to his mother, his teacher suspected that he might be retarded and asked to have him tested. This was in 1984. To the teacher's astonishment, Alex scored 158 on the Stanford-Binet. The school psychologist described him as "in the very superior range of intellectual ability" and recommended that he be placed in advanced classes with other highly gifted students. But according to his mother, the only thing that Alex's public elementary school was able to do was to group Alex with the six other children classified as gifted and have them "play games" once a week. Most of the children selected for this "pull-out program" would probably have been moderately, rather than profoundly, gifted, since the profoundly gifted are more rare.

As Alex continued through junior and senior high school, he was often disruptive, and most of his teachers did not like him. Their major concern was that he become more "studious." Eventually, his mother removed him from school and enrolled him in a correspondence course to obtain a college-entrance high school diploma. "I took him out of the system, which had no place for him, and he did the rest," she told me. Today, as a young adult, Alex is a successful and entrepreneurial computer graphics designer.

Second story: Peter S. was a child like David and Michael Kearney—profoundly academically gifted in both the verbal and mathematical domains. His profile was typical of other such gifted children: reading and begging to do math (including algebra) at age three; plunging himself deeply into a study of anatomy by reading his mother's college textbooks at age four; then moving on to other intense, idiosyncratic pursuits; and reading ten books at a time by age seven. Peter S.'s mother, Julia, and the hospital staff noticed his startling alertness as a newborn. His parents (who were also extremely precocious as children) immediately realized that their son was bright. But since he was their first child, they did not realize just *how* unusual he was, even when he was found reading at age three.

Peter S.'s family lives in rural Arkansas on a farm. His mother took him to the local elementary school at age three and asked whether there might be any program in which she could enroll him. The school superintendent advised her to put him in day care. "But he wants to do algebra," she protested. She explained that her son had recently asked her how to solve equations "when you don't know the numbers," showing her that he had grasped the concept of variables. But the superintendent was unhelpful, even hostile. Peter's mother recalled him saying something to the effect of: "Your child is ahead. Don't worry. He'll be ahead of the game when he starts kindergarten."

Julia convinced the superintendent to give her the kindergarten curriculum so that she could introduce it to her son at home. Soon she needed the curriculum for the first grade. Between the ages of three and four, Peter S. mastered the local school's curriculum from kindergarten through third grade. At four, Julia said, he began to make sudden and tremendous leaps in comprehension. Clearly, this was not a child who would thrive at age five in the local kindergarten. But the superintendent disagreed and urged her to enroll her son. He said that this child should get used to children of his own age and learn to deal with them. He urged that Peter be mainstreamed.

Had Julia complied, her son would have been eligible for the same kind of pull-out enrichment program that was given to Alex: after third grade, he would have had one twenty-five–minute period every two weeks when he would interact with other "gifted" children in the school. There is certainly some value in letting precocious children meet other precocious children, even if only for a limited amount of time each week. But Peter S. was so profoundly gifted that he would probably have felt almost as different from the other children in the pull-out program as from the children in his regular classroom. Children who are moderately academically gifted are very different in interests and proclivities from those who are at the high extremes, like Peter S. Moreover, how could such a small amount of time, no matter how stimulating or enriching, have compensated for the rest of the time when Peter S. would have been expected to learn at a level years below his capabilities, and to learn what he had mastered at age three?[4]

Peter S.'s mother realized all this. She also noticed that Peter seemed to become depressed if he spent even a day without some intellectual challenge. She recognized that Peter's younger sister was going to face similar problems as she got older. Thus, she chose to home school both, starting at age three. (Two more precocious children followed, too young at the time of the writing of this book to begin their home schooling.) The circumstances of this family made home schooling possible. They lived on a small, self-sustaining farmstead. The father thus worked at home and gave Julia his constant support, help, and encouragement in home schooling.

Julia pieced together a curriculum using the Arkansas

Public School course content guide as well as her imagination. Her curriculum included a math course for gifted children developed at Stanford University, creative writing, literature, current events, geography, Latin, and violin. For a history unit on civil rights, she selected serious literature for Peter's reading: Alex Haley's *Roots*, Richard Wright's *Black Boy*, Mark Twain's *Tom Sawyer*, and Harper Lee's *To Kill a Mockingbird*. For bedtime reading one week, their father read them George Orwell's *Animal Farm*.[5]

Julia felt that home schooling allowed her to advance at her children's pace and to challenge them to the limit. At five, Peter S. was doing fourth-grade math, ninth-grade English, and eleventh-grade anatomy. She did not want her children to think that learning comes without effort, a lesson she feared they would get in ordinary school.

Julia explained to me that two hours of home schooling were equivalent to about one full day of public school, given all the usual breaks schools have for lunch, recess, gym, and so on. Thus, she usually schooled her children only three times a week for about four hours at a stretch. But home schooling allowed her to be flexible. For instance, she often taught them in the evenings, because this was her children's best time. (Like Michael Kearney and his sister, Peter S. and his sister needed little sleep and were extremely active.) Sometimes they wanted to work twelve hours a day, and she accommodated them. If on some days they did not feel like working at all, they played. Neither liked to sit in chairs, so they did not have to.

This home school offered an extremely child-centered, personalized, progressive, challenging education. Such home schooling has the potential to be the best of what school can be, and Peter S. and his sister were fortunate that they had each other for company, even though they missed out on peer social experience. When I asked Julia why she had not chosen to accelerate her children radically, as Michael Kearney's parents had done, she replied that she saw no benefit in rushing them through an education. She felt that a solid and wide educational base was a more appropriate goal than a rapidly reached diploma. She also said that acceleration could destroy their "childlike sense of wonder." I felt that she was probably correct.

AN ARGUMENT WITH A MORAL FLAVOR

Advocates for gifted education disagree about whether gifted students should get an "enriched" or an "accelerated" education, and whether they should be grouped into special classes with children of like age and ability, or placed with older children by skipping grades. But the debate within the field of gifted education is mild compared to the heated controversy between those in favor of any kind of gifted education and those opposed. Each side fervently believes that it is in the right, and that the other is morally wrong. Each side believes that it cares about the interests of *all* children, while the other side cares only about the interests of some. The arguments pro and con are not specific to the United States but can be heard in most advanced countries today.

Ability Grouping: The Case Against

When gifted education means grouping children by ability, those opposed to gifted education argue that children left in the low track feel dumb. These children, they fear, will suffer from losing the academic leadership of the highest-achieving students. The low-tracked students are usually assigned the least experienced teachers. Teachers do not like to teach these children and become demoralized. The low expectations that teachers have for these students, and that these students adopt as a result of being in the low group, become self-fulfilling prophesies.

Grouping the gifted together is believed to harm not only

those left out but also those selected for the gifted track. Separating top students and placing them in their own class, it is argued, can only lead to arrogance and elitism. The harm that gifted education does to the nongifted far outweighs any value it may have for the gifted child, it is said.

In addition to being considered harmful, gifted grouping is also considered unnecessary. Gifted children are supposed to be able to challenge themselves and learn at their own pace in the regular classroom. It is also suggested that the gifted can help those less able to learn by teaching them and by setting an example. This is thought to be both of academic value (teaching someone else helps consolidate what one has learned) and of social value (gifted children learn to interact with children of all kinds of ability).

Ability grouping has also been accused of being racist and classist, since gifted programs in the United States, for example, are overrepresented by Asians, followed by whites, and underrepresented by blacks and Hispanics. A study by the U.S. Department of Education conducted in 1991 found that programs for gifted students had five times more students from families in the top socioeconomic quarter of the population than students from the lowest quarter. The most serious charge made is that these statistics demonstrate the existence of racist admission criteria. An only slightly less damning charge is that this demonstrates that gifted programs lead to racist outcomes. In any case, these numbers show that our tests are picking up achievement as moderated by socioeconomic and cultural factors, and they are not picking up native and often undeveloped potential. In one recent study, researchers showed that the use of the Ravens Progressive Matrices Test, a nonverbal, spatial test, along with a consideration of whether the child has been "disadvantaged," has led to somewhat more proportional representation of minority children. But note that this test is unlikely to pick out verbally gifted, nonspatial children.[6]

Ability Grouping: The Case For

The argument for ability grouping is usually made by researchers who specialize in education for the gifted, teachers of the gifted, and parents of the gifted. To eliminate ability grouping, they argue, is to cave in to a simplistic egalitarian political agenda. Elimination of ability grouping will lead to standards being set at the lowest level, and the resultant education will fail to meet the needs of high-ability students. True, minorities (with the exception of Asians) are underrepresented in programs for the gifted. But, they contend, this is a social problem, reflecting the fact that minorities are disadvantaged. In fact, elimination of gifted programs will hurt minority gifted children the most, it is said, for minority children all too often attend the worst schools in our nation (since schools are supported by local property taxes). These schools have the fewest resources for extracurricular activities and the lowest overall academic achievement levels. Moreover, parents of majority-culture children usually have the resources to seek alternatives, whereas parents of minority-culture gifted children often have no options other than whatever the public schools provide.

Acceleration: The Argument Against

When gifted education means acceleration rather than ability grouping, the charge of elitism and unfairness gives way to another charge. Parents who seek to accelerate their child by early admission to school or by grade skipping are seen as pushy parents willing to rob their child of a normal childhood for an early college degree. Principals believe that accelerated children will not fit in and will lack friends, because they will not be with children of their own age (and size). When a father in Australia requested acceleration for his profoundly gifted children, the principal refused, saying, among other things: "They need socialization with their peers. . . . If they can't kick a football properly, how can you expect them to fit in with other kids?" And then, "The other kids in the class wouldn't like it" (presumably because they would not accept someone younger and smaller as one of them).[7]

These comments sound much like those of the principal whom Peter S.'s mother approached. They reflect the belief that school is primarily for socialization, not learning, *and* that a child who is academically precocious still is happiest when socializing with children similar in age, irrespective of interests and abilities.

Acceleration: The Argument For

In contrast, those in favor of acceleration argue that keeping a child who can do sixth-grade work in a second-grade class is not saving that student's childhood but is instead robbing that child of the desire to learn. Those in favor of acceleration, including radical acceleration, argue that placing a child with intellectual peers is far more important than keeping that child with age peers. In response to the claim that profoundly gifted accelerated children will not fit in because they are too young to relate to their classmates, those in favor of acceleration reply that it is the profoundly gifted *non*accelerated children who do not fit in. When not accelerated, the profoundly gifted find they have no peers because they are too different from their classmates to relate to them. Why, it is argued, should age and physical size be more important grouping criteria than ability?

HOW GIFTED CHILDREN FARE IN OUR SCHOOLS

Four good "in principle" reasons can be offered in support of some form of special education for the gifted:

- American schools have low standards.
- Low standards lead to underachievement.

- Academically (as well as artistically and musically) gifted children often find that school plays little or no role in the development of their gifts.
- Gifted children from disadvantaged backgrounds suffer the most from the lack of special educational provisions.

The Low Standards of American Schools

American schools hold comparatively low expectations for their students. When foreigners come to the United States and place their children in our schools, they are typically shocked by how easy the schools are compared to what their children have experienced at home. American textbooks have become less demanding (by two grade levels) in the past twenty years. Publishers shy away from publishing textbooks aimed at the top third of students, because they know such books will not sell. When our students apply to college, they take multiple-choice aptitude and achievement tests, but when European students apply to a university, they must write lengthy answers to essay questions.[8]

Not surprisingly, American children fare poorly when compared to children in most other developed countries. A 1993 report issued by Secretary of Education Richard Riley presented some alarming comparisons. For instance, in a recent international study, 40 percent of Korean students showed an understanding of mathematical concepts, as compared with 9 percent of American students. A similar pattern was found for science: 33 percent of Korean students, 31 percent of British Columbian students, and 7 percent of American students were able to apply elementary science principles in problem solving.[9]

Low standards are bad for all students, but they are particularly bad for the ablest students. According to the Riley report, American students in the top 3 to 5 percent of the IQ range say they study less than one hour a day. The report also notes that compared to the top students in other countries, the best U.S. students have less rigorous curricula and read fewer challenging books. Not surprisingly, then, high-ability American students fare far worse than high-ability students in other countries. For instance, the top 10 percent of students in the United States were outperformed by the top 10 percent of students in Japan, Taiwan, and China in mathematics. In addition, the parents of the top American students were found to set lower standards for their children than did Japanese parents: American parents reported higher levels of satisfaction with their children's ability and performance than did Japanese parents.[10]

Thus, one strong argument in favor of gifted education is that our most academically strong students are our most underchallenged group, and they perform far lower than similarly able students in other developed countries. The comparative findings provide an argument not only for challenging our more gifted more, but for challenging *all* of our students more. These two goals are not in conflict.

Low Challenge, Underachievement, and Low Self-Esteem

The lack of challenge in our schools means that our children are not performing up to their potential. They are underachieving. While all our children are probably underachieving, the gap between potential and performance must be the highest for the most gifted. According to the Riley report, academically gifted children have mastered between a third and a half of the basic curriculum before they have even entered school. Since these children can already read and write and are precocious in math, and since reading, writing, and arithmetic form the major part of what is taught in the first few grades of school, naturally these children are not going to learn much that is new, and they are going to be underchallenged.[11]

Educator Leta Hollingworth estimated that gifted children waste much of their time in school and that profoundly gifted children waste *all* of their time in school. In her words:

Where the gifted child drifts in the school unrecognized, held to the lockstep which is determined by the capacities of the average, he has little to do. He receives daily practice in habits of idleness and daydreaming. His abilities are never genuinely challenged, and the situation is contrived to build in him expectations of an effortless existence. Children up to about 140 IQ tolerate the ordinary school routine quite well, being usually a little young for the grade through an extra promotion or two, and achieving excellent marks without serious effort. But above this status, children become increasingly bored with school work, if kept in or nearly in the lockstep. Children at or above 180 IQ, for instance, are likely to regard school with indifference, or with positive distaste, for they find nothing to do there.[12]

Note that 150 was the average IQ of participants in Lewis Terman's study, which could explain why Terman did not find that his subjects hated school!

The academically gifted child typically thrives in day care and preschool. The trouble that Hollingworth talks of usually starts with entrance into formal kindergarten, and the trouble is particularly acute for the profoundly gifted. Suddenly the child is expected to learn things she already knows. For instance, the child who is reading novels at home is asked to circle all of the pictures of objects whose names begin with the letter *B*. The child who plays math computer games is expected to count. The most compliant of these children go along with what is expected. But very often these children become bored, frustrated, and withdrawn, and come into conflict with their teachers. Many teachers, who have no special training in recognizing signs of giftedness, simply consider these children a problem and send home reports that the child is unmotivated, does not want to try, and cannot sit still. Such children may be referred to the school psychologist for testing to determine whether they are hyperactive, have a learning disability, or have an attention deficit disorder. We are far more likely to pathologize these children than to consider that they may be restless and inattentive because they are bored.

One of the leaders in the study of the underachievement syndrome in the gifted, Sylvia Rimm, suggests that the gifted are more at risk than other children for underachievement because the fit between child and school is least good for the gifted. These children learn that it takes no effort to succeed, a lesson that Rimm believes leads to the low self-esteem seen in underachievers. Because they can succeed without trying, they rarely exert much effort in their schoolwork. When the curriculum becomes somewhat more demanding in later grades, these children continue to slack off, and their performance then begins to decline. They begin to look like slow, rather than gifted, students, resulting in yet further decrements in self-esteem.[13]

Schools: An Unimportant Role?

Given the lack of fit between gifted students and their schools, it is not surprising that such students often have little good to say about their school experiences. In one study of 400 adults who had achieved eminence in all areas of life, researchers found that three-fifths of these individuals either did badly in school or were unhappy in school. Few MacArthur Prize fellows, winners of the MacArthur Award for creative accomplishment, had good things to say about their precollegiate schooling if they had not been placed in advanced programs. Anecdotal reports support this. Pablo Picasso, Charles Darwin, Mark Twain, Edvard Grieg, Stephen Vincent Benét, Oliver Goldsmith, and William Butler Yeats all disliked school. So did Winston Churchill, who almost failed out of Harrow, an elite British school. About Oliver Goldsmith, one of his teachers remarked, "Never was so dull a boy."

Often these children realize that they know more than their teachers, and their teachers often feel that these children are willful, arrogant, inattentive, or unmotivated.[14]

Some of these gifted people may have done poorly in school because their gifts were not scholastic. Maybe we can account for Picasso in this way. But most fared poorly in school not because they lacked ability but because they found school unchallenging and consequently lost interest. Yeats described the lack of fit between his mind and school: "Because I had found it difficult to attend to anything less interesting than my thoughts, I was difficult to teach." As noted earlier, gifted children of all kinds tend to be strong-willed nonconformists. Nonconformity and stubbornness (and Yeats's level of arrogance and self-absorption) are likely to lead to conflicts with teachers. This is what happened with Jacob, Peter B., and Alex. Children like this often educate themselves informally. They read a lot, they join after-school math clubs, or they work on the school newspaper. These experiences can be far more instructive than regular classes. "I always learned more out of school than in," said one MacArthur Prize fellow. This comment echoes Darwin, who said, "I consider that all I have learnt of any value has been self-taught."[15]

When highly gifted students in any domain talk about what was most important to the development of their abilities, they are far more likely to mention their families than their schools or teachers. A writing prodigy studied by David Feldman and Lynn Goldsmith was taught far more about writing by his journalist father than his English teacher. High-IQ children in Australia studied by Miraca Gross had much more positive feelings about their families than their schools. About half of the mathematicians studied by Benjamin Bloom had little good to say about school. They all did well in school and took honors classes when available, and some skipped grades. But they often knew more math than their teachers, and in elementary school their mathematical abilities usually went unnoticed. In the best situations, the teacher recognized their ability but could not teach at this level and simply sent the child off to the library to learn independently. While any group of people picked at random might describe their school experiences negatively, it is distressing to hear such evaluations from individuals with the kinds of minds that schools are supposed to nurture.

Here are several representative quotes from Bloom's mathematicians:

> School . . . really didn't have much to do with my life . . . or my ambitions or my hopes. It was something I did.

> Once I started studying on my own, I never learned any mathematics in school. I've had some inspiring teachers, but they've always been intelligent enough to see that I'm very independent and that the best thing that they could do for me was to give me the books and let me work on my own.

> I guess I never expected that teachers did much good. I sort of figured out that I wouldn't get any help. By the time I was thirteen, I was trying to teach myself calculus, and nobody who taught at my school knew calculus.

> I fell asleep in mathematics. In those days there was heterogeneous grouping, everybody was in the same classroom, doing the same thing, and you would go at the same rate as the slowest person in the class.

School only stimulated these students' intellectual lives when they entered college. Then, for the first time, they were with others like themselves; and for the first time, they began to think of math as a career. Like the mathematicians, the research neurologists studied by Bloom said that most of their learning about science had occurred outside of school and on their own. School was boring for them and did not nurture or encourage their scientific leanings.[16]

The same conclusion can be drawn from Csikszentmihalyi's previously described study of the experience of high school students gifted in math, science, music, art, and athletics. When beeped in class, these students said three-fourths of the time that they did not want to be doing what they were doing. The gifted students were far more critical of their teachers than were the control group members.

Of course, academically gifted children fortunate enough to go to unusually challenging public or private schools may not have such negative evaluations of school. But the typical story is one in which school is seen at best as irrelevant, and at worst as a negative intellectual (and social) experience. When gifted children are surrounded by children who lack their interests and abilities, they are likely to devalue their abilities and conform to the crowd.[17]

The kind of education these profoundly gifted children need is outside the scope of ordinary schools, and such students are often educated outside of school by a mentor. Many of the students who have won awards in the Westinghouse Science Talent Search did their research out of their school building, in a hospital or university laboratory. Usually a professor or laboratory supervisor acted as a mentor. And many children who enroll in summer programs for gifted children (run, for example, by the Center for Talented Youth) report that they found mentors there who were important to their later development.[18]

Schools are set up to teach academic skills, so it is particularly disturbing that students at the highest academic levels often feel they are learning little from school. It is perhaps less surprising, but no less disheartening, that students gifted in art or music also discount their school experiences. Bloom's sculptors, for example, did not find any value in their school art classes and often ridiculed them as silly. None of their teachers were professional artists. Art was not treated seriously, as a possible career, and these sculptors felt that they received no good formal training in art until they began to get professional art training after graduation from high school.

While artistically gifted children never mention school art teachers as people who taught them about art, they do mention adult artists who served as mentors. Like the students who win the Westinghouse Science Talent Search, future artists find their teachers outside of the classroom. For instance, Joel, the artistically gifted child studied by Constance Milbrath, never mentioned school art teachers, but he did talk about an artist who was a family friend and who taught him much about art. As mentioned, Wang Yani was kept out of school art classes by her father, who felt that the Chinese formulaic method of teaching art was destructive to artistic ability. Yani's father claimed he never explicitly taught his daughter. Nonetheless, it is highly likely that she learned from him, at least indirectly, as he watched over her painting development.

Schools in our country have minimal art programs, do not try to identify children with artistic ability, and would not even know what to do with such children if they did identify them. Recall the school psychologist's recommendation upon discovering the extent of Peter B.'s gift: find him an art program or an art teacher somewhere; neither can be found in school.

If we looked for artistic ability in schoolchildren, we would surely find it. In the early part of the twentieth century, an art educator from Munich, Georg Kerschensteiner, asked fifty thousand public schoolchildren to make drawings both from observation and from memory. He identified a group of children with high ability, almost all of whom were from poor families. These children, whose artistic gift had not been noticed by their schools, were then enrolled in special art classes, where their abilities flourished. More recently, a summer program was set up at Indiana University for artistically gifted adolescents. Almost all those selected said that they needed more advanced instruction than what their regular schools offered.[19]

Most children with artistic gifts are not lucky enough to find their way to the few appropriate programs that exist. Since art is not a highly valued skill in our culture, our schools do not make art a priority. It is thus families who must nurture artistic ability. But most do not do so for the same reason that schools fail to do so—because of the devaluing of art by our society.

Musically gifted children also have the same negative things to say about school music classes. Reynard, a student at Juilliard who is on his way to becoming a concert cellist, told me that he learned "zilch" from the music teachers at his school—and this despite the fact that he had attended a public elementary school and a high school in an affluent university community that boasted some of the best schools in the country. Unlike artistically gifted children, musically gifted children typically have formal out-of-school training in their domain of gift. Private music teachers play an enormously important role in shaping musical giftedness. If artistically gifted children received formal art training outside of school, they might well cite their art teachers as central to their development.

Gifted Programs and the Disadvantaged

The argument that gifted programs discriminate because certain minority groups are underrepresented in these programs can be countered by the argument that such programs are actually *more* important for the disadvantaged gifted than for the advantaged gifted. In suburban schools without gifted programs, children who seek challenges can often join math or chess clubs after school. By high school, musical children in these schools can join the school orchestra. Moreover, even if these children attend schools lacking in extracurricular activities that might stimulate them, they are likely to have parents who value and have the means to supply such enriching experiences as travel, museum trips, books, and concerts. Contrast these children to ones from poor families in rural or inner-city schools. Such schools are our weakest, and thus the ones least likely to have challenging after-school activities. In addition, children who attend these schools are far less likely than affluent ones to have educated parents with the time and resources to provide the enrichment that schools do not.

Although children whose parents are less educated are less likely to achieve in school, they can be helped to achieve if they are provided with challenging opportunities. Eliminating gifted programs in our public schools will result in even more of an exodus from public to private schools: the affluent gifted will be sent to private schools, while the poor gifted will remain probably unrecognized and certainly unnurtured. One of the most important federal actions concerning gifted education was the Javits Act of 1987, which had as its priority the identification and nurturance of gifted children from minority groups. Abandoning gifted education means abandoning poor and minority children far more completely than the children of the affluent.[20]

There is another reason why gifted programs may be particularly important for minority children—at least for some minority groups. In our society, being smart carries no premium. Gifted students often pretend they are less able in order to fit in and to avoid being labeled as "nerds." This problem is particularly marked in some minority groups, as mentioned earlier. For instance, while Asians value high academic achievement, black students often view doing well in school as caving in to white values. Elimination of gifted programs means that gifted students from some minority groups will

have no other children like themselves with whom to identify. One of the most potentially powerful outcomes of a math
and science program for gifted black university students was
that, for the first time, these students felt it was not "uncool"
to be smart.[21]

A variant of this argument can be made for girls who are
gifted in mathematics and science. These girls excel in an area
traditionally seen as appropriate for boys. If we eliminate
gifted math and science programs, girls who excel in these
areas will lack other girls with whom to identify, and they may
not feel encouraged to develop their skills.[22]

OPTIONS FOR ACADEMICALLY GIFTED CHILDREN TODAY

Many different options exist for gifted children in this country.
Most are geared toward the moderately gifted, but they are
not available to the majority of children who would qualify,
and they currently are under threat of extinction. There is no
national agreement on what kind of education gifted children
should get. Thus, much depends on the child's school district
and the parents' choice. There have always been private
schools, many of which require achievement or even IQ tests
for admission. For public school students, there are specialized
schools for the gifted at both the elementary and the secondary levels, magnet schools for particular kinds of giftedness
(art, science), gifted classrooms within regular schools, and
pull-out programs in which gifted children are grouped
together for two or three hours a week. There are also intensive private summer programs, such as the CTY, in which students can master a year's worth of material in a few weeks.

Until the mid-nineteenth century, gifted children of the
affluent were schooled at home by private tutors, or they
attended private schools and were allowed to skip more than

one grade. In the first half of the twentieth century, a few special schools for gifted children existed, but the usual practice was to accelerate such children, not to group them together. The movement to establish formal gifted programs, and to group gifted children of the same age together for instruction, began in force in reaction to the Soviet launching of *Sputnik* in 1957. Ability grouping thus began to replace acceleration as the way to deal with the gifted. However, even today, only a small portion of our gifted children (defined to include the moderately gifted) are enrolled in some kind of special class for the gifted. Those in the gifted education movement have always believed that special provisions are needed not only for the extremely gifted but also for the moderately gifted (which is why IQ cutoffs have usually been set at around 130 for special school programs).[23]

In 1972, the U.S. Office of Education issued a report on the status of education for the "gifted and talented," informally called the Marland report, after Sidney Marland, then the U.S. Commissioner of Education. According to this report, only 4 percent of gifted children (broadly defined) were getting any kind of special service. Half of the superintendents surveyed said that they had no gifted children in their school systems. (This may well have been accurate if the superintendents meant no *profoundly* gifted children. But the Marland report does not confine itself only to the profoundly gifted.) The report said that gifted children were the most deprived and "retarded" group in school because of the large discrepancy between their abilities and what schools could offer them. Marland argued that the gifted be made a national priority in our education system. He also suggested that the definition of *giftedness* be broadened to include the arts, creativity, leadership, and athletics.

In reaction to this report, Congress established an Office of the Gifted and Talented in the Office of Education. The government office, however, lacked power and could only advocate. As for the broadened definition of *giftedness*, schools paid lip service to this new view but continued to create programs whose sole criterion of admission was IQ or scholastic achievement.

In 1981, the Office of the Gifted and Talented was eliminated. Thereafter, the gifted were supposed to come under the jurisdiction of the Council for Exceptional Children. The gifted were to be treated specially, just as were the disabled. But when a parent recently sued the state of Connecticut in order for her gifted child to receive special education, the state ruled that only disabled children have a law mandating that they get special educational treatment. Special education for the gifted, the state ruled, was optional.[24]

Today only about a fifth of our states include the gifted as special education students covered by the law for the handicapped (Education for all Handicapped Children Act, Public Law 94-142). This law requires that all special education students be given Individualized Education Programs (IEPs). These are programs, like the one developed for David, worked out jointly by parents, teachers, and school psychologists and other officials. IEPs are in theory excellent, as each child with an IEP is given a hand-tailored education. However, IEPs are extremely difficult to carry out well.[25]

The Javits Act led to the creation of a federally funded National Research Center on the Gifted and Talented, directed by Joseph Renzulli at the University of Connecticut. This center has developed programs of gifted education all across the country, using more than 200 schools as experimental sites.

A little over twenty years after the Marland report, Secretary of Education Richard Riley issued his report, in 1993. The Riley report again deplored the state of gifted education in our country. According to the report, about two-thirds of our public schools have some kind of gifted program. But in 1990, only two cents out of every 100 dollars spent on education in kindergarten through high school were spent on gifted programs. And the typical gifted program is a paltry, part-time, "pull-out" program of only several hours a week. All our gifted programs taken together were estimated in the Riley report to serve only a fraction of our gifted population (again, broadly defined to include the moderately gifted). And the situation is even worse in music and art: children receive at best one class period a week in each of these domains; many elementary school systems have been forced to cut their art teachers; and those that do teach typically have to teach students at many schools and so can never come to know students individually.[26]

In fact, we provide far more services to retarded children than to gifted ones. Children with IQs of two standard deviations below the mean are given special help, but those with IQs two standard deviations above the mean (that is, 130) are usually not given advanced instruction. Those with IQs three standard deviations below the mean are enrolled in a partial or full-day program; those four standard deviations below the mean receive continuous supervision and are placed in special institutions. But children with IQs three or even four standard deviations above the mean (that is, 145 to 160) could easily get no special attention.[27]

States differ in how they provide for the gifted in public schools, but in all states, gifted programs are seen as a frill and are the first to go in a budget crisis. And as already mentioned, they are also under constant attack as undemocratic, elitist, and racist. Thus, for both financial and ideological reasons, gifted programs are being cut today. Currently, only those states that have both mandates and money have stable or expanding programs; the rest are in the process of cutting back. Where there are no state mandates, decisions are made at the local level, by individual principals, usually in response to parental pressure. Rural schools have, by and large, the fewest provisions for the gifted.[28]

In addition, because of the belief that children should not be denied a normal childhood, there is a trend against early entrance to kindergarten and grade skipping of any kind. Parents who feel that their child should be accelerated must fight for this and often lose. When grade skipping is permitted, it is usually a skip of only one year. But a one-year advancement has been shown to be of little benefit for extremely gifted children, and this is why it is children at the extremes who have the most difficulties in school.[29]

Although programs explicitly labeled as for the gifted are being cut today, most elementary school teachers use some de facto ability grouping in certain subject areas, such as reading. And at the high school level, where students have choices in the courses they take, it is usually possible to choose between more and less advanced courses. Nonetheless, even when these are not officially called courses for the gifted, they are under attack, and some communities are considering dismantling honors classes at the high school level.[30]

As this brief history should make clear, the United States is profoundly ambivalent about how to educate the academically gifted, torn between the goals of excellence and equity. All other countries have shown a similar ambivalence. Some have resolved the issue more strongly in favor of gifted programs, while others have gone in the opposite direction. In Japan, for instance, while there is no tracking in elementary school, there are four levels of high school and admission is determined by competitive examination. In contrast, Australia and Scandinavian countries oppose gifted education at all levels.[31]

IS EDUCATION FOR THE GIFTED BENEFICIAL?

Policies about gifted education are far more likely to be based on political values and ideology than on research findings, even though a considerable body of research exists on the effects of various kinds of gifted education. In 1991, over 300 studies on the effects of acceleration had been published, and over 750 on the effects of ability grouping. Ability grouping can mean either an across-the-board approach for all students (commonly called tracking or streaming) or grouping just for the most gifted (commonly called gifted education), and it can mean grouping for all subject matters or only for particular ones. Acceleration can mean either skipping grades or taking fast-paced courses. Acceleration and ability grouping begin to blur together when we talk of advanced courses, for these not only are accelerated but are taught to students of similar high ability. It is important to try to keep these distinctions in mind when evaluating the research on the effects of education for the gifted.

The many studies do not always come to the same conclusion, and everyone can find a study to support a particular point of view, just as everyone can cite stories in which a gifted program was helpful to a particular gifted child or hurtful to a child left out. However, a look at the bulk of the studies shows that, by and large, special provisions for the profoundly academically gifted are needed and beneficial. But the question of tracking across the board (which means separate classes for average, below-average, and above-average, moderately gifted students) is a separate issue. Here the research indicates that comprehensive ability grouping for all children is useful only if it is done by particular subject areas, and if it entails differentiated curricula and instruction at each level. But the benefits of ability grouping for all children are far less clear and far weaker than are the benefits of special education for the gifted.[32]

Ability Grouping

At least according to surveys from several decades ago, the majority of teachers favor some kind of ability grouping. One of the strongest and most widely cited attacks against ability grouping today has been made by educator Jeannie Oakes, who argued that grouping is unfair and harmful to those not included in the high track. She showed how students in the low track felt discriminated against and labeled as stupid by their teachers and peers. They were given material that was unchallenging, they learned little, and their self-esteem suffered. Oakes based her conclusions on case studies of twenty-five junior and senior high schools. This may seem like a large research base, but since hundreds of studies have been carried out on the issue of grouping, any conclusion must be based on the findings of these studies taken together.[33]

The most systematic way to make sense of the hundreds of studies is to use the statistical technique called meta-analysis, in which many studies are combined into one overall study. In any such analysis, it is important to compare how students of particular ability levels fare when placed in heterogeneous versus ability-grouped environments. While Oakes showed that low-tracked students learned little, it is important to go further and investigate whether these same kinds of students would learn *more* if they had not been taught separately from higher-ability students.

Special Classrooms for the Academically Gifted

James and Chen-Li Kulik, two psychologists at the University of Michigan, have conducted meta-analyses of studies of various kinds of programs for the gifted, all of which have entrance criteria that admit both the moderately and the profoundly gifted. Their studies have shown that gifted children educated separately perform somewhat better than do equally gifted children who remain in heterogeneous classrooms. The benefit seems to be a modest one. In the typical study, only a small majority of the children in the gifted class (63 percent) outperformed the gifted children in the heterogeneous class. But note that these studies all define *giftedness* to include the moderately gifted. They do not tell us about the consequences of separate education just for the profoundly gifted.

According to these studies, being placed in a gifted class does not make children arrogant, nor does it lower their self-esteem because they are no longer the biggest fish in the pond. What these studies do not tell us, however, are the potentially negative effects on the nongifted students when they lose the peer leadership of the most gifted students. Two leading educational psychologists have argued that lower-ability students without high-ability leaders become "leaderless aggregations of discouraged and alienated students." If this is indeed true, we should provide separate classes only for the most profoundly gifted students, especially in light of the relatively modest benefits of gifted classes revealed by the Kuliks' meta-analyses.[34 35]

Enrichment Pull-out Programs for the Academically Gifted

The most common form of ability grouping at the elementary school level is the pull-out program, the form of ability grouping that involves periodic "enrichment" times. Enrichment classes have tended to be child-centered and individualistic: children may work independently or in small groups to pursue questions that interest them, conduct experiments, and so on.

Pull-out programs are weak solutions to the problems faced by the profoundly gifted. They take up only two or three hours a week, and the rest of the time the child is given no differentiated instruction. The activities in which the children engage in pull-out programs are often unrelated to the specific forms of giftedness they possess. There is little continuity from week to week, and students do not gain the experience of studying something systematically. All too often these programs consist of games, movies, field trips, and scattered projects.

Some informal research on pull-out programs bears out these criticisms. Children can rarely recall what they did in the enrichment sessions. In response to one survey, only 16 percent of pull-out programs were judged to be substantial by the schools using them. And in response to another survey, many schools said that their pull-out programs were too superficial, too short, and too unsystematic. Recall the description given by Alex's mother, reported at the opening of this chapter: her son's pull-out program meant getting the handful of gifted children together once a week just to play games. While she may have been exaggerating in her frustration, I have heard this kind of comment from parents and gifted children too often to discount it.[36]

Gifted children in pull-out programs show achievement gains on standardized tests, in comparison to groups of similarly gifted children *not* in such programs. But in all of the studies of such programs, gains were modest. Moreover, students of all ability levels would probably benefit from these enrichment programs. None of the studies to date have proved that they would not. Moreover, students in these studies were usually not assigned randomly to either a pull-out class or a regular one. Only with random assignment can we be sure that gains experienced by the children in the pull-out group are due to the program, and not to preexisting differences between the two groups of children. Psychologist Joseph Renzulli is trying to take the best features of enrichment programs—such as active, hands-on, project-based learning—and infuse them into school for all children.[37]

Comprehensive Tracking

In 1919, a form of grouping was introduced in Detroit that today seems insidious, though the practice can still be found in some districts. Starting in first grade, students were separated into three classes, based on their IQ scores. The idea behind this effort was to reduce variation among students and thus make the teacher's job easier. No explicit changes in curriculum across the three groups were made.[38]

In a meta-analysis of studies of such comprehensive tracking, the Kuliks found a positive but very small effect for the high-ability group. No effects were found for students in the low or middle groups. This finding suggests that tracking does not harm the academic performance of the low-track students, contrary to what has been argued by Oakes and others. But this finding also provides no strong evidence that tracking does much to elevate the performance of the high-track students. Note that the same conclusion was drawn from meta-analyses of studies of gifted classes, mentioned earlier: the gifted benefit, but the benefits are very modest.[39]

In a meta-analysis of tracking at the secondary school level, the Kuliks looked separately at thirteen studies in which students of equal ability were randomly assigned to either tracked or untracked classes versus thirty-eight in which students were assigned by some other means (such as teacher selection and self-selection). Overall, tracking offered only very small benefits. Moreover, all the benefits came from the studies in which students had been assigned nonrandomly. Thus, it may well be that high-ability students do a bit better in tracked classes because they are the highest-ability students to begin with, as measured by the fact that someone decided to place them in the high-track class. Only studies in which equal-ability students are randomly assigned to tracked and untracked classes can reveal whether tracking per se makes a difference.[40]

When tracking means taking more advanced courses, as it often does by secondary school, a more positive picture emerges, and we find that high-track students improve more over a year than do low-track students. But this is hardly surprising, since students in the high track are more likely to be taking advanced academic courses (for instance, French rather than shop), as well as more academic courses altogether.[41]

One of the strongest arguments against tracking is that it harms the self-esteem of those tracked into low groups. But the Kuliks' meta-analysis showed that self-esteem rose somewhat for students in the low track and declined for students in the high track. Self-esteem among those in the low track may rise because these students no longer have to compare themselves to higher achievers; self-esteem may decline in the high track because students now must compare themselves to others who achieve at an equally high level.

Hollingworth noted that when students were placed in a special school for the gifted, many had their first experience at being equaled or surpassed. "Conceit was corrected, rather than fostered, by the experience of daily contact with a large number of equals." This may well be a good thing.[42]

Within-Class Grouping

At the elementary school level, tracking usually means grouping children by ability *within a class*. The different ability groups usually also receive differentiated instruction. There are positive but small effects for students at all ability levels, in both elementary and high schools.[43]

Cross-Grade Grouping

One of the charges against ability grouping is that teachers assigned to teach a low group do not expect much of their students, and their low expectations become self-fulfilling prophesies. A solution sometimes believed to avert this problem is ability grouping across grade levels. Here, a teacher might be assigned to teach a group of high-achieving younger students along with a group of low-achieving older students. But students in this kind of group can still be classified by the teacher as high or low, since the teacher knows full well the student's age level and ability.

This form of grouping was first instituted for reading in the late 1950s and was called the Joplin plan. A meta-analysis by the Kuliks of fourteen studies (ranging from kindergarten through twelfth grade) showed a small positive effect across all subject areas whenever this form of grouping was used. Two of the studies reported effects separately by ability level. These studies showed something surprising: the students most helped by this form of ability grouping were the low-ability ones. Again, this finding contradicts the view that ability grouping should be abolished because of its harmful effects on children assigned to low groups.[44]

Acceleration

Children who are extremely gifted academically are sometimes allowed to skip a grade or two, a practice called modest acceleration. Radical acceleration involves skipping many grades, and graduating from high school and entering college many years ahead of schedule. Meta-analyses by the Kuliks have shown that children who are moderately gifted academically clearly benefit from a one- or two-year grade skip. But as noted earlier, such modest acceleration is of little benefit to children who are five or six years ahead of their age peers.[45]

Terman believed that any child beginning school at the age of six and a half, with a mental age of ten, could be brought up to fourth-grade level before the end of first grade. He argued that such children should skip several grades and enter college by age sixteen, though he opposed more radical acceleration. On the report that Terman sent to parents after their children had been tested, he wrote: "When school achievement is two or three grades above that in which the child is located, an extra promotion is usually desirable. . . . Probably few children, however bright, should enter high school before the age of 11 or 12, or college before the age of 15 or 16. Advancement much more rapid than this involves the risk of defective social development."[46]

When Terman compared the accelerated and nonaccelerated children in his high-IQ sample, he found a link between early college entrance and later high career achievement. Of course, such a correlation does not allow us to conclude that the acceleration led to the high levels of professional achievement, for it could be that the most able children were also the ones who accelerated. However, this comparison does demonstrate that some acceleration is not harmful. In fact, no study has shown that acceleration is harmful either cognitively or socially and emotionally. And this is surely an important finding.[47]

No large-scale study of *radical* grade skipping has been conducted, however; only case studies are available. For example, Gross has described cases in which profoundly gifted children were not accelerated, or were accelerated only modestly, and suffered boredom, frustration, and social isolation.[48]

Acceleration does not always mean grade skipping. It can also mean entering kindergarten early or enrolling in advanced courses, such as advanced placement or college classes, or intensive summer programs like those offered by the Study of Mathematically Precocious Youth (SMPY) or its cousin, the Center for Talented Youth (CTY). But now the line between ability grouping and acceleration begins to blur, since students in advanced courses are grouping themselves with other similar peers.

Both CTY and SMPY identify gifted children around ages eleven to thirteen and offer them acceleration outside of school, during the summer, in their area of gift. To qualify for these programs, students must achieve a score equivalent to that of the average college-bound high school senior on the SAT before age thirteen. For instance, to qualify for a math program, students must score at least 500 on the math portion of the SAT, or at least 930 on the combined math and verbal SAT portions. Thus, those who qualify are profoundly, not moderately, gifted. Children accepted take intensive summer courses in which an entire year's curriculum is mastered in three weeks. This approach, pioneered by Julian Stanley at Johns Hopkins University, is being replicated in universities all over the country, and even in China.[49]

Students selected for these courses have been studied and compared to students who qualified but who for some reason chose not to enroll. The outcomes were positive. SMPY students, who engaged in various forms of acceleration, including early school entrance, grade skipping, college courses taken in high school, and fast-paced SMPY summer courses, did better in college than those equally qualified who chose not to accelerate in any of these ways.[50]

Studies by Stanley and his colleagues have also shown that students who skip several grades and graduate from college anywhere between ages seventeen and nineteen have no problems academically, and no problems in social and emotional adjustment. However, the nonaccelerants were not harmed, and also did very well. This study thus does more to show that acceleration is not harmful than it does to show that a failure to accelerate a child can result in harm.[51]

It may be that the kinds of summer acceleration offered by programs such as CTY or SMPY exert their strongest effects socially rather than cognitively. Students in these programs often report that the most important thing for them was to meet people like themselves and find out that it is okay to be smart. Listen to what some of these students have to say:

> I've made better friends here than back at school, at least more good, deep friends.

> There is an intense social experience that occurs when you make the revelation that there are people out there like you.

> We've discovered a place where we can be ourselves, and not be afraid to stand out or to voice our opinions. . . . [At home] . . . I have a hard time finding people enough like me to make real friendships work.[52]

Of all the forms of gifted programs, acceleration in its various forms is the most clearly positive in effect, though we do not know much about the skipping of more than a few grades. While high school students can accelerate by taking advanced courses, elementary school students are usually not allowed to accelerate. As noted earlier, school officials are typically hesitant to allow a child to skip a grade and are hostile to the idea of allowing a child to skip several grades, fearing its social and emotional consequences. But grade skipping, at least in moderate form, is in many ways a good option: it avoids the charges of elitism and separatism that come with ability grouping, it costs nothing, and it may be the only solution when there is no critical mass of gifted children.[53]

OTHER SOLUTIONS

Other solutions for gifted children besides grouping within and between classes, pull-out programs, and acceleration also exist. An extreme solution that I would consider to be one of last resort is the solution of home schooling described in the opening of this chapter. Home schooling is a fast-growing movement in the United States, with about one million children currently being home schooled. This solution, of course, can work only for parents who are willing and able (cognitively, emotionally, and economically). Many prodigies throughout history were home schooled, and this will probably always be an option for extremely gifted children from privileged families. I would consider it to be a last choice because it means children do not have the experience of being with their peers.[54]

Another extreme solution is to create entirely separate schools for the gifted. The Nueva School in California, mentioned earlier, is one of the few U.S. schools explicitly designed for academically gifted children. Most children are admitted as kindergarteners, and they must score 125 or above on an IQ test. Applicants also must spend time in the classroom, and qualitative observations are used to select students who are creative as well as gifted. When I visited this school, I saw students engaged in small, challenging classes. I also saw a high level of personalized instruction. For example, one student who excelled in nonfiction writing was given an individual assignment. Her task was to go to the library and dig up examples of good and bad writing, and then determine the qualities of writing that made some styles better than others.

There have always been such special schools for the gifted. Many private schools are de facto schools for gifted children, since they require achievement tests or even IQ tests for admission. The Illinois Math and Science Academy is one of a handful of public schools (some residential, some not) that are reserved for the gifted, mostly at the high school level, and mostly focusing on math and science. The California Academy of Math and Science, founded in 1990, seeks out gifted minority students, and almost 90 percent of its students are in fact minorities.[55]

These schools often have longer classes than do regular schools (some last for two consecutive periods), and students are encouraged to engage in independent research. Students from these schools often win the Westinghouse Science Talent Search, and many go on to become scientists.[56]

The highly successful profile of graduates from these schools makes these schools seem like ideal places to send gifted children. Of course, the kinds of students enrolled in these schools perhaps would have flourished anywhere. No researchers have randomly assigned gifted students to specialized versus ordinary schools and compared their development. And no such studies will be forthcoming, since families and schools are unlikely to allow such random assignment. However, it seems foolish to conclude that these students would have done just as well in ordinary schools because this would mean that there are no benefits to having challenging courses and classmates of extremely high ability.

Yet another solution is to have nongraded classrooms in which all levels of students can proceed at their own pace. This solution has not been very widely implemented, probably because of the extraordinary demands such a classroom places on the teacher.[57]

Another less extreme solution is to have individualized instruction for gifted children within a regular classroom. This solution avoids the problem of separating gifted children into elite groups. Sometimes these children are given IEPs such as the one worked out for David. (This solution is one that is *mandated* for handicapped students who can be kept in a regular classroom.) This solution can prove quite labor intensive: in David's case, the program was worked out by the classroom teacher, the guidance counselor, the specialist in gifted education, the math resource teacher, and David's mother. The plan, a flexible one that was continually updated, allowed David to work at his math level with the math resource teacher two or three times a week, and to work with a teacher's aide writing stories when his classmates were learning to sound out words. He was allowed to work on his own in the class when the others were working on material that David already knew, and he could go to the library or to the gifted specialist whenever he wanted to find the answer to a question. Although the school had suggested a one-year grade skip, David's parents decided against it. David was already the youngest child in his class, he was small for his age, and his emotional and social development was only at age level. Moreover, a one-year skip would have done little to close the gap for a child reading at the sixth-grade level in first grade.

Individualized instruction for a very advanced child is more commonly carried out without a formal IEP: the teacher simply tries to teach the one or two gifted children in the classroom in a more challenging way. Gifted students may be given special research projects or be assigned mentors. They may be allowed to skip material they already know. The more that projects are open-ended, the more that children can all go at their own pace. This solution, if well done, is far better than teaching gifted children just like all others for most of the time and then sending them to a specialist once or twice a week.

One problem with any kind of individualized instruction for a gifted child, however, is that those taught in this way will not have the stimulation of learning together with other children of similar ability. Moreover, individualized instruction is a difficult thing to do well, and it requires that the teacher instruct one child very differently or find a resource person to help out. Given the constraints within which teachers must work (such as large classes, diverse student bodies with many learning and behavior problems), individualized instruction is not an ideal solution in most cases.

Moreover, teachers are not very successful at differentiating among students in a heterogeneous classroom. While teachers do give more advanced projects and more difficult worksheets to the students they perceive to be most able, the instruction provided is typically passive: the ablest students are simply given more difficult materials and expected to figure things out on their own. In a large-scale survey of third- and fourth-grade teachers, only half said they had any training in teaching gifted children. These teachers said that they made only minor modifications in the regular curriculum for students considered to be gifted. When third- and fourth-grade teachers were observed as they interacted with high- and average-ability children, most of the time they made no differentiation at all. The gifted students often appeared bored, inattentive, and uninvolved. And even when students are really given individualized instruction according to ability, meta-analyses have shown only modest positive effects. Teachers with formal training in teaching gifted children, however, have been shown to make better curriculum modifications for the gifted in their classrooms.[58]

The solution that appeals to our egalitarian values—though not one that is necessarily the most fair to the gifted, or the most effective—is to set up cooperative learning environments in which children of widely varying ability levels learn together. In such an arrangement, students work together in small mixed-ability groups to solve problems. When done right, cooperative learning can be very effective. Some argue that gifted children can learn well in such groups and that they do not need to be with children of equally high ability. But what this means, usually, is that gifted children become the teachers of the less gifted. This could be useful, though, since being able to explain something means that one must first make sure one understands it. However, the very gifted are not necessarily good teachers: they cannot conceive of not understanding a simple math problem, since they themselves simply *see* the answer. Moreover, if gifted children are always engaged in teaching skills that they already know and are never stretched to master things at their own level, school will become a place where they do not fulfill their potential. We do not know the real costs and benefits of cooperative learning for gifted children, because we do not have enough research comparing gifted children placed in cooperative mixed-ability groups with those placed in homogeneous high-ability groups.[59]

In addition, we cannot assume that the gifted child in the cooperative learning classroom will serve as a role model and stimulate the other children to higher performance levels. For this to happen, the lower-ability children would have to perceive that they could change and that they are not too different from the gifted children. In addition, the high-ability child would have to continue to perform at a high level and not become an underachiever due to insufficient stimulation.

TEACHING TO THE TOP AND
BRINGING EVERYONE UP

When teachers teach at a high level, students at all levels rise to meet the challenge. This is the guiding philosophy of the Stanford educational psychologist Hank Levin, who founded the Accelerated Schools Project in response to the negative effects of remedial education on high-risk students. Levin reasoned that schools make things worse for at-risk students by placing them in less demanding classrooms or giving them remedial, less demanding work in a regular classroom. This commonly used approach has the opposite of its intended effects: students develop low expectations because teachers have low expectations. And the gap between these students and others is widened.

Levin's accelerated schools are fast paced and high level for all students. In one inner-city school in Los Angeles's Watts neighborhood, students who score below average on standardized tests read and perform Rossini's *Barber of Seville* in sixth grade, get their spelling words from poetry, and discuss the First Amendment. These schools treat low-achieving children like gifted children, accelerating their education rather than slowing it down. Studies comparing low-achieving children in remedial versus accelerated classes have shown that these children achieve more in accelerated classes. This is powerful evidence that if we raise standards for all, we bring the level up and narrow the gap between high- and low-achieving students.[60]

SOME RECOMMENDATIONS

We are wasting what few resources we have for gifted education on the moderately academically gifted. We would do far better if we elevated the level of instruction for all students and concentrated our gifted resources only on the extreme children, the kinds described in this book.

Most children who qualify for gifted programs are the moderately gifted, since very few children, by definition, are at the high extreme. The moderately gifted child would not need special programs if we raised our standards for all children. Some teachers and some entire schools have shown this to be true. For instance, when teachers take materials designed for gifted programs and use them in ordinary classrooms, all children thrive. I saw this when my son's teacher had her fourth- and fifth-graders perform *Macbeth* using a script provided by the California Gifted and Talented Education program. Her students all had parts, all learned lines in Shakespearean English, and all were challenged and stimulated.

Recently, Albert Shanker, the head of the American Federation of Teachers, made this same point in his weekly column in the *New York Times*. He described one high school in New York that had eliminated the lower track entirely and integrated the students previously in the lower track into the more demanding "Regents" track (in which top students prepare for the competitive Regents exam). Teachers were not told which students would have been non-Regents students, and high demands were made on all students. Surprisingly, a greater percentage of students passed the Regents exam once this was instituted.[61]

It will not be easy to raise educational standards significantly in the United States. One factor working against high standards is the fact that our schools are entirely decentralized. Local, rather than national, school boards make the decisions. In addition, our school population is extremely diverse culturally, and many people do not feel that one kind of curriculum is valid for all. And finally, our culture is anti-intellectual and is guided by misplaced and false egalitarianism. I say false because to deny high standards and to offer a middle-level pabulum for all is fair to no one, least of all the gifted.

If we raise our standards and expectations for all children, they will all do better, as the previously cited examples and the international comparisons show us. In addition, the moderately gifted would no longer be understimulated and in need of special programs. But the real extremes, the profoundly gifted children, would still need special provisions. It is these children that we should be trying to identify, and these in whom we ought to invest special resources set aside for the gifted.

Instead of *gifted programs,* I would prefer the more precise term *advanced class.* And rather than using a numerical score (with an arbitrary cutoff) that is supposed to predict what the student might achieve, why not use what the student has actually achieved? No diving coach uses a test with an arbitrary cutoff to determine who gets on the team. Rather, the coach observes the student diving and makes a qualitative judgment about whether this student has achieved a high level and shows promise. To decide who gets to join the school orchestra or who gets a part in a play, we have tryouts and make qualitative, informed judgments. Why not use criteria such as those used by athletics, or in the arts? Programs for the gifted have paid little attention to psychologists' critiques of IQ tests as narrow, and of standardized tests in general as assessing test-taking skills rather than the ability to think and understand.[62]

Some will argue that if we do not use tests, we will miss the gifted underachievers, those children who are not achieving at a high level but who have the potential to do so. But if we had more challenging classrooms to begin with, we would have fewer underachievers. And an astute teacher who looks closely at young children can tell the difference between those who are really having trouble learning and those who are bored. One sure sign of an underachieving gifted child is a high achievement pattern outside of school. These children, for instance, often read widely at home and have many unusual interests. If we wait until high school to identify these children, doing so may be far more difficult, as patterns of school alienation will have set in more deeply. These children need to be identified as soon as possible, preferably in the first few years of school.[63]

Some will also worry that if we use achievement as a criterion, we will miss the disadvantaged child who has potential but who has not ever been pushed to work. Yet if our schools held high expectations for these children and gave them challenging problems, giftedness would be apparent. One program in a New York inner-city school is currently experimenting with the use of portfolios of student work, as well as observations of students' attention span over time, to identify disadvantaged gifted children.[64]

If achievement serves as an entrance criterion, it should also serve as an exit criterion. Students who fail to perform at a high level in an advanced class should not continue in it. Students should realize that being placed in an advanced class is not simply a pat on the back but an indication that they must work at a higher level. Students not able or willing to do this should not be kept in the class. This of course assumes that teachers and administrators will be strong enough to stand up to angry parents whose children are not kept in the class.

In addition, students who get special resources ought to feel special responsibility and engage in some form of community service. This viewpoint is one of the guiding tenets of the Israel Arts and Science Academy, a residential high school in Jerusalem for highly gifted students (both Jewish and Arab). Here, all students must become involved in projects in which they contribute something of value to their community.

I also believe that identification should be domain-specific. Students should be identified as needing advanced instruction in mathematics or literature, for example, but not necessarily as needing advanced instruction in all subjects. Subjects in which a student is not advanced can be taught to the student in the regular classroom.

As for how these children should be taught, we need to take far more drastic measures than we do now. It is not enough to pull them out into a special enrichment class for several hours a week, but there is no one best approach. Profoundly gifted children can be well served by being grouped together by ability in their areas of giftedness. Advanced instruction given to a group of similar-age children is in my view preferable to radical grade skipping, for with such radical acceleration come the social problems of a much younger child trying to gain acceptance by much older classmates.

If we cannot provide advanced instruction to these extremely gifted children in school, either by ability grouping or by grade skipping, then we could at least borrow the Eastern European and Asian system of offering rich, stimulating extracurricular activities in science, math, art, and music. Why not have all-day school programs in which, from midafternoon on, children could select an after-school activity at the appropriate level of challenge?

All educational choices for academically gifted children involve compromises. Radical acceleration means that the child does not mix with children similar in age, and this brings its own problems. And ability grouping means that children do not mix with a heterogeneous group of children, which has its own drawbacks. However, if we cut out advanced instruction for our most extremely gifted children, we are wasting their potential. We ought to treat children with profound academic gifts the way we treat children with profound musical gifts, with high-level, demanding instruction at the appropriate level of challenge.

Ten

WHAT HAPPENS TO GIFTED CHILDREN WHEN THEY GROW UP?

The drawing prodigy Eitan, who drew with such brilliance at so young an age, has today, in his twenties, lost his passion for art. At the time of this writing, he plans to go into computer graphics, an occupation only indirectly related to his drawing talent. The math prodigy William James Sidis hated math as an adult and worked at a low-level job until his early and isolated death. Out of more than seventy musical prodigies who blossomed in San Francisco in the 1920s and 1930s, only six (including Yehudi Menuhin and Leon Fleischer) went on to become well-known soloists. We do not know what happened to the others, but probably some became orchestra members or music teachers, while others left music altogether.[1]

In sharp contrast to these stories are those of child prodigies who went on to make major creative contributions to their domains as adults—Yo-Yo Ma, Norbert Wiener, Jean Piaget, and Pablo Picasso, to name just a few. Two young violinists today, Midori and Sarah Chang, show every promise of going on to become major adult performers. And the painting prodigy Wang Yani, now in her late adolescence, shows no signs of losing interest in the visual arts and may well go on to become an important painter, though it is still too early to tell.

We are more likely to hear about the Picassos, Midoris, and Yo-Yo Mas of the world than about the Eitans and the Sidises. And thus we may come to the faulty conclusion that child prodigies typically stick to their chosen domains and go on to make major contributions.

The myth that prodigies have brilliant futures is strengthened by the fact that many eminent and creative people throughout history showed exceptional abilities as children. We forget that this does not imply the reverse—that exceptional children become adult creators. Most gifts never fully develop. Many gifted children burn out. A major difficulty in probing the connection between childhood giftedness and adult creativity is that we so rarely have any record of the many gifted children who have stopped developing their abilities.

To make matters worse, the labels "gifted" and "creative" are often blurred when they ought to be clearly distinguished. Just as intelligence and creativity are not the same thing, neither are giftedness and creativity. As I have argued, the gifted child is the child who is born with an unusual ability to master a particular domain (or domains). The prodigy is simply a more extreme version of a gifted child, able to perform at an adult level while still a child. These children are often creative in the "little *c*" sense—that is, they discover the rules and technical skills of their domain on their own, with minimum adult scaffolding, and often invent unusual strategies by which to solve problems. While children can be creative in this sense, they are rarely if ever creative in the "big *C*" sense. By this I mean stretching, altering, or even transforming a domain. When domains are changed by children, it is only because an adult connected to the domain recognizes something of value in children's work and is influenced by it. This is what happened when twentieth-century artists were influenced by children's art, as well as the art of other "outsiders" such as primitive and schizophrenic artists.[2]

Consider these four possible relationships between childhood giftedness/prodigiousness and adult creativity, in its fullest sense.[3]

Gifted children who drop out. There are, first of all, the gifted children like Eitan or William James Sidis who lose interest in their domain of talent and either burn out bitterly (as did Sidis), or simply turn to other interests (as did Eitan). While there are numerous published reports of such "failures" in all domains—mathematics, chess, writing, art, music, athletics, and so on—there are undoubtedly countless more who have lapsed into oblivion. The fact that we call such cases failures shows that we see prodigies as having some kind of obligation to themselves and to the world to persevere in the area in which they first dazzled us.[4]

It is easy to come up with after-the-fact explanations for these cases of dropout. Children who drop out, we reason, must have been pushed too hard or encouraged too little, or they must have had other interests they wished to pursue. But could anyone have predicted that Wiener would go on to invent the field of cybernetics, while Sidis would end up working at a low-level job and expressing a hatred for mathematics? Both were pushed hard by their fathers, who were professors at Harvard and knew each other as friends. Likewise, could anyone have predicted that Erwin Nyiregyhazi would drop out of music for fifty years, returning to it only at the end of his life, while Yo-Yo Ma would become the greatest cellist of his generation? Both had equally illustrious beginnings and equally determined parents. There are simply too many interacting factors that shape a child prodigy into an adult creator for us to be able to predict which ones will make it into the halls of the greats.

Gifted children who become experts. Then there are gifted

children who neither drop out nor become creators. Rather, they become experts in the domain of their gift. Expertise is not creativity. Experts perform at a very high level within a well-established domain, but they do not alter the domain. These are the musical children who become first-violinists in an orchestra or the high-IQ children who become successful lawyers, doctors, and professors. Most of the children studied by Lewis Terman fit clearly into this category. These children may not be very different, as adults, from similarly successful adults who were not recognized as gifted as children.[5]

Only a few people will ever revolutionize a domain of knowledge. These people must be born when the zeitgeist is right—when a domain is ready for the kind of change that the creator envisions. Moreover, a domain can change only so much and thus can accommodate only a very few creators. The factors that predict who will become a creator, thus, include not only the traits of the individuals in question but also historical and cultural factors.

Of that tiny minority who revolutionize a domain of knowledge, I would distinguish two further types:

Gifted children who become adult creators. A few go from being a gifted child or prodigy in a domain to being an adult creator in that domain—a pattern exemplified by Mozart and Picasso. Those who traverse this route must make the profound transition from being an expert in an established domain to being someone who disrupts the domain and remakes it, leaving it forever altered. To follow this route requires not only extreme early ability but also a rebellious personality, a desire to shake up the status quo.

Late bloomers. And then there are the late bloomers—children who are not picked out early on as gifted in any clearly defined domain but who in young adulthood discover a domain in which they can make a contribution, and who go on to become genuinely creative in that area. Darwin was such a late bloomer, as were the composers Igor Stravinsky and Anton Bruckner. Late bloomers are certainly not ordinary as children—they show unusual interests and high levels of curiosity—but no one would predict, from the child, what the adult would become. Often these children discover their domain in college, where they are first introduced to it. They then take off, looking much like prodigies who discovered their domain in childhood. These individuals typically master their domain virtually on their own, refusing to conform to the demands of the college curriculum, or even dropping out of college, as, for example, in the case of Bill Gates, the founder of Microsoft; Edwin Land, the founder of Polaroid; or futurist and inventor Buckminster Fuller.

We can investigate the link between childhood giftedness and adult creativity in either of two ways. We can start with adult creators. From what they are like as adults, and what we know about their childhoods, we can come up with some of the cognitive and personality factors that predict adult creativity. This retrospective method has the obvious flaw that it tells us nothing about those who may start out as gifted children but not end up as creative adults.[6]

We can also follow gifted children longitudinally. This is a more difficult and more time-consuming method, and we only have a few such studies. These studies are valuable because they allow us to characterize the differences between those who do and do not become creative as adults.[7]

No one factor has ever been shown to be either necessary or sufficient in the prediction of adult creativity. Moreover, so many factors are involved, factors interacting in ways we do not fully understand, that it is impossible to predict the future trajectory of any individual gifted child, just as it is impossible to predict with certainty any child's future interests and choice of work. Nonetheless, the enterprise is by no means hopeless. We can say with some certainty what factors *typically* play a role in the equation leading from gifted child to adult creator. And we can say with equal certainty what factors by themselves play little or no role. One thing we have learned is that above a certain point, levels of ability play a less important role than do personality and motivational factors.[8]

DOES HIGH IQ PREDICT CREATIVE ACCOMPLISHMENT IN ADULTHOOD?

A look at the life course of the Terman subjects shows us that high intelligence by itself does not predict adult creativity. A look at the Terman subjects also tells us something intriguing about the relationship of creativity to stress. It appears that a certain level of stress in childhood may be conducive to creativity, though whether stress stimulates creativity, or is simply likely to characterize those who are also creative, we cannot say for sure. Maybe the Terman subjects had too little stress in their childhoods for major creativity to develop.

Beulay Fabris, now in her early eighties, was one of the original Terman subjects. She had skipped kindergarten because she could read by three, and she sped through school, graduating from Stanford in three years at age twenty. She had shown mathematical aptitude as a child, and over her husband's objections, she took a job as an accountant for a bank. She loved playing with numbers and making everything fit together. When I met her, she was a retired widow, but still speeding along. As a child, she had read voraciously, and she told me she currently reads a book a day. She also travels frequently on nature photography trips. Before a trip she reads all about the geography, history, and customs of the countries she is about to visit. She had just completed her autobiography.

In her mental and physical energy, Beulay Fabris was like another Terman subject I met, Russell Robinson, a retired engineer. When I arrived to interview him at his house, I noticed a three-thousand–piece jigsaw puzzle that he and his wife were completing. Russell told me that knowing he had an IQ high enough to be in Terman's group had given him great confidence throughout his life. The knowledge sustained him when tackling difficult problems of his research career.

The striking mental energy that I saw in Beulay Fabris and Russell Robinson was typical of the Terman subjects late in life. Compared to the elderly population at large, the Terman subjects report more reading, travel, physical activity, and community service. However, although the Terman people maintained high energy levels throughout their lives, they did not for the most part become highly creative or eminent as adults.[9]

Adult creators stand out far more clearly in personality and motivational factors than they do in IQ. To be sure, most eminent and creative adults are of above-average intelligence. And a number of studies have demonstrated a minimum level of intellectual ability required for creativity. However, above an IQ of around 120, there is no relation between IQ and creative accomplishment.[10]

Since, as I have argued, intelligence and creativity are domain-specific, it makes more sense to ask about the relationship between having a high ability in a particular domain and being creative in that domain. We would not expect inventors to have high verbal IQs, and in fact they often do not (some inventors have verbal IQs as low as 60). When we pose the question in this domain-specific way, the answer is the same: a certain reasonably high baseline level of competence is required, but above some level, personality factors are more predictive of creative accomplishment than are ability levels.[11]

The Terman study shows us how having a high IQ as a child leads most typically to success, perhaps even expertise in some cases, but not necessarily to appreciable creative accomplishment. The Termites grew up, by and large, to be healthy, stable, and happy. Most became respected professionals—doctors, lawyers, professors, engineers, and businessmen—an outcome that could as well have been predicted by their edu-cated, middle-class family backgrounds as by their high IQs. Fewer than half the women were employed, but this was clearly due to the times. When the twenty-six Termites with IQs over 180 were compared to twenty-six Termites chosen at random, no marked differences in accomplishment were found. No Terman children grew up to become creative geniuses. Two future Nobel laureates, William Schockley, who invented the transistor, and Luis Alvarez, who won the prize in physics, were actually rejected from the study because their IQs did not test high enough! When asked to rate what was most important to them, the Termites listed family, friends, civic responsibility, and integrity—just the things that creators sacrifice for their work.[12]

Yet, although none have come to be considered geniuses, it is not fair to dismiss all Terman subjects as uncreative. At least one became a film director, and in a group of forty female Terman subjects selected as a representative sample, half were found to be unusually creative as amateurs in their later life. These women had also been creative as children—they had acted, written for the school literary magazine, or tried to become artists.[13]

Terman expected that his subjects would go on to make great creative accomplishments, but he came to realize that other factors must be involved in creative achievement besides high IQ. As we will see, having the right kind of personality and drive turns out to be more important than having the right IQ score. Moreover, as I hinted earlier, there is consider-able evidence that creative adults had stressful childhoods, a point to be discussed later. Most of the Termites did not seem to experience particularly high levels of tension and stress in their lives. The Termites who were the most well adjusted and popular in childhood were less likely to maintain their intel-lectual skills as adults than were those who were less popular. Being too well adjusted may not be conducive to creativity.[14]

The same kind of findings came out of a study of children who attended the Hunter College Elementary School in New York City between 1948 and 1960. This school was set up for high-IQ children in 1941, and the average score of the students on the Stanford-Binet IQ test was 157, just about the same as the average of the Terman children. Graduates of this school became productive professionals just like the Termites. They became doctors, lawyers, professors, dentists, journalists, and accountants. Like the Termites, they did not show the passion and ruthlessness that characterize creators. One said, for instance, "I really wanted to direct movies, to write movies, but I wasn't willing to cut the corners necessary." Their main motive in life was to enjoy themselves, and like the Terman subjects, they valued family life far more than does the typical creator. The only difference between the Terman and Hunter outcomes was that while most of Terman's women became housewives, the Hunter women, growing up in a time when women's roles were radically changing, often became professionals.[15]

Probably the fundamental reason high IQ in childhood does not predict creativity in adulthood is that, as already stated, intelligence and creativity are not the same things. Intelligence in a domain, like giftedness in a domain, means the ability to function at a high level in that domain, but creativity involves asking new questions and altering the domain. One can be highly intelligent but rigid, noncreative, or lacking in the kind of single-minded passion that drives creators. Take the oft-cited example of Marilyn (née vos Savant) Jarvik, the person with the highest recorded IQ ever, listed in the *Guinness Book of World Records* as 228. She now writes a Sunday magazine column called "Ask Marilyn," in which she replies to questioners who try to stump her. She may be quick, she may be clever, but no one would call her significantly creative in the big *C* sense.[16]

Creativity tests are not much better than IQ tests in predicting real-life creativity. Creativity tests usually measure divergent thinking, or what we might call "cleverness"—the ability to come up with novel associations, unusual uses for ordinary objects, and the like. Scores on divergent-thinking tests have some modest ability to predict creative accomplishments in adult work. But they do not correlate highly with "real" creative accomplishments—writing poetry, solving math problems in new ways, composing music, and so on.[17]

IQ not only fails to predict creativity in adulthood but also predicts school success imperfectly. IQ is even less useful as a predictor of success and achievement in adulthood. We know that IQ tests measure a narrow band of intelligence—verbal and numerical abilities, but not, for example, abilities in music, art, or athletics. In addition, IQ tests tell us nothing about the kinds of abilities that are undoubtedly critical for getting along in the world, abilities such as understanding of others, understanding of oneself, "practical" intelligence (that is, solving practical problems faced in real life), and resilience. If you are skeptical of the claim that a high IQ is not sufficient for success in life, just visit a meeting of an elite high-IQ society such as MENSA, the Four Sigma Society, or the Mega Society. Those who join such organizations are often unemployed misfits who have no other professional organization to join. Their high IQs are their only claim to self-esteem.[18]

IQ tests are also useless in predicting the kind of work that a person will eventually choose, since they are measures of "general" ability. Measures of domain-specific ability in childhood and adolescence give us some leverage in predicting adult occupation, though they tell us nothing about the extent to which an adult will make a creative contribution to that occupation. For instance, high scores on the math portion of the SAT in early adolescence are associated with high academic achievement later on in math and science. And adolescent hobbies such as computer programming, science experiments, math, and composition have been found often to match occupations in adulthood. And, according to one study, adults who go into occupations that grow out of adolescent interests reach higher levels of accomplishment than do those who go into occupations unrelated to earlier interests.[19]

DO CHILD PRODIGIES BECOME ADULT CREATORS?

Since childhood abilities and hobbies in particular domains are more predictive of adult occupational choices than is general IQ, we might expect to be able to predict the future course of prodigies, children who seem to be born into a domain and who are so gifted that they perform at an adult level. It is tempting to assume that prodigies will stick to their domains in adulthood and become major creators.

If we begin with adult creators and ask whether they were prodigies in their domains as children, the answer is mixed. Some were; many were not.

A study of classical composers by the psychologist Dean Keith Simonton showed that the greatest (as measured by productivity and fame) tended to have been prodigies as children. These greatest (presumably also the most creative) composers began to compose before their teenage years, while the lesser ones usually began to compose only in their late teens. The greats took three fewer years, on average, from the onset of formal training to the age of the first composition. And they also took about three fewer years between their first composition and their first masterpiece. Other studies have also shown that greater precocity in childhood is associated with greater eminence in adulthood. Prodigies take less time to become great, and by and large they reach greater heights.[20]

However, other studies tell a different story. Many creators did not start out as prodigies. Two-thirds of the group of 317 eminent twentieth-century individuals studied by the clinical psychologist Victor Goertzel were not even described as precocious, much less as prodigies. Of a sample of 100 creators studied by Csikszentmihalyi, many were not prodigies. And of the seven major twentieth-century creators studied by the psychologist Howard Gardner, only Picasso was a prodigy. Igor Stravinsky did not compose seriously until about twenty. Martha Graham did not dance until twenty. Einstein, an uneven student, was at first rejected from the Zurich Polytechnic, and he could not get a teaching job after receiving his physics doctorate. T. S. Eliot and Sigmund Freud were good students, but it took both many years to find their ultimate chosen domains. Eliot began in philosophy and turned to poetry at age twenty. Freud switched his interests regularly until his thirties, and it was only at forty that he began the investigation that culminated in psychoanalysis. And Mahatma Gandhi was unremarkable as a youth and did not find his calling as a leader until his early thirties.[21]

It may well be more important to be a prodigy in some domains than it is in others. Prodigies appear most often in formal, well-structured domains such as music and chess, and it is in these domains that eminent adults most often started out as prodigies. In the domains of writing and the visual arts, eminent adults were typically not prodigies as children. And in more loosely structured domains to which children would typically have no access, such as law or medicine, prodigies are almost never found. The psychologist Jean Piaget was a scientific prodigy who published a paper on biology at age eleven. But I would not count him as an exception, since where he excelled as a child was in the ability to make fine, subtle observations of the natural world. The natural world is a domain to which children typically have access, and the making of fine discriminations in this domain is something that children are often good at. Children's interest in discriminating kinds of sneakers or kinds of cars may be a modern manifestation of this ability.[22]

This does not mean that adults who are eminent in "non-prodigy" domains were not exceptional as children. They most likely were, if one knew how to look and what to look for. The 100 creators studied by Csikszentmihalyi showed intense curiosity at an early age. The seven creators studied by Gardner all worked systematically as children, and they clearly had unusual abilities. However, they did not discover their ultimate domains until their early adult years, often after some kind of crystallizing experience in which by chance they encountered something that made them fall in love with a particular domain. When the teenage Graham saw Ruth St. Dennis dance, she was mesmerized. "From that moment on my fate was sealed. I couldn't wait to learn to dance as the goddess did," she said. Only after Bruckner heard the music of Wagner, in his late thirties, did he begin to compose symphonies.[23]

Not only is being a prodigy not necessary for adult creative accomplishment, but it is also not sufficient, even in the domains in which prodigies are most common—music and chess. The list of failed prodigies, or of prodigies who became successful but not eminent, is a long one.

Of the six prodigies chronicled by David Feldman and Lynn Goldsmith, only one chose a career directly connected to the domain in which he had been prodigious. The child, who was a violin prodigy, was, at age twenty-seven, a world-class violin soloist. The child who was a writing prodigy went to work as a writer for a music magazine. Thus, his work was connected to his early literary skill, but this work has not yet led to major creative accomplishments in writing. Adam, mentioned in chapter 7, who was an omnibus prodigy gifted in music, mathematics, and language, attended an ordinary college at an early age and had a spotty academic record. At the time of this writing, he plans to go to graduate school in music composition. The math prodigy entered college at age thirteen, graduated with degrees in English, physics, and astronomy, and went to work at the Goddard Space Center.

The two chess prodigies stopped playing chess by ages ten and eleven, respectively. One did poorly in school; the other went to law school.[24]

As children, prodigies dazzle by their precocity. But every prodigy eventually becomes an ex-prodigy. If precocity and technical skill are all that they have, as adults they are no longer special. Late bloomers have caught up with them.

To go on to creative accomplishments, prodigies must remake themselves. They must learn how to transform sheer technical skill into something more conceptual, interpretative, and original. Prodigies in art must go beyond the technical skill of drawing and have something to express. An art prodigy named Peggy Somerville never was able to go beyond painting skilled impressionist landscapes. Hence, what looked astonishing for a child seemed fairly plebeian for an adult. Mathematicians must ask new questions, or solve old ones in new ways. Chess masters must invent new strategies to keep ahead of those who have studied their games. Musical prodigies who stun the world with their technical virtuosity are forgotten if they cannot play interpretively and expressively as adults. At twelve, the violinist Sarah Chang seems already to have achieved this. She was described as having an ability to "remake a piece with each performance, suffusing it with passionate musicality."

It is in the need to go beyond technical precocity that many prodigies falter. Jeanne Bamberger writes of the common identity crisis of adolescent musical prodigies, who realize that they now must come up with their *own* interpretations. These children, she notes, face a turning point when they have to integrate their original and intuitive understanding of music, based on phrasing and a bodily feel for their instruments, with a more conscious, formal mode of understanding. It is also at this point that they begin to ask themselves whether they are playing music for their parents, their teachers, or themselves.

When things go too smoothly for prodigies, they may never shift from being experts to being creators. Creativity is often spurred by failure. Creators have to be prepared to fail and fail again, and be invigorated by this process to boot.[25]

Another factor may also play a role in determining a prodigy's future. When the skills of a child prodigy match the skills valued by adult creators in that same domain, the prodigy may be more likely to succeed in that domain. Prodigies in drawing typically stand out in their ability to draw realistically. But realism in the visual arts is valued only in some cultures in particular eras. Perhaps Eitan lost his interest in drawing because what he was so good at was not what was then valued in the adult art world. Varda, another Israeli child of the same age who drew more expressively but less realistically as a child, has chosen to become an artist. In chess, the situation is more fixed. What counts as being good in chess does not change from era to era. And what chess prodigies can do well is just what is valued in adult chess masters. Perhaps then, chess prodigies are more likely to continue in chess than are prodigies in music and art. But we have little evidence for this speculation because too few prodigies have been followed into adulthood.[26]

PERSONALITY TRAITS THAT PREDICT LATER CREATIVITY

For those who do make it into the roster of creators, a certain set of personality traits proves far more important than having a high general IQ, or a high domain-specific ability, even one at the level of a prodigy. Creators are hard-driving, focused, dominant, independent risk takers. They have experienced stressful childhoods, and they often suffer from forms of psychopathology. This picture of creators suggests that high-ability children without at least some of these factors have little hope of becoming major creators as adults.

Drive and Energy

Creators are workaholics. The most creative people are also the most prolific. Eminent scientists studied by psychologist Anne Roe worked sixty- or seventy-hour weeks. Picasso created about 20,000 works; Freud had 330 publications; Edison obtained 1,093 patents.[27]

Creators must be able to persist in the face of difficulty and overcome the many obstacles in the way of creative discovery. They must persist because of what has become known among creativity researchers as the "ten-year rule"—the dictum that it takes about ten years of hard work in a domain to make a breakthrough. Even Mozart did not produce his first masterpiece until after about ten years of composing. A willingness to toil and to tolerate frustration and persist in the face of failure is crucial. Howard Gruber, in a study of the evolution of Darwin's thought, pointed out that what predicts great achievement is a passionate and prolonged involvement with a subject, a quality not measurable on standardized intelligence or achievement tests.[28]

Longitudinal studies tell the same story. Drive and energy in childhood are more predictive of success, if not creativity, than is IQ or some more domain-specific ability. As noted before, when the twenty-six Termites with IQs over 180 were compared to twenty-six Termites chosen at random, no marked differences in accomplishment were found. When the more successful Termites were compared with the less successful ones (for example, the lawyers versus the salesclerks), they were found to differ only by seven IQ points: the more successful averaged IQs of 157, and the less successful averaged 150. But where they really differed was in their childhood ratings of motivation. The more successful group had been rated as more persistent, driven, lively, and engaged in a greater number of extracurricular activities. And when Csikszentmihalyi compared those gifted adolescents in his study who did remain committed to their particular domain of gift at the end of high school with those who did not, he found the same thing: those who remained committed were those who earlier had shown higher achievement motivation and greater endurance. The kind of energy shown by the children I have described in earlier chapters would suggest that these children might be among those who will go on to become eminent. But only time will tell whether this childhood energy will continue during the adolescent years, when more disciplined and sustained work is required. Recall also that it is at adolescence that gifted children face the painful choice between intimacy and excellence.[29]

The kind of intense, focused drive that creators show has its personal costs. Creators must be willing to sacrifice comfort, relaxation, and personal relationships for the sake of their work. They are often ruthless and destructive of personal ties. In contrast, the Terman subjects, successful but not creative, tended to rate personal ties and civic duties very highly.[30]

While it is indisputable that intense drive is a necessary precondition of adult creativity, we cannot say where this drive comes from. It seems unlikely that such high drive can exist in the absence of high ability, because (with the exception of gamblers) people do not persist at what they are not good at. But why some people with high ability also have high drive, while others do not, is an unanswered question. Whether drive is an inborn characteristic or whether it comes about through role models is not clear. True, Terman's most successful adults were more likely than the least successful ones to have fathers in professional fields and a strong educational tradition in the family. But it is certainly possible that underlying both the parent's and child's success is inborn drive, or energy level.

Attention, Interest, and Flow

Related to motivation is the ability to maintain undivided, focused attention. Adult creators focus intensely while working. And in Csikszentmihalyi's study, those gifted adolescents most able to show undivided attention while at work in their domain of ability were those who made the most progress in their area at the end of high school. Those who were unable to shut out the daily distractions of adolescent life and focus were less able to develop their talent.[31]

The ability to focus is also a product of enjoyment. Adult creators do not distinguish between work and play, nor did the gifted children described in this book. Jacob played his guitar, Peter B. drew, David read, and Michael Kearney solved math problems not because they were told to do so but because these activities were what they most loved to do.[32]

But only those who can continue to merge work and play will go on to become adult creators. Adolescents in Csikszentmihalyi's study who reported feeling cheerful, strong, excited, open, and successful while working in their domain of gift were the ones who remained committed and did not lose interest and drop out. These were the adolescents who reported flow while working: they reported concentration so intense that they noticed nothing besides what they were working on. The ability of these adolescents to attain a state of flow while working in their area of gift was far more predictive of commitment than was academic ability, family support, or other personality factors.[33]

Dominance, Confidence, and Tolerance of Competition

Creators are strong, dominant personalities with an unshakable belief in themselves. They must be able to believe in themselves, for otherwise, they would be felled by the inevitable attacks that come when one goes against the established point of view. They set challenging goals for themselves and believe that they can achieve what they aspire to.[34]

Those who would be recognized must also be able to tolerate competition—some may even thrive on it. And they must be thick-skinned enough to sell themselves: artists must convince gallery owners to show their work; musicians must convince agents to take them on. William James Sidis and Erwin Nyiregyhazi were both isolated and overprotected by their parents, and they may have thus failed to develop the kinds of tough real-world social skills needed to convince their fields' gatekeepers of their creativity.[35]

Independence and Introversion

Creators are independent and nonconforming. Abiding by the norms of society is not a priority for them. Caring about pleasing everyone cannot be a priority for anyone who is going to challenge an established tradition.[36]

Accompanying independence is introversion and a high tolerance for solitude. Preferring to stay home alone and write, Charles Dickens refused social invitations. As he explained: "These are the penalties paid for writing books. Who ever is devoted to an art must be content to deliver himself wholly up to it." As seen in earlier chapters, independence, introversion, and a tolerance for solitude usually also characterize gifted children. Among Csikszentmihalyi's gifted adolescents, those who could not tolerate solitude dropped out of their talent domain at the end of high school, despite high ability in the domain. On the other hand, some have noted that creative people have a tendency toward *both* introversion and extroversion and are able to pass back and forth freely between these two states.[37]

Risk Taking and a Desire to Shake Things Up

Creators have to be willing to risk failure, since anything new is likely initially to be denounced. Moreover, the most successful creators are also those with the most failures to their names. As Simonton has documented, creators who produce the most works are most likely to produce a masterpiece, but they also produce the most failed works. Since creators have high self-confidence, they are less likely to be destroyed by a vicious review or an ignored composition.[38]

Perhaps most important of all is the desire to set things straight, to alter the status quo and shake up the established tradition. Creators do not accept the prevailing view. They are oppositional and discontented. And those who succeed in altering the tradition must have a vision good and important enough to become accepted eventually.[39]

Birth order plays a fascinating role here. First-borns tend to identify with their parents, and hence with the status quo. They tend to be successful high achievers with a traditional outlook. Later-borns identify less with their parents and are more rebellious, possibly because they are jealous of the privileges accorded to the first-born. This rebellious, antiauthority tendency of later-borns could account for the fact that we find many later-borns in domains in which it is expected that one will be unconventional. This seems to be the case in the domain of writing, for example: Dostoevsky, Eliot, Twain, and Wordsworth, to name just a few, were later-borns. Later-borns also are disproportionately more likely than first-borns to become political revolutionaries and to support revolutionary scientific theories such as Darwin's theory of evolution. Eighty-three percent of Darwin's supporters were later-borns, and Darwin himself was a later born. Since gifted children are disproportionately first-born, it is not surprising that while most become successful they do not turn out to be revolutionary creators.[40]

GENDER

Males have a better chance of succeeding as adult creators. Sadly, this is still true today in all domains, and there is no need to catalogue all the obvious social causes for this inequity. One piece of evidence that academically gifted girls are less likely than similar boys to fulfill their potential is the striking decrease in the number of girls in gifted school programs in later grades. Girls make up about half the population in these programs in kindergarten through third grade, but by junior high school they make up less than 30 percent. Girls show lower self-confidence and lower career aspirations than do boys of equal ability. The ambitions of bright girls decline in high school, even though they tend to get higher grades than boys. And girls are more likely to hide their abilities in order to be socially accepted.[41]

Thus, it is not surprising that more gifted boys than girls become adult creators. Those women who do become creators often adopt traditionally male lifestyles. Women who become eminent are four times more likely than equally distinguished men to be unmarried. And those who do marry are three times more likely to be childless than are successful married men. It is no doubt extremely difficult to find the time for creative accomplishment when one also has the job of being a wife and mother (which, unfortunately, still takes more time than the job of being a husband and father).[42]

Girls with high ability and no brothers are also more likely to become eminent than those with brothers. Brothers may overshadow their sisters and get all the parents' attention. The sisters of Mozart, Mendelssohn, and Yo-Yo Ma may have been equally gifted, but their parents poured all their resources into their sons.[43]

FAMILY FACTORS THAT PREDICT LATER CREATIVITY

"All happy families are like one another; each unhappy family is unhappy in its own way," wrote Tolstoy in the opening lines of *Anna Karenina.* "Hatred of one parent or the other can make an Ivan the Terrible or a Hemingway; the protective

love, however, of two devoted parents can absolutely destroy an artist," wrote Gore Vidal. Retrospective portraits of the families of individuals who became creators in adulthood clash strikingly with the benevolent picture of the families of gifted children painted by Csikszentmihalyi, Bloom, and others. The future creator seems to grow up in a family that is much less child-centered and supportive, and far more stress-filled than does the gifted child not destined to become a creator.[44]

Three-fourths of the eminent creators studied by the Goertzels experienced some kinds of extreme stress in their early family life: poverty; death of a parent; divorced or estranged parents; rejecting, abusive, or alcoholic parents; fathers who experienced professional failure or bankruptcy; and so on. They came from atypical families—irritable, explosive families, often prone to depression or to large-scale mood swings. In a later study of eminent twentieth-century individuals, the Goertzels found that 85 percent came from stress-filled families.[45]

Particularly shocking is the frequency with which eminent individuals have lost a parent in childhood. A few who lost a parent in the first decade of life include Tolstoy, Dante, Michelangelo, Raphael, J. S. Bach, Wagner, and Charlie Chaplin. In Cox's study of major creators, over a fifth had lost one or both parents in childhood. Levels of early parental loss in creators are over three times as high as levels in the population at large, which have been reported to be somewhere between 6 percent and 8 percent. The only other groups with such high levels of parental loss are delinquents and depressive or suicidal psychiatric patients.[46]

It is instructive to compare the typical creator family to that described by Csikszentmihalyi as optimal for the development of talent, because the contrast is striking. The typical family in the Goertzels' studies would have been classified by Csikszentmihalyi as "differentiated"—high in intellectual stimulation, low in support. Families that combined intellectual stimulation and drive with emotional support, families that would have been classified by Csikszentmihalyi as "integrated," were in the clear minority.[47]

Family trauma more often characterized those who became writers, artists, musicians, and actors, in comparison to those who became scientists, physicians, and political leaders in Goertzels' study of eminent twentieth-century figures. Eighty-nine percent of the novelists and playwrights, 83 percent of the poets, and 70 percent of the artists had difficult family lives, while this was true for only 56 percent of the scientists. The same distinction was found in a comparison between Nobel Prize winners in science versus literature: those in literature were more likely to come from unstable family environments. Literature winners were also eight times more likely to have lost a parent in childhood. This fact is certainly consistent with the conventional wisdom that artists are more tormented and disturbed than are scientists, and it also fits with the finding, discussed later, that artists are more prone to psychopathology than are scientists. Of course, these findings come from studies of twentieth-century Western artists and scientists, and it is not at all clear that the same would have held true in the eighteenth century or in non-Western cultures.[48]

There may be something about the experience of stress in childhood that actually promotes creativity, even though this same level of stress may destroy more often than promote. A variety of hypotheses might account for the association of stress in childhood with creativity in adulthood.

Stress could lead a gifted child to escape into an obsessive, solitary focus on an area of talent. Obstacles and hardship could teach lessons in perseverance and resilience, two ingredients needed for later creativity. Trauma could make a child feel different from the start and thus lead to a willingness to *be* different. The perception that one's environment is unpredictable may lead to the desire to achieve in order to gain control over one's destiny. A sense of deprivation could lead a child to be creative in order to gain positive recognition from the world. But it is not possible to draw definitive conclusions about causality. Creative individuals and their parents could share genetic traits that lead to both stress and creativity. Thus, rather than trauma stimulating creativity, creativity and trauma could be spurred on by some independent, inherited factor.[49]

Other explanations might account for the association of early parental loss with later creativity. Children who have suffered loss of a parent learn to tolerate solitude, which creative work demands. In addition, the child who has lost a parent does not have to compete with, and perhaps triumph over, a living parent. The child is free to achieve more than the parent. Jean-Paul Sartre wrote that the death of his father was "the big event of my life . . . [it] gave me freedom." Alternatively, the child who has lost a parent may feel a strong responsibility to live up to some imaginary projection of what the parent would have expected.[50]

Loss of a parent may also lead to a kind of compensation—desire to replace the lost object by creating one's own object, whether a work of art or a scientific theory. A horror of the void left by death could stimulate a child to create an ideal world and to lose herself in its creation. The desire to replace emptiness and the lost object with an ideal created world may be so strong that the individual is not overly critical. Too much self-censorship always works against novelty.

A genetic explanation is also conceivable. Perhaps individuals who are extremely driven and creative choose to have children later in life, and thus are more likely to die before their children are grown. Such parents could pass on the capacity for drive and creativity to their children.

A bolder hypothesis, but one for which there is increasingly strong evidence, is that stress is associated with creativity through the intervening factor of psychopathology. Stress-filled families may be prone to various kinds of psychopathology that are themselves often associated with creativity. Stress-creating parents could either genetically transmit psychopathology to their children or create psychopathology through trauma. And abundant evidence exists in support of a strong link between certain forms of psychopathology and creativity, especially creativity in the arts. For instance, a study of American creative writers showed that 80 percent had been diagnosed with some form of mood disorder (for example, depression, mania), and that over half of them had bipolar disorder, experiencing both depression and states of mania. And a study of British artists and writers found that 38 percent had been treated for a mood disorder, a percentage that is very high considering the fact that only one in three people with mood disorders ever seeks treatment.[51]

But what underlies this association between creativity and mood disorders? First, the experience of mood disorder can lead a person to create as a therapeutic enterprise. And the experience of suffering can provide the subject for works of art. In addition, mood disorders, particularly mania of low intensity, called hypomania, can lead to unusual thought processes associated with creative episodes: sharpened and focused thinking, novel associations, overinclusive categories (perceiving similarities between things normally seen as different), and speed of thought, as well as the kind of drive so often found in creative people.[52]

Certainly, most people with affective disorders do not become creators. And most creators do not suffer from affective disorders. Yet the higher incidence of such disorders in creators suggests that one predictor of creativity might be a tendency toward an affective disorder, as well, of course, as a high ability in some domain. But along with this combination, there must also be a high degree of ego strength and self-confidence. Creators' unshakable belief in their own vision must keep them from disintegrating.

LUCK

The role of chance in affecting adult eminence should not be underestimated. Many of the factors that predict creativity are ones over which a person has no control. Birth order, gender, an encounter with a crystallizing experience, and the kind of family one is born into, for instance, can be thought of as random lucky or unlucky accidents. There are brilliant people with doctorates in philosophy who are driving taxis merely because so few university openings for philosophers exist. The gifted child must have abilities that the domain is ready for. If the abilities are too out of synch with the domain, the gifts may never be recognized or may only be recognized centuries later. And the child must grow into an adult who succeeds in convincing the sometimes arbitrary gatekeepers of the domain—universities, publishers, museum curators, music recorders, and so on—that his or her abilities are exceptional.[53]

It would be satisfying to be able to conclude this book with a list of factors that would allow us to predict those gifted children who will drop out, those who will become experts, and those who will alter their domains. But this is not—and may never be—possible. We cannot predict what ordinary people will become, so why should we expect to be able to predict what atypical people will become? Early high ability is a very imperfect predictor of ultimate achievement in adulthood because so many other factors play a role—family, educational opportunity, personality, and luck. We will never know how many high-ability children fail to develop their gifts because they did not have the right kind of family, education, crystallizing experience, or personality. The characteristics that I have described are neither necessary nor sufficient for the emergence of an adult creator. All that we can say is that these characteristics are often associated with creativity in adulthood, and we can speculate about why. Nevertheless, I venture the following best guess about the factors that predict the four possible combinations of gifted child and adult outcome described in the beginning of this chapter.

- Those gifted children most likely to develop their talent to the level of an expert will be those who have high drive and the ability to focus and derive flow from their work; those who grow up in families that combine stimulation with support; and those who are fortunate to have inspiring teachers, mentors, and role models.

- Those gifted children most likely to leave their creative mark on a domain in adulthood will also have high drive, focus and flow, and inspiring mentors and models. But in two other areas they should be different. They should be willing to be nonconforming, take risks, and shake up the established tradition. And they should be more likely than those who become experts to have grown up in stressful family conditions. (While stress may be a facilitating factor, it is surely not sufficient, and is not a factor for parents to strive for!) Many are also likely to develop some form of affective disorder. In addition, they must be born when the times are right: their domains must be ready for the kinds of changes they envision, and there must not be too many others likely to beat them in revolutionizing the domain first.

- Those gifted children predicted to burn out are those whose parents push them to extremes and are overinvolved in their development. These parents differ from those who produce creative children. Parents of future creators cause stress in their children's lives, but they are not overinvolved. Instead, they pursue their own interests, and they encourage independence in their offspring. But the difficulty of prediction is brought home by the fact that John Stuart Mill, who was excessively pushed by his father, did not drop out, whereas William James Sidis did.[54]

- Those gifted children not "born into"
  a domain often discover their ultimate calling in adulthood when they are catalyzed by a crystallizing experience, a life-changing event in which a gift is discovered and self-doubts are dispelled.

There will always be exceptions to every generalization when we are trying to predict something as complex as what people will make of their lives. Nonetheless, the more we learn about the factors typically associated with the blossoming of talent—whether the talent blossoms into expertise or into revolutionary creativity—the more we can do to foster that talent and prevent future Sidises from burning out.

Eleven

SORTING MYTH FROM REALITY

What can we say, now, about giftedness and its myths? I began with nine questionable assumptions about giftedness. I offer the following conclusions in place of these myths.

MYTH 1: GLOBAL GIFTEDNESS

Myth: Academically gifted children have a general intellectual power that makes them gifted in all school subjects.

Reality: Rarely are children gifted across the board in academic domains. Rather, gifts tend to be clearly defined and domain-specific. Uneven profiles are far more common than even ones, with most high-IQ children excelling more clearly in either mathematical or verbal areas. Highly verbal children can often do well in math using verbal strategies, but verbal abilities in the absence of spatial ones can only take one so far in math. Children can also be gifted in one scholastic area and actually learning disabled in another.

MYTH 2: TALENTED BUT NOT GIFTED

Myth: The gifted are those children with high ability in academic areas. Children with high ability in music and art are talented.

Reality: There is no justification for calling academic children "gifted" and artistic ones "talented." Although the domain in which they are exceptional differs, these children are alike in showing precocity, divergence, and drive. The same generalizations apply across all forms of high-ability children: their exceptional abilities are in part inborn; their abilities develop as a result of some of the same kinds of family forces; they face the same kinds of educational needs; and because they are introverted and different from others, they are at risk for social isolation. It is a false distinction to classify some as gifted and others as talented.

MYTH 3: EXCEPTIONAL IQ

Myth: Giftedness in any domain depends on having a high IQ.

Reality: Children can be extremely gifted in music or art without having exceptional overall IQs. However, musically gifted children tend to perform better in scholastic areas than do artistically gifted children. Why musical children do well in school is not known, but a likely factor is the learning of music notation, which may then generalize to the notations of language and number, along with the daily drill of disciplined practice. The best evidence for gifts operating independently of IQ comes from savants, individuals with extremely low IQs who are nonetheless able to perform at dazzling levels in a few well-structured, formal domains, notably calculation, piano playing, realistic drawing, and chess.

MYTHS 4 AND 5: BIOLOGY VERSUS ENVIRONMENT

Commonsense Myth: Giftedness is entirely inborn.

Psychologists' Myth: Giftedness is entirely a matter of hard work.

Reality: No matter how early they begin and how hard they work, most children will never learn as rapidly, nor make as much progress, as those born with exceptional abilities. This does not mean that hard work and training are irrelevant to the development of talent. Gifted children (and savants) work extremely hard and acquire far more extensive experience in their domains than do most children, and this experience is critical to the development of their talent. However, gifted children and savants do not get to be where they are simply through hard work and rigorous disciplined practice. Rather, it is the high ability with which these children are born that drives them to work so hard. Their motivation and hence their extensive practice are a *result* of their gift, not its cause. There is considerable evidence in favor of the position that gifted children and savants are born with atypical brains, and that gifts are to some extent a product of one's genes and of hormonal influences during gestation.

Those rare ordinary children who are disciplined to work extremely hard can also achieve high levels of skill. However, these children never achieve without extensive support and instruction from adults, and they never achieve as much as do children born with an unusual fit between their minds and some domain. Gifted children have a lucky combination of a special proclivity to master some domain along with an obsessive drive to master that domain. Gifted children as well as savants need minimum instruction and support, discover rules on their own, and often approach their domain in unusual ways, inventing idiosyncratic ways of solving problems.

MYTH 6: THE DRIVING PARENT

Myth: Gifted children are created by pushy parents driving their children to overachieve; when pushed too hard by over-ambitious parents, these children burn out.

Reality: No matter how gifted, children do not develop their gifts without a parent or surrogate parent behind them encouraging, stimulating, and pushing. But the parents do not create the gift. The children are usually pushing the parents, sending out clear signals of their need for a stimulating environment. Parents try to accommodate.

But parents can destroy a gift. When parents live vicariously through their child's gift, caring more about their child's achievements than her emotional life, they are likely to end up with a bitter dropout.

MYTH 7: GLOWING WITH PSYCHOLOGICAL HEALTH

Myth: Gifted children are better adjusted, more popular, and happier than average children.

Reality: Extremely gifted children do not have interests in common with their peers, and they are considered odd by their classmates. They are extremely intense, they are introverted, and they like solitude. The rewards of solitude are great because time alone can lead to the development of skill and the acquisition of knowledge. If being well adjusted means fitting in and being like others, these children are certainly not well adjusted. They are different from others, and they know it. And unless they can find others like themselves who share their passion for mastery and learning, they become isolated, lonely, and discouraged. They also risk becoming arrogant and contemptuous of others, on the one hand, or underachievers lacking in self-esteem, on the other.

MYTH 8: ALL CHILDREN ARE GIFTED

Myth: All children are gifted, and thus there is no special group of children that needs enriched or accelerated education in our schools.

Reality: While all children have relative strengths and weaknesses, some children have extreme strengths in one or more areas. Extreme giftedness creates a special educational need, just as does retardation or learning disability.

The belief that all children are gifted and thus that no child is gifted enough to need special education leads to discrimination against the gifted. Children who are gifted in music typically receive music education appropriate to their level. Because schools do not pretend to accommodate such children, they get their training outside of school. Children gifted in art also are not accommodated by school art classes, and the kinds of art classes offered by regular schools play little or no role in the development of the artistic child's ability. Artistically gifted children are usually self-taught and do not receive training in art at an early age. This is unfortunate, as artistic gifts need stimulation and training as much as do musical ones. Children gifted in a bodily-kinesthetic domain receive training outside of school: they study gymnastics, skating, swimming, tennis, or ballet from high-powered coaches in private or group lessons.

For children gifted in academic areas, it is another story indeed. These children are treated like artistically gifted children. They receive little special education, and it is assumed that they can teach themselves. Either they get an education no different from that offered for typical children, or they receive minimal intervention. Usually this means they leave their classroom once or twice a week for an enrichment class in which they may be given training in creative and critical thinking, and in which they work on projects that may or may not be related to their domain of gift. The typical criterion for admission into such programs is an IQ at the moderately gifted level: 130 or higher. This is also the criterion for admission into full-time "gifted and talented" classes, and into schools reserved entirely for the gifted.

But what this means is that the resources we spend on the gifted in our schools are spent primarily on the moderately gifted. If we elevated the academic standards and expectations for all children and made our schools more like those in Western Europe and Japan, then the moderately gifted would no longer be underchallenged. For most of those who still remained underchallenged, skipping a grade or linking up with a mentor would suffice.

But there will still be some who need something more— those rarer children who are "severely" gifted, who work at five or six years above grade level. These children remain poorly served today even by the best programs, classes, and schools for the gifted, and would still be underchallenged were we to elevate standards for all. There is a vast difference between a child with an IQ of 180 and a child with an IQ of 130, and they should not be treated as belonging to the same group with the same kinds of educational needs. What resources we spend on the gifted would be more profitably spent on the profoundly gifted. These children would then be more likely to develop their potential and find others like themselves as friends.

Children with extreme verbal or mathematical abilities are identical in needs to children with extreme artistic or musical gifts. They hunger for stimulation and challenge. Perhaps if we focused the resources we have reserved for the gifted on these kinds of children, more such children would develop their talent and go on to become experts or creators in their domains as adults.

MYTH 9: GIFTED CHILDREN BECOME EMINENT ADULTS

Myth: Gifted children, especially prodigies, go on to become eminent and creative adults.

Reality: Many gifted children, even prodigies, do not become eminent in adulthood, and many eminent adults were not prodigies. Gifted children are certainly creative in that they make discoveries in their domain on their own, and they solve problems in novel ways. But they cannot be creative in the sense of transforming their domain. No one transforms a domain without years of hard work (the minimum number of years seems to be around ten), so it is no wonder that children do not do so.

But most gifted children do not transform their domains even as adults. Most cannot go beyond the kind of precocity and technical skill that made them stand out as children. Some continue to work in the same area and become skilled professionals operating within an established domain. Some move on to other areas of interest, where they show competence, but not brilliance. Some, usually those made into showpieces by their parents, want nothing to do with their early domain of gift.

Only a few ever go on to disrupt a domain and reshape it for all those to come. Those who become adult creators differ from those who become skilled experts within a domain. But where they differ is in personality, not in level of ability. They have discontents that have often been nurtured from an early age by a stress-filled family life. They are the nonconformists, the risk takers, the ones who want to shake things up and change the status quo. Sometimes they are also those with psychopathology—the depressives, the manics, the manic-depressives. Whether their mood disorders are environmentally created by traumatic childhoods and parental loss, or also genetically transmitted by parents whose affective states create trauma in childhood, is not known, but it is plausible that both environmental and genetic causes play an important role.

∽

Gifted children are not just faster than normal children but are also different. Because they require minimal structured support, because they make discoveries on their own and invent novel ways of understanding, and because they have such a rage to master, they are different from children who just work extremely hard. Gifted children, especially the extreme ones we call prodigies, are far more like savants than like hard-working but otherwise normal children. But we can as yet only speculate about how the brains of gifted children and savants diverge from the norm. With the new and continually improving brain imaging techniques, we may some day have a definitive answer on the nature of the brains of gifted people.

Psychology should have theories that account for the development of the atypical as well as the typical. We should not have entirely separate theories to explain learning and development in ordinary, retarded, autistic, learning-disabled, and gifted children. Too often we have researchers devoted to one of these populations, with the result that we have separate explanatory accounts of each population. Ultimately, psychological theory must account for all of the various ways in which the mind and brain develop. We need universal theories of development, but these theories must be able to incorporate special populations, whether these are special because of pathology, giftedness, or both.

Notes

One
NINE MYTHS ABOUT GIFTEDNESS

1. For more on how the gifted have been feared, see Anastasi and Foley (1941) and Zigler and Farber (1985).
2. Studies of morality, leadership, and eminence conducted (respectively) by Colby and Damon (1992), Gardner (1995), and Simonton (1994) represent exceptions. For a discussion of how giftedness has not been incorporated into mainstream psychology, see Jackson (1993). For more on giftedness as a privilege rather than a problem, see Zigler and Farber (1985).
3. For a critique of giftedness as an elitist construct, see Margolin (1994).
4. For evidence of the ten-year rule for mastery and creativity, see Gardner (1993a) and Simonton (1994).
5. For a discussion of flow states, see Csikszentmihalyi (1990). For other definitions of *giftedness,* see Sternberg and Davidson (1986). Renzulli (1986b) defined *giftedness* as a combination of ability, creativity, and task commitment. Sternberg (1991) defined *giftedness* as superior access to and ability to use basic intellectual strategies. The U.S. Office of Education defined gifted children as those capable of high performance in general intellectual ability, specific academic aptitude, creative or productive thinking, leadership, the visual and performing arts, and psychomotor ability (Marland, 1971).
6. Feldman and Goldsmith (1991) defined a *prodigy* as a child who achieves adult mastery by or before the age of ten.
7. For a description of domains where prodigies are and are not

found, see Feldman and Goldsmith (1991) and Csikszentmihalyi, Rathunde, and Whalen (1993). Piaget published a paper in biology at the age of eleven. For a discussion of Darwin's childhood interests in nature, see Bowlby (1990). For more on E. O. Wilson's early naturalist abilities, see Wilson (1994). For a more general consideration of giftedness in the biological domain, see Gardner (1996).

8. For a discussion of the Pueblo conception of giftedness, see Romero (1994). For an additional cross-cultural discussion of giftedness, see Callahan and McIntire (1994). For a discussion of how the domains in which we find gifted children are culturally determined, see Tannenbaum (1994).

9. Gagné (1995) distinguishes between gifts as the starting point and talents as the end point. My point is that all high early abilities should be called either gifts or talents.

10. The quotation is by the British psychologist Hans J. Eysenck, in Eysenck and Barrett (1993, p. 115). For a critique of efforts to define *giftedness* by IQ, see Gardner (1983, 1993b), Getzels and Jackson (1962), and Sternberg (1981, 1982, 1985, 1986, 1991, 1993).

11. The quotation about parents producing a child prodigy is from Howe (1990, p. 138).

12. For the Terman quotation, see Subotnik and Arnold (1993, pp. 17–18).

13. For more on the notion of giftedness as an elitist social construct, see Margolin (1994).

14. For a discussion of discrimination against gifted children, see Silverman (1993c).

15. For an empirical differentiation between high IQ and creativity in children, see Getzels and Jackson (1962).

Two
GLOBALLY GIFTED:
THE CHILDREN BEHIND THE MYTH

1. For the view that no child can learn to read without a great deal of help, see Howe (1990), who wrote: "When a young child has learned to read earlier than most, before going to school, a close examination of the circumstances almost always reveals that the child has received considerable assistance from

an adult or an older child who has been prepared to spend a good deal of time working with the young learner" (p. 79). For a similar point of view, see Fowler (1990). For studies of precocious readers, see Crain-Thoreson and Dale (1992), Jackson (1992), Jackson, Donaldson, and Cleland (1988), Jackson, Donaldson, and Mills (1993), and Mills and Jackson (1990).

2. Doman, G. (1964). For evidence that adult creators are involved in many projects at the same time, see Gruber (1981), who described creators as involved in a "network of enterprise," a network of related problems they are pursuing.

3. For more on parents of prodigies who believe their children have supernatural powers, see Feldman and Goldsmith (1991).

4. For a similar example, see Goertzel and Goertzel (1962), who quoted a mother about her son, as follows: "He is the one who does all the pushing of those around him in his search for answers" (p. 285).

5. For the quotes from Michael and his father, see Castro and Grant (1994, p. 100).

6. There have been numerous other reports of extreme prodigies like Michael. For instance, Feldman and Goldsmith (1991) described Adam, a child who spoke in sentences at three months, carried on complex conversations at six months, read children's classics at eighteen months, and discussed logarithms at three years. Gross (1993a) described several children who said their first word before six months. Howe (1990) and Radford (1990) described famous prodigies such as J. S. Mill, who learned Greek at age three. Hollingworth (1942) described children with IQs over 180 who have shown similar extraordinary early abilities.

7. Terman's study appeared in a series of volumes, listed here in order of appearance: Terman (1925), Burks, Jensen, and Terman (1930), Terman and Oden (1947, 1959), Holahan and Sears (1995). The second volume, by Cox (1926), is based on a historical sample of eminent adults.

8. For a discussion of the artificial nature of items on the Stanford-Binet, see Gardner (1983).

9. For statistics about percentages of children scoring at various levels on IQ tests, see Gross (1993b), Marland (1971), Sattler (1982), and Simonton (1994). For average IQs of Ph.D. holders, see Simonton (1994).

10. Terman and Oden (1947) reported on the reading ability of the children in their study with IQs of 170 or above. They noted that nearly 43 percent of the 170-plus group were reading at age five, while only 18 percent of the entire group were able to read at this age. Thirteen percent of the 170-plus group read before age four. Hollingworth (1942) found that out of twelve children with IQs of 180 or higher, all read before school: four read at two, three read at three, and three read at four. Many others have also reported a relationship between early reading and high IQ: e.g., Freeman (1979), Gross (1993a, b), and Terrassier (1985). In a study by Leroy-Boussion (1971, cited in Terrassier [1985]) done in France, children were offered the chance to learn to read with only half the usual amount of instruction. Only those children with IQs of 130 or higher succeeded. However, early reading is not a necessary predictor of later high IQ. Jackson (1992) noted cases of children who read early but who had only average IQs.

11. Ceci (1990a) discussed how the Terman study confounded IQ with social class.

12. The more recent longitudinal study of high-IQ children that did not depend on teacher nominations was conducted by Gottfried, Gottfried, Bathurst, and Guerin (1994). IQ tests are constructed so that they will not be biased in favor of either sex. Thus, one would expect screening by IQ tests to yield equal numbers of boys and girls.

13. Whitmore (1986) discussed teachers' reluctance to consider children with a learning disability as gifted. Getzels and Jackson (1962) found that children who scored high on creativity tests but were average in IQ performed as well in school as did those who scored high on IQ tests but only at average level on creativity tests. Despite the equal academic performance of these two groups of children, teachers preferred the high-IQ children. Teachers may have sensed that the high-IQ children were more diligent and less likely to make trouble. Ceci (1990a) noted the possibility of a social class bias and a halo effect in Terman's teacher nominations.

14. For studies showing that parents are good detectors of IQ giftedness, see Ciha, Harris, Hoffman, and Potter (1974), Robinson and Robinson (1992), and Silverman (1993c). Kaufmann and Sexton (1983) found that 83 percent of ninety-eight parents were aware of their child's gifts before school. Lewis and

Louis (1991) and Roedell (1989) reported that parents are most likely to notice signs of alertness and responsiveness, and precocity in language, memory, and abstract reasoning.

15. The characteristics listed here are discussed in much of the literature on high-IQ children. For examples, see Albert (1971, 1975), Cox (1926), Freeman (1991), Gross (1993a), Hildreth (1966), Hollingworth (1926, 1931, 1942), Kincaid (1969), Lehman (1953), Lewis and Louis (1991), Ochse (1990), Piirto (1994), Raskin (1936), Robinson (1993a), Roe (1952), Roeper (1982, 1990), Silverman (1993c), Subotnik, Kassan, Summers, and Wasser (1993), Terman (1925), and Zixiu (1985).

16. The study showing a relation between infant memory and later IQ was conducted by Fagan and McGrath (1981). See also Bornstein and Sigman (1986) and Lewis (1975) for more on signs of giftedness in infancy.

17. For more on studies showing a relationship between preference for novelty in infancy and IQ, see Lewis and Brooks-Gunn (1981).

18. For evidence of precocious physical development, see Gross (1993a) and Kincaid (1969).

19. For more on the concept of flow, see Csikszentmihalyi (1990). For a description of how high-IQ children solve the Tower of Hanoi problem, see Kanevsky (1992).

20. For more on how high-IQ children are "metacognitive" (that is, aware of the strategies they use) and how they think differently, see Kanevsky (1992), Rogers (1986), Shore and Kanevsky (1993), and Sternberg (1981, 1986).

21. For a discussion of the dyssynchrony between handwriting and other skills in high-IQ children, see Terrassier (1985).

22. Alexander, Carr, and Schwanenflugel (1995) noted the metaphysical discourse in which such children engage. Hollingworth (1942) noted the example of Goethe, who at nine devised his own religion.

23. Greenacre (1956). For mystical, hypomanic states in creators, see Jamison (1993, 1995).

24. For evidence that high-IQ children often have IQs higher than their parents, see Benbow, Zonderman, and Stanley (1983).

25. For an early discussion and critique of the fact that IQ tests are the primary way in which giftedness is assessed, see Get-

zels and Jackson (1962). For a more recent discussion of the same issue, see Feldhusen and Jarwan (1993). Sattler (1982) pointed out that most gifted programs use a cutoff of 130, which yields the upper 2 to 3 percent of the school population.

26. For a discussion of how IQ tests may be unfair to certain groups, see Ford (1994) and Frasier (1993). For observational measures as a better way to identify gifted minority children, see Borland and Wright (1994).

27. Feldman and Goldsmith (1991) administered Piagetian tests of logic, spatial understanding, role taking, and moral reasoning to several of their prodigies and found that the prodigies performed like normal children of their age. This finding was used to demonstrate that giftedness is highly domain-specific. Those who have criticized the equation of giftedness with general intelligence, and who have argued for a more multidimensional view of giftedness, include Feldhusen (1986, 1989), Feldman and Goldsmith (1991), Gagné (1995), Gardner (1983), Heller (1991), Marland (1971), Piirto (1994, 1995), and Treffinger and Renzulli (1986). For in-depth considerations of how IQ tests measure only a narrow set of abilities, see Gardner (1983) and Sternberg (1985, 1991).

28. For more on new tests of academic giftedness, see Mönks (1992), Renzulli (1978), Sternberg (1985), and Sternberg and Davidson (1986). For more on the finding that normal-IQ children selected for other qualities fared as well on many dimensions as high-IQ children in a gifted program, see Hunsaker et al. (1995). For a discussion of alternatives to IQ tests for identifying gifted minority students, see Ford (1994) and Frasier (1993).

Three
UNEVENLY GIFTED,
EVEN LEARNING DISABLED

1. Norbert Wiener and William James Sidis are often cited as examples of math prodigies. Howe (1990), Feldman and Goldsmith (1991), and Radford (1990) described mathematical and literary prodigies. Howe (1990, p. 142) mentioned Winifred Sackville Stoner and Nika Turbina, who wrote

poetry, and Daisy Ashford, who wrote a short novel. Feldman and Goldsmith (1991) studied Randy McDaniel, also a writing prodigy who began writing stories at three and by six could write poems, stories, and plays, and had researched essays.

2. For a discussion of the conflict between how gifted children solve math problems and what schools require, see Feldhusen, VanTassel-Baska, and Seeley (1989, chap. 6).

3. The example of the solution by the gifted child is from ibid.

4. Krutetskii (1976) described how mathematically gifted children mathematize everyday experience. Children who are fascinated by numbers were described by Piirto (1994). Edward Teller was described by Blumberg and Panos (1990). Radford (1990) discussed the kinds of early mathematical interests that are predictive of one's becoming a mathematician.

5. This quote is from the Center for Talented Youth, Study of Exceptional Talent, newsletter #33, Sept./Oct. 1994, p. 5.

6. The two quotes are from Terman (1925, pp. 339 and 636, respectively). For the lack of strong special interests in art and music, see Terman (1925, p. 369, table 139). Hollingworth (1926) recognized that extremely high-IQ children could be weak in some areas, and noted that her children with IQs over 180 often had difficulty with a particular school subject.

7. For more on unevenness in academically gifted children, see Benbow and Minor (1990), Mueller, Dash, Matheson, and Short (1984), and Silver and Clampit (1990). Lewis (1985) described children with large discrepancies between verbal and spatial subscores. For more on the finding that high-IQ adults show lower correlations among subabilities, see Detterman (1991, 1993) and Detterman and Daniel (1989). For more on the finding that children with IQs of 120 or higher had sharp verbal-performance discrepancies, see Wilkinson (1993). For a discussion of the possibility that a ceiling on subabilities exists in people with lower IQs, see Detterman (1991).

8. For more on the study of over a thousand gifted individuals, see Achter, Lubinski, and Benbow (1996). For a description of the SMPY program, as well as discrepancies between verbal and mathematical scores, see Stanley (1988). For more on the retrospective study of math, see Bloom (1985).

9. The study of verbally precocious children was conducted by

Benbow and Minor (1990). See also Benbow, Stanley, Kirk, and Zonderman (1983) for findings that mathematically gifted children are often weak verbally, but that verbally gifted children usually are also strong in math. See Stanley and Benbow (1986) for a discussion of why overall IQ should not be used for entrance into special classes.

10. For more on gifted and learning-disabled children, see Baum (1984), Baum and Owen (1988), Boodoo et al. (1989), Feiring and Taft (1985), Feldhusen and Jarwan (1993), Fox, Brody, and Tobin (1983), Hemmings (1985), Reis, Neu, and McGuire (1995), Schiff, Kaufman, and Kaufman (1981), Whitmore (1981), and Yewchuk (1985). Some information on giftedness and attention disorder can be found in Durden and Tangherlini (1993). For more on underachieving gifted children, see Butler-Por (1993) and Whitmore (1980). The estimated number of gifted learning-disabled students comes from Davis and Rimm (1985). The estimate on the number of high-IQ children with reading disabilities comes from Fox (1983). For more on the school problems of gifted learning-disabled students, see Reis, Neu, and McGuire (1995).

11. For more on the point that math involves spatial thinking, see Gardner (1983) and Krutetskii (1976). For more on studies showing a relationship between high math and high spatial ability, see Benbow and Minor (1990), Benbow, Stanley, Kirk, and Zonderman (1983), and Hermelin and O'Connor (1986a). For more on the point that this is truest for those most gifted in math, see Benbow, Stanley, Kirk, and Zonderman (1983). For evidence that college math and science majors are skilled spatially, see Casey and Brabeck (1989), Casey, Winner, Brabeck, and Sullivan (1990), and D'Amico and Kimura (1987).

12. For more on the relationship between scores on the math SAT, verbal SAT, and Ravens Progressive Matrices, see Stanley (1988).

13. Krutetskii (1976) described the three kinds of children with math gifts.

14. For more on information-processing methods and assumptions, see Gardner (1985).

15. Dark and Benbow (1991) conducted the study comparing working memory in verbally gifted students versus mathematically gifted ones. For similar findings, see Puckett and

Kausler (1984), who found that memory-scanning rate for digits predicts quantitative ability in college, and that scan rate for words and letters predicts verbal ability in college. See also Palmer, McLeod, Hunt, and Davidson (1985), who showed that reading ability correlates with performance on tasks with words, but not letters.

16. Roe (1952) noted that scientists reported using visual imagery. Hermelin and O'Connor (1986a) showed that mathematically gifted children were better than verbal IQ-matched controls in remembering patterns. Casey, Winner, Brabeck, and Sullivan (1990) showed that college students who were best at recalling a complex design were those majoring in areas requiring extensive math.

17. The study of retrieval of semantic information was conducted by Dark and Benbow (1991). Other researchers who have also shown that speed of accessing verbal information in long-term memory is a correlate of high verbal ability include Hunt, Frost, and Lunneborg (1973) and Hunt, Lunneborg, and Lewis (1975).

18. For more on the claim that priming effects are smaller for good readers, see Carr (1981) and Fischler and Goodman (1988).

19. Chase and Ericsson (1982) and Chi (1978) discussed memory in chess experts. Feldman (1980) and Gardner (1983) discussed how high abilities in one area do not predict high ability in another area.

20. Dark and Benbow (1991) also claimed that mathematically gifted children excel over the verbally gifted in continually updating information in working memory, whether this information is linguistic or numerical. They showed this when they asked mathematically and verbally gifted children to recall letters paired with other letters, numbers, or locations on a grid. Those with mathematical talent outperformed those with verbal talent, even when the stimuli were letters. This finding is consistent with the idea that at the core of mathematical talent is the ability to handle long chains of reasoning (Gardner, 1983). However, Dark and Benbow did not use words on this task, and it was with words that the verbal group stood out in the first task. Only if subjects had been asked to recall letters paired with words, and the math group had still excelled, would I feel confident in reaching Dark and Benbow's conclusion.

21. For more on sex differences in math, see Benbow (1988) and Benbow and Stanley (1980b, 1983a). For evidence that sex differences persist and predict later math and science achievement, see Benbow and Stanley (1982). For more on the role of spatial ability in sex differences in math, see Burnett, Lane, and Dratt (1979) and Casey, Nuttal, Pezaris, and Benbow (1995).

22. The lowered male-female ratios among Asians are reported in Benbow (1988). For the argument that Asian parents place more stress on visual-spatial thinking than do other groups, see Storfer (1990).

23. For the argument favoring achievement tests over full-scale IQ scores or subscores, see Stanley (1995).

Four
ARTISTIC AND MUSICAL CHILDREN

1. For accounts of gifted drawing development see Cane (1951), Gardner (1980), Goldsmith (1992), Golomb (1992a, 1992b, 1995), Golomb and Hass (1995), Gordon (1987), Milbrath (1987, 1995, in preparation), Paine (1987), Pariser (1987, 1991), Richardson (1991), Vasari (1979), Wilson and Wilson (1976), Winner and Martino (1993), Zhensun and Low (1991), and Zimmerman (1992). For accounts of gifted musical development, see Bamberger (1982, 1986), Feldman and Goldsmith (1991), and Shuter-Dyson (1982, 1986).

2. For more on the late acquisition of color terms, see Soja (1994).

3. Eitan was studied by Golomb (1992a, 1995).

4. Milbrath (1995) described the child who drew dinosaurs with scientific accuracy.

5. Richardson (1991) reported how Picasso drew from non-canonical starting points.

6. A study of depth techniques used by normal and gifted drawers was carried out by Milbrath (1995). She found that foreshortening was used in 50 percent of the gifted children's drawings by age seven and eight; comparable levels in the normal sample were reached only by ages thirteen and fourteen, six years later.

7. For more on the claim that gifted children use a figural, rather

than a conceptual, strategy, and that perspective is first local, see Milbrath (1987, 1995). Willats (1977) studied the development of perspective in normal children and found it to be a late development.

8. The comparison of orientations used by gifted and ordinary drawers was made by Milbrath (1995).

9. A study of composition in gifted children was conducted by Milbrath (in preparation). Arnheim (1974) writes about kinds of pictorial balance.

10. For more on realism in the childhood drawings of artists, see Gordon (1987). The sculptors studied by Bloom (1985) also drew realistically as children. The advanced realism of Millais was noted by Paine (1987); that of Landseer was noted by Goldsmith and Feldman (1991); that of Seargent was noted by Cox (1992); and that of Klee, Picasso, and Toulouse-Lautrec was noted by Pariser (1987, 1991).

11. The three quotes by Picasso are from Richardson (1991, pp. 29, 45, and 29, respectively).

12. The two artists who did not begin with realism were described by Golomb (1992b) and Golomb and Hass (1995). Similar cases were described by Hurwitz (1983), Kerschensteiner (1905), and Lark-Horowitz, Lewis, and Luca (1973).

13. Gombrich (1960) discussed the development of Western perspective, beginning with the Renaissance.

14. Yani was described by Goldsmith (1992), Goldsmith and Feldman (1989), and Zhensun and Low (1991).

15. Gardner (1980) studied a child who used cartooning as an escape from realism. But Milbrath (1995) described a child who could draw equally well in cartoon and realistic styles.

16. Goldsmith and Feldman (1989) noted the contrast between Yani's painting and calligraphy. Manuel (1919) found no relation between drawing and handwriting in Western children.

17. The quote is from Wilson and Wilson (1976, p. 46).

18. Crystallizing experiences, ones that catalyze a gifted child into a domain, were described by Walters and Gardner (1986).

19. I am indebted to Bill Eldridge, Jacob's teacher, for his insights into Jacob's playing.

20. I am indebted to Nina Grimaldi, Stephen's piano teacher, and Judy Ross, his theory teacher, for their insights into Stephen's abilities.

21. For more on the claim that musical giftedness emerges early,

see Scott and Moffett (1977) and Shuter-Dyson (1986). The Mozart anecdotes are reported in Schonberg (1970). The survey of forty-seven musicians was conducted by Shuter-Dyson and Gabriel (1981), as was the finding that the majority of great violinists were prodigies. However, Sloboda (1985) noted some counterexamples of concert pianists who were not recognized as musically gifted in early childhood. For the anecdote about Lorin Hollander, see Winn (1979).

22. Radford (1990), Miller (1989), Scott and Moffett (1977), and Sosniak (1985) discussed how the earliest sign is a strong response to musical sound. Sloboda (1985) discussed how sheer auditory discrimination ability is not a sign of musical giftedness.

23. Judd (1988) argued that musical memory is the central indicator of musical giftedness.

24. For the typical age when singing emerges, see Sloboda (1985). For earlier emergence of singing in the gifted, see Shuter-Dyson (1982). Revesz (1925) studied the Hungarian musical prodigy Erwin Nyiregyhazi and also made the point about Handel.

25. For more on when children can sing accurately, see Gardner, Davidson, and McKernon (1981) and Sloboda (1985). For more on accurate singing in musically gifted children, see Revesz (1925).

26. For a discussion of musically gifted children's ability to imitate songs, see Miller (1989). Schonberg (1970) discussed the early abilities of Mozart. Richet (1900) studied Pepito Areola. Winn (1979) wrote about Rubinstein. Henson (1977) made the point about Mozart's memory for the *Miserere*. Bamberger (personal communication) observed young performers imitating famous performers' styles.

27. All the information about Erwin Nyiregyhazi is from Revesz (1925).

28. Bamberger (1986) found that musically gifted children say they cannot imitate a piece if they think too much about it as they are playing it.

29. The incidence of perfect pitch in the normal population was estimated by Bachem (1955). Winn (1979) discussed Lorin Hollander. Mozart's perfect pitch was discussed by Winn (1979) and Schonberg (1970).

30. For more on composers who did and did not have perfect

pitch, see Slominsky (1988) and Sacks (1995a). Walters, Krechevsky, and Gardner (1985) found that not all musically gifted children had perfect pitch.

31. Sergent and Roche (1973) found that earlier onset of instruction was associated with having perfect pitch. Takehuchi and Hulse (1993) found that perfect pitch could be trained in normal children between ages three and five.

32. Merritt Schader, a student at Princeton who had studied at the San Francisco Music Conservatory, was the musician who told me of the problems that come with perfect pitch. Sacks (1995a) noted that perfect pitch may interfere with musical enjoyment and performance.

33. Walters, Krechevsky, and Gardner (1985) reported that sight-reading is not consistently associated with giftedness in music. Mozart's sight-reading abilities were reported by Scott and Moffet (1977). Glenn Gould's ability to read notes before words was reported in the film *Thirty-two Short Films About Glenn Gould*.

34. Sloboda (1985) discussed the development of singing in normal children. For a discussion of the decline of inventiveness in drawing, see Gardner (1980) and Winner (1982).

35. The musician who picked tunes off the radio is quoted in Walters, Krechevsky, and Gardner (1985). Areola was studied by Richet (1900). Mozart's improvisational abilities were discussed by Scott and Moffett (1977) and Schonberg (1970).

36. Revesz (1925) noted how rare it is to find a very young child gifted in composition.

37. Composers who began to compose before ten are noted by Schwartz (1984), Revesz (1925), and Radford (1990).

38. Bamberger (1986).

39. Bamberger (1982) discussed the midlife crisis in musical prodigies.

40. Milbrath (1987) developed the analogy between shifting from figural to formal in drawing and in music.

Five

THE IQ MYTH

1. For more on reports of children with high IQ, but with no particular drawing ability, see Holland (1961), Hollingworth

(1926, 1942), Lewerenz (1928), Wallach and Wing (1969), and Welsh (1975). Terman's special ability cases are discussed in Terman (1925, p. 47).

2. Csikszentmihalyi, Rathunde, and Whalen (1993) conducted the study of teenagers gifted in various domains. Getzels and Csikszentmihalyi (1976) found that art students rated aesthetics more highly than theology students rated religion.

3. Milbrath (1995) discussed the case of Joel. Frith (1980) and Phillips (1987) reported that artists have difficulty with written language.

4. See Gardner (1983) for a discussion of the independence of visual-spatial ability from other forms of intelligence.

5. Milbrath (1995) described another gifted child artist who also saw forms in patterns, and cited Temkin (1987) as having made this observation about both Ernst and Klee.

6. For evidence that gifted drawers excel in recognition of hidden shapes and incomplete figures, that they can readily store and access images, and that these abilities are IQ independent, see O'Connor and Hermelin (1983) and Hermelin and O'Connor (1986a).

7. Vasari (1979) described Michelangelo's visual memory. Morelock and Feldman (1993) discussed Yani. Richardson (1991) described Picasso's visual memory. Rosenblatt and Winner (1988) found that gifted drawers excelled in visual memory for pictures.

8. The study of memory for pictures was conducted by Rosenblatt and Winner (1988). The study of memory for Persian letters was conducted by Hermelin and O'Connor (1986a).

9. Correlations between musical ability and IQ are discussed by Shuter-Dyson (1982). Radford (1990) made the point about Erwin Nyiregyhazi's academic precocity and Mendelssohn's translations. The IQs of Terman's special ability music cases are reported in Terman (1925, p. 47).

10. Csikszentmihalyi, Rathunde, and Whalen (1993).

11. Radford (1990) noted the IQs of the Yehudi Menuhin School students. Shuter-Dyson (1986) mentioned the student at this school with the lowest IQ who won a music prize.

12. For more on academic performance levels of adolescents gifted in athletics, music, and art, see Csikszentmihalyi, Rathunde, and Whalen (1993, pp. 67–68).

13. For the claim that musicians, painters, and writers have prodigious visual and auditory memories, see Waterhouse (1988).

For findings that the musically gifted perform well on visual-spatial-perceptual tasks, see Barrett and Barker (1973), Hassler (1990), Hassler, Birbaumer, and Feil (1985, 1987), and Karma (1979). Comparisons between spatial abilities in musicians versus painters were made by Hassler (1990). The findings showing a relationship between music lessons and spatial skills were presented at the meeting of the American Psychological Association: see Rauscher, Shaw, Levine, Ky, and Wright (1994). For more on the relationship between listening to Mozart and spatial reasoning, see Rauscher, Shaw, and Ky (1993, 1995). The findings by Rauscher and colleagues are surprising enough that they ought to be independently replicated before they are accepted.

14. Savants were originally called "idiots savants" by a British psychiatrist, Dr. J. Langdon Down, in 1887, a man better known for the discovery of Down's syndrome, a genetic abnormality that causes retardation. For reviews of the savant syndrome, see Howe (1990) and Treffert (1989). Treffert (1989) used the term "savant syndrome" and reported that savants' IQs range between 40 and 70. Treffert (1989) reported the figure of fewer than 100 cases.

15. For general discussions of the nature of autism, see Frith (1989), Gillberg and Coleman (1992), Happé (1995), Kanner (1944), Rimland (1964), and Wing (1976).

About 10 percent of autistic individuals show savant signs (Rimland [1978]), while only .06 percent of retarded people do (Hill [1978]). The estimate of .06 percent is very low because it is based on the institutionalized population, and therefore includes many with IQs under 40, the lower cutoff for savantism. Since retardation is a far more common condition than autism, there are more retarded savants than autistic ones. The incidence of early infantile autism is estimated to be about 4 to 10 in 10,000 (Happé [1995]). Selfe (1995) claimed that all savants have some autisticlike symptoms.

A tiny minority of savants are found among children who become schizophrenic in late childhood or early adolescence, and among children who suffer brain damage either before birth, at birth, or in childhood after experiencing an injury or an illness. Thus, while the savant syndrome is usually congenital, it can also be acquired. For a discussion of acquired savant syndrome, see Treffert (1989).

16. For more on heightened spatial abilities in autistics, see Frith

and Hermelin (1969). Shah and Frith (1983) showed that autistics recognize hidden figures well and note how they solve jigsaw puzzles.

17. For the foreign-language–learning savant, see Smith and Tsimpli (1995). Sometimes hyperlexia, the ability to read without comprehension at the sentence or text level, is considered a form of savantism. But here I focus only on prodigious savants, those whose skills would be extraordinary if they were found in a normal adult. Hyperlexics show us skills that are extraordinary only in comparison to their total lack of skill in other areas.

18. For discussions of Nadia, see Park (1978) and Selfe (1977, 1983, 1985, 1995). Selfe (1995) stated that all the drawing savants she had seen were autistic or had autistic symptoms. Although most savants draw very realistically, some savants work in an expressionistic style, as can be seen in Cathy's figure 5.2 (see Buck, Kardeman, and Goldstein [1985]).

19. Rimland (1964) described feats of musical memory in autistic children. See also Happé (1995) and Frith (1989).

20. Selfe (1983) compared Nadia to four other autistic artists and noted similarities among them. Morgan (1987) also described an autistic artist with poor gross-motor coordination. The foreshortened drawing by the fifteen-year-old autistic child is from Park (1978).

21. Park (1978) argued against the hypothesis that language destroyed Nadia's drawing talent. She noted that her own daughter, also an autistic artist, continued to draw as her language improved.

22. Wiltshire (1987, 1991). For a discussion of Wiltshire, see Sacks (1993, 1995b).

23. See Morgan (1987) for a description of another child with these same preferences for implements that make fine lines.

24. Morishima and Brown (1977) studied the Japanese savant.

25. Park (1978) and Selfe (1983) suggested that savants are more interested in process than product and are unaffected by praise.

26. Selfe (1983) noted that the five autistic artists she studied could all place initially disconnected details on various parts of the page and end up with a perfectly connected set of lines. Wiltshire was also able to do this.

27. The study of E. C. was carried out by Mottron and Belleville (1993).

28. O'Connor and Hermelin (1987) compared savants and retarded individuals matched in IQ on the Draw-a-Person Test.

29. Treffert (1989) noted that sometimes savant memories are described as "eidetic," but that the term *photographic memory* more accurately describes savant memory. Eidetic images are vivid visual afterimages that last but a short time; photographic memories allow accurate recall of information (not necessarily visual) long after it has been experienced. Some form of vivid, detailed, photographic memory, which operates automatically, meaning without conscious effort, always characterizes the savant.

   O'Connor and Hermelin (1983) showed that normally gifted children outperformed ordinary children in their ability to recognize incomplete pictures. O'Connor and Hermelin (1987) showed that savants excelled in precisely the same way. O'Connor and Hermelin (1987) demonstrated that savants show even more exceptional performance in reproducing (rather than just recognizing) a picture from memory. They seem to possess a superior motor-programming skill along with their superior visual memory.

30. Down (1887) used the phrase "verbal adhesion." Cain (1970) used the phrase "memory without reckoning." Rimland (1964) said that savants pay more attention to physical characteristics of the stimulus than its meaning. Down (1887) describes the savant who memorized *The Rise and Fall of the Roman Empire*. Selfe (1995) discussed Nadia's memory.

31. See Phillips, Hobbs, and Pratt (1978) for evidence that children copy designs more realistically than representations. See Edwards (1979) for evidence that people copy more faithfully when copying pictures upside down.

32. Selfe (1977) originally suggested an impairment in conceptualization as an explanation for Nadia's skill. See also Arnheim (1980) and Pariser (1981) for a consideration of this idea. Selfe (1995) has since questioned this hypothesis.

33. Arnheim (1974) discussed how children's schemas are generalizations.

34. The study in which savants were asked to reproduce representational and scrambled pictures was carried out by O'Connor and Hermelin (1987).

35. Pring and Hermelin (1993) conducted the study in which

savants and gifted children were tested for their memory of pictures related either by shape or by category.

36. Sacks (1985, p. 20).
37. I am indebted to Constance Milbrath for the point about the lack of visual narrative and humor in savants' drawings.
38. Rimland and Hill (1984) noted that savants are most often found in music. Miller (1989) provided an extensive review of music savants. He pointed out that our understanding of music savants comes entirely from Western savants.
39. For a discussion of Wiltshire, see Sacks (1993–94, 1995b).
40. Rimland (1978) described the child who could listen to an opera but not sit still for *Sesame Street*. Miller (1989) described the child who was disturbed by loud noises, yet loved music. According to Schonberg (1970), loud sounds made Mozart physically ill.
41. Rimland and Fein (1988) noted the fidelity with which music savants play back music they have heard.
42. Miller (1989) suggested that the piano is the music savant's preferred instrument because of its one-to-one mapping and linear organization.
43. The kind of perfect pitch savants have is the most extreme form: they can identify any notes on any instrument. This is sometimes called "extended absolute pitch." For more on the incidence of perfect pitch in autistic populations, see Rimland and Fein (1988).
44. Miller (1989) and Treffert (1989) noted the confluence of blindness, retardation, and prematurity in music savants.
45. For further discussion of Blind Tom, see Miller (1989) and Treffert (1989).
46. Simonton (personal communication) noted that there are large discrepancies in the number of pieces Blind Tom was claimed to have memorized, but most sources give a figure between 500 and 700.
47. Simonton (personal communication) noted the need to be skeptical of possible exaggerations by Tom's owner, since Tom was exploited for profit.
48. The music savant N. P. was studied by Sloboda, Hermelin, and O'Connor (1985).
49. For further evidence that musical savants use musical structures such as scale and rhythm as they process and recall music, see Charness, Clifton, and MacDonald (1988).

50. Hermelin, O'Connor, and Lee (1987) carried out the study of composition in music savants.
51. Miller (1989) studied L. L. and noted his ability to compose.
52. Judd (1988) described the style of musical savants as devoid of feeling. Scheerer, Rothmann, and Goldstein (1945) characterized savants as pathologically concrete. For more on the claim that music savants play with feeling, see Viscott (1970) and Miller (1989).
53. Miller (1989) argued that musical savants have intact musical ability, while calculators and hyperlexics just have splinter skills. Mitchell (1907) discussed nonpathological calculators. Hyperlexia is also a splinter skill: hyperlexics can decode print but not extract meaning at the sentence or text level. Calendrical calculators were first described by Down (1887), then by Binet (1894).
54. Scripture (1891) described the calculator who counted words at a play.
55. Treffert (1989) discussed the case of Fuller.
56. Scripture (1891) noted calculators' ability to recall numbers from anywhere in the string.
57. Hermelin and O'Connor (1990b) studied calculating savants. Horowitz, Kestenbaum, Person, and Jarvik (1965) argued that calculators use rote memory. Ericsson and Faivre (1988) estimated the number of bits required to multiply any two 3-digit numbers. A comparison between a savant calculator and a psychologist with a math degree was conducted by Hermelin and O'Connor (1990b). The two subjects were asked, among other things, to generate prime numbers. The savant was quicker and more accurate, but both made the same kinds of errors. A follow-up study with the same results was conducted by Anderson, O'Connor, and Hermelin (n.d.).
58. The twins were described by Horowitz, Kestenbaum, Person, and Jarvik (1965).
59. Hermelin and O'Connor (1986a) noted that calendrical calculators have more difficulty with remote dates. They also showed that savants use calendrical regularities or rules.
60. Hamblin (1966) quoted the twins.

Six

THE BIOLOGY OF GIFTEDNESS

1. For further elaboration of this argument, see Ericsson and Faivre (1988), Ericsson, Krampe, and Tesch-Romer (1993), Howe (1990), Howe, Davidson, Moore, and Sloboda (1995), Sloboda (1996), Sloboda, Davidson, and Howe (1994), and Sloboda, Davidson, Howe, and Moore (in press). Suzuki is quoted in Herman (1981, p. 36). For a discussion of behaviorism and its demise with the cognitive revolution, see Gardner (1985).

2. Bloom (1985). Josh Waitzkin is discussed in Waitzkin (1984). See Walters, Krechevsky, and Gardner (1985) for the claim that music teachers say they can easily tell when they have a gifted student: these students learn rapidly, correct their own errors, and perform with confidence.

3. Ericsson, Krampe, and Tesch-Romer (1993). Similar claims were made by the British psychologist John Sloboda and his colleagues in a study called the Leverhulme Project, reported in Howe, Davidson, Moore, and Sloboda (1995), Sloboda and Howe (1991), Sloboda, Davidson, and Howe (1994), and Sloboda, Davidson, Howe, and Moore (in press). Parents of musician-children in this study said that they had seen no early signs of musicality. But the children studied here were not as profoundly gifted as were those studied by Bloom. Moreover, Sloboda's highest musical achievers had begun to recognize tunes by eighteen months, six months ahead of the others. Sloboda believes, however, that this could be simply because this group had more exposure to music in infancy.

4. Gruber (personal communication).

5. Charles was studied by Hildreth (1941). I am indebted to Rudolf Arnheim and Claire Golomb for bringing Hildreth's study to my attention as an example of what can be achieved with work but no exceptional talent.

6. For more on the Chinese method of teaching drawing, see Gardner (1989) and Winner (1989).

7. For more on the Suzuki method, see Suzuki (1969).

8. Schlaug, Jancke, Huang, and Steinmetz (1995). The anatomical distinction of the brains of those with perfect pitch is consistent with autopsy evidence from a musician with melody deafness who had damage in the left planum temporale, as

reported by Schlaug et al. (1995), and with Scheibel's (1988) report that the preserved brain of a musician with perfect pitch had an auditory area almost twice as large as usual. The neurons in the auditory area observed by Scheibel were not elevated in number, but were less densely packed than usual.

As mentioned, the left planum temporale is somewhat larger than the right planum temporale in most people, and it has been implicated in language dominance (Geschwind and Levitsky, 1968). Sacks (1995a) noted that we need MRIs of special populations with perfect pitch to see if they all have the considerably enlarged left planum temporale found in the musicians with perfect pitch.

These findings might seem at first to clash with the finding that the right hemisphere is activated during music listening, as reported by Zatorre, Evans, Meyer, and Gjedde (1992). However, while musically untrained people depend primarily on their right hemisphere when processing music, trained musicians have left-hemisphere involvement as well, as shown by Bever and Chiarello (1974). This is probably because people with training or with giftedness (these are difficult to disentangle) use a more analytic strategy when listening to music. For a critique, see Zatorre (1984).

9. The Russian study was reported on CBS's *60 Minutes* and discussed by Altman (1991).

10. For the study of Einstein's brain, see Diamond, Scheibel, Murphy, and Harvey (1985). For information on the functions of the parietal lobe, see Mesulam (1981). For information on the functions of glial cells, see Thompson (1985, pp. 45–47). What little we know about their functions suggests that these cells help to clear out cellular debris in the brain and also play a role in myelinization of the neurons, a process that radically speeds nerve conduction. Support for a relationship between low neuronal to glial cell ratios and high abilities comes from the fact that these ratios decrease as the phylogenetic scale is ascended in mammals from mice to humans (Bass, Hess, Pope, and Thalheimer, 1971).

11. For research showing that animals raised in stimulating environments develop more neurons, see Diamond (1988). For the study of violinists' brains, see Elbert et al. (1995). For an overview of the new brain imaging techniques, see Raichle (1994). For research on music, language, and the brain, see

Zatorre, Evans, Meyer, and Gjedde (1992). For research on imagery and the brain, see Kosslyn and Koenig (1992).

12. Jerison (1982) studied brain size across species. He reported a correlation of .995 between the brain size of the animal and the amount of cortical surface. The studies showing a relationship between brain size and IQ in humans, but only in males, were conducted by Willerman, Schultz, Rutledge, and Bigler (1991) and Yeo, Turkheimer, Raz, and Bigler (1987). Willerman et al. (1991) reported a correlation of .51 between brain size and IQ in college students with average versus high (130 or more) IQs. This means that brain size predicted 26 percent of the variance in IQ. The greatest size difference between average- and high-IQ brains was in the areas of the cortex involved in higher mental processes, such as the area in which Einstein had an enhanced number of glial cells. And Yeo et al. (1987) found a relationship between type of IQ score and side of brain. The greater the verbal IQ in relation to performance IQ, the greater the size of the left hemisphere (which is responsible for language in most people) in relation to the right.

13. For the report on the artist with a larger visual area, see Scheibel (1988).

14. Scheibel (1988) examined dendrite length and complexity in the brain.

15. Galton (1883).

16. Other studies in this same paradigm have measured "inspection time." Here a stimulus is briefly flashed on a screen, and a person must make a judgment about it, such as which of two lines is longer. The higher the IQ, the shorter the exposure needed to make an accurate judgment.

   The same criticisms made of the reaction-time measures can be made of the inspection-time measures. This task is more complex than it seems. It is not just a measure of the speed of sensory processing, but may be influenced by factors such as how quickly people adapt to sensory stimulation and what strategies they decide to use. Thus, this is not a basic biological measure of a person's neuronal intelligence.

   For studies using reaction time and inspection time to show that neuronal speed underpins intelligence, see Eysenck (1967), Jensen (1993), and Nettelbeck (1987). See Eysenck (1988) for the view that these underpinnings of intelligence are fixed and inherited. For critiques of reaction- and inspection-time studies, see Anderson (1992) and Ceci (1990a, b).

17. Studies of glucose metabolism during nonverbal reasoning tasks were carried out by Haier, Siegel, Neuchterlein et al. (1988), Haier, Siegel, MacLachlan et al. (1992), and Haier, Siegel, Tang et al. (1992). Subjects' brains were imaged while taking the Ravens Advanced Progressive Matrices test, a difficult task that calls on nonverbal reasoning. One might predict that high-ability brains would use more glucose, since they achieve more. However, just the opposite was found. People with higher test scores used less glucose while taking the test. Thus, they seemed to have more efficiently functioning brains. For the same finding with verbal tests, see Berent et al. (1988) and Parks et al. (1988). Thus, perhaps greater efficiency is a nonlocalized, general aspect of being skilled.

18. Despite statistically significant findings, however, the correlations between ability and glucose efficiency account for only about a quarter of the variance.

19. Oddly, individuals with higher verbal IQs showed the most pronounced increase in glucose use after Tetris training. This is difficult to explain, since Tetris is not a task that can be solved verbally. This just goes to show how difficult these new brain imaging studies are to interpret.

20. Diamond (1988) showed lower glucose use in rats raised in enriched environments. Other measures have also demonstrated some relationship between IQ and efficiency. For instance, we can measure brain waves (called evoked potentials) that result from a particular stimulus such as a flash of light. Studies have shown a strong positive relationship between IQ and consistency of brain-wave response in response to simple sensory stimuli. Thus, perhaps people with higher IQs have neurons that respond to sensory information more consistently, hence perhaps more efficiently. The relationship between IQ and brain-wave response was shown by Blinkhorn and Hendrickson (1982) and Hendrickson and Hendrickson (1980), and was replicated by Haier et al. (1983).

Evoked potentials have also been measured when people listened to clicks (Schafer, 1987). When the clicks were regular, rather than random, people with higher IQs showed less of an evoked potential response; but those with lower IQs did not. The conclusion drawn was that those with higher IQs were better able to ignore highly predictable events.

Both Ceci (1990a, b) and Anderson (1992) have critiqued studies using evoked potentials as direct measures of intelligence. Anderson has pointed out that evoked potentials vary as a function of skull thickness or spinal fluid properties. Until we understand the relation between brain waves and neurons, and between brain waves and cognitive processes, a correlation between EEG and IQ cannot help us understand the relationship between neurons and cognitive processes. Anderson concluded that while there is definitely some correlation between various kinds of low-level neural processes and IQ, it is not clear how to interpret such a relationship. Ceci pointed out that intelligence cannot be reduced to some low-level physiological property of the brain unrelated to motivation, training, education, or even test anxiety.

21. For more on the Geschwind-Galaburda theory, see Geschwind (1984) and Geschwind and Galaburda (1987).

22. For more on the role of the right hemisphere in math, music, and art, see Gardner (1975, 1983), Gervais (1982), and Zatorre, Evans, Meyer, and Gjedde (1992). For evidence that math involves spatial thinking, and thus is likely to involve the right hemisphere, see Krutetskii (1976). For evidence that math depends on both right- and left-hemisphere skills, see Gardner (1983). For a review of extensive evidence that the left posterior hemisphere is directly involved in language, see Gardner (1975).

    For evidence that delayed growth in the left hemisphere leads to enhancement of the right hemisphere, see Goldman-Rakic and Rakic (1984), who showed that damage to one side of a monkey's brain can result in increased growth on the other side.

23. Since anomalous dominance means having a more symmetrical brain, there is no telling which side of the brain will end up controlling handedness. Thus, those with anomalous dominance are sometimes right-handed, and sometimes non-right-handed. Geschwind and Galaburda (1987) estimated that only about a third of those with anomalous dominance are non-right-handed. In a minority of cases, people with anomalous dominance have reversed brain organization with language on the right side and visual-spatial skills on the left. For more information about the relationship between anomalous dominance and handedness, see Bryden, Hecaen, and DeAgostini (1983), Hecaen, DeAgostini, and Monzon-Montes (1981), and Satz, Achenbach, and Fennell (1967).

    Testosterone was only one factor in determining handedness, Geschwind recognized. For discussions of early left-sided brain damage as a cause of non-right-handedness, see Bakan (1971) and Satz (1973). For more on genetic contributions to handedness, see Annett (1985) and Levy and Nagylaki (1972).

24. See Geschwind and Behan (1982) for the argument that testosterone affects the development of the immune system. Animal research has also demonstrated that testosterone affects the developing immune system. For instance, administering testosterone to mice in utero yields baby mice with immune disorders (McCruden and Stimson [1991]). Animal research has also shown that an intact left hemisphere is important for an intact immune system. For instance, a lesion to the left, but not the right, hemisphere in mice can damage their immune system (Renoux [1988]).

25. See Geschwind and Galaburda (1987) for a discussion of the factors related to excess testosterone exposure. For more on sex differences in math, see Benbow (1988) and Benbow and Stanley (1980b, 1983a). For more on sex differences and handedness, see Oldfield (1971), Porac and Coren (1981), and Geschwind and Galaburda (1987). For more on sex differences and learning disorders, see Geschwind and Galaburda (1987). Bakan (1991) showed the relationship between stress and smoking and increased testosterone.

26. For a critical evaluation of the Geschwind-Galaburda theory, see the entire issue of *Brain and Cognition, 26*(2), 1994: For other critiques of the Geschwind hypothesis, and a discussion of conflicting evidence, see McManus and Bryden (1991), Pennington et al. (1987), Satz and Soper (1986), and Van Strien, Bouma, and Bakker (1987).

27. O'Boyle and Benbow (1990) showed that academically gifted adolescents used their right hemisphere more strongly during face perception than did average-ability subjects. O'Boyle, Alexander, and Benbow (1991) showed that the right hemispheres of mathematically gifted adolescents had enhanced electrical activity.

28. Annett and Kilshaw (1982) reported a higher incidence of left-handedness among mathematicians. Smith, Meyers, and Kline (1989) reported that college students who rate themselves as mathematically able are disproportionately non-right-handed. McNamara, Flannery, Obler, and Schachter (1994) conducted the study in which 20 percent of people who said they had a math gift were non-right-handed. Ben-

bow (1986) reported elevated rates of non–right-handedness among academically precocious youth.

29. See Zolog (1983) and Inouye, Shinosaki, Iyama, and Matsumoto (1993) for evidence that math computation is mediated by the left hemisphere. See Gardner (1983) for evidence that mathematical conceptualization is mediated by the right hemisphere.

30. Mebert and Michel (1980) conducted the study showing that 21 percent of art students are left-handed. Peterson (1979) also found that adults who study art are disproportionately non–right-handed. Smith, Meyers, and Kline (1989) showed that non–right-handers are also likely to rate themselves as having artistic talent. Rosenblatt and Winner (1988) reported the higher incidence of left-handedness in children gifted in drawing. Peterson and Lansky (1974) reported the higher number of non–right-handers in architecture. Cranberg and Albert (1988) found more non–right-handers among high-level male chess players.

31. The study reporting that 11 percent of musically gifted people were non–right-handed was conducted by McNamara, Flannery, Obler, and Schachter (1994). Oldfield (1969) found no relationship between musical ability and handedness. Other studies have found a relationship only to weak left-handedness, a finding that would not be predicted by the Geschwind and Galaburda model: Byrne (1974) found an overrepresentation of mixed-handers among students at a music conservatory, but this included both weak right-handers as well as weak left-handers; and Deutsch (1980) found that weak left-handers outperformed all other handedness types in memory for pitch in college students selected at large. For further studies of handedness in musicians, see Hassler (1990), Hassler and Birbaumer (1988), Hassler and Gupta (1993), and Peterson (1979). Enough studies have demonstrated a relationship to prohibit us from rejecting the music-handedness link.

32. See Rosenblatt and Winner (1988) for evidence that left-handed children gifted in art are no more gifted than are right-handed children gifted in art.

33. For a review of studies investigating whether non–right-handers have higher spatial abilities, see Annett (1985) and Porac and Coren (1981). Mebert and Michel (1980) suggested that the conflicting findings about left-handers' spatial abilities may be

due to the fact that left-handers are a mixed group in terms of dominance. For right-handers with anomalous dominance, see Casey and Brabeck (1989).

34. O'Boyle, Gill, Benbow, and Alexander (1994) carried out the finger-tapping study. An earlier study by O'Boyle and Benbow (1990) showed that not only mathematically but also verbally gifted adolescents use their right hemisphere as much as their left in processing language. However, it may well be that the verbally gifted students in this study were also mathematically gifted.

Some evidence exists that giftedness in music is also associated with some language in the right hemisphere. Some studies showed that musicians use their right hemisphere more than do nonmusicians to process words (Gordon [1970, 1978, 1980] and Hassler and Birbaumer [1988]). However, the picture is complicated by sex differences. Hassler (1990) found that female musicians and painters were more lateralized for language than were male musicians and painters (and even than a control group). This is just the opposite of what is found in nonmusical people, where females show more bilateral involvement than do males.

35. For evidence that dyslexic children score higher on IQ subtests assessing spatial abilities than they do on those assessing sequential ones, see Naidoo (1972), Rugel (1974), and Smith et al. (1977). See also Gordon and Harness (1977), who developed a battery of tests to assess right- and left-hemisphere functioning in learning-disabled children. They found that 97 percent of learning-disabled children scored higher than average on the right-hemisphere tests and lower than average on the left-hemisphere ones. For more anecdotal reports of visual-spatial gifts in dyslexic and autistic individuals, see Galaburda and Kemper (1979), Rimland (1964, 1978a, b), and Sano (1918).

36. Colangelo et al. (1993) showed that inventors did poorly in verbal, but not mathematical, areas in school. Hassler (1990) showed that artists did poorly on a test of verbal fluency. Winner, Casey, DaSilva, and Hayes (1991) showed self-reported reading problems in art students. Winner and Casey (1993) reported spelling problems in art students. Non–phonetically based errors are ones that, when sounded out, sound wrong (for example, "physicain" for "physician"); in contrast, phonet-

ically based errors are ones that, when sounded out, sound correct (for example, "phisician"). This tendency to make non–phonetically based errors was found even when SAT performance was partialed out, showing that the reading and spelling problems of these students were independent of the kinds of abilities assessed by the SAT. For a discussion of types of spelling errors and how they relate to reading problems, see Frith (1980) and Phillips (1987).

37. McNamara et al. (1994) showed the association between musical giftedness and learning disorders.

38. For a discussion of dyslexia in terms of evolution, see Geschwind and Galaburda (1987).

39. Geschwind and Behan (1982) found that extreme left-handers reported allergies 2.7 times as often as did extreme right-handers. Further evidence that autoimmune problems are associated with anomalous dominance comes from numerous studies showing that non–right-handers are more likely to have allergies than are right-handers: see Coren (1994), Hassler and Birbaumer (1988), Hassler and Gupta (1993), Martino and Winner (1995), McKeever and Rich (1990), Searleman and Fugagli (1987), and Smith (1987). And Hassler and Gupta (1993) showed that individuals with anomalous dominance (as indicated by right-hemisphere involvement in language processing) had elevated immunoglobulin E values, an indication that they had an excess of antibodies due to allergic reactions.

However, the link has held up only for some immune problems (allergies, asthma, colitis) but not others predicted by Geschwind, such as myasthenia gravis and arthritis. It is not clear why, and this finding is inconsistent with the Geschwind-Galaburda model.

Some studies have failed to show immune problems in left-handers. See Bishop (1986), Salcedo, Spiegler, Gibson, and Magilvay (1985), and Van Strien, Bouma, and Bakker (1987). For a study that failed to show a link between immune disorders and anomalous language dominance and spatial ability, see Rich and McKeever (1990).

Benbow (1986) reported immune problems in both mathematically and verbally gifted youth. The earlier report of immune problems in high-IQ children was from Hildreth (1966).

For other studies showing a link between immune disorders and giftedness, see Temple (1990), who found an elevated frequency of immune disorders in academics in the field of mathematics. Kolata (1983) reported immune disorders in the mathematically gifted.

A link between immune disorders and musical giftedness has been hinted at but not established. McNamara et al. (1994) reported an elevated incidence of self-reported immune problems in women gifted in various areas, including math, music, and art. Hassler and Birbaumer (1988) found that musicians also have an elevated rate of immune disorders, but this study did not disentangle handedness from musical ability. That is, left-handed musicians were compared to nonmusicians, most of whom were right-handed. Thus, we do not know whether the elevation in immune disorders was due to handedness or musical ability. In addition, Hassler and Gupta (1993) did not find an elevated rate of immune disorders in musicians.

40. Here are some of the major criticisms of the Geschwind-Galaburda model:

Loose definition of anomalous dominance. Anomalous dominance is loosely defined as any pattern deviating from the standard one. But this definition does not specify how deviant a brain has to be to be classified as anomalous in its organization. Anomalous dominance is usually assessed by determining a person's handedness, an imperfect index (and less frequently by determining whether the person has bilateral representation of language or visual-spatial skills). None of these are clear and unambiguous indications of anomalous dominance. We would be better off if anomalous dominance were defined entirely anatomically, as a brain in which the left planum temporale is equal to or smaller than the right planum temporale. But of course, this is much more difficult to determine than a person's handedness.

Has the role of testosterone been demonstrated? Bryden, McManus, and Bulman-Fleming (1994) stated that there is no evidence of testosterone actually functioning in the way the Geschwind-Galaburda model claims. The few direct studies that have measured both handedness (in children) and testosterone in utero (when the children were fetuses) did not support the model's predictions. See, for example, Grimshaw, Bryden, and Finegan (1993).

Clearly, we need direct tests of the testosterone hypothesis, in which we manipulate the amount and timing of prenatal testosterone. Thus far, most of the evidence we can use to assess the testosterone hypothesis is based on correlations among factors that are said to be affected by testosterone. Thus, the fact that males have more non-right-handedness, better spatial skills, and more dyslexia and stuttering has been used to support the testosterone claim, but this is a very indirect and thus weak kind of support. For a review of the kind of indirect evidence used to support the testosterone claim, see Halpern (1992).

But we do have a very little bit of direct evidence that does in fact support the Geschwind-Galaburda claim about testosterone. For instance, individuals with disorders associated with abnormally low prenatal hormones show cerebral dominance and levels of verbal and spatial abilities in the direction predicted by the Geschwind-Galaburda model (see Halpern [1994] for a discussion). Moreover, there is animal evidence about the effect of prenatal testosterone that supports the model. We also know from Bakan (1991) that smoking and stress during pregnancy increase testosterone levels and are associated with an elevated incidence of non-right-handedness.

Given the difficulty of testing the model directly, some researchers have looked at the effect of testosterone on adult cognitive abilities. Kimura (1985) showed that women whose testosterone levels are higher do better on spatial-reasoning tasks than do those with lower levels, as do those who have a masculine body type. But for men, just the opposite holds, suggesting some optimal level of testosterone for good spatial reasoning. Casey and Brabeck (1989) found that a subset of college women who were "tomboys" as children also showed superior spatial skills. This subset consisted of those who were majoring in the spatial fields of math or science, and who were right-handed but had non-right-handed family members. Being a tomboy may in part be a function of testosterone, but this is purely speculative at this time. For other evidence on spatial ability and body type, see Broverman, Klaiber, Kobayaski, and Vogel (1968) and Petersen (1976).

Have the other predicted relations been supported? Some of the other relationships predicted by the model have received some support. For instance, a strong relationship between language problems and non-right-handedness was reported by Coren (1994). There is also now quite a bit of evidence for an association between non-right-handedness and immune problems (see Kaplan and Crawford [1994]), and between language-related learning disabilities and immune problems (see Annett and Turner [1974]). For other studies showing relationships in the direction predicted by the model, see Casey and Brabeck (1989), Martino and Winner (1995), Schachter, Ransil, and Geschwind (1987), Smith, Meyers, and Kline (1989), and Winner and Casey (1993).

Has the theory been adequately tested? Because the Geschwind-Galaburda model predicts so many different kinds of associations, and because many of the factors that are predicted to cluster are extremely rare, the model is very difficult (though not impossible) to test. One problem is that each of the factors can be measured in so many different ways. Given the rarity of many of the conditions to be looked for (immune disorders, learning disabilities, giftedness, non-right-handedness), one really needs studies with thousands of subjects to demonstrate statistically significant findings in the direction predicted by the model (see Coren [1994] for this view). Although the evidence in support of the model is hardly clear and consistent, the theory has not yet been sufficiently tested, and this despite the massive numbers of studies that have been carried out.

41. For the view that savants have inherited their gifts and deficits, see Duckett (1976) and Rife and Snyder (1931). For the learning evidence, see Ericsson and Faivre (1988).

42. Treffert (1989) discussed the savant syndrome in terms of the Geschwind-Galaburda hypothesis of pathology of superiority. For a discussion of hyperlexia and visual-spatial skills, see Lewis (1985) and Sacks (1993/1994). For more on savants' difficulty in language, see Steel, Gorman, and Flexman (1984) and Treffert (1989).

43. For more on left-handedness and autism, see Lewin, Kohen, and Matthew (1993). For evidence on left-handedness and hyperlexia, see Aram and Healey (1988) and Healey, Aram, Horwitz, and Kessler (1982).

44. For a discussion of autopsy evidence on savants, see Treffert (1989). Selfe (1977) reported that Nadia had right-hemisphere abnormalities, but no details were given. Treffert (1989) wrote about Leslie Lemke. The music savant J. L. was described by Charness, Clifton, and MacDonald (1988). For evidence of left-hemisphere abnormalities in autistics, see Hauser, Delong,

and Rosman (1975). For conflicting evidence about the location of brain damage in autistics, see Happé (1995).

45. For more on pruning, see Hamburger and Oppenheim (1982).

46. Treffert (1989) relied on the work of Mishkin and Petri (1984) in his discussion of two kinds of memory systems.

47. Galton (1869) argued that genius is inherited. For a discussion of Galton's claims, see Simonton (1994) and Thompson and Plomin (1993). Terman's associate, Oden (1968), reported that the children in Terman's study had children with IQs averaging 133.

48. For the study of musical ability in twins, see Coon and Carey (1989).

49. For twin studies estimating the heritability of general intelligence, see Bouchard and McGue (1981), Bouchard et al. (1990), and Pedersen, Plomin, Nesselroade, and McClearn (1992). For studies of the heritability of specific abilities, see Benbow, Zonderman, and Stanley (1983), Cardon, Fulkner, DeFries, and Plomin (1992), DeFries, Plomin, Vanderberg, and Kuse (1981), McGee (1979), Rice, Fulker, and DeFries (1986), and Rose, Miller, Dumont-Driscoll, and Evans (1979).

50. Scarr and Weinberg (1978) showed that concordance rates between adopted (genetically unrelated) siblings drop from .32 in childhood to -.03 in adulthood, showing the decreasing role of the environment. For other studies consistent with this conclusion, see Loehlin, Horn, and Willerman (1989), Rice, Fulker, and DeFries (1986), and Teasdale and Owen (1984).

   For the argument that people select their environments and this selection is guided by genetic traits, see Scarr and McCartney (1983).

51. See Thompson and Plomin (1993). For more on studies comparing IQs of children and parents in normal populations, see Plomin and DeFries (1980) and Scarr and Weinberg (1978).

52. The concept of emergenesis was advanced by Lykken, McGue, Tellengen, and Bouchard (1992). Striking differences between identical and fraternal twin pairs were uncovered by Bouchard and his colleagues in the Minnesota Study of Twins Reared Apart (Bouchard et al. [1990]).

53. Simonton (1994) noted how some of Galton's geniuses fit the emergenesis model.

54. Benbow, Zonderman, and Stanley (1983). For Plomin's pre-

dictions about the future of behavioral genetics, see Plomin and Thompson (1993), and Plomin, Owen, and McGuffin (1994).

55. For critiques of the IQ measure, see Gould (1981) and Kamin (1974). Ceci (1990a) reanalyzed twin studies to show a stronger environmental effect than had been previously noted.

56. See Ceci (1990a, b) for the argument that what may be inherited is temperament, not IQ.

57. For this kind of critique of heritability studies, see Ceci (1990a) and Lerner (1991, 1992).

58. For the view that heritability does not imply fixity, see Scarr-Salapatek (1971).

Seven

GIFTEDNESS AND THE FAMILY

1. For a discussion of low standards in America, see Damon (1995). For comparisons to higher standards in Asia, see Stevenson, Lee, and Stigler (1986) and Stevenson and Stigler (1992). For nontechnological societies, see Whiting and Whiting (1975).

2. Those who support revolutionary theories, whether intellectual or political, are often later-borns, as demonstrated by Sulloway (1990) and discussed in chapter 10.

3. Albert (1980a) used the phrase "special positions" to refer to gifted children's positions as either first-borns or only-borns. For studies showing that gifted children and eminent adults are disproportionately first-borns, see Barbe (1956), Cox (1977), Ellis (1926), Feldman and Goldsmith (1991), Freeman (1979), Galton (1874), Goertzel, Goertzel, and Goertzel (1978), Gottfried, Gottfried, Bathurst, and Guerin (1994), Roe (1952), Sheldon (1954), and Terman (1925).

4. Adler (1938) argued that first-borns try to make up for their lost position of prominence. Zajonc (1986) proposed the confluence model, according to which first-borns receive more adult stimulation.

5. Gottfried, Gottfried, Bathurst, and Guerin (1994) showed that the homes of high-IQ children are enriched from infancy on. Freeman (1979) found that in comparison to average-IQ chil-

dren, high-IQ children in England grew up in homes with more books and were read to at an earlier age. Cox, Daniel, and Boston's (1985) study of MacArthur fellows shows how academically gifted children have parents who provide intellectual stimulation. For an example of how parents of high-IQ children interact at a sophisticated verbal level with their children, see Moss (1990).

6. Feldman and Goldsmith (1991), p. 100.

7. The gifted children studied by Bloom (1985), Csikszentmihalyi, Rathunde, and Whalen (1993), Feldman and Goldsmith (1991), and Terman (1925) all grew up in highly educated families. Tomlinson-Keasey and Little (1990) showed that in the Terman sample, parental education was the strongest predictor of the level of education and occupation attained by the child. The predictive power of parental education is just as strong for ordinary children: as shown by Jencks (1972), the father's education and occupation are the strongest determinants of the child's eventual socioeconomic level. Fathers' education may lead to achievement because educated fathers create enriched environments. But fathers' education may also lead to achievement simply because our schools and guidance counselors have higher expectations for children of professional-level families than of working-class ones.

In Csikszentmihalyi's study, over 80 percent of the parents of the gifted adolescents had at least a college degree. The difference between the level of education attained by parents in the gifted versus the average sample was especially great for mothers. While only a third of the mothers in an average sample had graduated from college, 82 percent of those in the gifted sample had.

These findings are echoed in numerous studies. Benbow and Stanley (1980a) reported the following high educational profile for parents of children identified as mathematically gifted by the Study for Mathematically Precocious Youth: 66 percent of the fathers and 24 percent of the mothers were college graduates; and 45 percent of the fathers had postcollegiate education.

In a study of the families of Nobel Prize–winning scientists, Berry (1981) found that most came from professional or business families, and 40 percent had fathers who were either holders of a university position or medical doctors. Roe

(1952) found that half of a sample of eminent male scientists were sons of professional fathers, a rate eighteen times higher than that of the general population. High parental education in families of high-IQ children was also reported by Barbe (1956), Gottfried, Gottfried, Bathurst, and Guerin (1994), Hollingworth (1942), Kincaid (1969), and Sheldon (1954). High-IQ children also tend to have highly educated grandparents, as shown by Galton (1869) and Gross (1993a, b).

8. Freeman (1991) and Radford (1990) showed that families of low socioeconomic status with identified gifted children provide enriched environments. Cox, Daniel, and Boston (1985) described MacArthur fellows with immigrant parents who were not well educated but who valued education. Comer's story can be found in Comer (1988). Frasier (1993) discussed problems in assessing giftedness in children from poor backgrounds. For evidence that middle- and upper-middle-class children are disproportionately identified as gifted, see Astin (1964), who showed this to be true of National Merit Scholars, and Benbow and Stanley (1980a), who found this for students admitted to SMPY.

9. Effects of understimulation on the development of humans have been documented by Clarke and Clarke (1976) and Kagan and Klein (1973).

10. Simonton (1994) discussed the logical possibility that high ability is genetically transmitted and is unrelated to the presence of enriched environments that high-ability parents provide. Gottfried, Gottfried, Bathurst, and Guerin (1994) showed that high-IQ children demand more extracurricular activities. Adam's omnivorous demands are described in Feldman and Goldsmith (1991). The argument that children select their environments was made by Scarr and McCartney (1983).

11. The parents of the children described in this book all noticed signs of high ability in infancy, as did the parents of the prodigies described by Feldman and Goldsmith (1991). Gottfried, Gottfried, Bathurst, and Guerin (1994) showed that parents of high-IQ children also notice giftedness in their infants.

12. Gottfried, Gottfried, Bathurst, and Guerin (1994) showed that environments of high-IQ children were enriched as early as infancy but became more so as the children grew older.

13. Child-centered families of the gifted are described by Bloom (1985), Csikszentmihalyi, Rathunde, and Whalen (1993), Feld-

man and Goldsmith (1991), Gross (1993a), and Olszewski, Kulieke, and Buescher (1987). Feldman and Goldsmith (1991, p. 216) reported the story about the Menuhin family.

14. A study of very high IQ children showed that 87 percent had received extensive training at home by one or both parents, typically the mother. Freeman (1979) found that parents of her gifted sample were very involved in their children's learning and worked with their children.

15. Howe (1990) reported about the Menuhin family and the Polgar family. Bloom (1985) noted that there is room for only one elite performer per family. Yo-Yo Ma and his sister were both musical prodigies, but only Yo-Yo was pushed to become a professional performer. See Goldsmith (1987) for a discussion of female prodigies.

16. For a description of Tara Lipinski, see Longman (1994).

17. Deakin (1972) described this Welsh mother of four prodigies.

18. Feldman and Goldsmith (1991, pp. 112–13).

19. Richardson (1991) and Gardner (1993a) wrote about Picasso's father; Goldsmith (1992) wrote about Yani's father. The parents of artistically gifted children studied by Bloom (1985) and by Csikszentmihalyi, Rathunde, and Whalen (1993) all provided strong support for their children's artistic development.

20. For evidence that there is almost always a parent or parent surrogate who pushes and models hard work, see Bloom (1985), Csikszentmihalyi, Rathunde, and Whalen (1993), Feldman and Goldsmith (1991), and Gardner (1993a). Goertzel and Goertzel (1962) found that it was the mothers who pushed, but who also conveyed a strong belief in their child's ability to achieve. Jin Li (personal communication), who is from China and is now a student of creativity at Harvard Graduate School of Education (and mother of KyLee in chapter 3), told me that in China both parents play an equal role. There are certainly famous cases of fathers who pushed: the fathers of J. S. Mill, Mozart, William James Sidis, and Yo-Yo Ma, for example. For information on the role of the mother in the Meyerhoff program, see Ames (1990).

21. Waitzkin (1984, p. 122). For other studies showing that high parental expectations are associated with high achievement motivation in children, see Chamrad and Robinson (1986), McClelland, Atkinson, Clark, and Lowell (1953), Nichols (1964), and Olszewski, Kulieke, and Buescher (1987). Colan-

gelo and Dettman (1983) noted the difference between the standards set by parents of high- and low-achieving academically gifted children.

22. For evidence about the importance of modeling along with high expectations, see Freeman (1979). The claim that achieving parents who are not at the peak of achievement are more effective as parents than the highest achievers is my own speculation.

23. Bloom (1985, p. 74).

24. For other studies of value placed on intellectual activity in families of the academically gifted, see Cox, Daniel, and Boston (1985) and Roe (1952). Goldsmith (in press) discussed the need for parents to be directive early, and to let go later.

25. Van Tassel-Baska (1989b) reported the study of family importance among disadvantaged gifted adolescents. For information on the role of the family in the Meyerhoff students' experience, see Ames (1990) and Marriott (1992). Clark (1983) found that parental values played a very important role in the achievement of black children.

26. Stevenson and Stigler (1992) compared Japanese and American students' performance. For more on Hungarian performance, see Csapo (1995). Damon (1995) discussed the destructive effects of American parents' low expectations. There is a downside often found in societies with very high standards, though it is not a necessary one. Often in such societies children get locked in at an early age to a track that is either university bound or not. In contrast, we allow late bloomers a second chance. Thus, in the end we may conserve as much talent as these more rigid societies. I am indebted to Dean Keith Simonton (personal communication) for reminding me of this. However, there is no reason that we could not have high expectations without locking children in and denying them a second chance.

27. Numerous studies showing that parents of gifted children allow their children freedom to make their own decisions are reported in a review by Colangelo and Dettman (1983). Dweck and Elliott (1983) and Henderson and Dweck (1990) showed that achievement motivation develops when children have the chance to master challenges independently. Feldman and Goldsmith (1991) showed that parents of their prodigies were responsive rather than controlling. Terman and Oden

(1947) reported that the parents of the Terman sample encouraged initiative and independence. Karnes, Schwedel, and Steinberg (1984) found that parents of high-IQ preschoolers encouraged independence more than did parents of lower-IQ children. Piper and Naumann (1974) showed that mothers of two- to three-year-olds with high IQs allowed their children more independence and decision making than did mothers of children with average IQs, who were more authoritarian and controlling. Weissler and Landau (1992) showed that fathers in families with no academically gifted children were more authoritarian than fathers in families with one academically gifted child. Similar findings can be found in Freeburg and Payne (1967) and Geppert and Kuster (1983). Getzels and Jackson (1962) discovered that parents of children with high IQs but little creativity tend to be parents who grant their children little autonomy. They pressure their children to conform and behave well. But parents of children who are creative (as measured by paper-and-pencil creativity tests), though only average in IQ, tend to be more permissive. They do not pressure their children to conform, and they grant them a measure of autonomy.

28. Baumrind (1971) used the term "authoritative" parenting and showed the effectiveness of this kind of parenting. A correlation between extreme parental pushing and underachievement has been shown by Fine (1977) and Karnes et al. (1961).

29. Cornell (1984), Freeman (1979), and Gottfried et al. (1994) showed that families of the gifted are more cohesive. Lower divorce rates were shown by Barbe (1956). The recent study reporting no difference in divorce rates was by Gottfried, Gottfried, Bathurst, and Guerin (1994).

30. Albert (1971, 1980a, b) and Robinson and Noble (1991) reported evidence of positive relationships between gifted children and their parents. Gross (1993a) showed that out of seventeen very high IQ children, five attained the maximum score on "family self-esteem, " seven had above-average scores, and five had average scores. None had low scores. This is in striking contrast to the low scores they attained on "school self-esteem," as discussed in chapter 8. Karnes et al. (1961) showed that achievement correlates with having affectionate parents.

31. Csikszentmihalyi, Rathunde, and Whalen (1993).

32. Elkind (1981) and Damon (1995).

33. For a discussion of Wiener's relationship to his father, see Wiener (1953, pp. 71–72; 1956, p. 18). Howe (1990) discussed parental pushing in the case of Ruskin, Mill, and Wiener. See Jamison (1993) for mood disorders in the eminent. The quotation from Wiener is Wiener (1953, p. 67). Music educators who do not believe in public performances at too young an age include Gary Graffman, the director of the Curtis Institute of Music in Philadelphia. The cellist Msitislav Rostropovich apparently shared this view. See Hoffman (1993) for a discussion. The quote from Yeou-Cheng Ma is in Hoffman (1993, p. 38).

34. For more on Adragon De Mello, see Cone (1994). The quote is from p. 19.

35. Montour (1977) and Manley (1937) discussed the case of Sidis. Montour (1977) made the case that Sidis's problem was not acceleration but emotional deprivation.

36. The quote about running an adding machine is in Manley (1937, p. 26).

37. The quotes about bitterness and irresponsibility are in Manley (1937, pp. 25 and 26, respectively).

38. Montour (1977) referred to such parents as "creator" parents and noted that the fathers of Norbert Wiener and J. S. Mill credited their sons' achievements to the training they provided as fathers.

39. Miller (1981). McGuffog (1985) discussed the problems that gifted children experience as a result of overly demanding parents. Fabri (1964) discussed the case of an artistically gifted child whose parents stopped supporting his gift when he decided to become an artist. Goldsmith (in press) discussed the importance of nurturing the emotional needs of the gifted child.

40. For a discussion of how giftedness affects the family, see Albert and Runco (1986) and Silverman (1993a).

Eight
SO DIFFERENT FROM OTHERS:
THE EMOTIONAL LIFE OF
THE GIFTED CHILD

1. Hollingworth (1942). For a discussion of the need for clinical intervention, see Delisle (1986) and Silverman (1993a, b). Janos and Robinson (1985) estimated the rate of 20 percent to 25 percent.

2. For other studies besides Terman's claiming gifted children to be well adjusted, see Brody and Benbow (1986), Gallagher and Crowder (1957), Galluci (1988), Mönks and Van Boxtel (1985) [in Holland], and Subotnik, Karp, and Morgan (1989). For a review of the social and emotional side of giftedness, see Janos and Robinson (1985). For an example of the assertion that the gifted are popular and self-confident, see Mayseless (1993, p. 135).

3. Waitzkin (1984); Feldman and Goldsmith (1991).

4. For studies showing high achievement motivation and perseverance in gifted children, see Bloom (1985), Bogle and Buckhalt (1987), Csikszentmihalyi, Rathunde, and Whalen (1993), Janos and Robinson (1985), and Renzulli (1978). Stevenson, Chen, and Lee (1993) showed that high achievers in Taiwan, China, Japan, and the United States were more intrinsically motivated than were average achievers. The quote from the Westinghouse finalist is in Belluck (1995, p. B8).

5. Studies showing that academically gifted children believe their achievement is due to effort use a measure called "locus of control," which assesses whether one believes one is shaped by internal versus external factors. Effort is an internal factor, luck is external. Gifted children (including those studied by Terman) show a belief in internal, rather than external, locus of control. See, for example, Brody and Benbow (1986), Davis and Connell (1985), Lucito (1964), and Milgram and Milgram (1976).

6. For reports of perfectionism in the gifted, see, for example, Hollingworth (1926), Kerr (1991), Robinson and Noble (1991), Roeper (1990), and Silverman (1993c).

7. For evidence on the positive academic self-esteem of the academically gifted, see Gross (1993a) and Hoge and Renzulli (1993).

8. Csikszentmihalyi, Rathunde, and Whalen (1993). The study showing sex differences in self-esteem in the academically gifted is by Kelly and Colangelo (1984).

9. For reports on low academic self-esteem in underachieving gifted students, see Butler-Por (1987) and Kanoy, Johnson, and Kanoy (1980). For a report on low academic self-esteem in gifted children with learning disabilities, see Waldron, Saphire, and Rosenblum (1987).

10. For a discussion of the pernicious effects of an excessive focus on self-esteem in our schools, see Damon (1995).

11. Hollingworth (1942) pointed out how extremely high IQ children can be very critical of others.

12. For studies showing independence, dominance, and nonconformism in the academically gifted, see Feldhusen and Hoover (1986), Freeman (1979), Haier and Denham (1976), Hogan (1980), Hogan et al. (1977), Janos and Robinson (1985), Lucito (1964), Olszewski-Kubilius, Kulieke, and Krasney (1988), Silverman (1993a, c), Terman (1925), Viernstein and Hogan (1975), and Viernstein, McGinn, and Hogan (1977). Csikszentmihalyi, Rathunde, and Whalen (1993) found that gifted adolescents scored high on dominance.

13. The sophisticated moral and philosophical concerns of high-IQ children were noted by Carroll (1940), Hollingworth (1942), and Silverman (1993c, 1994).

14. Piaget (1932); Kohlberg (1963, 1964, 1969).

15. For studies demonstrating a positive relationship between IQ and level of moral reasoning, see Arbuthnot (1973), Boehm (1962), Grant, Weiner, and Ruchton (1976), Gross (1993b), Hallahan and Kauffman (1982), Janos and Robinson (1985), Kohlberg (1964), Maccoby (1980), and Thorndike (1940). Level of social problem solving and social reasoning are also correlated with IQ; see Janos and Robinson (1985) for a review.

16. See Colby and Damon (1992) for the study of adults who have led selfless, moral lives. For an example of the claim that the high-IQ gifted are more morally sensitive than the average child, see Silverman (1994).

17. Freeman (1991, 1994) reported that higher-IQ children were more pessimistic about nuclear war. Galbraith (1985) reported the finding about concern with world problems. For other studies showing that high-IQ children feel pessimistic about

the world, see George and Gallagher (1978), Landau (1976), and Torrance (1983). For evidence that high-IQ children read the newspaper more than do average children, see Clark and Hankins (1985) and Freeman (1979).

18. Ritchie, Bernard, and Shertzer (1982) showed that IQ does not predict interpersonal sensitivity; Silverman mentioned the lack of advanced social skills during a September 1994 presentation to a local support group for parents of gifted children, run by Annemarie Roeper, in Oakland, California.

19. On formal measures of introversion versus extroversion, assessed by a self-report, forced-choice paper-and-pencil test called the Myers–Briggs Type Indicator, the IQ-gifted score highly on introversion. The Myers–Briggs Type Indicator is described by Myers (1987), and the test is published as Myers (1962). For a review of the introversion/extroversion dimension as it relates to giftedness, see Eysenck (1993).

Linda Silverman (1993b), director of the Gifted Child Development Center in Denver, finds that introversion increases with IQ. She reported that about 75 percent of the children she counsels with IQs over 160 are introverted, while about 50 percent of the moderately gifted (whose IQs are not as high as 160, but are still in the gifted range) are introverted. This estimate is consistent with that of a large study of 1,725 students in gifted programs, in which half of the students were classified as introverted. These percentages contrast sharply with the norms in this country, where about 75 percent of the population are extroverts. Thus, the extremely IQ gifted are the mirror image of the norm. For further evidence that high-IQ giftedness correlates with introversion, see Albert (1978) and Janos and Robinson (1985). Gallagher (1990) showed that half of the 1,725 students in her study were introverted.

20. Silverman (1993a, b) noted that some gifted children are ostracized. Csikszentmihalyi, Rathunde, and Whalen (1993) made the point that gifted children derive pleasure from solitude and need solitude for talent development.

21. For more on the hypersensitivity of the gifted child, see Cruickshank (1963), Dabrowski (1964), Dabrowski and Piechowski (1977), Gallagher (1985), McGuffog (1985), Piechowski (1979, 1995), Piechowski and Colangelo (1984), Robinson (1993 a, b), and Silverman (1983). For more on the claim about Elvis Presley, see Wright's (1994) review of Gural-

nick's (1994) biography. The claim about Schweitzer can be found in Goertzel and Goertzel (1962).

22. Greenacre (1956). The British psychologist Hans J. Eysenck, who developed scales to measure introversion versus extroversion, noted that introverts are overly sensitive to stimulation. The Polish psychiatrist Kazimierz Dabrowski dubbed this quality as "overexcitability." The relationship between extreme inhibition, or shyness, and intensity of sensory response was reported by Kagan (1994).

23. For evidence of social isolation in the high-IQ gifted, see Austin and Draper (1981), Barbe and Renzulli (1975), Brody and Benbow (1986), Freeman (1979), Gallagher (1985), Khatena (1982), Laycock (1979), Newland (1976), Powell and Haden (1984), and Silverman and Kearney (1989). Csikszentmihalyi, Rathunde, and Whalen (1993) reported that teenagers gifted in art and music face some of the same problems. The English musical children were described by Howe and Sloboda (1992). For Wiener's autobiography, see Wiener (1953). Studies of eminent adults who recall loneliness as children include Albert (1980a), Goertzel and Goertzel (1962), Ochse (1990), and Radford (1990).

24. The mother's remark is unpublished. Terman's report on the social problems of the profoundly gifted can be found in Burks, Jensen, and Terman (1930). The quote from Terman is cited in Gross (1993a, p. 242).

25. The finding that Terman's most successful adults had problems in adolescence can be found in Oden (1968).

26. The acute problems of high-IQ children were noted by Hollingworth (1926, 1942).

27. For reports on the social alienation of the highly gifted, see Freeman (1994), Gross (1993a), Mönks and Ferguson (1983), Roedell (1984), and Schneider (1987). See also a study by Janos, Marwood, and Robinson (1985), in which the researchers reported that it is the children with IQs of 168 on average who were more likely to have no close friends and to play less often with friends in contrast to more moderately gifted children whose IQs ranged from 120 to 140. Mayseless (1993) showed that gifted adolescents report lower intimacy with same-sex friends in comparison to a control group. For reports on the positive family relations in gifted populations, see Bloom (1985), Getzels and Jackson (1961), and Sheldon (1954).

28. Gross's (1993a) study of extremely high IQ children confirmed the finding that these children have unusually sophisticated play interests. The child who read Gibbon is described in Terman and Oden (1947).

29. Evidence for the high-IQ gifted preferring older friends can be found in Gross (1989, 1993a), Hollingworth (1931), Janos, Marwood, and Robinson (1985), Robinson and Noble (1991), Silverman (1993a, b), and Terman (1925).

30. Cross, Coleman, and Stewart (1992) reported that the gifted are aware of being classified as different. Freeman (1994) noted that most feel proud of being different. For more on the rewards of solitude, see Storr (1988).

31. See Gross (1993a). For suicide, see Delisle (1986) and Farrell (1989).

32. Positive peer ratings are reported by Robinson and Noble (1991) and Schneider, Ledingham, Crombie, and Clegg (1986). Wiener's remark can be found in Wiener (1956, p. 19). The relationship between feeling different and having fewer friends and lower social self-esteem is reported by Janos, Marwood, and Robinson (1985).

33. The lack of social and sexual confidence among talented adolescents is reported by Whalen and Csikszentmihalyi (1989). The less positive body image among the IQ-gifted was reported by Milgram and Milgram (1976). Sexual attitudes are discussed in Csikszentmihalyi, Rathunde, and Whalen (1993).

34. For more on the Freudian model of sublimation as the defense mechanism used by creative artists and by scientists, see Freud (1957, 1959, 1961).

35. Freeman (1994). See also studies by Cornell (1989) and Cornell and Grossberg (1989). One piece of evidence that the labeled children in Freeman's (1994) study were odder to begin with is that the labeled children were described by their parents as having poor physical coordination and asthma more often than were the unlabeled children. Even though the two groups were equal in IQ, it is possible that the children whose parents joined the gifted association were more odd, more creative, or more rebellious, and that these qualities caused their parents to label them and to join the association.

36. One piece of evidence that the academically gifted perform at less than their ability level comes from a study by Painter (1976), who found that out of 160 British children whose IQs

ranged from moderately gifted (123) to extremely gifted (212), over 60 percent were performing at more than four years below their tested achievement levels. Gross (1989) discusses the conflict between intimacy and excellence.

37. The comparison between gifted and nongifted boys and girls in terms of popularity was carried out by Luftig and Nichols (1991). Silverman (1993a) noted how dominance in gifted boys is perceived as leadership, while the same trait in girls is perceived as bossiness.

38. Gross (1989, 1993a) discussed the conflict between excellence and intimacy. For evidence that girls are more likely than boys to underachieve to seem normal, see Robinson and Noble (1991), Silverman (1993a, b), and Tannenbaum (1983). The finding that girls with high grades are more symptomatic than boys was reported by Locksley and Douvan (1980). At the University of Maryland Baltimore County's Meyerhoff Scholarship Program for high-achieving black students in science and technology, students reported that they had faced hostility from their black peers in high school for being "nerds." In the Meyerhoff program, they are with other black students who value learning, and they are no longer persecuted for being studious. For information on the Meyerhoff program, see Ames (1990) and Marriott (1992). For Ogbu's studies, see Fordham and Ogbu (1986) and Ogbu (1988). See also Fordham (1988), who found that black adolescents who do well in school are perceived as acting white. Lindstrom and Van Sant (1986) and Passow (1972) made the same observation.

39. Storr (1988) wrote about the importance of solitude for creativity.

40. The quote about Josh Waitzkin is in *Searching for Bobby Fischer*, p. 19.

Nine
SCHOOLS: HOW THEY FAIL,
HOW THEY COULD HELP

1. The quote is from Mayor Kenneth Reeves of Cambridge, Massachusetts, cited in Bloom (1993, p. 25). Bloom noted that while somewhat over half of the states mandate some special attention to the gifted, Massachusetts requires none.

2. For broader definitions of intelligence than IQ, see Gardner (1983) and Sternberg (1985). For a discussion of the claim that all children are gifted, see Feldhusen (1992b). For the argument against this view, see Gagné (1995).

3. American ambivalence toward the intellect was noted long ago by de Tocqueville (1899). This issue is discussed in the Department of Education's "Riley report" (Riley [1993]). See Singal (1991) for a discussion of hostility toward the gifted by schools and by school psychologists.

4. Hollingworth (1942) noted the striking difference between moderately and profoundly gifted children.

5. The Stanford math program is a computer program called Educational Program for Gifted Youth (EPGY).

6. For arguments against ability grouping, see Good and Brophy (1993), Margolin (1994), National Education Association (1968), Oakes (1985), and Slavin (1989/1990, 1990). For statistics on the overrepresentation in gifted programs of whites, Asians, and students from upper-middle-class families, and the underrepresentation of blacks, Hispanics, and poor children, see Margolin (1994), Riley (1993), U.S. Department of Education (1991), and VanTassel-Baska (1991). According to the Riley report, 17.6 percent of Asians, 9 percent of whites, 7.9 percent of blacks, 6.7 percent of Hispanics, and 2.1 percent of Native Americans are enrolled in gifted programs. The recent study using the Ravens Standard Progressive Matrices Test was conducted by Saccuzzo and Johnson (1995).

7. The quotes from Australian school officials are reported by Gross (1993a, p. 281).

8. See Toom (1993) for an account of a foreigner's reaction to American schools. Reis (1994) documented the decline in textbook level over the past twenty years. Kirst (1982) noted that publishers refuse to publish textbooks aimed at too high a level.

9. Riley (1993) summarized findings from international studies. See also Stevenson, Chen, and Lee (1993), Stevenson, Lee, and Stigler (1986), and Stevenson and Stigler (1992) for comparisons of American students to those in other countries.

10. The comparison of the top 10 percent of students in the United States, Japan, Taiwan, and China was carried out by Stevenson, Chen, and Lee (1993). Riley (1993) noted other similarly disturbing findings comparing top students interna-

tionally. In biology, top American students ranked the lowest of top students in twelve nations. In math and science, the top 10 percent of American students ages nine to thirteen ranked near the bottom in comparison to students from nineteen other countries. In another math study carried out by the International Association of Education Achievement, the top American students performed lower than top students in ten other countries; in addition, average students in Japan performed better than the highest 5 percent of American students. At the highest level of mathematics, where students are asked to interpret data, only 1 percent of American students succeeded, in comparison to 5 percent of students from Korea, the top-scoring country (see Riley [1993]).

11. VanTassel-Baska (1991) cited many studies demonstrating that about half of U.S. students in the top 5 percent of IQ range are underachieving. See also Reis (1994).

12. The quote is from Hollingworth (1931, p. 5).

13. Rimm (1986) pointed out the relationship between low challenge and low self-esteem, and showed how underachievers have low self-esteem. See also Davis and Rimm (1985), Kanoy, Johnson, and Kanoy (1980), and Whitmore (1980).

14. Goertzel and Goertzel (1962) conducted the study of 400 eminent adults. For the study of MacArthur fellows, see Cox, Daniel, and Boston (1985). Hildreth (1966) listed famous people who disliked school and cited Goldsmith's teacher (p. 94).

15. Hildreth (1966, p. 94) cited Yeats. The MacArthur Fellow Robert Root-Bernstein is quoted in Cox, Daniel, and Boston (1985, p. 23). Darwin is quoted in Gruber (1981, p. 71).

16. Feldman and Goldsmith (1991) studied the writing prodigy. Gross (1993a) reported on high-IQ children's far more positive feelings about family than school. The quotes from mathematicians are from Bloom (1985, pp. 291, 292–93, 302, and 308, respectively).

17. Csikszentmihalyi, Rathunde, and Whalen (1993). See Coleman (1960) for a discussion of the negative effects of a peer culture that devalues intellectual pursuits.

18. Subotnik (1988a, b) discussed how students who won honors or who were semifinalists and finalists in the Westinghouse Science Talent Search had important mentors outside of school science classes. Zuckerman (1977) found that about half of the Nobel laureates she studied had another Nobel laureate as a

mentor. The importance of mentors in the CTY program is discussed by Durden and Tangherlini (1993).

19. For a discussion of Kerschensteiner's study, see Stern (1911). For more on the Indiana University Summer Arts Institute, see Clark and Zimmerman (1995). Clark and Zimmerman (1995) are currently trying to identify and nurture rural minority children with artistic gifts. Some art educators today argue for formal measures by which to identify artistic giftedness. For example, Clark (1993) developed the Clark Drawing Abilities Test. In my opinion, it is usually so clear when a child is artistically gifted that no formal test is needed.

20. Benbow, Arjmand, and Walberg (1991) note that underachievers who come from undereducated families increase their achievement when exposed to challenging courses.

21. For the claim that black students sometimes feel that excelling in school is a white value, see Fordham and Ogbu (1986) and Ogbu (1988). Black students at the University of Maryland Baltimore County's Meyerhoff program for gifted black students in science and technology say that in high school they encountered hostility from other blacks for being high achieving. For information, see Ames (1990) and Marriott (1992).

22. Benbow, Arjmand, and Walberg (1991) showed that advanced courses in math and science are more important for girls than boys if these students are to remain in a science major in college.

23. For a history of gifted education, see Tannenbaum (1993) and Whitmore (1980). Statistics for the number of children in gifted programs in different years were compiled by the National Center for Educational Statistics (1992) and are cited in Margolin (1994). Schools for the gifted founded near the turn of the century were the Horace Mann School, the Speyer School, the Hunter College School, and the State of Iowa Experimental School.

24. The story of the Connecticut suit is reported by Diegmueller (1994, p. 8).

25. For more on the inclusion of the gifted in the law for the handicapped requiring IEPs and for a discussion of the difficulty of creating IEPs, see Passow and Rudnitski (1993).

26. The estimate of 2 cents per 100 dollars is from Riley (1993).

27. Silverman (1993c) made these comparisons between those with retarded and gifted IQs.

28. Purcell (1993) reported that only states with both mandates and money are not cutting back on gifted education. Fetterman (1988) provided a case study of gifted education in California and described how expenditures for gifted education are declining in this state.

29. See Elkind (1981) for the view that children should not be unduly pushed. Gross (1993a) found that a one-year acceleration for children with extremely high IQs had little effect on the children studied. Terman and Oden (1947) favored grade skipping and advised a series of grade skips for the highly gifted.

30. Slavin (1989/1990) reported that most teachers use some ability grouping in elementary school. For this he cited the National Education Association Research Division (1968) and Wilson and Schmits (1978).

31. For a review of options for gifted children in the United States, see Cox, Daniel, and Boston (1985) and Shore, Cornell, Robinson, and Ward (1991). For international comparisons of gifted education, see Fetterman (1988) and Gallagher (1985). At the egalitarian extreme is Scandinavia, where there are no special provisions for the academically gifted and where such children are told to seek private lessons after school to nurture their interests (Urban and Sekowski [1993]). Australia is also opposed to education for the gifted, and the profoundly gifted Australian children studied by Miraca Gross suffered as a result. Somewhat more ambivalent is Japan (see Stevenson, Chen, and Lee [1993] and Wu and Cho [1993]). At the elementary school level in Japan there is no grade skipping, there are no special classes or tracks for the gifted, and there is no ability grouping of any kind. While there are clear achievement differences among children at this level, the term *gifted* is taboo and all subscribe to the view that differences in achievement are due to differences in effort, not to innate ability. At the high school level, tracking begins in earnest: there are four levels of high school, and students gain entrance into the top level of school by scoring highly on very competitive examinations. Again, however, the at-least explicit belief is that those who make it into the top schools have done so because they have worked harder in the lower grades. Thus, Japan strives for egalitarianism in the early school years but does not maintain this stance at the high school level, where the striving to create an elite, educated class takes over.

Under Marxism, the Soviet Union and other Eastern European countries (Poland, Hungary, Czechoslovakia) made no special provisions for the academically gifted, though they always had special training for children gifted in art, music, and athletics (Urban and Sekowski [1993]). Children gifted in ballet, acrobatics, or athletics were carefully groomed and sent off to win international competitions. These countries had not only specialized schools to train such children but also a large extracurricular system in which children could focus, after school, on an art form, music, a sport, or an academic area. With the fall of Marxism, provisions for the academically gifted in school have been coming back into favor, as they are today in China.

China, which pays lip service to the egalitarian ideals of Marxism, has special programs for the gifted (Zixiu [1993]), and there is little ambivalence about encouraging, even pushing, gifted children (Jin Li, personal communication). Western European countries, such as England, Germany, and the Netherlands, also all make some provisions for the gifted, in the form of both tracking and acceleration, though all remain profoundly ambivalent.

32. Rogers (1991) reported the number of studies carried out on ability grouping and acceleration by 1991. For a review of programs for the gifted, see Cox, Daniel, and Boston (1985).

33. A National Education Association report in 1968 showed that the majority of teachers favored ability grouping. Oakes (1985).

34. Kulik and Kulik (1991, 1992) conducted a meta-analysis of twenty-five studies of special classes for the gifted and found these results. In an earlier meta-analysis of fourteen studies of only secondary school gifted versus nongifted classes, Kulik and Kulik (1982) found that the students in these gifted classes did better on average than those in nongifted classes. While the Kuliks found no decline in the self-esteem of gifted children in high-ability classes, Hoge and Renzulli (1993) found some decline. Thus, the effects of ability grouping on the self-esteem of gifted children have not been consistently demonstrated. The quote about leaderless aggregations is from Good and Brophy (1993, p. 269). They note the negative effects on lower-ability students when high-ability students are removed from the classroom and no longer assume a peer leadership position.

35. Where there are not enough children to constitute an entire

class for the gifted, cluster grouping is sometimes used (see Weinbrenner and Devlin [1993] for a description). Suppose there are eight gifted children at the fifth-grade level in a school with three fifth grades. Cluster grouping would mean placing all eight children in the same classroom. The aim of such grouping is to allow one teacher to alter the curriculum for these students, rather than having all three fifth-grade teachers making adjustments for two or three such students. This is a form of grouping, but it only involves grouping at the very high end. A meta-analysis again carried out by Kulik and Kulik (1991) (on four studies only) revealed an overall positive effect: the grouped gifted children did better than the scattered ones, in all academic areas tested. The effect was strong.

36. According to Riley (1993), 72 percent of elementary school gifted programs use a pull-out program only. Cox, Daniel, and Boston (1985) also find this to be the most common form of gifted education at the elementary school level. One of the most widely used pull-out programs is Renzulli's Enrichment Triad Model (Renzulli [1977] and Renzulli and Reis [1985]). In this program, students work individually or in small groups to investigate problems, conduct experiments, or create things.

Renzulli (1986a), who has pushed for pull-out programs because he believes they alleviate the boredom of the gifted child, has nonetheless been very critical of the superficial way in which enrichment is typically carried out. Davis and Rimm (1985) have criticized these programs as involving only "games."

Fetterman (1988) reported that children in pull-out programs can rarely recall what they actually did in these sessions. Cox, Daniel, and Boston (1985) conducted the survey in which only 16 percent of schools felt their pull-out programs were substantial. For the survey in which many schools criticized their own pull-out programs, see Gallagher et al. (1983). See also Gagné (1995) for a critique of enrichment pull-out programs as minimal and as not tailored to individual children's domain-specific gifts.

37. For studies of the effects of pull-out programs, see Delcourt, Loyd, Cornell, and Goldberg (1994), Treffinger, Callahan, and Baughn (1991), and Vaughan, Feldhusen, and Asher (1991). Renzulli (1994) is trying to take the best features of enrichment programs and adapt them to entire schools.

38. Jere Brophy (personal communication) pointed out to me the need to be skeptical about the claim, made by the Kuliks, that the instruction received at each level was the same.

39. Kulik and Kulik (1992). Slavin (1987, 1990) reported no benefits to such tracking at any ability level.

40. The lack of effect for randomly assigned studies can be seen by examining table 1 of Kulik and Kulik (1982).

41. Slavin (1990) pointed to studies showing that high-track students improve more rapidly than do low-track students, but Slavin noted that in these studies, being in a higher track also meant taking more advanced courses. Thus, these comparisons confound ability grouping with level and kind of instruction.

42. The self-esteem finding was reported by Kulik and Kulik (1992). The quotation is from Hollingworth (1931, p. 445). Only a few studies have measured self-esteem and more studies are clearly needed.

43. Kulik and Kulik (1992) conducted a meta-analysis of within-class ability grouping and reported positive effects for elementary and high schools. Slavin (1987) carried out a "best evidence synthesis" of the research on ability grouping in elementary schools for math and reading. He found academic gains for children in math at all ability levels when grouped, but he could not find support for within-class ability grouping in reading, even though this practice is very common.

44. Kulik and Kulik (1992) conducted the meta-analysis of cross-grade grouping. Slavin (1987) also found, in a best evidence synthesis, that grouping across grades was beneficial for reading at the elementary school level; he also reported that one study showed this procedure as being beneficial for math.

45. A meta-analysis of eleven studies in which accelerated gifted students were compared to nonaccelerated gifted students of the same age showed the accelerants to be achieving at a higher level (Kulik and Kulik [1984, 1992]). About 81 percent of the accelerants outperformed the nonaccelerants by almost one year, a strong effect. A meta-analysis of the twelve studies comparing accelerated and nonaccelerated gifted students in the same grade (but differing in age) showed that the accelerants performed as well as their older classmates (Kulik and Kulik [1984, 1992]). This also is impressive. It means, for example, that a gifted seven-year-old who skips a grade will perform just as well as a gifted eight-year-old who did not

skip. A word of caution, however: these meta-analyses were based on a mixed bag of studies in which acceleration included skipping grades as well as taking advanced classes.

A few of the studies the Kuliks examined included self-report paper-and-pencil measures of social outcomes such as adjustment, popularity, and attitude toward school. These studies showed no clear trends in either a positive or negative direction. Given the few studies and the crude measures, we are better off relying on the kinds of case-study evidence presented, for instance, by Miraca Gross (1993a). The highly gifted children whom Gross studied who were allowed to accelerate through school had higher self-esteem than those who did not. One of her most gifted students was permitted no acceleration (or any other kind of special education), and this student had the lowest self-esteem and was frustrated and socially isolated.

46. Terman and Oden (1947) argued for grade skipping. The report Terman sent to parents is unpublished and is in the Terman archives at Stanford University.

47. Terman and Oden compared children in the Terman sample who entered college early to those who did not.

48. Gross (1993a).

49. See Tangherlini and Durden (1993) for a description of the criteria for admission to SMPY or CTY. See Gallagher et al. (1983) for a discussion of how these programs are being used in universities throughout the country. See Stanley, Huang, and Zu (1986) for a discussion of such programs in China.

50. Swiatek and Benbow (1991a, b) carried out a ten-year longitudinal study of SMPY accelerants. For other similar kinds of evidence that acceleration is beneficial, not harmful, see Benbow (1983), Daurio (1979), Feldhusen (1989), Janos, Robinson, and Lunneborg (1989), Robinson (1983), Rogers (1991), and VanTassel-Baska (1989a).

These findings were replicated by Benbow and Arjmand (1990) and by Benbow, Arjmand, and Walberg (1991), who reported the benefits of taking intensive summer courses in math and science. Students who take such courses are more likely to remain in math and science, and to achieve highly in these subjects, than equally gifted students who do not take such courses or any other kind of advanced courses.

51. For evidence that accelerants do better than nonaccelerants,

see Benbow (1991), Stanley and Benbow (1983), Swiatek (1992), and Swiatek and Benbow (1991a, b). A recently initiated twenty-year follow-up of SMPY students by Lubinski and Benbow should shed further light on what happens to accelerated students.

52. These quotes are from Enersen (1993, p. 173). Some colleges have set up programs for high school students to take college courses full-time yet still be grouped with other high school students of equal ability. One such program is Simon's Rock Early Entrance College, part of Bard College, started in 1966, which admits students one to two years younger than usual, with or without a high school degree. Others include the Clarkson School, a one-year program at Clarkson University, and the Texas Academy of Mathematics and Science, a two-year program at the University of North Texas.

53. VanTassel-Baska (1989a, p. 15) noted that while acceleration is clearly supported by research, it is an option rarely offered. See Feldhusen and Kennedy (1989) for a description of the kinds of advanced courses offered by U.S. high schools.

54. For more on statistics about home schooling, see Kearney (1989). See Robinson and Noble (1991) for a discussion of historical figures who were home schooled.

55. Other public schools for the gifted include Bronx High School of Science, Brooklyn's Midwood High School, Hunter College Campus School, Stuyvesant High School (all four in New York City), North Carolina School of Science and Mathematics, and Texas Academy of Math and Science. Among those that specialize in the arts are LaGuardia High School of Music and Performing Arts in New York, High School for the Performing and Visual Arts in Houston, and North Carolina School of the Arts. A more comprehensive survey can be found in Cox, Daniel, and Boston (1985).

  Like Nueva, these schools have highly selective admissions criteria. In an effort to find more gifted minority students, who may not score as well on tests, some schools, such as the Bronx High School of Science, are starting to place greater weight on teacher nominations rather than relying only on test scores.

56. See Berger (1994) for a description of the way in which these schools engage students in the *doing* of science. Sixty-five per-

cent of graduates from Bronx High School of Science have become scientists over a fifty-year period (Pyrt, Masharov, and Feng [1993]).

57. Nongraded classrooms were discussed by Goodlad and Anderson (1987). For a review of such classrooms, see Pavan (1973). Rogers (1991) conducted a best evidence synthesis of nongraded classrooms and reported positive academic outcomes.

58. For a discussion of how teachers can successfully teach gifted children in regular classrooms, see Willis (1995). Slavin is one of the leading educational researchers today who argues for keeping the gifted child in the regular classroom and allowing the teacher to teach to different levels in the classroom. The study of third- and fourth-grade teachers was conducted by Westberg et al. (1993). Bangert, Kulik, and Kulik (1983) conducted a meta-analysis of individualized instruction studies in grades six through twelve. Hartley (1978) conducted a meta-analysis of studies of individualized math instruction at the elementary and secondary levels. For the finding that teachers with formal training in teaching the gifted make more modifications, see Brown et al. (1995).

59. Slavin (1987, 1990) showed that under certain circumstances, cooperative learning is more effective than traditional forms of learning. However, as noted by Robinson (1990), there is no research supporting the placing of gifted students in cooperative settings in regular classrooms. For this we would need, as Slavin (1987) pointed out, studies comparing cooperative learning in heterogeneous settings versus ability grouping for gifted children. No such studies have been carried out.

60. For more on Levin's schools, see Levin (1987a, 1987b, 1994). For studies showing the effectiveness of accelerated learning for low-achieving students, see Peterson (1989) and Knight and Stallings (in press). For the description of the accelerated school in Watts, see Stout (1992).

61. Shanker (1995).

62. According to Riley (1993), 73 percent of U.S. school districts surveyed nationally said that they had adopted the Marland (multidimensional) definition of giftedness. However, almost all also said that they used either IQ scores or teacher recommendations for general intelligence for admission into a gifted program and ignored the other dimensions of giftedness that

form part of the Marland definition. Critics of the use of IQ include Gardner (1983, 1993b) and Sternberg (1985, 1991).

63. Butler-Por (1993) found that underachievers show high achievement outside of school.

64. For more on the project in New York using portfolios, see Borland and Wright (1994) and Wright and Borland (1993).

Ten
WHAT HAPPENS TO GIFTED CHILDREN WHEN THEY GROW UP?

1. Goldsmith (in press) discussed the San Francisco music prodigies. For a study of how few talented art students ever make it as artists, see Getzels (1979).

2. See Csikszentmihalyi (1996), Gardner (1993b), and Zuckerman (1977) for a similar definition of creativity as domain transforming.

3. Three of these possible relationships are described by Gardner (1993c).

4. For reports of prodigies who dropped out, see Goldsmith (in press).

5. Terman (1925).

6. For examples of this retrospective approach, see Cox (1926), Galton (1874), Goertzel and Goertzel (1962), Goertzel, Goertzel, and Goertzel (1978), and Roe (1952).

7. For examples of this longitudinal approach, see Goldsmith (in press), Perleth and Heller (1994), Subotnik and Arnold (1993, 1994), Subotnik, Kassan, Summers, and Wasser (1993), and, of course, the Terman studies.

8. For more on the difficulty of predicting, see Feldman and Goldsmith (1991), Goldsmith and Feldman (1989), Howe (1990), Simonton (1994), and Trost (1993).

9. The Terman subjects late in life are discussed in Holahan and Sears (1995), and compared to average elderly.

10. For studies showing no correlation between IQ and creativity above an IQ of 120, see Barron (1968), Bloom (1963), Cox (1926), Drevdahl (1956), Getzels and Jackson (1962), Helson and Crutchfield (1970), Ochse (1990), Roe (1952), Simonton (1994), and Torrance (1962).

11. Piirto (1994) noted that some inventors studied by Berkeley's

Institute for Personality Assessment Research (IPAR) scored as low as 60 in verbal IQ, in contrast to some of the writers studied, who scored 160.

12. Feldman (1984) compared the twenty-six Termites with IQs over 180 to twenty-six Termites chosen at random. Ceci (1990a) noted that the success of Terman's subjects could be predicted by their socioeconomic background. Willis and Olszewski (1988) found income to be more important than race in determining academic success.

13. The study of creative Terman women was conducted by Vaillant and Vaillant (1990).

14. For a description of the Termites in adulthood, see Terman and Oden (1959). The study showing that the most adjusted Termites did not maintain their intellectual skills was conducted by Tomlinson-Keasey and Little (1990).

15. Subotnik, Kassan, Summers, and Wasser (1993) studied the Hunter College Elementary School graduates. The quote is from p. 86.

16. Gallagher and Crowder (1957) showed that high-IQ children often lack creativity and become intellectually rigid in the middle grades of school. Getzels and Jackson (1962) showed that IQ and creativity are independent. Marilyn Jarvik's IQ is listed in McFarlan (1989, p. 26).

17. Torrance (1972, 1992), however, reported a correlation (between .46 and .58) between scores in high school on the Torrance Tests of Creative Thinking and adult creative accomplishments. For more on the lack of validity of creativity tests, see Baer (1991) and Piirto (1994).

18. For evidence that IQ is a poor predictor of achievement, see McClelland (1973) and Wallach (1976). For evidence that IQ is only an imperfect predictor even of school success, see Duncan, Featherman, and Duncan (1973). For a discussion of the kinds of abilities ignored by IQ tests, see Gardner (1983). For a discussion of the independence of IQ from practical and social intelligence, see Sternberg and Wagner (1986). For more on the independence of IQ and ego resilience (defined as the ability to be open to new experience, recover from stress, and be flexible), see Block and Kremen (1995). The observation that high-IQ society members are often misfits was made by Simonton (1994); I made the same observation when I visited a MENSA conference in 1994.

19. Benbow (1992) noted the relationship between high math SAT scores and later math/science achievement but also found that many leave the field of math, especially women. Milgram and Hong (1993) showed the connection between adolescent interests and adult occupations: these were matched in 35 percent of the forty-eight subjects studied. For another longitudinal study showing that domain-specific tests are better predictors of later achievement than IQ tests, see Heller (1991).

20. Simonton (1991) studied 120 classical composers who were famous to varying degrees. For other studies showing that greater precocity is associated with greater adult eminence, see Cox (1926) and Shuter-Dyson and Gabriel (1981).

21. For the study of 100 creators, see Csikszentmihalyi (1996). For the study of Freud, Eliot, Einstein, Gandhi, Graham, Stravinsky, and others, see Gardner (1993a). Studies showing that top performers (not necessarily major creators) were not prodigies as children include Bloom (1985) and Sloboda (1985).

22. For a discussion of the early signs of naturalist intelligence, see Gardner (1996).

23. Csikszentmihalyi (1996). For more on the importance of crystallizing experiences for children not "born into" a particular domain, see Simonton (1994) and Walters and Gardner (1986). Martha Graham is quoted in Gardner (1993a, p. 269). For more on the crystallizing experience of Bruckner, see Simonton (1994).

24. Goldsmith (1987, in press) described the adult choices of these prodigies.

25. For more on how prodigies must remake themselves, see Gardner (1993c) and Goldsmith (in press). For more on Peggy Somerville, see Dinnage (1993). For the description of Sarah Chang, see Hoffman (1993). Bamberger (1982) discussed the identity crisis in music prodigies. Gardner and Wolf (1988) posited the necessity of some experience of failure, or what they called a "fruitful asynchrony," for later creative accomplishment.

26. Golomb and Hass (1995) studied Varda.

27. The prolific outputs of Picasso, Freud, Edison, and many others have been documented by Simonton (1994). He has pointed out that in any domain, about 10 percent of people

account for about half of the creative breakthroughs in that domain.

28. The ten-year rule has been noted by Ericsson, Krampe, and Tesch-Romer (1993), Gardner (1993a), Hayes (1989), and Simon and Chase (1973). Gardner (1993a) also noted that each subsequent breakthrough occurs at approximately ten-year intervals. Simonton (1994) noted that prodigies may achieve their first masterpiece in somewhat less than ten years, but even prodigies still take years. For the study of Darwin, see Gruber (1981).

29. For the comparison of more versus less successful Termites, see Terman and Oden (1959, p. 148), and Oden (1968). Csikszentmihalyi, Rathunde, and Whalen (1993) compared adolescents who did and did not remain committed to science, math, art, music, and sports.

30. Gardner's (1993a) seven creators made what he called a Faustian bargain with their work, giving up personal ties for immortality.

31. Rathunde and Csikszentmihalyi (1993) showed the importance of undivided attention in predicting later achievement.

32. Csikszentmihalyi (1996) studied 100 eminent adults who remained creative throughout their lives. He found that for these people, work was a form of play.

33. See Csikszentmihalyi, Rathunde, and Whalen (1993). While flow predicted commitment across all five domains studied, the relative importance of immediate versus deferred pleasure varied by domain. Teenagers gifted in math and science felt less engaged and excited by their work than did teenagers gifted in art, music, or sports, perhaps because there is less sensory involvement in work in math and science. However, those in math and science felt that they would gain rewards for their work in the future, since careers in these domains are prestigious and pay well, while those in art, music, and sports do not. They knew full well that only a few can make it "big" in these domains. Csikszentmihalyi speculated that the ability to enjoy work and achieve flow may be more predictive of long-term commitment in math and science, while the ability to relate present enjoyment of work to a future plan of action may be more predictive of long-term commitment in art, music, and sports.

34. Cattell (1965) demonstrated dominance in scientists. The

belief that one can achieve what one aspires to is often referred to as "self-efficacy" (Taylor, Locke, Lee, and Gist [1984]). Barron (1958) and MacKinnon (1965) found that creators in various domains who were studied at Berkeley's Institute for Personality Assessment Research all scored high on ego strength and self-confidence. For further evidence that creators have high self-confidence and low self-doubt, see Gardner (1993a).

35. For a discussion of the social skills necessary to sell oneself to the field, see Getzels and Csikszentmihalyi (1976).

36. Cattell (1963, 1965) showed that writers, artists, and scientists are independent, "radical" rather than conservative, and low on "group super-ego" (that is, low in concern for group norms). See also Crutchfield (1962) and Helson and Crutchfield (1970) for evidence of independence and nonconformism in creators.

37. For evidence that creators are introverts, see Cattell (1963). The Dickens quote is cited in Simonton (1994, p. 269). Storr (1988) wrote about the importance of solitude for creators. According to Kay Jamison (personal communication), creators are both introverted and extroverted. Csikszentmihalyi (1996) found that creative people are characterized by oppositional states.

38. Simonton (1994) documented that the ratio of great works to failures is the same for more prolific creators and less prolific ones. It follows that the most prolific creators produce the most masterpieces as well as the most failures.

39. MacKinnon (1962) showed that creative architects, mathematicians, and scientists differed from the merely competent ones not in ability but in personality: the creative ones were oppositional and discontented, while the merely competent ones were passive and content. See also Albert and Runco (1986).

40. Simonton noted the presence of later-borns among writers and political revolutionaries. Sulloway (1990) documented the association between being a later-born and supporting revolutionary, antiestablishment scientific theories.

41. The decline in the number of girls in school programs for the gifted was noted by Silverman (1986). The lower self-confidence of high-ability girls was noted by Subotnik and Arnold (1993). Reis and Callahan (1989) showed that the ambitions of bright girls decline in high school, and they

argued that this is because girls are given less attention. Noble (1989) found that academically gifted women recalled hiding their abilities to fit in.

42. For the finding that eminent women are less likely to marry and to have children than eminent men, see Simonton (1994).

43. Helson (1980, 1990) showed that women without brothers were more likely to become eminent in math.

44. Tolstoy (1961, p. 17). Vidal is quoted in Ochse (1990, p. 34). Reports of the high levels of stress and trauma in families of future creators can be found in Albert (1971, 1978, 1980a, b), Cox (1926), Goertzel and Goertzel (1962), Goertzel, Goertzel, and Goertzel (1978), Howe (1990), McCurdy (1960), Ochse (1990), Olszewski, Kulieke, and Buescher (1987), Radford (1990), Roe (1952), Simonton (1994), Walberg, Rasher, and Hase (1978), and Weisberg and Springer (1961). For the lack of intense closeness in families of creative children, see Weisberg and Springer (1961).

45. Goertzel and Goertzel (1962) and Goertzel, Goertzel, and Goertzel (1978). See also Ludwig (1995).

46. These individuals are cited by Simonton (1994), who compiled a long list of eminent figures who lost a parent in childhood. For studies showing high parental loss in creators, see Cox (1926), Csikszentmihalyi (1996), Eisenstadt (1978), Goertzel, Goertzel, and Goertzel (1978), Goertzel and Goertzel (1962), Roe (1952), Silverman (1994), Simonton (1994), and Walberg, Rasher, and Parkerson (1980). Albert (1980a) reported an 8 percent base rate of early parental death; Roe (1952) reported that 6 percent of college students have lost a parent by age ten. A lower estimate was reported by Hathaway and Monachesi (1963), who found that 8 out of a survey of 11,329 adolescents had suffered parental loss. Comparisons to other groups with high parental loss were made by Albert (1980a), Brown (1968), Eisenstadt (1978), Ochse (1990), and Tomlinson-Keasey, Warren, and Elliott (1986). Albert (1980a) reported a rate of early parental loss in criminals of 32 percent, and in psychiatric patients of 27 percent. But see Ludwig (1995), who did not find this, and who cautions that most studies did not use a control group from the same historical time.

47. Most of the studies showing that families of creators are stress-filled and not very child-centered are retrospective and

recount families of an earlier era. Since today's families are in general more child-centered, it is possible that today's families of future creators are more like the families typical of gifted children.

48. Goertzel, Goertzel, and Goertzel (1978). The comparison between science and literature Nobel laureates was conducted by Berry (1981). Simonton (1994) reported similar statistics. Note, however, a methodological problem that might or might not have influenced these findings: Nobel Prize–winning scientists are Western, while prize-winning writers come from all over the world.

49. Ochse (1990) and Simonton (1994) offered some of these speculations to account for the association between stress in childhood and adult creativity. Bouchard pointed out the impossibility of drawing causal connections from the correlational studies of family environment and creativity (see Bouchard's comments in Csikszentmihalyi and Csikszentmihalyi [1993, p. 205]).

50. Sartre (1964, p. 11). For further consideration of why parental loss can lead to creativity, see Eisenstadt (1978) and Simonton (1994). I am indebted to Mardi Horowitz for his insights on this matter (personal communication).

51. The study of eminent American writers was conducted by Andreasen (1987). The study of British artists and writers was conducted by Jamison (1989, 1993). For other studies of the link between affective disorders and creativity, see Arieti (1976), Barron (1969), Ellis (1926), Goertzel, Goertzel, and Goertzel (1978), Götz and Götz (1979a, b), Juda (1949), Karlson (1970), Ludwig (1995), MacKinnon (1962), Richards (1994), and Rothenberg (1990). See Simonton (1994) for a review. For a comparison between creators and leaders showing that it is creators, but not leaders, who become ill, see Goertzel, Goertzel, and Goertzel (1978) and Ludwig (1992). Jamison (1989, 1993) found no affective disorders in biographers, in contrast to the arguably more creative novelists, poets, playwrights, and artists. For the comparison between artists and writers versus scientists, see Cattell and Butcher (1968). See also Ludwig (1995) and Eysenck (1995).

52. For evidence that mood disorders lead to unusual and creative thought processes, see Barron (1969) and MacKinnon (1962), who found, using the Minnesota Multiphasic Personality

Inventory, that creative people score midway between average people and psychotic patients on unusual thought processes, openness to expression of impulses, and depression. Götz and Götz (1979a, b) found that artists score higher than average on the psychoticism scale of the Eysenck Personality Questionnaire (EPQ). For a discussion of the advantages that mania confers, see Jamison (1989, 1993, 1995) and Richards (1981). For evidence that mania leads to overinclusive categories, see Andreasen and Canter (1974). See also Isen and Daubman (1984) and Isen, Johnson, Mertz, and Robinson (1985) for evidence that induction of elevated moods also leads to overinclusive categories. Richards (1995, personal communication) suggested to me that gifted children who so typically show high drive, focus, and energy may be mildly manic. See Jamison (1995) for a vivid personal account of the relationship between creativity and mania.

53. For a discussion of the readiness of the domain and acceptance by the field, see Csikszentmihalyi (1988). For more on the role of chance, see Tannenbaum (1983, 1994).

54. Goertzel, Goertzel, and Goertzel (1978) described parents of creators as pursuing their own interests and encouraging independence.

References

Achter, J. D., Lubinski, D., & Benbow, C. P. (1996). *Multipotentiality among the intellectually gifted: It was never there in the first place, and already it's vanishing*. Unpublished manuscript.

Adler, A. (1938). *Social interest*. (Trans. J. Linton & R. Vaughan). London: Faber & Faber.

Albert, R. S. (1971). Cognitive development and parental loss among the gifted and the creative. *Psychological Reports, 29,* 19–26.

Albert, R. S. (1975). Toward a behavioral definition of genius. *American Psychologist, 30,* 140–151.

Albert, R. S. (1978). Observations and suggestions regarding giftedness, familial influence and the achievement of eminence. *Gifted Child Quarterly, 28,* 201–211.

Albert, R. S. (1980a). Family positions and the attainment of eminence: A study of special family positions and special family experiences. *Gifted Child Quarterly, 24* (2), 87–95.

Albert, R. S. (1980b). Exceptional creativity and achievement. In R. S. Albert (Ed.), *Genius and eminence: The social psychology of creativity and exceptional achievement* (pp. 19–35). New York: Oxford University Press.

Albert, R. S., & Runco, M. A. (1986). The achievement of eminence: A model of exceptional boys and their parents. In R. J. Sternberg & J. E. Davidson (Eds.), *Conceptions of giftedness* (pp. 332–357). New York: Cambridge University Press.

Alexander, J. M., Carr, M., & Schwanenflugel, P. J. (1995). Development of metacognition in gifted children: Directions for future research. *Developmental Review, 15*(1), 1–37.

Altman, L. K. (1991, Sept. 24). Can the brain provide clues to intelligence? *New York Times*.

Ames, M. H. (1990, Fall). The Meyerhoff scholars: Names you'll hear in Maryland's future. *University of Maryland Baltimore County Review, 9*(2), 3.

Anastasi, A., & Foley, J., Jr. (1941). A survey of the literature on artistic behavior in the abnormal: I. Historical and theoretical background. *Journal of General Psychology, 25*, 111–142.

Anderson, M. (1992). *Intelligence and development: A cognitive theory.* Oxford: Blackwell.

Anderson, M., O'Connor, N., & Hermelin, B. (n.d.). *Intelligence and cognition—A case study of a mentally retarded, savant prime number calculator.* Unpublished manuscript.

Andreasen, N. C. (1987). Creativity and mental illness: Prevalence rates in writers and their first-degree relatives. *American Journal of Psychiatry, 144*, 1288–1292.

Andreasen, N. C., & Canter, A. (1974). The creative writer: Psychiatric symptoms and family history. *Comprehensive Psychiatry, 15*, 123–131.

Annett, M. (1985). *Left, right, hand and brain: The right shift theory.* Hillsdale, NJ: Erlbaum.

Annett, M., & Kilshaw, D. (1982). Mathematical ability and lateral asymmetry. *Cortex, 18*, 547–568.

Annett, M., & Turner, A. (1974). Laterality and the growth of intellectual abilities. *British Journal of Educational Psychology, 44*, 37–46.

Aram, D. M., & Healey, J. M. (1988). Hyperlexia: A review of extraordinary word recognition. In L. K. Obler & D. Fein (Eds.), *The exceptional brain* (pp. 70–102). New York: Guilford Press.

Arbuthnot, J. (1973). Relationship between maturity of moral judgment and measures of cognitive abilities. *Psychological Reports, 33*, 945–946.

Arieti, S. (1976). *Creativity.* New York: BasicBooks.

Arnheim, R. (1974). *Art and visual perception: A psychology of the creative eye. The new version.* Berkeley, CA: University of California Press.

Arnheim, R. (1980). The puzzle of Nadia's drawings. *The Arts in Psychotherapy, 7*, 79–85.

Astin, A. W. (1964). Socioeconomic factors in the achievements and aspirations of the Merit Scholar. *Personnel and Guidance Journal, 42*, 581–586.

Austin, A. B., & Draper, D. C. (1981). Peer relationships of the academically gifted: A review. *Gifted Child Quarterly, 25*(3), 129–134.

Bachem, A. (1955). Absolute pitch. *Journal of the Acoustical Society of America, 27* (6), 1100.

Baer, J. (1991). Generality of creativity across performance domains. *Creativity Research Journal, 4* (1), 23–39.

Bakan, P. (1971). Handedness and birth order. *Nature, 229*, 195.

Bakan, P. (1991). Handedness and maternal smoking during pregnancy. *International Journal of Neuroscience, 56*, 161–168.

Bamberger, J. (1982). Growing up prodigies: The mid-life crisis. In D. H. Feldman (Ed.), *Developmental approaches to giftedness*. San Francisco, CA: Jossey-Bass, 265–279.

Bamberger, J. (1986). Cognitive issues in the development of musically gifted children. In R. J. Sternberg & J. Davidson (Eds.), *Conceptions of giftedness* (pp. 388–413). New York: Cambridge University Press.

Bangert, R. L., Kulik, J. A., & Kulik, C.-L. C. (1983). Individualized systems of instruction in secondary schools. *Review of Educational Research, 53*, 143–158.

Barbe, W. B. (1956). A study of the family background of the gifted. *Journal of Educational Psychology, 47*, 302–309.

Barbe, W. B., & Renzulli, J. (1975). *Psychology and education of the gifted*. New York: Wiley.

Barrett, H. G., & Barker, H. R., Jr. (1973). Cognitive pattern perception and musical performance. *Perceptual and Motor Skills, 36*, 1187–1193.

Barron, F. (1958). The psychology of imagination. *Scientific American, 199*(3), 151–166.

Barron, F. (1968). *Creativity and personal freedom*. New York: Van Nostrand Reinhold.

Barron, F. (1969). *Creative person and creative process*. New York: Holt, Rinehart & Winston.

Bass, N. H., Hess, A., Pope, A., & Thalheimer, C. (1971). Quantitative cytoarchitectonic distribution of neurons, glia and DNA in rat cerebral cortex. *Journal of Comparative Neurology, 148*, 481–490.

Baum, S. (1984, September). Meeting the needs of learning disabled gifted students. *Roeper Review*, 16–19.

Baum, S., & Owen, S. V. (1988). High ability/learning disabled students: How are they different? *Gifted Child Quarterly, 32*(3), 321–326.

Baumrind, D. (1971). Current practices of parental authority. *Developmental Psychology Monograph, 4*(4), 1–103.

Beck, W. (1928). *Self-development in drawing. As interpreted by the genius of Romano Dazzi and other children.* New York: G. P. Putnam's Sons.

Belluck, P. (1995, January 25). At 15, Westinghouse finalist grasps "Holy Grail" of math. *New York Times,* pp. A1, B8.

Benbow, C. P. (1983). Adolescence of the mathematically precocious. In C. P. Benbow & J. C. Stanley (Eds.), *Academic precocity: Aspects of its development* (pp. 9–37). Baltimore, MD: Johns Hopkins University Press.

Benbow, C. P. (1986). Physiological correlates of extreme intellectual precocity. *Neuropsychologia, 24,* 719–725.

Benbow, C. P. (1988). Sex differences in mathematical reasoning ability in intellectually talented preadolescents: Their nature, effects, and possible causes. *Behavioral and Brain Sciences, 11,* 169–232.

Benbow, C. P. (1991). Meeting the needs of gifted students through acceleration: A neglected resource. In M. C. Wang, M. C. Reynolds, & H. J. Walberg (Eds.), *Handbook of special education: Research and practice: Vol. 4. Emerging programs* (pp. 23–36). Elmsford, NY: Pergamon Press.

Benbow, C. P. (1992). Academic achievement in mathematics and science of students between ages 13 and 23: Are there differences among students in the top one percent of mathematical ability? *Journal of Educational Psychology, 84*(1), 51–61.

Benbow, C. P., & Arjmand, O. (1990). Predictors of high academic achievement in mathematics and science by mathematically talented students: A longitudinal study. *Journal of Educational Psychology, 82,* 440–441.

Benbow, C. P., Arjmand, O., & Walberg, H. J. (1991). Educational productivity predictors among mathematically talented students. *Journal of Educational Research, 84*(4), 215–223.

Benbow, C. P., & Benbow, R. M. (1986). Physiological correlates of extreme intellectual precocity. *Mensa Research Journal, 21,* 54–87.

Benbow, C. P., & Benbow, R. M. (1987). Extreme mathematical talent: A hormonally induced ability? In D. O. Hossu (Ed.), *Duality and unity of the brain.* New York: Macmillan.

Benbow, C. P., & Minor, L. L. (1990). Cognitive profiles of verbally and mathematically precocious students: Implications for identification of the gifted. *Gifted Child Quarterly, 34,* 21–26.

Benbow, C. P., & Stanley, J. C. (1980a). Intellectually talented students: Family profiles. *Gifted Child Quarterly, 24*(3), 119–128.

Benbow, C. P., & Stanley, J. C. (1980b). Sex differences in mathematical ability: Fact or artifact? *Science, 210,* 1262–1264.

Benbow, C. P., & Stanley, J. C. (1982). Consequences in high school and college of sex differences in mathematical reasoning ability: A longitudinal perspective. *American Educational Research Journal, 19,* 598–622.

Benbow, C. P., & Stanley, J. C. (1983a). Sex differences in mathematical reasoning ability: More facts. *Science, 222,* 1029–1031.

Benbow, C. P., & Stanley, J. C. (1983b). *Academic precocity: Aspects of its development.* Baltimore, MD: Johns Hopkins University Press.

Benbow, C. P., Stanley, J. C., Kirk, M. K., & Zonderman, A. B. (1983). Structure of intelligence in intellectually precocious children and in their parents. *Intelligence, 7,* 129–152.

Benbow, C. P., Zonderman, A. B., & Stanley, J. C. (1983). Assortive marriage and familiarity of cognitive abilities in families of extremely gifted students. *Intelligence, 7,* 153–161.

Berent, S., Giordani, B., Lehtinen, S., Markel, D., Penny, J. B., Buchtel, H. A., Starosta-Rubinstein, S., Hichwa, R., & Young, A. B. (1988). Positron emission tomographic scan investigations of Huntington's disease: Cerebral metabolic correlates of cognitive function. *Annals of Neurology, 23,* 541–546.

Berger, J. (1994). *The young scientists: America's future and the winning of the Westinghouse.* Reading, MA: Addison-Wesley.

Bergman, J. P., & Escalona, S. (1949). Unusual sensitivities in very young children. *Psychoanalytic Study of Children, 3–4,* 333–352.

Berry, C. (1981). The Nobel scientists and the origins of scientific achievement. *British Journal of Sociology, 32,* 381–391.

Bever, T., & Chiarello, R. (1974). Cerebral dominance in musicians and non-musicians. *Science, 185,* 537–539.

Binet, A. (1894). *Psychologie des grandes calculateurs (et de jouers d'echecs).* Paris: Hachette.

Birns, B., & Golden, M. (1972). Prediction of intellectual performance at 3 years from infant tests and personality measures. *Merrill Palmer Quarterly, 18,* 53–58.

Bishop, D. V. M. (1986). Is there a link between handedness and hypersensitivity? *Cortex, 22,* 289–296.

Blinkhorn, S., & Hendrickson, D. (1982). Average evoked responses and psychometric intelligence. *Nature, 295,* 596–597.

Block, J., & Kremen, A. (1995). *IQ and ego-resiliency: The conceptual and empirical connections and separateness.* Unpublished manuscript, University of California at Berkeley.

Bloom, B. (1963). Report on the creativity research by the Examiners' Office of the University of Chicago. In C. W. Taylor & F. Barron (Eds.), *Scientific creativity: Its recognition and development* (pp. 251–264). New York: Wiley.

Bloom, B. (1982). The role of gifts and markers in the development of talents. *Exceptional Children, 48*(6), 510–521.

Bloom, B. (Ed.). (1985). *Developing talent in young people.* New York: Ballantine Books.

Bloom, J. K. (1993, November 1). Panel recommends Cambridge schools end tracking. *Boston Globe,* pp. 17, 25.

Blumberg, S. A., & Panos, L. G. (1990). *Edward Teller: Giant of the golden age of physics.* New York: Macmillan.

Boden, M. (1991). *The creative mind: Myths and mechanisms.* New York: BasicBooks.

Boehm, L. (1962). The development of conscience: A comparison of American children of different mental and socioeconomic levels. *Child Development, 33,* 575–590.

Bogle, C. E., & Buckhalt, J. A. (1987). Reactions to failure and success among gifted, average, and EMR students. *Gifted Child Quarterly, 31,* 70–74.

Boodoo, G. M., Bradley, C. L., Frontera, R. L., Pitts, J. R., & Wright, L. B. (1989). A survey of procedures used for identifying gifted learning disabled children. *Gifted Child Quarterly, 33* (3), 110–114.

Borland, J. H., & Wright, L. (1994). Identifying young, potentially gifted, economically disadvantaged students. *Gifted Child Quarterly, 38*(4), 164–171.

Bornstein, M., & Sigman, M. (1986). Continuity in mental development from infancy. *Child Development, 57,* 251–274.

Bouchard, T. J., & McGue, M. (1981). Familial studies of intelligence: A review. *Science, 212,* 1055–1059.

Bouchard, T. J., Lykken, D. T., McGue, M., Segal, N. L., & Tellegen, A. (1990). Sources of human psychological differences: The Minnesota Study of Twins Reared Apart. *Science, 250,* 223–228.

Bowlby, J. (1990). *Charles Darwin: A new life.* New York: Norton.

Brody, L. E., & Benbow, C. P. (1986). Social and emotional adjustment of adolescents extremely talented in verbal or mathematical reasoning. *Journal of Youth and Adolescence, 15,* 1–18.

Broverman, D. M., Klaiber, E. L., Kobayaski, Y., & Vogel, W. (1968).

Roles of activation and inhibition in sex differences in cognitive abilities. *Psychological Review, 75,* 23–50.

Brown, F. (1968). Bereavement and lack of a parent in childhood. In E. Miller (Ed.), *Foundations of Child Psychiatry* (pp. 435–455). Oxford: Pergamon Press.

Brown, S. W., Archambault, F. X., Jr., Zhang, W., & Westberg, K. L. (1995, Spring). A follow-up study of the interaction effects on the classroom practices survey. University of Connecticut: *The National Research Center on the Gifted and Talented Newsletter,* 6–9.

Bryden, M. P., Hecaen, H., & DeAgostini, M. (1983). Patterns of cerebral organization. *Brain and Language, 20,* 249–262.

Bryden, M. P., McManus, I. C., & Bulman-Fleming, M. B. (1994). Evaluating the empirical support for the Geschwind-Behan-Galaburda Model of Cerebral Lateralization. *Brain and Cognition, 26,* 103–167.

Buck, L. A., Kardeman, E., & Goldstein, F. (1985). Artistic talent in "autistic" adolescents and young adults. *Empirical Studies of the Arts, 3* (1), 81–104.

Bull, B. L. (1985). Eminence and precocity: An examination of the justification of education for the gifted and talented. *Teachers College Record, 87*(1), 1–19.

Burks, B. S., Jensen, D. W., & Terman, L. M. (1930). *Genetic studies of genius: Vol. 3. The promise of youth: Follow-up studies of a thousand gifted children.* Stanford, CA: Stanford University Press.

Burnett, S., Lane, D., & Dratt, L. (1979). Spatial visualization and sex differences in quantitative ability. *Intelligence, 3,* 345–354.

Butler-Por, N. (1987). *Underachievers in school: Issues and intervention.* Chichester: Wiley.

Butler-Por, N. (1993). Underachieving gifted students. In K. A. Heller, F. J. Monks, & A. H. Passow (Eds.), *International handbook of research and development of giftedness and talent* (pp. 649–668). Oxford: Pergamon Press.

Byrne, B. (1974). Handedness and musical ability. *British Journal of Psychology, 65,* 279–281.

Cain, A. C. (1970). Special isolated abilities in severely psychotic young children. *Psychiatry, 33,* 137–149.

Callahan, C. M., & McIntire, J. A. (1994). *Identifying outstanding talent in American Indian and Alaska native students.* Washington, DC: U.S. Department of Education.

Cane, F. (1951). *The artist in each of us.* New York: Pantheon.

Cardon, L. R., Fulkner, D. W., DeFries, J. C., & Plomin, R. (1992).

Multivariate genetic analysis of specific cognitive abilities in the Colorado Adoption Project at age seven. *Intelligence, 16*, 338–400.

Carr, T. H. (1981). Building theories of reading ability: On the relation between individual differences in cognitive skills and reading comprehension. *Cognition, 9*, 73–114.

Carroll, H. A. (1940). *Genius in the making*. New York: McGraw-Hill.

Casey, M. B., & Brabeck, M. (1989). Exceptions to the male advantage in a spatial task: Family handedness and college major as factors identifying women who excel. *Neuropsychologia, 27*, 689–696.

Casey, M. B., Nuttal, R., Pezaris, E., & Benbow, C. P. (1995). The influence of spatial ability on gender differences in mathematics college entrance test scores across diverse samples. *Developmental Psychology, 31*(4), 697–705.

Casey, M. B., Winner, E., Brabeck, M., & Sullivan, K. (1990). Visual-spatial abilities in art, math, and science majors: Effects of sex, family handedness, and spatial experience. In K. Gilhooly, M. Keane, R. Logie, & G. Erdos (Eds.), *Lines of thinking: Reflections on the psychology of thought*. New York: Wiley.

Castro, P., & Grant, M. (1994, October 24). Small wonder. *Psychology Today*, 99–100.

Cattell, R. B. (1963). The personality and motivation of the researcher from measurements of contemporaries and from biography. In C. W. Taylor & F. Barron (Eds.), *Scientific creativity* (pp. 119–131). New York: Wiley.

Cattell, R. B. (1965). *The scientific analysis of personality*. Baltimore: Penguin.

Cattell, R. B., & Butcher, H. J. (1968). *The prediction of achievement and creativity*. Indianapolis: Bobbs-Merrill.

Ceci, S. J. (1990a). *On intelligence . . . more or less: A bio-ecological treatise on intellectual development*. Englewood Cliffs, NJ: Prentice Hall.

Ceci, S. J. (1990b). On the relation between microlevel processing efficiency and macrolevel measures of intelligence: Some arguments against current reductionism. *Intelligence, 14*, 141–150.

Center for Talented Youth (1994). Newsletter *33*, Sept/Oct., p. 5. Study of Exceptional Talent, Johns Hopkins University.

Chamrad, D. L., & Robinson, N. M. (1986). Parenting the intellectually gifted preschool child. *Topics in Early Childhood Special Education, 6*, 74–87.

Charness, N., Clifton, J., & MacDonald, L. (1988). Case study of a musical "mono-savant": A cognitive psychological focus. In

L. K. Obler & D. Fein (Eds.), *The exceptional brain: Neuropsychology of talent and special abilities* (pp. 277–293). New York: Guilford Press.

Chase, W. G., & Ericsson, K. A. (1982). Skill and working memory. In G. H. Bower (Ed.), *The psychology of learning and motivation* (Vol. 16, pp. 1–58). New York: Academic Press.

Chi, M. (1978). Knowledge structures and memory development. In R. S. Siegler (Ed.), *Children's thinking: What develops?* (pp. 73–96). Hillsdale, NJ: Erlbaum.

Ciha, T. E., Harris, R., Hoffman, C., & Potter, M. W. (1974). Parents as identifiers of giftedness, ignored but accurate. *Gifted Child Quarterly, 18,* 191–195.

Clark, G. A. (1993). Judging children's drawings as measures of art abilities. *Studies in Art Education, 34*(2), 72–81.

Clark, G. A., & Zimmerman, E. D. (1995). You can't just scribble: Art talent development. *Educational Forum, 59*(4), 400–408.

Clark, R. (1983). *Family life and school achievement: Why poor black children succeed or fail.* Chicago, IL: University of Chicago Press.

Clark, W. H., & Hankins, N. E. (1985). Giftedness and conflict. *Roeper Review, 8,* 50–53.

Clarke, A. M., & Clarke, A. D. B. (Eds.). (1976). *Early experience: Myth and evidence.* London: Open Books.

Colangelo, N., Assouline, S., Kerr, B., Huesman, R., & Johnson, D. (1993). Mechanical inventiveness: A three-phase study. In G. R. Bock & K. Ackrill (Eds.), *The origins and development of high ability* (pp. 160–174). New York: Wiley.

Colangelo, N., & Dettman, D. F. (1983). A review of research on parents and families of gifted children. *Exceptional Children, 50*(1), 20–27.

Colby, A., & Damon, W. (1992). *Some do care: Contemporary lives of moral commitment.* New York: Free Press.

Coleman, J. S. (1960). The adolescent subculture and academic achievement. *American Journal of Sociology, 65,* 337–347.

Comer, J. (1988). *Maggie's American dream: The life and times of a black family.* New York: New American Library.

Cone, T. (1994, October 30). Living backward. *San Jose Mercury News,* West Magazine section, pp. 8–11, 16–19.

Coon, H., & Carey, G. (1989). Genetic and environmental determinants of musical ability in twins. *Behavior Genetics, 19,* 183–193.

Coren, S. (1994). Methodological problems in determining the relationship between handedness and immune system function. *Brain and Cognition, 26,* 168–173.

Cornell, D. G. (1984). *Families of gifted children.* Ann Arbor, MI: UMI Research Press.

Cornell, D. G. (1989). Child adjustment and parent use of the term "gifted." *Gifted Child Quarterly, 33,* 59–64.

Cornell, D. G., & Grossberg, I. N. (1989). Parent use of the term "gifted": Correlates with family environment and child adjustment. *Journal for the Education of the Gifted, 12,* 218–230.

Cox, C. (1926). *Genetic studies of genius: Vol. 2. The early mental traits of three-hundred geniuses.* Stanford, CA: Stanford University Press.

Cox, J., Daniel, N., & Boston, B. (1985). *Educating able learners: Programs and promising practices.* Austin: University of Texas Press.

Cox, M. (1992). *Children's drawings.* London: Penguin.

Cox, R. L. (1977). Background characteristics of 456 gifted students. *Gifted Child Quarterly, 21,* 261–267.

Crain-Thoreson, C., & Dale, P. S. (1992). Do early talkers become early readers? Linguistic precocity, preschool language, and emergent literacy. *Developmental Psychology, 28,* 421–429.

Cranberg, L. D., & Albert, M. J. (1988). The chess mind. In L. K. Obler & D. Fein (Eds.), *The exceptional brain: Neuropsychology of talent and special abilities* (pp. 156–190). New York: Guilford Press.

Cross, T. L., Coleman, L. J., & Stewart, R. A. (1992). The social cognition of gifted adolescents: An exploration of the stigma of giftedness paradigm. *Roeper Review, 16*(1), 37–40.

Cruickshank, W. (1963). *Psychology of exceptional children and youth.* Englewood Cliffs, NJ: Prentice-Hall.

Crutchfield, R. (1962). Conformity and creative thinking. In H. E. Gruber, G. Terrell, & M. Wertheimer (Eds.), *Contemporary approaches to creative thinking* (pp. 120–140). New York: Atherton Press.

Csapo, B. (1995). A comparison of Hungarian and U.S. school performance. Paper presented at Center for Advanced Study in the Behavioral Sciences, Stanford University, Stanford, California.

Csikszentmihalyi, M. (1990). *Flow: The psychology of optimal experience.* New York: Harper & Row.

Csikszentmihalyi, M. (1996). *Creativity.* New York: HarperCollins.

Csikszentmihalyi, M., & Csikszentmihalyi, I. S. (1993). Family influences on the development of giftedness. In G. R. Bock & K. Ackrill (Eds.), *The origins and development of high ability* (pp. 187–200). New York: Wiley.

Csikszentmihalyi, M., Rathunde, K., & Whalen, S. (1993). *Talented teenagers: The roots of success and failure*. New York: Cambridge University Press.

Csikszentmihalyi, M., & Robinson, R. E. (1986). Culture, time and the development of talent. In R. J. Sternberg & J. E. Davidson (Eds.), *Conceptions of giftedness* (pp. 264–284). New York: Cambridge University Press.

Dabrowski, K. (1964). *Positive disintegration.* London: Little, Brown.

Dabrowski, K., & Piechowski, M. M. (1977). *Theory of levels of emotional development* (Vol. 1). Oceanside, NY: Dabor Science.

D'Amico, C., & Kimura, D. (1987). *Evidence for subgroups of adextrals based on speech lateralization and cognitive patterns* (Research Bulletin No. 664). Ontario: University of Western Ontario, Department of Psychology.

Damon, W. (1995). *Greater expectations: Overcoming the culture of indulgence in America's homes and schools*. New York: Free Press.

Dark, V. J., & Benbow, C. P. (1990). Enhanced problem translation and short-term memory: Components of mathematical talent. *Journal of Educational Psychology, 82*(3), 420–429.

Dark, V. J., & Benbow, C. P. (1991). Differential enhancement of working memory with mathematical versus verbal precocity. *Journal of Educational Psychology, 83*(1), 48–60.

Daurio, S. P. (1979). Educational enrichment versus acceleration: A review of the literature. In W. C. George, S. J. Cohn, & J. C. Stanley (Eds.), *Educating the gifted: Acceleration and enrichment* (pp. 13–63). Baltimore: Johns Hopkins University Press.

Davidson, J. E. (1986). The role of insight in giftedness. In R. J. Sternberg & J. E. Davidson (Eds.), *Conceptions of giftedness* (pp. 201–243). New York: Cambridge University Press.

Davis, G. A., & Rimm, S. (1985). *Education of the gifted and talented.* Englewood Cliffs, NJ: Prentice-Hall.

Davis, H. B., & Connell, J. P. (1985). The effect of aptitude and achievement status on the self-system. *Gifted Child Quarterly, 29*(3), 131–136.

Deakin, M. (1972). *The children on the hill.* Indianapolis: Bobbs-Merrill.

DeFries, J., Plomin, R., Vanderberg, S., & Kuse, A. (1981). Parent-offspring resemblance for cognitive abilities in the Colorado Adoption Project. *Intelligence, 5,* 245–277.

Delcourt, M. A. B., Loyd, B. H., Cornell, D. G., & Goldberg, M. D. (1994). *Evaluation of the effects of programming arrangements on student learning outcomes* (Research Monograph No. 94107). University of Connecticut: The National Research Center on the Gifted and Talented.

Delisle, J. R. (1986). Death with honors: Suicide among gifted adolescents. *Journal of Counseling and Development, 64*, 558–560.

Detterman, D. K. (1991). Reply to Dreary and Pagliari: Is g intelligence or stupidity? *Intelligence, 15*, 251–255.

Detterman, D. K. (1993). Giftedness and intelligence: One and the same. In G. R. Bock & K. Ackrill (Eds.), *The origins and development of high ability* (pp. 22–31). New York: Wiley.

Detterman, D. K., & Daniel, M. H. (1989). Correlations of mental tests with each other and with cognitive variables are highest for low IQ groups. *Intelligence, 15*, 349–359.

Deutsch, D. (1980). Handedness and memory for tonal pitch. In J. Herron (Ed.), *Neuropsychology of lefthandedness* (pp. 263–272). New York: Academic Press.

Diamond, M. (1988). *Enriching heredity: The impact of environment on the anatomy of the brain.* New York: Free Press.

Diamond, M. C., Scheibel, A. B., Murphy, G. M., Jr., & Harvey, T. (1985). On the brain of a scientist: Albert Einstein. *Experimental Neurology, 88*, 198–206.

Diegmueller, K. (1994, March 30). Gifted programs not a right, Conn. court rules. *Education Week*, p. 8.

Dinnage, R. (1993, May 14). Ability island. *Times Literary Supplement*, p. 20.

Doman, G. (1964). *How to teach your baby to read.* New York: Random House.

Down, J. L. (1887). *On some of the mental affections of childhood and youth.* London: Churchill.

Drevdahl, J. E. (1956). Factors of importance for creativity. *Journal of Clinical Psychology, 12*, 21–26.

Duckett, J. (1976). *Idiot savants: Super-specialization in mentally retarded persons.* Unpublished doctoral dissertation, University of Texas at Austin, Department of Special Education.

Duncan, O. D., Featherman, D., & Duncan, B. (1973). *Socioeconomic background and achievement.* New York: Seminar Press.

Durden, W. G., & Tangherlini, A. E. (1993). *Smart kids: How academic talents are developed and nurtured in America.* Toronto: Hogrefe & Huber.

Dweck, C. S., & Elliott, E. S. (1983). Achievement motivation. In E. M. Hetherington (Ed.), *Handbook of child psychology: Vol. 4. Socialization, personality, and social development* (4th ed., pp. 343–391). New York: Wiley.

Edwards, B. (1979). *Drawing on the right side of the brain.* Los Angeles: Tarcher.

Eisenstadt, J. M. (1978). Parental loss and genius. *American Psychologist, 33,* 211–223.

Elbert, T., Pantev, C., Wienbruch, C., Rockstroh, B., & Taub, E. (1995). Increased cortical representation of the fingers of the left hand in string players. *Science, 270,* 305–307.

Elkind, D. (1981). *The hurried child.* Reading, MA: Addison-Wesley.

Ellis, H. (1926). *A study of British genius* (rev. ed.). Boston: Houghton Mifflin.

Enersen, D. L. (1993). Summer residential programs: Academics and beyond. *Gifted Child Quarterly, 37*(4), 169–176.

Ericsson, K. A., & Faivre, I. A. (1988). What's exceptional about exceptional abilities? In L. K. Obler & D. A. Fein (Eds.), *The exceptional brain: Neuropsychology of talent and special abilities* (pp. 436–473). New York: Guilford Press.

Ericsson, K. A., Krampe, R. T., & Tesch-Romer, C. (1993). The role of deliberate practice in the acquisition of expert performance. *Psychological Review, 100*(3), 363–406.

Eysenck, H. J. (1967). Intelligence assessment: A theoretical approach and experimental approach. *British Journal of Educational Psychology, 37,* 81–98.

Eysenck, H. J. (1988). *A model for intelligence.* New York: Springer-Verlag.

Eysenck, H. J. (1993). Creativity and personality: Suggestions for a theory. *Psychological Inquiry, 4,.* 147–148.

Eysenck, H. J. (1995). *Genius: The natural history of creativity.* New York: Cambridge University Press.

Eysenck, H. J., & Barrett, P. T. (1993). Brain research related to giftedness. In K. A. Heller, F. J. Mönks, & A. H. Passow (Eds.), *International handbook of research and development of giftedness and talent* (pp. 115–131). Oxford: Pergamon Press.

Fabri, R. (1964). Tribulations of the artistic child (and its parents). *Gifted Child Quarterly, 8,* 64–66.

Fagan, J. F., & McGrath, S. K. (1981). Infant recognition and later intelligence. *Intelligence, 5,* 121–130.

Farrell, D. M. (1989). Suicide among gifted students. *Roeper Review, 11,* 134–139.

Fein, D., Humes, M., Kaplan, E., Lucci, D. E., & Waterhouse, L. (1984). The question of left hemisphere dysfunction in infantile autism. *Psychological Bulletin, 95,* 258–281.

Feiring, C., & Taft, L. T. (1985). The gifted learning disabled child: Not a paradox. *Pediatric Annals, 14*(10), 729–732.

Feldhusen, J. F. (1986). A new conception of giftedness and programming for the gifted. *Illinois Council for the Gifted Journal, 5*, 5–26.

Feldhusen, J. F. (1989). Synthesis of research on gifted youth. *Educational Leadership, 46*, 6–11.

Feldhusen, J. F. (1991). Identification of gifted and talented youth. In M. C. Wang, M. C. Reynolds, & H. J. Walberg (Eds.), *Handbook of special education: Research and practice: Vol. 4. Emerging programs* (pp. 7–22). Oxford: Pergamon Press.

Feldhusen, J. F. (1992a). Early admission and grade advancement for young gifted learners. *The Gifted Child Today, 15*(92), 45–49.

Feldhusen, J. F. (1992b). *Talent identification and development in education (TIDE).* Sarasota, FL: Center for Creative Learning.

Feldhusen, J. F., & Hoover, S. M. (1986). A conception of giftedness: Intelligence, self-concept and motivation. *Roeper Review, 8*(3), 140–143.

Feldhusen, J. F., & Jarwan, F. A. (1993). Identification of gifted and talented youth for educational programs. In K. A. Heller, F. J. Monks, & A. H. Passow (Eds.), *International handbook of research and development of giftedness and talent* (pp. 233–251). New York: Pergamon Press.

Feldhusen, J. F., & Kennedy, D. M. (1989). Effects of honors classes on secondary students. *Roeper Review, 11*(3), 153–156.

Feldhusen, J. F., VanTassel-Baska, J. L., & Seeley, K. (Eds.). (1989). *Excellence in educating the gifted.* Denver: Love.

Feldman, D. H. (1980). *Beyond universals in cognitive development.* Norwood, NJ: Ablex.

Feldman, D. H. (1984). A follow-up study of subjects who scored above 180 (IQ in Terman's "Tenetic studies of genius"). *Exceptional Children, 50*, 518–523.

Feldman, D. H., with Goldsmith, L. T. (1991). *Nature's gambit: Child prodigies and the development of human potential.* New York: Teachers College Press. (Original work published 1986)

Feldman, R. D. (1982). *Whatever happened to the Quiz Kids? Perils and profits of growing up gifted.* Chicago: Chicago Review Press.

Fetterman, D. M. (1988). *Excellence and equality: A qualitatively different perspective on gifted and talented education.* Albany: State University of New York Press.

Fine, M. J. (1977). Facilitating parent–child relationships for creativity. *Gifted Child Quarterly, 21*, 487–500.

Fischler, I., & Goodman, G. O. (1988). Latency of associative activation in memory. *Journal of Experimental Psychology: Human Perception and Performance, 4*, 455–470.

Fisher, K. (1990, April). Interaction with infants is linked to later abilities. *APA Monitor*, 10.

Ford, D. Y. (1994). Desegregation of gifted educational program: The impact of *Brown* on underachieving children of color. *Journal of Negro Education, 63*(3), 358–375.

Fordham, S. M. (1988). Racelessness as a strategy in Black students' school success: Pragmatic strategy or pyrrhic victory? *Harvard Educational Review, 58*(1), 54–84.

Fordham, S. M., & Ogbu, J. U. (1986). Black students' school success: Coping with the burden of "acting white." *Urban Review, 18*, 176–206.

Fowler, W. (1990). Early stimulation and the development of verbal talents. In M. J. A. Howe (Ed.), *Encouraging the development of exceptional abilities and talents*. Leicester: British Psychological Society.

Fox, L. H. (1983). Gifted students with reading problems: An empirical study. In L. H. Fox, L. Brody, & D. Tobin (Eds.), *Learning disabled/gifted children: Identification and programming* (pp. 117–140). Baltimore: University Park Press.

Fox, L. H., Brody, L., & Tobin, D. (Eds.). (1983). *Learning disabled/gifted children: Identification and programming*. Baltimore: University Park Press.

Frasier, M. M. (1993). Issues, problems and programs in nurturing the disadvantaged and culturally different talented. In K. A. Heller, F. J. Monks, & A. H. Passow (Eds.), *International handbook of research and development of giftedness and talent* (pp. 685–692). Oxford: Pergamon Press.

Freeburg, N. E., & Payne, D. T. (1967). Parental influence on cognitive development in early childhood. *Child Development, 38*, 65–87.

Freeman, J. (1979). *Gifted children: Their identification and development in a social context*. Lancaster: MPT Press Limited.

Freeman, J. (1991). *Gifted children growing up*. Portsmouth, NH: Heinemann Educational; London: Cassell.

Freeman, J. (1993). Parents and families in nurturing giftedness and talent. In K. A. Heller, F. J. Monks, & A. H. Passow (Eds.), *International handbook of research and development of giftedness and talent* (pp. 669–684). Oxford: Pergamon Press.

Freeman, J. (1994). Some emotional aspects of being gifted. *Journal for the Education of the Gifted, 17*(2), 180–197.

Freud, S. (1957). Leonardo da Vinci and a memory of his childhood. In J. Strachey (Ed. and Trans.), *The standard edition of the complete psychological works of Sigmund Freud* (Vol. 11, pp. 63–137). London: Hogarth Press. (Original work published 1910)

Freud, S. (1959). Creative writers and day-dreaming. In J. Strachey (Ed. and Trans.), *The standard edition of the complete psychological works of Sigmund Freud* (Vol. 9, pp. 143–153). London: Hogarth Press. (Original work published 1908)

Freud, S. (1961). Dostoevsky and parricide. In J. Strachey (Ed. and Trans.), *The standard edition of the complete psychological works of Sigmund Freud* (Vol. 21, pp. 177–194). London: Hogarth Press. (Original work published 1928)

Frith, U. (1980). *Cognitive processes in spelling.* New York: Academic Press.

Frith, U. (1989). *Autism: Explaining the enigma.* Oxford: Blackwell.

Frith, U. (Ed.). (1991). *Autism and Asperger syndrome.* Cambridge: Cambridge University Press.

Frith, U., & Hermelin, B. (1969). The role of visual and motor cues for normal, subnormal, and autistic children. *Journal of Child Psychology and Psychiatry, 10,* 153–163.

Gagné, F. (1991). Toward a differentiated model of giftedness and talent. In N. Colangelo & G. A. Davis (Eds.), *Handbook of gifted education* (pp. 65–80). Boston: Allyn & Bacon.

Gagné, F. (1995). Hidden meaning of the "Talent Development" concept. *Educational Forum, 59*(4), 349–362.

Galaburda, A. M., & Kemper, T. L. (1979). Cytoarchitectonic abnormalities in developmental dyslexia: A case study. *Annals of Neurology, 6,* 94.

Galbraith, J. (1985). The eight great gripes of gifted kids: Responding to special needs. *Roeper Review, 8,* 15–18.

Gallagher, J. J. (1985). *Teaching the gifted child* (3rd ed.). Boston: Allyn & Bacon.

Gallagher, J. J., & Crowder, T. (1957). The adjustment of gifted children in the regular classroom. *Exceptional Children, 23*(7), 306–312, 317–319.

Gallagher, J. J., Weiss, P., Oglesby, K., & Thomas, T. (1983). *The status of gifted/talented education: United States survey of needs, practices and policies.* Los Angeles: Leadership Training Institute.

Gallagher, S. A. (1990). Personality patterns of the gifted. *Understanding Our Gifted, 3*(1), 1, 11–13.

Galluci, N. (1988). Emotional adjustment of gifted children. *Gifted Child Quarterly, 32,* 273–276.

Galton, F. (1869). *Hereditary genius: An inquiry into its laws and consequences.* London: Macmillan.

Galton, F. (1874). *English men of science: Their nature and nurture.* London: Macmillan.

Galton, F. (1883). *Inquiries into human faculty and its development.* London: Macmillan.

Gardner, H. (1975). *The shattered mind: The person after brain damage.* New York: Knopf.

Gardner, H. (1980). *Artful scribbles: The significance of children's drawings.* New York: BasicBooks.

Gardner, H. (1983). *Frames of mind: The theory of multiple intelligences.* New York: BasicBooks.

Gardner, H. (1985). *The mind's new science: A history of the cognitive revolution.* New York: BasicBooks.

Gardner, H. (1989). *To open minds: Chinese clues to the dilemma of contemporary education.* New York: BasicBooks.

Gardner, H. (1993a). *Creating minds: An anatomy of creativity seen through the lives of Freud, Einstein, Picasso, Stravinsky, Eliot, Graham and Gandhi.* New York: BasicBooks

Gardner, H. (1993b). *Multiple intelligences: The theory in practice.* New York: BasicBooks.

Gardner, H. (1993c). The relationship between early giftedness and later achievement. In G. R. Bock & K. Ackrill (Eds.), *The origins and development of high ability* (pp. 175–182). New York: Wiley.

Gardner, H. (1995). *Leading minds: An anatomy of leadership.* New York: BasicBooks.

Gardner, H. (1996). Are there additional intelligences? In J. Kane (Ed.), *Education, information, and transformation.* New York: Prentice-Hall.

Gardner, H., Davidson, L., & McKernon, P. (1981). The acquisition of song: A developmental approach. In *Documentary Report of the Ann Arbor Symposium. Music Educators' National Conference.* Reston, VA.

Gardner, H., & Wolf, C. (1988). The fruits of asynchrony: Creativity from a psychological point of view. *Adolescent Psychiatry, 15,* 106–123.

Gardner, J. (1961). *Excellence: Can we be excellent and equal too?* New York: Harper & Row.

George, P. G., & Gallagher, J. J. (1978). Children's thoughts about the future: A comparison of gifted and nongifted students. *Journal for the Education of the Gifted, 2,* 33–42.

Geppert, U., & Kuster, U. (1983). The emergence of "wanting to do it oneself": A precursor of achievement motivation. *International Journal of Behavioral Development, 6,* 355–365.

Gervais, A. (1982). Complex math for a complex brain. *Science News, 121,* 58.

Geschwind, N. (1984). The biology of cerebral dominance: Implications for cognition. *Cognition, 17,* 193–208.

Geschwind, N., & Behan, P. (1982). Lefthandedness: Association with immune disease, migraine, and developmental learning disorder. *Proceedings of the National Academy of Science, 79,* 5097–5100.

Geschwind, N., & Galaburda, A. M. (1987). *Cerebral lateralization.* Cambridge, MA: MIT Press.

Geschwind, N., & Levitsky, W. (1968). Human brain: Left right asymmetries in temporal speech region. *Science, 161,* 186–187.

Getzels, J. W. (1979). From art student to fine artist: Potential, problem finding, and performance. In A. H. Passow (Ed.), *The gifted and talented: Their education and development* (78th Yearbook of the National Society for the Study of Education; pp. 372–387). Chicago: University of Chicago Press.

Getzels, J. W., & Csikszentmihalyi, M. (1976). *The creative vision: A longitudinal study of problem finding in art.* New York: Wiley.

Getzels, J. W., & Jackson, P. (1961). Family environment and cognitive style: A study of the sources of highly intelligent and of highly creative adolescents. *American Sociological Review, 26*(3), 251–360.

Getzels, J. W., & Jackson, P. W. (1962). *Creativity and intelligence: Explorations with gifted students.* New York: Wiley.

Gillberg, C., & Coleman, M. (Eds.). (1992). *The biology of the autistic syndromes* (2nd. ed.). London: MacKeith.

Goertzel, M. G., Goertzel, V., & Goertzel, T. G. (1978). *Three hundred eminent personalities.* San Francisco: Jossey-Bass.

Goertzel, V., & Goertzel, M. G. (1962). *Cradles of eminence.* Boston: Little, Brown.

Goldman-Rakic, P., & Rakic, P. (1984). Experimental modification of gyral patterns. In N. Geschwind & A. M. Galaburda (Eds.), *Cerebral dominance: The biological foundations* (pp. 179–192). Cambridge, MA: Harvard University Press.

Goldsmith, L. T. (1987). Girl prodigies: Some evidence and some speculations. *Roeper Review, 10*(2), 74–82.

Goldsmith, L. T. (1992). Stylistic development of a Chinese painting prodigy. *Creativity Research Journal, 5*(3), 281–293.

Goldsmith, L. T. (in press). *Tracking trajectories of talent: Child prodigies growing up. Proceedings of the Third Annual Esther Katz Rosen Symposium on the Psychological Development of Gifted Children.* University of Kansas, Manhattan, KS.

Goldsmith, L. T., & Feldman, D. H. (1989). Wang Yani: Gifts well given. In W. C. Ho (Ed.), *Yani: The brush of innocence* (pp. 51–62). New York: Hudson Hills Press.

Golomb, C. (1992a). Eitan: The early development of a gifted child artist. *Creativity Research Journal, 5*(3), 265–279.

Golomb, C. (1992b). *The child's creation of a pictorial world.* Berkeley: University of California Press.

Golomb, C. (1995). Eitan: The artistic development of a child prodigy. In C. Golomb (Ed.), *The development of gifted child artists: Selected case studies* (pp. 171–196). Hillsdale, NJ: Erlbaum.

Golomb, C., & Hass, M. (1995). Varda: The development of a young artist. In C. Golomb (Ed.), *The development of gifted child artists: Selected case studies* (pp. 71–100). Hillsdale, NJ: Erlbaum.

Gombrich, E. H. (1960). *Art and illusion.* London: Phaidon Press.

Good, T. L., & Brophy, J. E. (1993). *Looking in classrooms* (6th ed.). New York: HarperCollins College.

Goodenough, F. L., & Harris, D. B. (1963). *Children's drawings as measures of intellectual maturity.* New York: Harcourt Brace & World.

Goodlad, J. I., & Anderson, R. H. (1987). *The nongraded elementary school.* New York: Teachers College Press.

Gordon, A. (1987). Childhood works of artists. *Israel Museum Journal, 6,* 75–82.

Gordon, H. W. (1970). Hemisphere asymmetry in the perception of musical chords. *Cortex, 6,* 387–398.

Gordon, H. W. (1978). Left-hemisphere dominance of rhythmic elements in dichotically presented melodies. *Cortex, 14,* 58–70.

Gordon, H. W. (1980). Degree of ear asymmetry for perception of dichotic chords and for illusory chord localization in musicians of different levels of competence. *Journal of Experimental Psychology: Perception and Performance, 6,* 516–527.

Gordon, H. W., & Harness, B. Z. (1977). A test battery for the diagnosis and treatment of developmental dyslexia. *Journal of Speech and Hearing Disorders, 8,* 1–7.

Gottfried, A. W., Gottfried, A. E., Bathurst, K., & Guerin, D. W. (1994). *Gifted IQ: Early developmental aspects. The Fullterton longitudinal study.* New York: Plenum.

Götz, K. O., & Götz, K. (1979a). Personality characteristics of professional artists. *Perceptual and Motor Skills, 49,* 919–924.

Götz, K. O., & Götz, K. (1979b). Personality characteristics of successful artists. *Perceptual and Motor Skills, 49,* 327–334.

Gould, S. J. (1981). *The mismeasure of man.* New York: Norton.

Grant, J. E., Weiner, A., & Ruchton, J. P. (1976). Moral judgment and generosity in children. *Psychological Reports, 39,* 451–454.

Greenacre, P. (1956). Experiences of awe in childhood. *Psychoanalytic Study of the Child, 11*, 9–80.

Grimshaw, G. M., Bryden, M. P., & Finegan, J. K. (1993). Relations between prenatal testosterone and cerebral lateralization at age 10. *Journal of Clinical and Experimental Neuropsychology, 15*, 39–40.

Gross, M. U. M. (1989). The pursuit of excellence or the search for intimacy? The forced-choice dilemma of gifted youth. *Roeper Review, 11*(4), 189–194.

Gross, M. U. M. (1993a). *Exceptionally gifted children.* London: Routledge.

Gross, M. U. M. (1993b). Nurturing the talents of exceptionally gifted individuals. In K. A. Heller, F. J. Monks, & A. H. Passow (Eds.), *International handbook of research and development of giftedness and talent* (pp. 473–490). Oxford: Pergamon Press.

Gruber, H. (1981). *Darwin on man.* Chicago: University of Chicago Press.

Guralnick, P. (1994). *Last train to Memphis: The rise of Elvis Presley.* Boston: Little, Brown.

Haier, R. J., & Denham, S. A. (1976). A summary profile of the non-intellectual correlates of mathematical precocity in boys and girls. In D. P. Keating (Ed.), *Intellectual talent: Research and development.* Baltimore: Johns Hopkins University Press.

Haier, R. J., Robinson, D. L., Braden, W., & Williams, D. (1983). Electrical potentials of the cerebral cortex and psychometric intelligence. *Personality and Individual Difference, 4*, 591–599.

Haier, R. J., Siegel, B. V., MacLachlan, A., Soderling, E., Lottenberg, S., & Buchsbaum, M. S. (1992). Regional cerebral glucose metabolic changes after learning a complex visuospatial/motor task: A positron emission tomographic study. *Brain Research, 570*, 134–143.

Haier, R. J., Siegel, B. V., Neuchterlein, K. N., Hazlett, E., Wu, J. C., Paek, J., Browning, H. L., & Bushbaum, M. S. (1988). Cortical glucose metabolic rate correlates of abstract reasoning and attention studied with positron emission tomography. *Intelligence, 12*, 199–217.

Haier, R. J., Siegel, B. V., Tang, C., Abel, L., & Buchsbaum, M. S. (1992). Intelligence and changes in regional cerebral glucose metabolic rate following learning. *Intelligence, 16*, 415–426.

Hallahan, D. P., & Kauffman, J. (1982). *Exceptional children.* Englewood Cliffs, NJ: Prentice-Hall.

Halpern, D. F. (1992). *Sex differences in cognitive abilities* (2nd ed.). Hillsdale, NJ: Erlbaum.

Halpern, D. F. (1994). Evaluating support for the Geschwind-

Behan-Galaburda model: With a rubber ruler and a thumb on the scale. *Brain and Cognition, 26,* 185–190.

Hamblin, D. J. (1966, March 18). They are idiot savants—wizards of the calendar. *Life, 60,* 106–108.

Hamburger, V., & Oppenheim, R. W. (1982). Naturally occurring neuronal death in vertebrates. *Neuroscience Commentaries, 1,* 39–55.

Happé, F. (1995). *Autism: An introduction to psychological theory.* Cambridge, MA: Harvard University Press.

Hartley, S. S. (1978). Meta-analysis of the effects of individually paced instruction in mathematics. *Dissertation Abstracts International,* 38(7-A), 4003. (University Microfilms No. AAD00-06641)

Hassler, M. (1990). Functional cerebral asymmetric and cognitive abilities in musicians, painters, and controls. *Brain and Cognition, 13,* 1–17.

Hassler, M., & Birbaumer, N. (1988). Handedness, musical attributes, and dichaptic and dichotic performance in adolescents: A longitudinal study. *Developmental Neuropsychology, 4*(2), 129–145.

Hassler, M., Birbaumer, N., & Feil, A. (1985). Musical talent and visual-spatial abilities: A longitudinal study. *Psychology of Music, 13,* 99–113.

Hassler, M., Birbaumer, N., & Feil, A. (1987). Musical talents and visual-spatial ability: Onset of puberty. *Psychology of Music, 15,* 141–151.

Hassler, M., & Gupta, D. (1993). Functional brain organization, handedness, and immune vulnerability in musicians and nonmusicians. *Neuropsychologia, 31,* 655–660.

Hathaway, S. R., & Monachesi, E. G. (1963). *Adolescent personality and behavior.* Minneapolis: University of Minnesota Press.

Hauser, S. L., Delong, G. R., & Rosman, N. P. (1975). Pneumographic findings in the infantile autism syndrome. *Brain, 98,* 667–688.

Hayes, J. R. (1989). *The complete problem solver* (2nd ed.). Hillsdale, NJ: Erlbaum.

Healey, J. M. (1982). The enigma of hyperlexia. *Reading Research Quarterly, 3,* 319–338.

Healey, J. M., Aram, D. M., Horwitz, S. J., & Kessler, J. W. (1982). A study of hyperlexia. *Brain and Language, 17,* 1–23.

Hécaen, H., De Agostini, M., & Monzon-Montes, A. (1981). Cerebral organization in left-handers. *Brain and Language, 12,* 261–284.

Heller, K. (1991). The nature and development of giftedness: A longitudinal study. *European Journal for High Ability, 2,* 174–188.

Helson, R. (1980). The creative woman mathematician. In L. H. Fox, L. Brody, & D. Tobin (Eds.), *Women and the mathematical mystique* (pp. 23–54). Baltimore: Johns Hopkins University Press.

Helson, R. (1990). Creativity in women: Outer and inner views over time. In M. A. Runco & R. S. Albert (Eds.), *Theories of creativity* (pp. 46–58). Newbury Park, CA: Sage.

Helson, R., & Crutchfield, R. S. (1970). Mathematicians: The creative researchers and the average Ph.D. *Journal of Consulting and Clinical Psychology, 34,* 250–257.

Hemmings, B. C. (1985). The gifted/handicapped: Some basic issues. *Exceptional Child, 32*(1), 57–62.

Henderson, V. L., & Dweck, C. S. (1990). Motivation and achievement. In S. S. Feldman & G. R. Elliot (Eds.), *At the threshold: The developing adolescent.* Cambridge, MA: Harvard University Press.

Hendrickson, D. E., & Hendrickson, A. E. (1980). The biological basis of individual differences in intelligence. *Personality and Individual Differences, 1,* 3–33.

Henson, R. A. (1977). Neurological aspects of musical experience. In M. Critchley & R. A. Henson (Eds.), *Music and the brain: Studies in the neurology of music.* London: William Heinemann Medical Books.

Herman, E. (1981). *Shinichi Suzuki: The man and his philosophy.* Athens, OH: Ability Associates.

Hermelin, B. (1983). The idiot savant: Flawed genius or clever Hans? *Psychological Medicine, 13,* 479–481.

Hermelin, B., & O'Connor, N. (1986a). Spatial representations in mathematically and in artistically gifted children. *British Journal of Educational Psychology, 56,* 150–157.

Hermelin, B., & O'Connor, N. (1986b). Idiot-savant calendrical calculators: Rules and regularities. *Psychological Medicine, 16,* 885–893.

Hermelin, B., & O'Connor, N. (1990a). Art and accuracy: The drawing ability of idiots-savants. *Journal of Child Psychology and Psychiatry, 31,* 217–228.

Hermelin, B., & O'Connor, N. (1990b). Factors and primes: A specific numerical ability. *Psychological Medicine, 20,* 163–169.

Hermelin, B., & O'Connor, N. (in press). Aspects of graphic development in normal and savant children. *Journal of Art and Design Education.*

Hermelin, B., O'Connor, N., & Lee, S. (1987). Musical inventiveness of five idiots-savants. *Psychological Medicine, 17,* 685–694.

Hildreth, G. (1941). *The child mind in evolution*. New York: Kings Crown Press.

Hildreth, G. (1966). *Introduction to the gifted*. New York: McGraw-Hill.

Hill, A. L. (1978). Savants: Mentally retarded individuals with special skills. In N. R. Ellis (Ed.), *International Review of Research in Mental Retardation* (Vol. 9, pp. 277–298). New York: Academic Press.

Hoffman, J. (1993, October 3). After child's play, what comes next? *New York Times*, pp. C-1, 38–39.

Hogan, R. (1980). The gifted adolescent. In J. Adelson (Ed.), *Handbook of Adolescent Psychology*. New York: Wiley.

Hogan, R., Viernstein, M. C., McGinn, P. V., Bohannon, W., & Daurio, S. P. (1977). Verbal giftedness and sociopolitical intelligence: Terman revisited. *Journal of Youth and Adolescence, 6*(2), 107–116.

Hoge, R. D., & Renzulli, J. S. (1993). Exploring the link between giftedness and self-concept. *Review of Educational Research, 63*(4), 449–465.

Holahan, C. K., & Sears, R. R. (1995). *The gifted group in later maturity*. Stanford: Stanford University Press.

Holland, J. G. (1961). Creative and academic performance among talented adolescents. *Journal of Educational Psychology, 52*, 136–147.

Hollingworth, L. S. (1926). *Gifted children: Their nature and nurture*. New York: Macmillan.

Hollingworth, L. S. (1931). The child of very superior intelligence as a special problem in social adjustment. *Mental Hygiene, 29*, 3–16.

Hollingworth, L. S. (1942). *Children above 180 IQ, Stanford-Binet origin and development*. Yonkers, NY: World Book.

Horowitz, W. A., Kestenbaum, C., Person, E., & Jarvik, L. (1965). Identical twin—"idiots savants"—calendar calculators. *American Journal of Psychiatry, 121*, 1075–1079.

Howe, M. J. A. (1990). *The origins of exceptional abilities*. Oxford: Blackwell.

Howe, M. J. A., Davidson, J. W., Moore, D. G., & Sloboda, J. A. (1995). Are there early signs of musical ability? *Psychology of Music, 23*, 162–176.

Howe, M. J. A., & Sloboda, J. A. (1992). Problems experienced by talented young musicians as a result of the failure of other children to value musical accomplishments. *Gifted Education International, 8*, 16–18.

Hunsaker, S. L., Frasier, M. M., Frank, E., Finley, V., & Klekotka, P. (1995). *Performance of economically disadvantaged students placed in gifted programs through the research-based assessment plan.* University of Connecticut: The National Research Center on the Gifted and Talented.

Hunt, E., Frost, N., & Lunneborg, C. L. (1973). Individual differences in cognition: A new approach to intelligence. In G. Bower (Ed.), *Learning and motivation* (Vol. 7, pp. 87–122). New York: Academic Press.

Hunt, E., Lunneborg, C., & Lewis, J. (1975). What does it mean to be high verbal? *Cognitive Psychology, 7,* 194–227.

Hurwitz, A. (1983). *The gifted and talented in art. A guide to program planning.* Worcester, MA: Davis Publications.

Inouye, T., Shinosaki, K., Iyama, A., & Matsumoto, A. (1993). Localization of activated areas and directional EEG patterns during mental arithmetic. *Electroencephalography and Clinical Neurophysiology, 86,* 224–230.

Isen, A. M., & Daubman, K. A. (1984). The influence of affect on categorization. *Journal of Personality and Social Psychology, 47,* 1206–1217.

Isen, A. M., Johnson, M. M. S., Mertz, E., & Robinson, G. F. (1985). The influence of positive affect on the unusualness of word associations. *Journal of Personality and Social Psychology, 48,* 1413–1426.

Jackson, N. E. (1992). Precocious reading of English: Origins, structure, and predictive significance. In P. S. Klein & A. J. Tannenbaum (Eds.), *To be young and gifted* (pp. 171–203). Norwood, NJ: Ablex.

Jackson, N. E. (1993). Moving into the mainstream? Reflections on the study of giftedness. *Gifted Child Quarterly, 37*(1), 46–50.

Jackson, N. E., Donaldson, G., & Cleland, L. N. (1988). The structure of precocious reading ability. *Journal of Educational Psychology, 80,* 234–243.

Jackson, N. E., Donaldson, G., & Mills, J. R. (1993). Components of reading skill in postkindergarten precocious readers and level-matched second graders. *Journal of Reading Behavior, 25,* 181–208.

Jamison, K. R. (1989). Mood disorders and patterns of creativity in British writers and artists. *Psychiatry, 52,* 125–134.

Jamison, K. R. (1993). *Touched with fire: Manic depressive illness and the artistic temperament.* New York: Free Press.

Jamison, K. R. (1995). *An unquiet mind.* New York: Knopf.

Janos, P. M., Marwood, K. A., & Robinson, N. M. (1985). Friendship patterns in highly intelligent children. *Roeper Review, 8*(1), 46–49.

Janos, P. M., & Robinson, N. M. (1985). Psychosocial development in intellectually gifted children. In F. D. Horowitz & M. O'Brien (Eds.), *The gifted and talented: Developmental perspectives* (pp. 149–195). Washington, DC: American Psychological Association.

Janos, P. M., Robinson, N. M., & Lunneborg, C. E. (1989). Markedly early entrance to college: A multi-year comparative study of academic performance and psychological adjustment. *Journal of Higher Education, 60,* 496–518.

Jencks, C. (1972). *Inequality.* New York: BasicBooks.

Jensen, A. (1993). Why is reaction time correlated with psychometric g? *Current Directions in Psychological Science, 2*(2), 53–56.

Jerison, H. (1982). The evolution of biological intelligence. In R. J. Sternberg (Ed.), *The handbook of intelligence* (pp. 723–791). New York: Cambridge University Press.

Juda, A. (1949). The relationship between highest mental capacity and psychic abnormalities. *American Journal of Psychiatry, 106,* 296–307.

Judd, T. (1988). The varieties of musical talent. In L. Obler & D. Fein (Eds.), *The exceptional brain: Neuropsychology of talent and special abilities* (pp. 127–155). New York: Guilford Press.

Kagan, J. (1994). *Galen's prophecy: Temperament in human nature.* New York: BasicBooks.

Kagan, J., & Klein, R. E. (1973). Cross-cultural perspectives on early development. *American Psychologist, 28,* 947–961.

Kamin, L. (1974). *The science and politics of IQ.* Hillsdale, NJ: Erlbaum.

Kanevsky, L. (1992). The learning game. In P. S. Klein & A. J. Tannenbaum (Eds.), *To be young and gifted* (pp. 204–243). Norwood, NJ: Ablex.

Kanner, L. (1944). Early infantile autism. *Journal of Pediatrics, 25,* 200–217.

Kanoy, R. C., Johnson, B. W., & Kanoy, K. W. (1980). Locus of control and self-concept in achieving bright elementary students. *Psychology in the Schools, 17,* 395–399.

Kaplan, B. J., & Crawford, S. G. (1994). The GBG model: Is there more to consider than handedness? *Brain and Cognition, 26,* 291–299.

Karlson, J. I. (1970). Genetic association of giftedness and creativity with schizophrenia. *Hereditas, 66,* 177–182.

Karma, K. (1979). Musical, spatial, and verbal abilities. *Bulletin of Council on Research in Music Education, 75,* 23–32.

Karnes, M. B., McCoy, G. F., Zerback, R. R., Wellersheim, J., Clarizio, H. G., Gostin, L., & Stanley, L. (1961). Factors associated with the underachievement and overachievement of intellectually gifted children. *Exceptional Child, 27,* 167–175.

Karnes, M. B., Schwedel, A. M., & Steinberg, D. (1984). Styles of parenting among parents of young gifted children. *Roeper Review, 6,* 232–235.

Kaufmann, F. A., & Sexton, D. (1983). Some implications for home–school linkages. *Roeper Review, 14,* 154–158.

Kearney, K. (1989). Homeschooling gifted children. *Understanding Our Gifted, 1*(3), 1, 12–13, 15–16.

Kelly, K. R., & Colangelo, N. (1984). Academic and social self-concepts of gifted, general and special students. *Exceptional Children, 50,* 551–554.

Kerschensteiner, G. (1905). *Die entwicklung der zeichnerischen Begabung* [The development of graphic talent]. Munich: Gerber.

Kerr, B. A. (1991). *A handbook for counseling the gifted and talented.* Alexandria, VA: American Counseling Association.

Khatena, J. (1982). *Educational psychology of the gifted.* New York: Wiley.

Kimura, D. (1985, November). Male brain, female brain: The hidden difference. *Psychology Today,* 50–58.

Kincaid, D. (1969). A study of highly gifted elementary pupils. *Gifted Child Quarterly, 13,* 264–267.

Kirst, M. (1982). How to improve schools without spending more money. *Phi Delta Kappa, 64,* 6–8.

Knight, S., & Stallings, J. (in press). The implementation of the Accelerated School Model in an urban elementary school. In R. Allington & S. Walmsley (Eds.), *No quick fix: Rethinking literacy programs in American elementary schools.* New York: Teachers College Press.

Kohlberg, L. (1963). The development of children's orientations toward a moral order: 1. Sequence in the development of moral thought. *Vita Humana, 6,* 11–33.

Kohlberg, L. (1964). Development of moral character and moral ideology. In M. Hoffman & L. Hoffman (Eds.), *Review of child development research* (pp. 383–431). New York: Russell Sage Foundation.

Kohlberg, L. (1969). Stage and sequence: The cognitive-developmental approach to socialization. In D. A. Goslin (Ed.), *Handbook of socialization theory and research*. New York: Rand McNally.

Kolata, G. (1983). Math genius may have hormonal basis. *Science, 222,* 1312.

Kosslyn, S., & Koenig, O. (1992). *Wet mind: The new cognitive neuroscience*. New York: Free Press.

Krutetskii, V. A. (1976). *The psychology of mathematical abilities in school children*. Chicago: University of Chicago Press.

Kulik, C.-L. C., & Kulik, J. A. (1984). Effects of accelerated instruction on students. *Review of Educational Research, 54*(3), 409–425.

Kulik, J. A., & Kulik, C.-L. C. (1982). Effects of ability grouping on secondary school students: A meta-analysis of evaluation findings. *American Educational Research Journal, 19*(3), 415–428.

Kulik, J. A., & Kulik, C.-L. C. (1991). Ability grouping and gifted students. In N. Colangelo & G. Davis (Eds.), *Handbook of gifted education* (pp. 178–196). Boston, MA: Allyn & Bacon.

Kulik, J. A., & Kulik, C.-L. C. (1992). Meta-analytic findings on grouping programs. *Gifted Child Quarterly, 36*(2), 73–77.

Landau, E. (1976). Children ask questions about the future of mankind. In J. Gibson & P. Chennels (Eds.), *Gifted children looking to their future* (pp. 268–275). London: Latimer.

Lark-Horowitz, B., Lewis, H., & Luca, M. (1973). *Understanding children's art for better teaching* (2nd ed.). Columbus, OH: Merrill.

Laycock, F. (1979). *Gifted children*. Glenview, IL: Scott Foresman.

Lee, M. (1989). When is an object not an object? The effect of meaning upon the copying of line drawings. *British Journal of Psychology, 80,* 15–37.

Lehman, H. C. (1953). *Age and achievement*. Princeton, NJ: Princeton University Press.

Lerner, R. M. (1991). Changing organism-context relations as the basic process of development: A developmental contextual perspective. *Developmental Psychology, 27,* 27–32.

Lerner, R. M. (1992). The demise of the nature–nurture controversy. A review of *Individual development and evolution: The genesis of novel behavior* by G. Gotlieb. *Human Development, 36,* 119–124.

Leroy-Boussion, I. (1971). Maturité mentale et apprentissage de la lecture ["Mental maturity and learning to read"]. *Enfance, 3.*

Levin, H. M. (1987a). Accelerating schools for disadvantaged students. *Educational Leadership, 44*(6), 19–21.

Levin, H. M. (1987b). New schools for the disadvantaged. *Teacher Education Quarterly, 14*(4), 60–83.

Levin, H. M. (1994). The necessary and sufficient conditions for achieving educational equity. In R. Berne & L. O. Picus (Eds.), *Outcome equity in education.* Thousand Oaks, CA: Corwin Press.

Levy, J., & Nagylaki, T. (1972). A model for the genetics of the hand. *Genetics, 72,* 117–128.

Lewerenz, A. S. (1928). I.Q. and the ability in art. *School and Society, 27,* 489–490.

Lewin, J., Kohen, D., & Matthew, G. (1993). Handedness in mental handicap: Investigation into populations of Down's syndrome, epilepsy and autism. *British Journal of Psychiatry, 163,* 674–676.

Lewis, M. (1975). The development of attention and perception in the infant and young child. In W. M. Cruickshank & D. P. Hallahan (Eds.), *Perception and learning disabilities in children.* New York: Syracuse University Press.

Lewis, M. (1985). Gifted or dysfunctional: The child savant. *Pediatric Annals, 14*(10), 733–742.

Lewis, M., & Brooks-Gunn, J. (1981). Attention and intelligence. *Intelligence, 5,* 231–238.

Lewis, M., & Louis, B. (1991). Young gifted children. In N. Colangelo & G. A. Davis (Eds.), *Handbook of gifted education* (pp. 365–381). Needham Heights, MA: Allyn & Bacon.

Light, P. (1985). The development of view-specific representation. In N. Freeman & M. Cox (Eds.), *Visual order.* Cambridge: Cambridge University Press.

Lindsley, O. (1965). Can deficiency produce specific superiority: The challenge of the idiot savant. *Exceptional Children, 31,* 225–232.

Lindstrom, R. R., & Van Sant, S. (1986). Special issues in working with gifted minority adolescents. *Journal of Counseling and Development, 64,* 583–586.

Locksley, A., & Douvan, E. (1980). Stress on female and male high school students. In R. E. Muuss (Ed.), *Adolescent behavior and society: A book of readings* (3rd ed., pp. 275–291). New York: Random House.

Loehlin, J. C., Horn, J. M., & Willerman, L. (1989). Modeling I.Q. change: Evidence from the Texas adoption project. *Child Development, 60,* 993–1004.

Longman, J. (1994, October 11). Sacrifices to keep a prodigy skating. *New York Times,* p. B-12.

Lubinski, D., Benbow, C. P., & Sanders, C. E. (1993). Reconceptualizing gender differences in achievement among the gifted. In K. A. Heller, F. J. Monks, & A. H. Passow (Eds.), *International handbook of research and development of giftedness and talent* (pp. 693–707). Oxford: Pergamon Press.

Lucito, L. J. (1964). Independence–conformity behavior as a function of intellect: Bright and dull children. *Exceptional Children, 30,* 5–13.

Ludwig, A. (1992). Creative achievement and psychopathology: Comparison among professions. *American Journal of Psychotherapy, 46,* 330–356.

Ludwig, A. (1995). *The price of greatness: Resolving the creativity and madness controversy.* New York: Guilford Press.

Luftig, R. L., & Nichols, M. L. (1991). An assessment of the social status and perceived personality and school traits of gifted students by non-gifted peers. *Roeper Review, 13*(3), 148–152.

Lykken, D. T., McGue, M., Tellengen, A., & Bouchard, T. J. (1992). Emergenesis: Genetic traits that may not run in families. *American Psychologist, 47,* 1565–1577.

Maccoby, E. E. (1980). *Social development.* New York: Harcourt.

MacKinnon, D. W. (1962). The nature and nurture of creative talent. *American Psychologist, 17,* 484–495.

MacKinnon, D. W. (1965). Personality and the realization of creative potential. *American Psychologist, 20,* 273–281.

Madeja, S. S. (1983). *Gifted and talented in art education.* Reston, VA: National Art Education Association.

Manley, J. (1937, August 14). Where are they now? April fool! *New Yorker, 37,* 22–26.

Manuel, H. T. (1919). *Talent in drawing: An experimental study of the use of tests to discover special ability.* Bloomington, IL: Public School Publishing Co.

Margolin, L. (1994). *Goodness personified: The emergence of gifted children.* New York: Aldine de Gruyter.

Marland, S. P., Jr. (1972). *Education of the gifted and talented: Report to the Congress of the United States by the Commissioner of Education.* Washington, DC: U.S. Government Printing Office.

Marriott, M. (1992, March 18). Blacks in science program shatter stereotype. *New York Times,* Metro section.

Martino, G., & Winner, E. (1995). Talents and disorders: The relationship between sex, handedness, and college major. *Brain and Cognition, 29,* 66–84.

Mayseless, O. (1993). Gifted adolescents and intimacy in close same-sex friendships. *Journal of Youth and Adolescence, 22*(2), 135–146.

McClelland, D. (1973). Testing for competence rather than for intelligence. *American Psychologist, 28*, 1–14.

McClelland, D. C., Atkinson, J. W., Clark, R. A., & Lowell, E. L. (1953). *The achievement motive.* New York: Appleton-Century.

McCruden, A. B., & Stimson, W. H. (1991). Sex hormones and immune function. In R. Ader, D. L. Felton, & N. Cohen (Eds.), *Psychoneuroimmunology* (2nd ed.). New York: Academic Press.

McCurdy, H. G. (1960). The childhood pattern of genius. *Horizon, 2*, 33–38.

McFarlan, D. (Ed.). (1989). *The Guinness book of records.* New York: Bantam.

McGee, M. G. (1979). Human spatial abilities: Psychometric studies and environmental, genetic, hormonal, and neurological influences. *Psychological Bulletin, 86*(5), 889–917.

McGuffog, C. (1985). Problems of gifted children. *Pediatric Annals, 14*(10), 719, 723–724, 726.

McKeever, W. F., & Rich, D. A. (1990). Left handedness and immune disorders. *Cortex, 26*, 33–40.

McManus, I. C., & Bryden, M. P. (1991). Geschwind's theory of cerebral lateralization: Developing a formal causal model. *Psychological Bulletin, 110*, 237–253.

McNamara, P., Flannery, K. A., Obler, L. K., & Schachter, S. (1994). Special talents in Geschwind's and Galaburda's theory of cerebral lateralization: An examination in a female population. *International Journal of Neuroscience, 78*, 167–176.

Mebert, C. J., & Michel, G. F. (1980). Handedness in artists. In J. Herron (Ed.), *Neuropsychology of left-handedness* (pp. 273–279). New York: Academic Press.

Mesulam, M. M. (1981). A cortical network for directed attention and unilateral neglect. *Annals of Neurology, 10*, 309–325.

Milbrath, C. (1987). Spatial representations of artistically gifted children: A case of universal or domain specific development? *Genetic Epistemologist, 25*, 1–5.

Milbrath, C. (1995). Germinal motifs in the work of a gifted child artist. In C. Golomb (Ed.), *The development of artistically gifted children. Selected case studies* (pp. 101–134). Hillsdale, NJ: Erlbaum.

Milbrath, C. (in preparation). *Patterns of artistic development.* New York: Cambridge University Press.

Milgram, R. M. (Ed.). (1989). *Teaching gifted and talented learners in regular classrooms.* Springfield, IL: Thomas.

Milgram, R. M., & Hong, E. (1993). Creative thinking and creative performance in adolescents as predictors of creative attainments in adults: A follow-up study after 18 years. *Roeper Review, 15*(3), 135–139.

Milgram, R. M., & Milgram, N. A. (1976). Personality characteristics of gifted Israeli children. *Journal of Genetic Psychology, 129,* 185–194.

Miller, A. (1981). *Prisoners of childhood.* New York: BasicBooks.

Miller, L. K. (1989). *Musical savants: Exceptional skill in the mentally retarded.* Hillsdale, NJ: Erlbaum.

Mills, J. R., & Jackson, N. E. (1990). Predictive significance of early giftedness: The case of precocious reading. *Journal of Educational Psychology, 82,* 410–419.

Mishkin, M., & Petri, H. L. (1984). Memories and habits: Some implications for the analysis of learning and retention. In L. R. Squire & N. Butters (Eds.), *Neuropsychology of memory.* New York: Guilford Press.

Mitchell, F. D. (1907). Mathematical prodigies. *American Journal of Psychology, 18,* 61–143.

Mönks, F. J. (1992). Development of gifted children: The issue of identification and programming. In F. J. Monks & W. A. M. Peters (Eds.), *Talent for the future* (pp. 191–202). Assen/Maastricht, The Netherlands: Van Gorcum.

Mönks, F. J., & Ferguson, T. (1983). Gifted adolescents: An analysis of their psychosocial development. *Journal of Youth and Adolescence, 12,* 1–18.

Mönks, F. J., & Van Boxtel, H. (1985). Gifted adolescents: A developmental perspective. In J. Freeman (Ed.), *The psychology of gifted children.* Chichester: Wiley.

Montour, K. (1977). William J. Sidis, the broken twig. *American Psychologist, 32,* 265–279.

Morelock, M. J., & Feldman, D. H. (1993). Prodigies and savants: What they have to tell us about giftedness and human cognition. In K. A. Heller, F. J. Monks, & A. H. Passow (Eds.), *International handbook of research and development of giftedness and talent* (pp. 161–181). Oxford: Pergamon Press.

Morgan, M. (1987). David Downes: Drawings from 4 to 10 years. In S. Paine (Ed.), *Six children draw* (pp. 23–37). New York: Academic Press.

Morishima, A., & Brown, L. F. (1977). A case report on the artistic talent of an autistic idiot savant. *Mental Retardation, 15,* 33–36.

Moss, E. (1990). Social interaction and metacognitive development in gifted preschoolers. *Gifted Child Quarterly, 34,* 16–20.

Mottron, L., & Belleville, S. (1993). A study of perceptual analysis in a high-level autistic subject with exceptional graphic abilities. *Brain and Cognition, 23,* 279–309.

Moulton, R. H. (1915). A twelve-year-old wonder child. *American Magazine, 79,* 56–58.

Mueller, H. H., Dash, U. N., Matheson, D. N., & Short, R. H. (1984). WISC-R subtest patterning of below average, average and above average IQ children: A meta-analysis. *Alberta Journal of Educational Research, 30,* 68–85.

Myers, I. B. (1962). *Manual: The Myers-Briggs Type Indicator.* Palo Alto, CA: Consulting Psychologists Press.

Myers, I. B. (1987). *Introduction to type: A description of the theory and applications of the Myers-Briggs Type Indicator.* Palo Alto, CA: Consulting Psychologists Press.

Naidoo, S. (1972). *Specific dyslexia.* New York: Wiley & Sons.

National Association for Gifted Children. (1992). National Association for Gifted Children policy statement on ability grouping. *Gifted Child Quarterly, 36,* 2.

National Commission on Excellence in Education. (1983). *A nation at risk.* Washington, DC: U.S. Department of Education.

National Education Association Research Division. (1968). *Ability grouping. (Research Summary 1968–1953).* Washington, DC: National Education Association.

Nettelbeck, T. (1987). Inspection time and intelligence. In P. A. Vernon (Ed.), *Speed of information processing and intelligence.* New York: Ablex.

Newland, R. (1976). *The gifted in socioeducational perspective.* New York: Macmillan.

Nichols, R. C. (1964). Parental attitudes of mothers of intelligent adolescents and the creativity of their children. *Child Development, 35,* 1041–1049.

Noble, K. D. (1989). Living out the promise of high potential: Perceptions of 100 gifted women. *Advanced Development, 1,* 57–75.

Oakes, J. (1985). *Keeping track: How schools structure inequality.* New Haven, CT: Yale University Press.

O'Boyle, M. W., Alexander, J., & Benbow, C. P. (1991). Enhanced right hemisphere activation in the mathematically precocious:

A preliminary EEG investigation. *Brain and Cognition, 17,* 138–153.

O'Boyle, M. W., & Benbow, C. P. (1990). Enhanced right hemisphere involvement during cognitive processing may relate to intellectual precocity. *Neuropsychologia, 28,* 211–216.

O'Boyle, M. W., Gill, H. S., Benbow, C. P., & Alexander, J. E. (1994). Concurrent finger-tapping in mathematically gifted males: Evidence for enhanced right hemisphere involvement during linguistic processing. *Cortex, 30,* 519–526.

Ochse, R. (1990). *Before the gates of excellence: The determinants of creative genius.* Cambridge: Cambridge University Press.

O'Connor, N. (1989). The performance of the "idiot savant": Implicit and explicit. *British Journal of Disorders of Communication, 24,* 1–20.

O'Connor, N., & Hermelin, B. (1983). The role of general ability and specific talents in information processing. *British Journal of Developmental Psychology, 1,* 389–403.

O'Connor, N., & Hermelin, B. (1984). Idiot savant calendrical calculators: Maths or memory? *Psychological Medicine, 14,* 801–806.

O'Connor, N., & Hermelin, B. (1987). Visual and graphic abilities of the idiot-savant artist. *Psychological Medicine, 17,* 79–90.

O'Connor, N., & Hermelin, B. (1990). The recognition failure and graphic success of idiot-savant artists. *Journal of Child Psychology and Psychiatry, 31*(2), 203–215.

O'Connor, N., & Hermelin, B. (1991). Talents and preoccupations in idiots-savants. *Psychological Medicine, 21,* 959–964.

Oden, M. H. (1968). The fulfillment of promise: Forty-year follow-up of the Terman gifted group. *Genetic Psychology Monographs, 77,* 3–93.

Ogbu, J. (1988). Cultural diversity and human development. In D. Slaughter (Ed.), *Black children and poverty: A developmental perspective* (New Directions in Child Development No. 42, pp. 11–28). San Francisco: Jossey-Bass.

Oldfield, R. C. (1969). Handedness in musicians. *British Bulletin of Psychology, 60,* 91–99.

Oldfield, R. C. (1971). The assessment and analysis of handedness: The Edinburgh Inventory. *Neuropsychologia, 9,* 97–114.

Olszewski, P. M., Kulieke, M., & Buescher, T. (1987). The influence of the family environment on the development of talent: A literature review. *Journal for the Education of the Gifted, 11,* 6–28.

Olszewski-Kubilius, P., Kulieke, M. J., & Krasney, N. (1988). Personality dimensions of gifted adolescents: A review of the empirical literature. *Gifted Child Quarterly, 2*, 347–352.

Paine, S. (Ed.). (1987). *Six children draw*. New York: Academic Press.

Painter, F. (1976). *Gifted children: A research study*. Herts, England: Pullen Publication.

Palmer, J., McLeod, C. M., Hunt, E., & Davidson, J. E. (1985). Information processing correlates of reading. *Journal of Memory and Language, 24*, 59–88.

Pariser, D. (1981). Nadia's drawings: Theorizing about an autistic child's phenomenal ability. *Journal of Studies in Art Education, 22*, 2, 20–31.

Pariser, D. (1987). The juvenile drawings of Klee, Toulouse-Lautrec and Picasso. *Visual Arts Research, 13*, 53–67.

Pariser, D. (1991). Normal and unusual aspects of juvenile artistic development in Klee, Lautrec, and Picasso. *Creativity Research Journal, 4*, 51–65.

Park, C. C. (1978). Review of Nadia: A case of extraordinary drawing ability in an autistic child. *Journal of Autism and Childhood Schizophrenia, 8*, 457–472.

Parks, R. W., Loewenstein, D. A., Dodrill, K. L., Barker, W. W., Yoshii, F., Chang, J. Y., Emran, A., Apicella, A., Sheramata, W., & Duara, R. (1988). Cerebral metabolic effects of a verbal fluency test: A PET scan study. *Journal of Clinical & Experimental Neuropsychology, 10*, 565–575.

Passow, A. H. (1972). The gifted and the disadvantaged. *National Elementary Principal, 51*, 22–36.

Passow, A. H. (Ed.). (1979). *The gifted and talented: Their education and development*. Chicago: University of Chicago Press.

Passow, A. H., & Rudnitski, R. A. (1993, October). *State policies regarding education of the gifted as reflected in legislation and regulation*. University of Connecticut: The National Research Center on the Gifted and Talented Collaborative Research Study No. CRS93301.

Pavan, B. N. (1973). Good news: Research on the nongraded elementary school. *Elementary School Journal, 73*, 333–342.

Pedersen, N. L., Plomin, R., Nesselroade, J. R., & McClearn, G. E. (1992). A quantitative genetic analysis of cognitive abilities during the second half of the lifespan. *Psychological Science, 3*, 346–353.

Pennington, B. F., Smith, S. D., Kimberling, W. J., Green, P. A., & Haith, M. M. (1987). Left-handedness and immune disorders in familial dyslexics. *Archives of Neurology, 44*, 634–639.

Perkins, D. N. (1981). *The mind's best work*. Cambridge, MA: Harvard University Press.

Perleth, C., & Heller, K. A. (1994). The Munich longitudinal study of giftedness. In R. Subotnik & K. D. Arnold (Eds.), *Beyond Terman: Contemporary longitudinal studies of giftedness and talent* (pp. 11–114). Norwood, NJ: Ablex.

Petersen, A. C. (1976). Physical androgeny and cognitive functioning in adolescence. *Developmental Psychology, 12*, 524–533.

Peterson, J. M. (1979). Left-handedness: Differences between student artists and scientists. *Perceptual and Motor Skills, 48*, 961–962.

Peterson, J. M. (1989). Remediation is no remedy. *Educational Leadership, 46*(6), 24–25.

Peterson, J. M., & Lansky, L. M. (1974). Left-handedness among architects: Some facts and some speculations. *Perceptual and Motor Skills, 38,* 547–550.

Phillips, I. (1987). *Word recognition and spelling strategies in good and poor readers*. Unpublished doctoral dissertation, Harvard University, Cambridge, MA.

Phillips, W., Hobbs, S., & Pratt, F. (1978). Intellectual realism in children's drawings of cubes. *Cognition, 6*, 15–34.

Piaget, J. (1932). *The moral judgment of the child*. New York: Harcourt, Brace.

Piechowski, M. M. (1979). Developmental potential. In N. Colangelo & R. T. Saffrann (Eds.), *New voices in counseling the gifted* (pp. 25–57). Dubuque: Kendall/Hunt.

Piechowski, M. M. (1995). Emotional giftedness: The measure of intrapersonal intelligence. In N. Colangelo & G. A. Davis (Eds.), *The handbook of gifted education* (2nd ed.). Needham Heights, MA: Allyn & Bacon.

Piechowski, M. M., & Colangelo, N. (1984). Developmental potential of the gifted. *Gifted Child Quarterly, 28,* 80–88.

Piirto, J. (1994). *Talented children and adults: Their development and education*. New York: Macmillan.

Piirto, J. (1995). Deeper and broader: The pyramid of talent development in the context of a giftedness construct. *Educational Forum, 59*(4), 363–370.

Piper, L. M., & Naumann, T. F. (1974). Home environment variables and gifted young children: An ecological inquiry. *Child Study Monographs, 1.*

Plomin, R. (1985). Behavioral genetics. In D. Detterman (Ed.), *Current topics in human intelligence* (Vol. 1). Norwood, NJ: Ablex.

Plomin, R., & DeFries, J. C. (1980). Genetics and intelligence: Recent data. *Intelligence, 4*, 15–24.

Plomin, R., Owen, M., & McGuffin, P. (1994). The genetic basis of complex human behaviors. *Science, 264*, 1733–1739.

Plomin, R., & Thompson, L. A. (1993). In G. R. Bock & K. Ackrill (Eds.), *The origins and development of high ability* (pp. 67–79). New York: Wiley.

Porac, C., & Coren, S. (1981). *Lateral preferences and human behavior.* New York: Springer-Verlag.

Powell, P., & Haden, T. (1984). The intellectual and psychosocial nature of extreme giftedness. *Roeper Review, 6*(3), 131–133.

Pring, L., & Hermelin, B. (1993). Bottle, tulip and wineglass: Semantic and structural picture processing by savant artists. *Journal of Child Psychology and Psychiatry, 34*(8), 1365–1385.

Puckett, J. M., & Kausler, D. H. (1984). Individual differences and models of memory span: A role for memory search rate. *Journal of Experimental Psychology: Learning, Memory, and Cognition, 10*, 72–82.

Purcell, J. H. (1993, Fall). A study of the status of programs for high ability students. *National Research Center on the Gifted and Talented Newsletter*, 6–7.

Pyrt, M. C., Masharov, Y. P., & Feng, C. (1993). Programs and strategies for nurturing talents/gifts in science and technology. In K. A. Heller, F. J. Monks, & A. H. Passow (Eds.), *International handbook of research and development of giftedness and talent* (pp. 453–472). Oxford: Pergamon Press.

Radford, J. (1990). *Child prodigies and exceptional early achievement.* London: Harvester.

Raichle, M. E. (1994). Visualizing the mind. *Scientific American, 270*(4), 58–64.

Raskin, E. (1936). Comparison of scientific and literary ability: A biographical study of eminent scientists in letters of the nineteenth century. *Journal of Abnormal and Social Psychology, 31*, 20–35.

Rathunde, K., & Csikszentmihalyi, M. (1993). Undivided interest and the growth of talent: A longitudinal study of adolescents. *Journal of Youth and Adolescence, 22*(4), 385–405.

Rauscher, F. H., Shaw, G. L., & Ky, K. N. (1993). Music and spatial task performance. *Nature, 365*, 611.

Rauscher, F. H., Shaw, G. L., & Ky, K. N. (1995). Listening to Mozart enhances spatial-temporal reasoning: Towards a neurophysiological basis. *Neuroscience Letters, 185*, 44–47.

Rauscher, F. H., Shaw, G. L., Levine, L. J., Ky, K. N., & Wright, E. L. (1994, August). *Music and spatial task performance: A causal relationship.* Paper presented at the annual meeting of the American Psychological Association, Los Angeles, CA.

Reis, S. M. (1994, April). How schools are shortchanging the gifted. *MIT Technology Review*, 39–45.

Reis, S. M., & Callahan, C. M. (1989). Gifted females: They've come a long way—or have they? *Journal for the Education of the Gifted, 12*(2), 99–117.

Reis, S. M., Neu, T. W., & McGuire, J. M. (1995). *Talents in two places: Case studies of high ability students with learning disabilities who have achieved.* University of Connecticut: The National Research Center on the Gifted and Talented Research Monograph No. 95113.

Renoux, G. (1988). The cortex relates the immune system and the activities of the T-cell specific immune potentiator. *International Journal of Neuroscience, 39*, 177–187.

Renzulli, J. S. (1977). *The enrichment triad model.* Mansfield Center, CT: Creative Learning Press.

Renzulli, J. S. (1978). What makes giftedness? Reexamining a definition. *Phi Delta Kappan, 60*, 180–184, 261.

Renzulli, J. S. (1986a). *Systems and models for developing programs for the gifted and talented.* Mansfield Center, CT: Creative Learning Press.

Renzulli, J. S. (1986b). The three-ring conception of giftedness: A developmental model for creative productivity. In R. J. Sternberg & J. Davidson (Eds.), *Conceptions of giftedness* (pp. 53–92). New York: Cambridge University Press.

Renzulli, J. S. (1994). *Schools for talent development: A practical plan for total school improvement.* Mansfield Center, CT: Creative Learning Press.

Renzulli, J. S., & Reis, S. M. (1985). *The schoolwide enrichment model.* Mansfield Center, CT: Creative Learning Press.

Revesz, G. (1925). *The psychology of a musical prodigy.* Freeport, NY: Books for Libraries Press. (Reprinted in 1970)

Rice, T., Fulker, D. W., & Defries, J. C. (1986). Multivariate path analysis of specific cognitive abilities in the Colorado Adoption Project. *Behavior Genetics, 16*, 107–125.

Rich, D. A., & McKeever, W. F. (1990). An investigation of immune system disorder as a "marker" for anomalous dominance. *Brain and Cognition, 12*, 55–72.

Richards, R. (1981). Relationships between creativity and psychopathology: An evaluation and interpretation of the evidence. *Genetic Psychology Monographs, 103*, 261–324.

Richards, R. (1994). Creativity and bipolar mood swings: Why the association? In M. P. Shaw & M. A. Runco (Eds.), *Creativity and affect* (pp. 44–72). Norwood, NJ: Ablex.

Richardson, J. (1991). *A life of Picasso.* New York: Random House.

Richet, G. (1900). Note sur un cas remarquable de precocité musicale ["A note on a remarkable case of musical precocity"]. IV Congrès Internationale de Psychologie. *Compte Rendu des Sciences*, 93–99.

Rife, D. C., & Snyder, L. H. (1931). Studies in human inheritance VI: A genetic refutation of the principles of "behavioristic" psychology. *Human Biology, 3*, 547–559.

Riley, R. (1993). *National excellence: A case for developing America's talent.* Washington, DC: U.S. Department of Education.

Rimland, B. (1964). *Infantile autism: The syndrome and its implication for a neural theory of behavior.* New York: Appleton-Century-Crofts.

Rimland, B. (1978). Inside the mind of the autistic savant. *Psychology Today, 12*(3), 68–80.

Rimland, B., & Fein, D. (1988). Special talents of autistic savants. In L. Obler & D. Fein (Eds.), *The exceptional brain: Neuropsychology of talent and superior abilities* (pp. 341–363). New York: Guilford Press.

Rimland, B., & Hill, A. (1984). Idiot savants. In J. Wortis (Ed.), *Mental retardation and developmental disabilities* (Vol. 13, pp. 155–169). New York: Guilford Press.

Rimm, S. B. (1986). *Underachievement syndrome: Causes and cures.* Watertown, WI: Apple.

Ritchie, A. C., Bernard, J. M., & Shertzer, B. E. (1982). A comparison of academically talented children and academically average children on interpersonal sensitivity. *Gifted Child Quarterly, 26*(3), 105–109.

Robinson, A. (1990). Point-counterpoint: Cooperation or exploitation? The argument against cooperative learning for talented students. *Journal for the Education of the Gifted, 14*, 9–27.

Robinson, H. B. (1983). A case for radical acceleration: Programs of the Johns Hopkins University and the University of Washington. In C. P. Benbow & J. C. Stanley (Eds.), *Academic precocity: Aspects of its development* (pp. 139–159). Baltimore, MD: Johns Hopkins University Press.

Robinson, N. M. (1993a). Identifying and nurturing gifted, very young children. In K. A. Heller, F. J. Monks, & A. H. Passow (Eds.), *International handbook of research and development of giftedness and talent* (pp. 507–524). New York: Pergamon Press.

Robinson, N. M. (1993b). *Parenting the very young, gifted child.* University of Connecticut: The National Research Center on the Gifted and Talented Technical Report No. 9307.

Robinson, N. M., & Noble, K. D. (1991). Social-emotional development and adjustment of gifted children. In M. C. Wang, M. C. Reynolds, & H. J. Walberg (Eds.), *Handbook of special education: Research and practice: Vol. 4. Emerging programs* (pp. 57–76). New York: Pergamon Press.

Robinson, N. M., & Robinson, H. B. (1992). The use of standardized tests with young gifted children. In P. S. Klein & A. Tannenbaum (Eds.), *To be young and gifted* (pp. 141–170). Norwood, NJ: Ablex.

Rodgers, B. (1979). *Effects of an enrichment program screening process on the self-concept and other-concept of gifted elementary children.* Unpublished doctoral dissertation, University of Cincinnati, Cincinnati, OH.

Roe, A. (1952). *The making of a scientist.* New York: Dodd, Mead.

Roedell, W. C. (1984). Vulnerabilities of highly gifted children. *Roeper Review, 6*(3), 127–130.

Roedell, W. C. (1989). Early development of gifted children. In J. VanTassel-Baska & P. Olszewski-Kubilius (Eds.), *Patterns of influence on gifted learners: The home, the self, and the school* (pp. 13–28). New York: Teachers College Press.

Roeper, A. (1982). How the gifted cope with their emotions. *Roeper Review, 5*(2), 21–24.

Roeper, A. (1990, June). Identifying the young gifted child. *Parents' Press, 13,* 22.

Rogers, K. B. (1986). Do the gifted think differently? A review of recent research and its implications for instruction. *Journal for the Education of the Gifted, 10*(1), 17–39.

Rogers, K. B. (1991). Grouping the gifted and talented: Questions and answers. *Roeper Review, 16,* 8–12.

Romero, M. F. (1994, Fall). Identifying giftedness among Keresan Pueblo Indians: The Keres study. *Journal of American Indian Education,* 35–58.

Rose, R. J., Miller, J. Z., Dumont-Driscoll, M., & Evans, M. M. (1979). Twin family studies of perceptual speed ability. *Behavioral Genetics, 9,* 71–86.

Rosen, B. C., & D'Andrade, R. G. (1959). The psychosocial origin of achievement motivation. *Sociometry, 22*, 185–218.

Rosenblatt, E., & Winner, E. (1988). Is superior visual memory a component of superior drawing ability? In L. K. Obler & D. Fein (Eds.), *The exceptional brain: Neuropsychology of talent and special abilities* (pp. 341–363). New York: Guilford Press.

Rothenberg, A. (1990). *Creativity and madness.* Baltimore, MD: Johns Hopkins University Press.

Rugel, R. P. (1974). WISC subject scores of disabled readers: A review with respect to Bannatyne's recategorization. *Journal of Learning Disabilities, 7*(1), 46–65.

Saccuzzo, D. P., & Johnson, N. E. (1995, Winter). Identifying traditionally underrepresented children for gifted programs. University of Connecticut: The National Research Center on the Gifted and Talented Newsletter, 4–5.

Sacks, O. (1985, April 25). The autistic artist. *New York Review of Books*, pp. 17–21.

Sacks, O. (1993, December 27/1994, January 3). A neurologist's notebook: An anthropologist on Mars. *New Yorker*, 106–125.

Sacks, O. (1995a, May 5). Musical ability [Letter]. *Science, 268*, 621.

Sacks, O. (1995b, January 9). A neurologist's notebook: Prodigies. *New Yorker*, 44–65.

Sadker, M., & Sadker, D. (1985). Sexism in the schoolroom of the '80s. *Psychology Today, 19*(3), 54–57.

Salcedo, J., Spiegler, B. J., Gibson, E. G., & Magilvay, D. B. (1985). The autoimmune disease systematic lupus erythematosus is not associated with left-handedness. *Cortex, 21*, 645–647.

Sano, F. (1918). James Henry Pullen, the genius of Earlswood. *Journal of Mental Science, 64,* 251–267.

Sartre, J. P. (1964). *The words.* (Trans. B. Frechtman). Greenwich, CT: Fawcett Publications.

Sattler, H. N. (1982). *Assessment of children's intelligence.* Philadelphia: Saunders.

Satz, P. (1973). Left handedness and early brain insult: An explanation. *Neuropsychologia, 11*, 115–117.

Satz, P., Achenbach, K., & Fennell, E. (1967). Correlations between assessed manual laterality and predicted speech laterality in a normal population. *Neuropsychologia, 5*, 295–310.

Satz, P., & Soper, H. V. (1986). Left-handedness, dyslexia, and autoimmune disorder: A critique. *Journal of Clinical and Experimental Neuropsychology, 8*, 453–458.

Scarr, S., & McCartney, K. (1983). How people make their own environments: A theory of genotype–environment effects. *Child Development, 54,* 424–435.

Scarr, S., & Weinberg, R. A. (1978). The influence of "family background" on intellectual attainment. *American Sociological Review, 43,* 674–692.

Scarr-Salapatek, S. (1971). Unknowns in the IQ equation. *Science, 174,* 1223–1228.

Schab, F. (1980). Deceit among the gifted. *Journal for the Education of the Gifted, 3*(3), 129–132.

Schachter, S. C., Ransil, B. J., & Geschwind, N. (1987). Associations of handedness with hair color and learning disabilities. *Neuropsychologia, 25,* 269–276.

Schafer, E. W. P. (1987). Neural adaptability: A biological determinant of g factor intelligence. *Behavioral and Brain Sciences, 10,* 240–241.

Scheerer, M., Rothmann, E., & Goldstein, K. A. (1945). A case of idiot-savant: An experimental study of personality organization. *Psychological Monographs, 58,* 1–16.

Scheibel, A. B. (1988). Dendritic correlates of human cortical function. *Archives Italiennes de Biologie, 126,* 347–357.

Schiff, M. M., Kaufman, A. S., & Kaufman, N. L. (1981). Scatter analysis of WISC-R profile for learning disabled children with superior intelligence. *Journal of Learning Disabilities, 14,* 400–404.

Schlaug, G., Jancke, L., Huang, Y., & Steinmetz, H. (1995). In vivo evidence of structural brain asymmetry in musicians. *Science, 267,* 699–701.

Schneider, B. H. (1987). *The gifted child in peer group perspective.* New York: Springer-Verlag.

Schneider, B. H., Ledingham, J. E., Crombie, G., & Clegg, M. R. (1986). *Social self-concepts of gifted children: Delusions of ungrandeur?* Paper presented at the annual meeting of the American Psychological Association, Washington, DC.

Schonberg, H. C. (1970). *The lives of the great composers.* New York: Norton.

Schwartz, T. (1984, December). Whiz kids. *New York, 17,* 34–43.

Scott, D., & Moffett, A. (1977). The development of early musical talent in famous composers: A biographical review. In M. Critchley & R. A. Henson (Eds.), *Music and the brain: Studies in the neurology of music* (pp. 174–201). London: Heinemann Medical Books.

Scripture, E. W. (1891). Arithmetical prodigies. *American Journal of Psychology, 4,* 1–59.

Searleman, A., & Fugagli, A. (1987). Suspected autoimmune disorders and left-handedness: Evidence from individuals with diabetes, Chron's disease, and ulcerative colitis. *Neuropsychologia, 25,* 367–374.

Selfe, L. (1977). *Nadia: A case of extraordinary drawing ability in an autistic child.* London: Academic Press.

Selfe, L. (1983). *Normal and anomalous representational drawing ability in children.* London: Academic Press.

Selfe, L. (1985). *Anomalous drawing development: Some clinical studies.* Cambridge: Cambridge University Press.

Selfe, L. (1995). Nadia reconsidered. In C. Golomb (Ed.), *The development of gifted child artists: Selected case studies* (pp. 197–236). Hillsdale, NJ: Erlbaum.

Sergent, D., & Roche, S. (1973). Perceptual shifts in the auditory information processing of young children. *Psychology of Music, 1,* 39–48.

Shah, A., & Frith, U. (1983). An islet of ability in autistic children: A research note. *Journal of Child Psychology and Psychiatry, 24,* 613–620.

Shanker, A. (1995, June 4). Where we stand: Raising the ceiling— and the floor. *New York Times,* p. E-7.

Shapiro, B. K., Palmer, F. B., Antell, S. E., Bilker, S., Ross, A., & Capute, A. J. (1989). Giftedness: Can it be predicted in infancy? *Clinical Pediatrics, 28,* 205–209.

Sheldon, P. M. (1954). The families of highly gifted children. *Marriage and Family Living,* 59–60, 67.

Shore, B. M., Cornell, D. G., Robinson, A., & Ward, V. S. (1991). *Recommended practices in gifted education: A critical analysis.* New York: Teachers College Press.

Shore, B. M., & Kanevsky, L. (1993). Thinking processes: Being and becoming. In K. A. Heller, F. J. Monks, & A. H. Passow (Eds.), *International handbook of research and development of giftedness and talent* (pp. 133–147). Oxford: Pergamon Press.

Shurkin, J. N. (1992). *Terman's kids: The groundbreaking study of how the gifted grow up.* Boston: Little, Brown.

Shuter-Dyson, R. (1982). Musical ability. In D. Deutsch (Ed.), *The psychology of music* (pp. 391–412). San Diego, CA: Academic Press.

Shuter-Dyson, R. (1986). Musical giftedness. In J. Freeman (Ed.), *The psychology of gifted children* (pp. 159–183). Chichester: Wiley.

Shuter-Dyson, R., & Gabriel, C. (1981). *The psychology of musical ability*. (2nd ed.). London: Methuen.

Silver, S. J., & Clampit, M. K. (1990). WISC-R profiles of high ability children: Interpretation of verbal-performance discrepancies. *Gifted Child Quarterly, 34,* 76–79.

Silverman, L. K. (1983). Personality development: The pursuit of excellence. *Journal for the Education of the Gifted, 6*(1), 5–19.

Silverman, L. K. (1986). What happens to the gifted girl? In C. J. Maker (Ed.), *Critical issues in gifted education. Vol. 1: Defensible programs for the gifted* (pp. 43–89). Rockville, MD: Aspen.

Silverman, L. K. (1993a). Counseling families. In L. K. Silverman (Ed.), *Counseling the gifted and talented* (pp. 151–178). Denver: Love.

Silverman, L. K. (1993b). A developmental model for counseling the gifted. In L. K. Silverman (Ed.), *Counseling the gifted and talented* (pp. 51–78). Denver: Love.

Silverman, L. K. (1993c). The gifted individual. In L. K. Silverman (Ed.), *Counseling the gifted and talented* (pp. 3–28). Denver: Love.

Silverman, L. K. (1994). The moral sensitivity of gifted children and the evolution of society. *Roeper Review, 17*(2), 110–116.

Silverman, L. K., & Kearney, K. (1989). Parents of the extraordinarily gifted. *Advanced Development, 1,* 1–10.

Simon, H. A., & Chase, W. G. (1973). Skill in chess. *American Scientist, 61,* 394–403.

Simonton, D. K. (1991). Emergence and realization of genius: The lives and works of 120 classical composers. *Journal of Personality and Social Psychology, 61,* 829–840.

Simonton, D. K. (1994). *Greatness: Who makes history and why.* New York: Guilford Press.

Singal, D. J. (1991). The other crisis in American education. *Atlantic Monthly, 268*(5), 59–74.

Slavin, R. E. (1987). Ability grouping and student achievement in elementary schools: A best-evidence synthesis. *Review of Educational Research, 57*(3), 293–336.

Slavin, R. E. (1989, December/1990, January). Research on cooperative learning: Consensus and controversy. *Educational Leadership,* 52–54.

Slavin, R. E. (1990). Achievement effects of ability grouping in secondary schools: A best-evidence synthesis. *Review of Educational Research, 60,* 471–499.

Sloboda, J. A. (1985). *The musical mind: The cognitive psychology of music.* Oxford: Clarendon Press.

Sloboda, J. A. (1996). The acquisition of musical performance expertise: Deconstructing the "talent" account of individual differences in musical expressivity. In K. A. Ericsson (Ed.), *The road to excellence: The acquisition of expert performance in the arts and sciences, sports and games.* Hillsdale, NJ: Erlbaum.

Sloboda, J. A., Davidson, J. W., & Howe, M. J. A. (1994). Is everyone musical? *Psychologist, 7*(8), 349–354.

Sloboda, J. A., Davidson, J. W., Howe, M. J. A., & Moore, D. G. (in press). The role of practice in the development of performing musicians. *British Journal of Psychology.*

Sloboda, J. A., Hermelin, B., & O'Connor, N. (1985). An exceptional musical memory. *Music Perception, 3,* 155–170.

Sloboda, J. A., & Howe, M. J. A. (1991). Biographical precursors of musical excellence: An interview study. *Psychology of Music, 19,* 3–21.

Slominsky, N. (1988). *Perfect pitch.* New York: Oxford University Press.

Smith, B. D., Meyers, M. B., & Kline, R. (1989). For better or for worse: Left-handedness, pathology, and talent. *Journal of Clinical and Experimental Neuropsychology, 11*(6), 944–958.

Smith, J. (1987). Left-handedness: Its association with allergic disease. *Neuropsychologia, 25,* 665–674.

Smith, M. D., Coleman, J. M., Dokecki, P. R., & Davis, E. E. (1977). WISC-R scores of learning-disabled children. *Journal of Learning Disabilities, 10,* 437–443.

Smith, N., & Tsimpli, I.-M. (1995). *The mind of a savant: Language, learning and modularity.* Oxford: Blackwell.

Soja, N. N. (1994). Young children's concept of color and its relation to the acquisition of color words. *Child Development, 6*(5), 918–937.

Sosniak, L. A. (1985). Learning to be a concert pianist. In B. S. Bloom (Ed.), *Developing talent in young people* (pp. 19–67). New York: Ballantine Books.

Stanley, J. (1988). Some characteristics of SMPY'S "700–800 on SAT-M before age 13 group": Youths who reason extremely well mathematically. *Gifted Child Quarterly, 32*(1), 205–209.

Stanley, J. C. (1995, April). *Varieties of giftedness.* Invited address, Annual Meeting of the American Educational Research Association, San Francisco.

Stanley, J. C., & Benbow, C. P. (1983). Extremely young college graduates: Evidence of their success. *College and University, 58*(4), 361–371.

Stanley, J. C., & Benbow, C. P. (1986). Youths who reason exceptionally well in mathematics. In R. J. Sternberg & J. E. Davidson (Eds.), *Conceptions of giftedness* (pp. 361–387). New York: Cambridge University Press.

Stanley, J. C., Huang, J. F., & Zu, X. M. (1986, Summer). SAT-M scores of highly selected students in Shanghai tested when less than 13 years old. *College Board Review, 140,* 10–13, 28–29.

Steel, J. G., Gorman, R., & Flexman, J. E. (1984). Neuropsychiatric testing in an autistic mathematical idiot-savant: Evidence for non-verbal abstract capacity. *Journal of American Academy of Child Psychiatry, 23,* 704–707.

Stern, W. (1911). The supernormal child. I and II. *Journal of Educational Psychology, 2,* 143–149, 181–190.

Sternberg, R. J. (1981). A componential theory of intellectual giftedness. *Gifted Child Quarterly, 25*(2), 86–93.

Sternberg, R. J. (1982). Lies we live by. *Gifted Child Quarterly, 26,* 157–161.

Sternberg, R. J. (1985). *Beyond I.Q.: A triarchic theory of human intelligence.* New York: Cambridge University Press.

Sternberg, R. J. (1986). A triarchic theory of intellectual giftedness. In R. J. Sternberg & J. E. Davidson (Eds.), *Conceptions of giftedness* (pp. 223–243). Cambridge: Cambridge University Press.

Sternberg, R. J. (1991). Giftedness according to the triarchic theory of human intelligence. In N. Colangelo & G. A. Davis (Eds.), *Handbook of gifted education* (pp. 45–54). Needham Heights, MA: Allyn & Bacon.

Sternberg, R. J. (1993). Procedures for identifying intellectual potential in the gifted: A perspective on alternative "metaphors of mind." In K. A. Heller, F. J. Mönks, & A. H. Passow (Eds.), International handbook of research and development of giftedness and talent (pp. 185–207). Oxford: Pergamon Press.

Sternberg, R. J., & Davidson, J. E. (Eds.). (1986). *Conceptions of giftedness.* Cambridge: Cambridge University Press.

Sternberg, R. J., & Wagner, R. K. (Eds.). (1986). *Practical intelligence: Nature and origins of competence in the everyday world.* New York: Cambridge University Press.

Stevenson, H. W., Chen, C., & Lee, S. (1993). Motivation and achievement of gifted children in East Asia and the United States. *Journal for the Education of the Gifted, 16,* 223–250.

Stevenson, H. W., Lee, S. Y., & Stigler, J. W. (1986). Mathematics achievement of Chinese, Japanese, and American children. *Science, 231,* 693–699.

Stevenson, H. W., & Stigler, J. W. (1992). *The learning gap: Why our schools are failing and what we can learn from Japanese and Chinese education*. New York: Simon & Schuster.

Storfer, M. D. (1990). *Intelligence and giftedness*. San Francisco: Jossey-Bass.

Storr, A. (1988). *Solitude*. New York: Free Press.

Stout, H. (1992, July 30). Remedial curriculum for low achievers is falling from favor. *Wall Street Journal*, pp. A1, A9.

Subotnik, R. (1988a). Adolescent attraction to scientific research questions: Guidance from without and choices from within. *Questioning Exchange: A Multidisciplinary Review, 2*, 61–66.

Subotnik, R. (1988b). The motivation to experiment: A study of gifted adolescents' attitudes toward scientific research. *Journal for the Education of the Gifted, 11*, 19–35.

Subotnik, R., & Arnold, K. D. (1993). Longitudinal studies of giftedness: Investigating the fulfillment of promise. In K. A. Heller, F. J. Mönks, & A. H. Passow (Eds.), *International handbook of research and development of giftedness and talent* (pp. 149–160). Oxford: Pergamon Press.

Subotnik, R., & Arnold, K. D. (Eds.). (1994). *Beyond Terman: Contemporary longitudinal studies of giftedness and talent*. Norwood, NJ: Ablex.

Subotnik, R., Karp, D., & Morgan, E. (1989). High IQ children at midlife. An investigation into the generalizability of Terman's genetic studies of genius. *Roeper Review, 11*(3), 139–144.

Subotnik, R., Kassan, L., Summers, E., & Wasser, A. (1993). *Genius revisited: High IQ children grown up*. Norwood, NJ: Ablex.

Sulloway, F. J. (1990, February). *Orthodoxy and innovation in science: Influence of birth order in a multivariate context*. Paper presented at the American Association for the Advancement of Science, New Orleans, LA.

Suzuki, S. (1969). *Nurtured by love*. New York: Exposition Press.

Swiatek, M. A. (1992). A decade of longitudinal research on academic acceleration through the Study of Mathematically Precocious Youth. *Roeper Review, 15*(3), 120–124.

Swiatek, M. A., & Benbow, C. P. (1991a). A ten-year longitudinal follow-up of participants in a fast-paced mathematics course. *Journal for Research in Mathematics Education, 22*(2), 138–150.

Swiatek, M. A., & Benbow, C. P. (1991b). Ten-year longitudinal follow-up of ability-matched accelerated and unaccelerated gifted students. *Journal of Educational Psychology, 83*(4), 528–538.

Takehuchi, A. H., & Hulse, S. H. (1993). Absolute pitch. *Psychological Bulletin, 13*, 345–361.

Tangherlini, A. E., & Durden, W. (1993). Strategies for nurturing verbal talents in youth: The word as discipline and mystery. In K. A. Heller, F. J. Mönks, & A. H. Passow (Eds.), *International handbook of research and development of giftedness and talent* (pp. 427–442). Oxford: Pergamon Press.

Tannenbaum, A. J. (1983). *Gifted children: Psychological and educational perspectives.* New York: Macmillan.

Tannenbaum, A. J. (1993). History of giftedness and "gifted education" in world perspective. In K. A. Heller, F. J. Mönks, & A. H. Passow (Eds.), *International handbook of research and development of giftedness and talent* (pp. 3–27). Oxford: Pergamon Press.

Tannenbaum, A. J. (1994). *The meaning and making of giftedness.* Unpublished manuscript, Teachers College, Columbia University.

Taylor, D. W. (1963). Variables related to creativity and productivity among men in two research laboratories. In C. W. Taylor and F. Barron (Eds.), *Scientific creativity* (pp. 228–250). New York: Wiley.

Taylor, M. S., Locke, E. A., Lee, C., & Gist, M. E. (1984). Type A behavior and faculty research productivity: What are the mechanisms? *Organizational Behavior and Human Performance, 34,* 402–418.

Teasdale, T. W., & Owen, D. R. (1984). Heredity and familial environment in intelligence and educational level: A sibling study. *Nature, 309,* 620–622.

Temkin, A. (1987). Klee and avant-garde 1912–1940. In C. Lanchner (Ed.), *Paul Klee* (pp. 13–37). New York: Museum of Modern Art.

Temple, C. M. (1990). Academic discipline, handedness and immune disorders. *Neuropsychologia, 28,* 303–308.

Terman, L. M. (1925). *Genetic studies of genius: Vol. 1. Mental and physical traits of a thousand gifted children.* Stanford, CA: Stanford University Press.

Terman, L. M., & Oden, M. H. (1947). *Genetic studies of genius: Vol. 4. The gifted child grows up.* Stanford, CA: Stanford University Press.

Terman, L. M., & Oden, M. H. (1959). *Genetic studies of genius: Vol. 5. The gifted group at mid-life: Thirty-five years' follow-up of the superior child.* Stanford, CA: Stanford University Press.

Terrassier, J.-C. (1985). Dyssynchrony—uneven development. In J. Freeman (Ed.), *The psychology of gifted children: Perspectives on development and education* (pp. 265–274). New York: Wiley.

Thelen, E., & Smith, L. B. (in press). *A dynamic systems approach to the development of cognition and action.* Cambridge, MA: MIT Press.

Thomas, B. (1984). Early toy preferences of four-year-old readers and nonreaders. *Child Development, 55*, 24–43.

Thompson, L. A., Detterman, D. K., & Plomin, R. (1993). *Genetic influence on low and high cognitive ability.* Unpublished manuscript.

Thompson, L. A., & Plomin, R. (1993). Genetic influence on cognitive ability. In K. A. Heller, F. J. Monks, & A. H. Passow (Eds.), *International handbook of research and development of giftedness and talent* (pp. 103–114). Oxford: Pergamon Press.

Thompson, R. F. (1985). *The brain: An introduction to neuroscience.* New York: Freeman.

Thorndike, R. (1940). Performance of gifted children on tests of developmental age. *Journal of Psychology, 9*, 337–343.

Tocqueville, A. de (1899). *Democracy in America.* New York: The Colonial Press.

Tolstoy, L. (1961). *Anna Karenina* (Trans. D. Magarshack). New York: New American Library.

Tomlinson-Keasey, C., & Little, T. D. (1990). Predicting educational attainment, occupational achievement, intellectual skill and personal adjustment among gifted men and women. *Journal of Educational Psychology, 82,* 442–455.

Tomlinson-Keasey, C., Warren, L. W., & Elliott, J. E. (1986). Suicide among gifted women: A prospective study. *Journal of Abnormal Psychology, 95*, 123–130.

Toom, S. (1993, Fall). A Russian teacher in America. *American Educator, 17*(3), 9–13.

Torrance, E. P. (1962). *Guiding creative talent.* Englewood Cliffs, NJ: Prentice-Hall.

Torrance, E. P. (1972). Predictive validity of the Torrance Tests of Creative Thinking. *Journal of Creative Behavior, 6*, 236–252.

Torrance, E. P. (1983). *Future images and characteristics of gifted children around the world.* Paper presented at meeting of the Fifth World Conference on the Gifted, Manila, Philippines.

Torrance, E. P. (1992). The beyonders in a thirty-year longitudinal study of creative achievement. *Roeper Review, 15*(3), 131–135.

Treffert, D. A. (1989). *Extraordinary people.* New York: Bantam Press.

Treffinger, D. J., Callahan, C., & Baughn, V. L. (1991). Research on enrichment efforts in gifted education. In M. C. Wang, M. C. Reynolds, & H. J. Walberg (Eds.), *Handbook of special education: Research and practice: Vol. 4. Emerging programs* (pp. 37–55). Oxford: Pergamon Press.

Treffinger, D. J., & Renzulli, J. S. (1986). Giftedness as potential for creative productivity: Transcending IQ scores. *Roeper Review, 8*(3), 150–154.

Trost, G. (1993). Prediction of excellence in school, university, and work. In K. A. Heller, F. J. Monks, & A. H. Passow (Eds.), *International handbook of research and development of giftedness and talent* (pp. 325–336). Oxford: Pergamon Press.

Urban, K. K., & Sekowski, A. (1993). Programs and practices for identifying and nurturing giftedness and talent in Europe. In K. A. Heller, F. J. Monks, & A. H. Passow (Eds.), *International handbook of research and development of giftedness and talent* (pp. 779–796). Oxford: Pergamon Press.

U.S. Department of Education. (1991). *Final report: Gifted and talented education programs for eighth-grade public school students* (National Educational Longitudinal Study No. 88). Washington, DC: U.S. Department of Education, Office of Planning, Budget, and Evaluation.

Vaillant, G. E., & Vaillant, C. O. (1990). Determinants and consequences of creativity in a cohort of gifted women. *Psychology of Women Quarterly, 14,* 607–616.

Van Strien, J. W., Bouma, A., & Bakker, D. (1987). Birth stress, autoimmune diseases, and handedness. *Journal of Clinical and Experimental Neuropsychology, 9,* 775–780.

VanTassel-Baska, J. L. (1989a). Appropriate curriculum for gifted learners. *Educational Leadership, 46,* 13–15.

VanTassel-Baska, J. L. (1989b). Characteristics of the developmental path of eminent and gifted adults. In J. L. VanTassel-Baska & P. Olszewski-Kubilius (Eds.), *Patterns of influence on gifted learners: The home, the self, and the school* (pp. 146–162). New York: Teachers College Press.

VanTassel-Baska, J. L. (1991). Research on special populations of gifted learners. In M. C. Wang, M. C. Reynolds, & H. J. Walberg (Eds.), *Handbook of special education: Research and practice: Vol. 4. Emerging programs* (pp. 77–101). Oxford: Pergamon Press.

VanTassel-Baska, J. L. (1993). Theory and research on curriculum development for the gifted. In K. A. Heller, F. J. Monks, & A. H. Passow (Eds.), *International handbook of research and development of giftedness and talent* (pp. 365–386). Oxford: Pergamon Press.

Vasari, G. (1979). *Artists of the Renaissance* (Trans. G. Bull). New York: Viking.

Vaughn, V., Feldhusen, J. F., & Asher, J. W. (1991). Meta-analysis and review of research on pull-out programs in gifted education. *Gifted Child Quarterly, 35,* 92–98.

Viernstein, M. C., & Hogan, R. (1975). Parental personality factors and achievement motivation in talented adolescents. *Journal of Youth and Adolescence, 4*(2), 183–190.

Viernstein, M. C., McGinn, P. V., & Hogan, R. (1977). The personality correlates of differential verbal and mathematical ability in talented adolescents. *Journal of Youth and Adolescence, 6*, 169–178.

Viscott, D. S. (1970). A musical idiot savant: A psychodynamic study, and some speculations on the creative process. *Psychiatry, 33*, 494–515.

Waitzkin, F. (1984). *Searching for Bobby Fischer: The world of chess observed by the father of a chess prodigy.* New York: Random House.

Walberg, H. J., Rasher, S. P., & Hase, K. (1978). IQ correlates with high eminence. In R. S. Albert (Ed.), *Genius and eminence: The social psychology of creativity and exceptional achievement* (pp. 52–56). New York: Oxford University Press.

Walberg, H. J., Rasher, S. P., & Parkerson, J. (1980). Childhood and eminence. *Journal of Creative Behavior 13*, 225–231.

Waldron, K. A., Saphire, D. G., & Rosenblum, S. A. (1987). Learning disabilities and giftedness: Identification based on self-concept, behavior, and academic patterns. *Journal of Learning Disabilities, 20*, 422–432.

Wallach, M. A. (1976). Tests tell us little about talent. *American Scientist, 64*, 57–63.

Wallach, M. A., & Wing, C. W. (1969). *The talented students: A validation of the creativity–intelligence distinction.* New York: Holt, Rinehart & Winston.

Walters, J., & Gardner, H. (1986). The crystallizing experience: Discovering an intellectual gift. In R. J. Sternberg & J. E. Davidson (Eds.), *Conceptions of giftedness* (pp. 306–331). New York: Cambridge University Press.

Walters, J., Krechevsky, M., & Gardner, H. (1985). Development of musical, mathematical, and scientific talents in normal and gifted children. Harvard University Graduate School of Education: Project Zero Technical Report No. 31.

Waterhouse, L. (1988). Speculations on the neuroanatomical substrate of special talents. In L. K. Obler & D. Fein (Eds.), *The exceptional brain: Neuropsychology of talent and special abilities* (pp. 493–512). New York: Guilford Press.

Weinbrenner, S., & Devlin, B. (1993). The practice of cluster grouping: Providing full-time educational services for gifted students. *Gifted Education Press Quarterly, 7*(2), 2–9.

Weintraub, S., & Mesulam, M. M. (1983). Developmental learning disabilities of the right-hemisphere: Emotional, interpersonal and cognitive components. *Archives of Neurology, 40*, 463–468.

Weisberg, P. S., & Springer, K. J. (1961). Environmental factors in creative function. *Archives of General Psychiatry, 5,* 554–564.

Weissler, K., & Landau, E. (1992). Characteristics of families with no, one, or more than one gifted child. *Journal of Psychology, 127*(2), 143–152.

Welsh, G. S. (1975). *Creativity and intelligence: A personality approach.* Chapel Hill: University of North Carolina at Chapel Hill, Institute for Research in Social Science.

Westberg, K. L., Archambault, F. X., Dobyns, S. M., & Salvin, T. J. (1993). The classroom practices observational study. *Journal for the Education of the Gifted, 16*(2), 120–146.

Whalen, S., & Csikszentmihalyi, M. (1989). A comparison of the self-image of talented teenagers with a normal adolescent population. *Journal of Youth and Adolescence, 18*(2), 131–146.

Whiting, B. B., & Whiting, J. W. M. (1975). *Children of six cultures: A psycho-cultural analysis.* Cambridge, MA: Harvard University Press.

Whitmore, J. R. (1980). *Giftedness, conflict, and underachievement.* Needham Heights, MA: Allyn & Bacon.

Whitmore, J. R. (1981). Gifted children with handicapping conditions: A new frontier. *Exceptional Children, 48*(2), 106–114.

Whitmore, J. R. (1986). Conceptualizing the issue of underserved populations of gifted students. *Journal for the Education of the Gifted, 10,* 141–153.

Wiener, N. (1953). *Ex-prodigy: My childhood and youth.* New York: Simon & Schuster.

Wiener, N. (1956). *I am a mathematician: The later life of a prodigy.* Cambridge, MA: MIT Press.

Wilkinson, S. C. (1993). WISC-R profiles of children with superior intellectual ability. *Gifted Child Quarterly, 37*(2), 84–91.

Willats, J. (1977). How children learn to represent three-dimensional space in drawings. In G. Butterworth (Ed.), *The child's representation of the world.* New York: Plenum Press.

Willerman, L., Schultz, R., Rutledge, A. N., & Bigler, E. D. (1991). *In vivo* brain size and intelligence. *Intelligence, 15,* 223–228.

Willis, G., & Olszewski, P. (1988). *Characteristics of gifted junior-high aged students.* Paper presented at the Annual Meeting of the American Educational Research Association, New Orleans, LA.

Willis, S. (1995, February 1). Mainstreaming the gifted. *Education Update, 37*(2), 4–5.

Wilson, B., & Schmits, D. (1978). What's new in ability grouping? *Phi Delta Kappan, 60,* 535–536.

Wilson, E. O. (1994). *Naturalist.* Washington, DC: Island Press.

Wilson, R., & Wilson, M. (1976). Visual narrative and the artistically gifted. *Gifted Child Quarterly, 20,* 432–447.

Wiltshire, S. (1987). *Drawings.* London: Dent.

Wiltshire, S. (1991). *Floating cities.* London: Michael Joseph.

Wing, L. (Ed.). (1976). *Early childhood autism* (2nd ed.). Oxford: Pergamon Press.

Winn, M. (1979, December 23). The pleasures and perils of being a child prodigy. *New York Times Magazine,* pp. 12–17, 38–45.

Winner, E. (1982). *Invented worlds: The psychology of the arts.* Cambridge, MA: Harvard University Press.

Winner, E. (1989). How can Chinese children draw so well? *Journal of Aesthetic Education, 23,* 41–63.

Winner, E., & Casey, M. B. (1993). Cognitive profiles of artists. In G. Cupchik & J. Laszlo (Eds.), *Emerging visions: Contemporary approaches to the aesthetic process* (pp. 154–170). New York: Cambridge University Press.

Winner, E., Casey, M. B., DaSilva, D., & Hayes, R. (1991). Spatial abilities and reading deficits in visual art students. *Empirical Studies of the Arts, 9*(1), 51–63.

Winner, E., & Martino, G. (1993). Giftedness in the visual arts and music. In K. A. Heller, F. J. Monks, & A. H. Passow (Eds.), *International handbook of research and development of giftedness and talent* (pp. 253–281). New York: Pergamon Press.

Wright, L., & Borland, J. H. (1993, May/June). Using early childhood developmental portfolios in the identification and education of young, economically disadvantaged, potentially gifted students. *Roeper Review,* 205–210.

Wright, S. (1994, October 30). Review of *Last train to Memphis. The rise of Elvis Presley. New York Times Book Review,* pp. 1, 18.

Wu, W.-T., & Cho, S. (1993). Programs and practices for identifying and nurturing giftedness and talent in Asia (outside the mainland of China). In K. A. Heller, F. J. Monks, & A. H. Passow (Eds.), *International handbook of research and development of giftedness and talent* (pp. 797–808). Oxford: Pergamon Press.

Yeo, R. A., Turkheimer, E., Raz, N., & Bigler, E. D. (1987). Volumetric asymmetries of the human brain: Intellectual correlates. *Brain and Cognition, 193,* 15–23.

Yewchuk, C. R. (1985). Gifted/learning disabled children: An overview. *Gifted Education International, 3*(2), 122–126.

Zajonc, R. B. (1986). The decline and rise of Scholastic Aptitude

Test scores: A prediction derived from the confluence model. *American Psychologist, 41*, 863–867.

Zatorre, R. Musical perception and cerebral function: A critical review. *Music Perception, 2*, 196–221.

Zatorre, R. J., Evans, A. C., Meyer, E., & Gjedde, A. (1992). Lateralization of phonetic and pitch discrimination in speech processing. *Science, 256*, 846–849.

Zhensun, A., & Low, A. (1991). *A young painter: The life and paintings of Wang Yani—China's extraordinary young artist.* New York: Scholastic.

Zigler, E., & Farber, E. A. (1985). *Commonalities between the intellectual extremes: Giftedness and mental retardation.* Chelsea, MI: Book Crafters.

Zimmerman, E. (1992). Factors influencing the graphic development of a talented young artist. *Creativity Research Journal, 5*(3), 295–311.

Zixiu, Z. (1985). The psychological development of supernormal children. In J. Freeman (Ed.), *The psychology of gifted children* (pp. 325–332). Chichester: Wiley.

Zixiu, Z. (1993). Programs and practices for identifying and nurturing giftedness and talent in the People's Republic of China. In K. A. Heller, F. J. Mönks, & A. H. Passow (Eds.), *International handbook of research and development of giftedness and talent* (pp. 809–814). Oxford: Pergamon Press.

Zolog, A. (1983). Speech disturbances in parietal lobe lesions. *Neurology et Psychiatrie, 21* (3), 165–167.

Zuckerman, H. (1977). *Scientific elite.* New York: Free Press.

Zuckerman, H. (1983). The scientific elite: Nobel laureates' mutual influences. In R. S. Albert (Ed.), *Genius and eminence: The social psychology of creativity and exceptional achievement* (pp. 241–252). New York: Oxford University Press.

Index

DATE DUE

GAYLORD   PRINTED IN U.S.A.